SCENES AND CHARACTERS OF THE
MIDDLE AGES.

King Henry the Eighth's Army.

SCENES AND CHARACTERS

OF THE

MIDDLE AGES.

By the Rev. EDWARD L. CUTTS, B.A.,
LATE HON. SEC. OF THE ESSEX ARCHÆOLOGICAL SOCIETY.

WITH ONE HUNDRED AND EIGHTY-TWO ILLUSTRATIONS.

LONDON:
J. S. VIRTUE & CO., Limited, 26, IVY LANE,
PATERNOSTER ROW.

Now Reissued by
Singing Tree Press
1249 Washington Blvd., Detroit, Michigan 1968

First published in 1872

Library of Congress Card Number: 67-27866

CONTENTS.

THE MONKS OF THE MIDDLE AGES.

CHAP.		PAGE
I.	THE ORIGIN OF MONACHISM	1
II.	THE BENEDICTINE ORDERS	6
III.	THE AUGUSTINIAN ORDER	18
IV.	THE MILITARY ORDERS	26
V.	THE ORDERS OF FRIARS	36
VI.	THE CONVENT	54
VII.	THE MONASTERY	70

THE HERMITS AND RECLUSES OF THE MIDDLE AGES.

I.	THE HERMITS	93
II.	ANCHORESSES, OR FEMALE RECLUSES	120
III.	ANCHORAGES	132
IV.	CONSECRATED WIDOWS	152

THE PILGRIMS OF THE MIDDLE AGES.

I.	PILGRIMS	157
II.	OUR LADY OF WALSINGHAM AND ST. THOMAS OF CANTERBURY	176

THE SECULAR CLERGY OF THE MIDDLE AGES.

CHAP.		PAGE
I.	THE PAROCHIAL CLERGY	195
II.	CLERKS IN MINOR ORDERS	214
III.	THE PARISH PRIEST	222
IV.	CLERICAL COSTUME	232
V.	PARSONAGE HOUSES	252

THE MINSTRELS OF THE MIDDLE AGES.

I.		267
II.	SACRED MUSIC	284
III.	GUILDS OF MINSTRELS	298

THE KNIGHTS OF THE MIDDLE AGES.

I.	SAXON ARMS AND ARMOUR	311
II.	ARMS AND ARMOUR, FROM THE NORMAN CONQUEST DOWNWARDS	326
III.	ARMOUR OF THE FOURTEENTH CENTURY	338
IV.	THE DAYS OF CHIVALRY	353
V.	KNIGHTS-ERRANT	369
VI.	MILITARY ENGINES	380
VII.	ARMOUR OF THE FIFTEENTH CENTURY	394
VIII.	THE KNIGHT'S EDUCATION	406
IX.	ON TOURNAMENTS	423
X.	MEDIÆVAL BOWMEN	439
XI.	FIFTEENTH CENTURY AND LATER ARMOUR	452

THE MERCHANTS OF THE MIDDLE AGES.

I.	BEGINNINGS OF BRITISH COMMERCE	461
II.	THE NAVY	475
III.	THE SOCIAL POSITION OF THE MEDIÆVAL MERCHANTS	487
IV.	MEDIÆVAL TRADE	503
V.	COSTUME	518
VI.	MEDIÆVAL TOWNS	529

THE MONKS OF THE MIDDLE AGES.

CHAPTER I.

THE ORIGIN OF MONACHISM.

WE do not aim in these chapters at writing general history, or systematic treatises. Our business is to give a series of sketches of mediæval life and mediæval characters, looked at especially from the artist's point of view. And first we have to do with the monks of the Middle Ages. One branch of this subject has already been treated in Mrs. Jameson's "Legends of the Monastic Orders." This accomplished lady has very pleasingly narrated the traditionary histories of the founders and saints of the orders, which have furnished subjects for the greatest works of mediæval art; and she has placed monachism before her readers in its noblest and most poetical aspect. Our humbler task is to give a view of the familiar daily life of ordinary monks in their monasteries, and of the way in which they enter into the general life without the cloister;—such a sketch as an art-student might wish to have who is about to study that picturesque mediæval period of English history for subjects for his pencil. The religious orders occupied so important a position in mediæval society, that they cannot be overlooked by the historical student; and the flowing black robe and severe intellectual features of the Benedictine monk, or the coarse frock and sandalled feet of the mendicant friar, are too characteristic and too effective, in contrast with the gleaming armour

B

and richly-coloured and embroidered robes of the sumptuous civil costumes of the period, to be neglected by the artist. Such an art-student would desire first to have a general sketch of the whole history of monachism, as a necessary preliminary to the fuller study of any particular portion of it. He would wish for a sketch of the internal economy of the cloister; how the various buildings of a monastery were arranged; and what was the daily routine of the life of its inmates. He would seek to know under what circumstances these recluses mingled with the outer world. He would require accurate particulars of costumes and the like antiquarian details, that the accessories of his picture might be correct. And, if his monks are to be anything better than representations of monkish habits hung upon "lay figures," he must know what kind of men the Middle Age monks were intellectually and morally. These particulars we proceed to supply as fully as the space at our command will permit.

Monachism arose in Egypt. As early as the second century we read of men and women who, attracted by the charms of a peaceful, contemplative life, far away from the fierce, sensual, persecuting heathen world, betook themselves to a life of solitary asceticism. The mountainous desert on the east of the Nile valley was their favourite resort; there they lived in little hermitages, rudely piled up of stones, or hollowed out of the mountain side, or in the cells of the ancient Egyptian sepulchres, feeding on pulse and herbs, and water from the neighbouring spring.

One of the frescoes in the Campo Santo, at Pisa, by Pietro Laurati, engraved in Mrs. Jameson's "Legendary Art," gives a curious illustration of this phase of the eremitical life. It gives us a panorama of the desert, with the Nile in the foreground, and the rock caverns, and the little hermitages built among the date-palms, and the hermits at their ordinary occupations : here is one angling in the Nile, and another dragging out a net; there is one sitting at the door of his cell shaping wooden spoons. Here, again, we see them engaged in those mystical scenes in which an over-wrought imagination pictured to them the temptations of their senses in visible demon-shapes—beautiful to tempt or terrible to affright; or materialised the spiritual joys of their minds in angelic or divine visions : Anthony driving out with his staff the beautiful demon from his cell, or rapt in ecstasy beneath the Divine apparition.* Such pictures of the early hermits are not infrequent in mediæval art—one, from a fifteenth century MS. Psalter in the British Museum (Domit. A. xvii. f. 4 v), will be found in a subsequent chapter of this book.

We can picture to ourselves how it must have startled the refined Græco-Egyptian world of Alexandria when occasionally some man, long lost to society and forgotten by his friends, reappeared in the streets and squares of the city, with attenuated limbs and mortified countenance, with a dark hair-cloth tunic for his only clothing, with a reputation for exalted sanctity and spiritual wisdom, and vague rumours of supernatural revelations of the unseen world; like another John Baptist sent to preach repentance to the luxurious citizens; or fetched, perhaps, by the Alexandrian bishop to give to the church the weight of his testimony to the ancient truth of some doctrine which began to be questioned in the schools.

Such men, when they returned to the desert, were frequently accompanied by numbers of others, whom the fame of their sanctity and the persuasion of their preaching had induced to adopt the eremitical life. It is not to be wondered at that these new converts should frequently build, or select, their cells in the neighbourhood of that of the teacher whom they had followed into the desert, and should continue to look up to him as their spiritual guide. Gradually, this arrangement became systematised; a number of separate cells, grouped round a common oratory, contained a community of recluses who agreed to certain rules and to the guidance of a chosen head; an enclosure wall was generally built around this group, and the establishment was called a *laura*.

The transition from this arrangement of a group of anchorites occupying the anchorages of a laura under a spiritual head, to that of a community

---

* We cannot put down all these supernatural tales as fables or impostures; similar tales abound in the lives of the religious people of the Middle Ages, and they are not unknown in modern days: *e.g.*, Luther's conflict with Satan in the Wartzburg, and Colonel Gardiner's vision of the Saviour. Which of them (if any) are to be considered true supernatural visions, which may be put down as the natural results of spiritual excitement on the imagination, which are mere baseless legends, he would be a very self-confident critic who professed in all cases to decide.

living together in one building under the rule of an abbot, was natural and easy. The authorship of this cœnobite system is attributed to St. Anthony, who occupied a ruined castle in the Nile desert, with a community of disciples, in the former half of the fourth century. The cœnobitical institution did not supersede the eremitical; both continued to flourish together in every country of Christendom.*

The first written code of laws for the regulation of the lives of these communities was drawn up by Pachomius, a disciple of Anthony's. Pachomius is said to have peopled the island of Tabenne, in the Nile, with cœnobites, divided into monasteries, each of which had a superior, and a dean to every ten monks; Pachomius himself being the general director of the whole group of monasteries, which are said to have contained eleven hundred monks. The monks of St. Anthony are represented in ancient Greek pictures with a black or brown robe, and often with a tau cross of blue upon the shoulder or breast.

St. Basil, afterwards bishop of Cesaræa, who died A.D. 378, introduced monachism into Asia Minor, whence it spread over the East. He drew up a code of laws founded upon the rule of Pachomius, which was the foundation of all succeeding monastic institutions, and which is still the rule followed by all the monasteries of the Greek Church. The rule of St. Basil enjoins poverty, obedience, and chastity, and self-mortification. The habit both of monks and nuns was, and still is, universally in the Greek Church, a plain, coarse, black frock with a cowl, and a girdle of leather, or cord. The monks went barefooted and barelegged, and wore the Eastern tonsure, in which the hair is shaved in a crescent off the fore part of the head, instead of the Western tonsure, in which it is shaved in a circle off the crown. Hilarion is reputed to have introduced the Basilican institution into Syria; St. Augustine into Africa; St. Martin of Tours into France; St. Patrick into Ireland, in the fifth century.

The early history of the British Church is enveloped in thick obscurity, but it seems to have derived its Christianity (indirectly perhaps) from an Eastern

---

* Besides consulting the standard authorities on the archæology of the subject, the student will do well to read Mr. Kingsley's charming book, "The Hermits of the Desert."

source, and its monastic system was probably derived from that established in France by St. Martin, the abbot-bishop of Tours. One remarkable feature in it is the constant union of the abbatical and episcopal offices; this conjunction, which was foreign to the usage of the church in general, seems to have obtained all but universally in the British, and subsequently in the English Church. The British monasteries appear to have been very large; Bede tells us that there were no less than two thousand one hundred monks in the monastic establishment of Bangor in the sixth century, and there is reason to believe that the number is not overstated. They appear to have been schools of learning. The vows do not appear to have been perpetual; in the legends of the British saints we constantly find that the monks quitted the cloister without scruple. The legends lead us to imagine that a provost, steward, and deans, were the officers under the abbot; answering, perhaps, to the prior, cellarer, and deans of Benedictine institutions. The abbot-bishop, at least, was sometimes a married man.

CHAPTER II.

THE BENEDICTINE ORDERS.

IN the year 529 A.D., St. Benedict, an Italian of noble birth and great reputation, introduced into his new monastery on Monte Cassino—a hill between Rome and Naples—a new monastic rule. To the three vows of obedience, poverty, and chastity, which formed the foundation of most of the old rules, he added another, that of manual labour (for seven hours a day), not only for self-support, but also as a duty to God and man. Another important feature of his rule was that its vows were perpetual. And his rule lays down a daily routine of monastic life in much greater detail than the preceding rules appear to have done. The rule of St. Benedict speedily became popular, the majority of the existing monasteries embraced it; nearly all new monasteries for centuries afterwards adopted it; and we are told, in proof of the universality of its acceptation, that when Charlemagne caused inquiries to be made about the beginning of the eighth century, no other monastic rule was found existing throughout his wide dominions. The monasteries of the British Church, however, do not appear to have embraced the new rule.

St. Augustine, the apostle of the Anglo-Saxons, was prior of the Benedictine monastery which Gregory the Great had founded upon the Celian Hill, and his forty missionaries were monks of the same house. It cannot be doubted that they would introduce their order into those parts of England over which their influence extended. But a large part of Saxon England owed its Christianity to missionaries of the native church sent forth from the great monastic institution at Iona and afterwards at Lindisfarne, and these would doubtless introduce their own monastic system. We find, in fact, that no uniform rule was observed by the Saxon monasteries; some seem to have kept the rule of Basil, some the rule of Benedict, and others seem to have modified the ancient rules, so as to adapt them to their own circumstances and wishes. We are not surprised to learn that under such circumstances some of the monasteries were lax in their discipline; from Bede's accounts we gather that some of them were only convents of secular clerks, bound by certain rules, and performing divine offices daily, but enjoying all the privileges of other clerks, and even sometimes being married. Indeed, in the eighth century the primitive monastic discipline appears to have become very much relaxed, both in the East and West, though the popular admiration and veneration of the monks was not diminished.

In the illuminations of Anglo-Saxon MSS. of the ninth and tenth centuries, we find the habits of the Saxon monks represented of different colours, viz., white, black, dark brown, and grey.* In the early MS. Nero C. iv., in the British Museum, at f. 37, occurs a very clearly drawn group of monks in white habits; another group occurs at f. 34, rather more stiffly drawn, in which the margin of the hood and the sleeves is bordered with a narrow edge of ornamental work.

About the middle of the ninth century, however, Archbishop Dunstan reduced all the Saxon monasteries to the rule of St. Benedict; not without opposition on the part of some of them, and not without rather peremptory treatment on his part; and thus the Benedictine rule became universal in the West. The habit of the Benedictines consisted of a white woollen cassock, and over that an ample black gown and a black hood. We give here an excellent representation of a Benedictine monk, from a book which formerly belonged to St. Alban's Abbey, and now is preserved in the British Museum (Nero D. vii. f. 81). The book is the official catalogue which each monastery kept of those who had been benefactors to the house, and who were thereby entitled to their grateful remembrance and their prayers. In many cases the record of a benefaction is accompanied by an illuminated portrait of the benefactor. In the present case, he is

---

* Strutt's "Dress and Habits of the People of England."

represented as holding a golden tankard in one hand and an embroidered cloth in the other, gifts which he made to the abbey, and for which he is thus immortalised in their *Catalogus Benefactorum*. Other illustrations of Benedictine monks, of early fourteenth century date, may be found in the Add. MS. 17,687, at f. 3; again at f. 6, where a Benedictine is preaching; and again at f. 34, where one is preaching to a group of nuns of the same order; and at f. 41, where one is sitting writing at a desk (as in the scriptorium, probably). Yet again in the MS. Royal 20 D. vii., is a picture of St. Benedict preaching to a group of his monks. A considerable number of pictures of Benedictine monks, illustrating a mediæval legend of which they are the subject, occur in the lower margin of the MS. Royal 10 E. iv., which is of late thirteenth or early fourteenth century date. A drawing of Abbot Islip of Westminster, who died A.D. 1532, is given in the "Vetusta Monumenta," vol. iv. Pl. xvi. In working and travelling they wore over the cossack a black sleeveless tunic of shorter and less ample dimensions.

Benedictine Monk.

The female houses of the order had the same regulations as those of the monks; their costume too was the same, a white under garment, a black gown and black veil, with a white wimple around the face and neck. They had in England, at the dissolution of the monasteries, one hundred and twelve monasteries and seventy-four nunneries.* For illustration of an abbess see the fifteenth century MS. Royal 16 F. ii. at f. 137.

The Benedictine rule was all but universal in the West for four centuries; but during this period its observance gradually became relaxed.

---

* This is the computation of Tanner in his "Notitia Monastica;" but the editors of the last edition of Dugdale's "Monasticon," adding the smaller houses or cells, swell the number of Benedictine establishments in England to a total of two hundred and fifty-seven.

We cannot be surprised if it was found that the seven hours of manual labour which the rule required occupied time which might better be devoted to the learned studies for which the Benedictines were then, as they have always been, distinguished. We should have anticipated that the excessive abstinence, and many other of the mechanical observances of the rule, would soon be found to have little real utility when simply enforced by a rule, and not practised willingly for the sake of self-discipline. We are not therefore surprised, nor should we in these days attribute it as a fault, that the obligation to labour appears to have been very generally dispensed with, and some humane and sensible relaxations of the severe ascetic discipline and dietary of the primitive rule to have been very generally adopted. Nor will any one who has any experience of human nature expect otherwise than that among so large a body of men—many of them educated from childhood * to the monastic profession—there would be some who were wholly unsuited for it, and some whose vices brought disgrace upon it. The Benedictine monasteries, then, at the time of which we are speaking, had become different from the poor retired communities of self-denying ascetics which they were originally. Their general character was, and continued throughout the Middle Ages to be, that of wealthy and learned bodies; influential from their broad possessions, but still more influential from the fact that nearly all the literature, and art, and science of the period was to be found in their body. They were good

---

* If a child was to be received his hand was wrapped in the hanging of the altar, "and then," says the rule of St. Benedict, "let them offer him." The words are "Si quas forte de nobilibus offert filium suum Deo in monasterio, si ipse puer minore ætate est, parentes ejus faciant petitionem et manum pueri involvant in pallu altaris, et sic eum offerunt" (c. 59). The Abbot Herman tells us that in the year 1055 his mother took him and his brothers to the monastery of which he was afterwards abbot. "She went to St. Martin's (at Tournay), and delivered over her sons to God, placing the little one in his cradle upon the altar, amidst the tears of many bystanders" (Maitland's "Dark Ages," p. 78). The precedents for such a dedication of an infant to an ascetic life are, of course, the case of Samuel dedicated by his mother from infancy, and of Samson and John Baptist, who were directed by God to be consecrated as Nazarites from birth. A law was made prohibiting the dedication of children at an earlier age than fourteen. At f. 209 of the MS. Nero D. vii., is a picture of St. Benedict, to whom a boy in monk's habit is holding a book, and he is reading or preaching to a group of monks.

landlords to their tenants, good cultivators of their demesnes; great patrons of architecture, and sculpture, and painting ; educators of the people in their schools; healers of the sick in their hospitals ; great almsgivers to the poor; freely hospitable to travellers; they continued regular and constant in their religious services; but in housing, clothing, and diet, they lived the life of temperate gentlemen rather than of self-mortifying ascetics. Doubtless, as we have said, in some monasteries there were evil men, whose vices brought disgrace upon their calling; and there were some monasteries in which weak or wicked rulers had allowed the evil to prevail. The quiet, unostentatious, every-day virtues of such monastics as these were not such as to satisfy the enthusiastical seeker after monastical perfection. Nor were they such as to command the admiration of the unthinking and illiterate, who are always more prone to reverence fanaticism than to appreciate the more sober virtues, who are ever inclined to sneer at religious men and religious bodies who have wealth, and are accustomed to attribute to a whole class the vices of its disreputable members.

The popular disrepute into which the monastics had fallen through their increased wealth, and their departure from primitive monastical austerity, led, during the next two centuries, viz., from the beginning of the tenth to the end of the eleventh, to a series of endeavours to revive the primitive discipline. The history of all these attempts is very nearly alike. Some young monk of enthusiastic disposition, disgusted with the laxity or the vices of his brother monks, flies from the monastery, and betakes himself to an eremitical life in a neighbouring forest or wild mountain valley. Gradually a few men of like earnestness assemble round him. He is at length induced to permit himself to be placed at their head as their abbot, requires his followers to observe strictly the ancient rule, and gives them a few other directions of still stricter life. The new community gradually becomes famous for its virtues ; the Pope's sanction is obtained for it ; its followers assume a distinctive dress and name ; and take their place as a new religious order. This is in brief the history of the successive rise of the Clugniacs, the Carthusians, the Cistercians, and the orders of Camaldoli and Vallombrosa and Grandmont ; they all sprang thus out of the Benedictine order, retaining the rule of Benedict as the groundwork of their several systems. Their departures from the Benedictine rule were comparatively few and trifling, and need not be enumerated in such a sketch as this: they were in fact only reformed Benedictines, and in a general classification may be included with the parent order, to which these rivals imparted new tone and vigour.

The following account of the foundation of Clairvaux by St. Bernard will illustrate these general remarks. It is true that the founding of Clairvaux was not technically the founding of a new order, for it had been founded fifteen years before in Citeaux; but St. Bernard was rightly esteemed a second founder of the Cistercians, and his going forth from the parent house to found the new establishment at Clairvaux was under circumstances which make the narrative an excellent illustration of the subject.

"Twelve monks and their abbot," says his life in the "Acta Sanctorum," "representing our Lord and his apostles, were assembled in the church. Stephen placed a cross in Bernard's hands, who solemnly, at the head of his small band, walked forth from Citeaux. . . . . . Bernard struck away to the northward. For a distance of nearly ninety miles he kept this course, passing up by the source of the Seine, by Chatillon, of schoolday memories, till he arrived at La Ferté, about equally distant between Troyes and Chaumont, in the diocese of Langres, and situated on the river Aube. About four miles beyond La Ferté was a deep valley opening to the east. Thick umbrageous forests gave it a character of gloom and wildness; but a gushing stream of limpid water which ran through it was sufficient to redeem every disadvantage. In June, A.D. 1115, Bernard took up his abode in the valley of Wormwood, as it was called, and began to look for means of shelter and sustenance against the approaching winter. The rude fabric which he and his monks raised with their own hands was long preserved by the pious veneration of the Cistercians. It consisted of a building covered by a single roof, under which chapel, dormitory, and refectory were all included. Neither stone nor wood hid the bare earth, which served for floor. Windows scarcely wider than a man's hand admitted a feeble light. In this room the monks took their frugal meals of herbs and water. Immediately above the refectory was the sleeping apartment. It was reached by a ladder, and was, in truth, a sort of loft. Here were the monks' beds, which were peculiar. They were made in the form of boxes or bins of wooden planks, long and wide enough for a man to lie down in. A small space, hewn out with an axe, allowed room for the sleeper to get in or out. The inside was strewn with chaff, or dried leaves, which, with the woodwork, seem to have been the only covering permitted. . . . . . The monks had thus got a house over their heads; but they had very little else. They had left Citeaux in June. Their journey had probably occupied them a fortnight, their clearing, preparations, and building, perhaps two months; and thus they would be near September when this portion of their labour was accomplished. Autumn and winter were approaching, and they had no store laid by. Their food during the summer had been a compound of leaves intermixed with coarse grain. Beech-nuts and roots were to be their main support during the winter. And now to the privations of insufficient food was added the wearing out of their shoes and clothes. Their necessities grew with the severity of the season, till at last even salt failed them; and presently Bernard heard murmurs. He argued and exhorted; he spoke to them of the fear and love of God, and strove to rouse their drooping spirits by dwelling on the hopes of eternal life and Divine recompense. Their sufferings made them deaf and indifferent to their abbot's words. They would not remain in this valley of bitterness; they would return to Citeaux. Bernard, seeing they had lost their trust in God, reproved them no more; but himself sought in earnest prayer for release from their difficulties. Presently a voice from heaven said, 'Arise, Bernard, thy prayer is granted thee.' Upon which the monks said, 'What didst thou ask of the Lord?' 'Wait, and ye shall see, ye of little faith,' was the reply; and presently came a stranger who gave the abbot ten livres."

William of St. Thierry, the friend and biographer of St. Bernard, describes the external aspect and the internal life of Clairvaux. We extract it as a sketch of the highest type of monastic life, and as a corrective of the revelations of corrupter life among the monks which find illustration in these pages.

"At the first glance as you entered Clairvaux by descending the hill you could see it was a temple of God; and the still, silent valley bespoke, in the modest simplicity of its buildings, the unfeigned humility of Christ's poor. Moreover, in this valley full of men, where no one was permitted to be idle, where one and all were occupied with their allotted tasks, a silence deep as that of night prevailed. The sounds of labour, or the chants of the brethren in the choral service, were the only exceptions. The order of this silence, and the fame that went forth of it, struck such a reverence even into secular persons that they dreaded breaking it—I will not say by idle or wicked conversation, but even by pertinent remarks. The solitude, also, of the place—between dense forests in a narrow gorge of neighbouring hills—in a certain sense recalled the cave of our father St. Benedict, so that while they strove to imitate his life, they also had some similarity to him in their habitation and loneliness. . . . . Although the monastery is situated in a valley, it has its foundations on the holy hills, whose gates the Lord loveth more than all the dwellings of Jacob. Glorious things are spoken of it, because the glorious and wonderful God therein worketh great marvels. There the insane recover their reason, and although their outward man is worn away, inwardly they are born again. There the proud are humbled, the rich are made poor, and the poor have the Gospel preached to them, and the darkness of sinners is changed into light. A large multitude of blessed poor from the ends of the earth have there assembled, yet have they one heart and one mind; justly, therefore, do all who dwell there rejoice with no empty joy. They have the certain hope of perennial joy, of their ascension heavenward already commenced. In Clairvaux they have found Jacob's ladder, with angels upon it; some descending, who so provide for their bodies that they faint not on the way; others ascending, who so rule their souls that their bodies hereafter may be glorified with them.

"For my part, the more attentively I watch them day by day, the more do I believe that they are perfect followers of Christ in all things. When they pray and speak to God in spirit and in truth, by their friendly and quiet speech to Him, as well as by their humbleness of demeanour, they are plainly seen to be God's companions and friends. When, on the other hand, they openly praise God with psalmody, how pure and fervent are their minds, is shown by their posture of body in holy fear and reverence, while by their careful pronunciation and modulation of the psalms, is shown how sweet to their lips are the words of God—sweeter than honey to their mouths. As I watch them, therefore, singing without fatigue from before midnight to the dawn of day, with only a brief interval, they appear a little less than the angels, but much more than men. . . . .

"As regards their manual labour, so patiently and placidly, with such quiet countenances, in such sweet and holy order, do they perform all things, that although they exercise themselves at many works, they never seem moved or burdened in anything, whatever the labour may be. Whence it is manifest that that Holy Spirit worketh in them who disposeth of all things with sweetness, in whom they are refreshed, so that they rest even in their toil. Many of them, I hear, are bishops and earls, and many illustrious through their birth or knowledge; but now, by God's grace, all acceptation of persons being dead among them, the greater any one thought himself in the world, the more in this flock does he regard himself as less than the least. I see them in the garden with hoes, in the meadows with forks or rakes, in the fields with scythes, in the forest with axes. To judge from their outward appearance, their tools, their bad and disordered clothes, they appear a race of fools, without speech or sense. But a true thought in my mind tells me that their life in Christ is hidden in the heavens. Among them I see Godfrey of Peronne, Raynald of Picardy, William of St. Omer, Walter of Lisle, all of whom I knew formerly in the old man, whereof I now see no trace, by God's favour. I knew them proud and puffed up; I see them walking humbly under the merciful hand of God."

The first of these reformed orders was the CLUGNIAC, so called because it was founded, in the year 927, at Clugny, in Burgundy, by Odo the Abbot. The Clugniacs formally abrogated the requirement of manual labour required in the Benedictine rule, and professed to devote themselves more sedulously to the cultivation of the mind. The order was first introduced into England in the year 1077 A.D., at Lewes, in Sussex; but it never became popular in England, and never had more than twenty houses here, and they small ones, and nearly all of them founded before the reign

The Benedictine Orders. 15

of Henry II. Until the fourteenth century they were all priories dependent on the parent house of Clugny; though the prior of Lewes was the High Chamberlain, and often the Vicar-general, of the Abbot of Clugny, and exercised a supervision over the English houses of the order. The English houses were all governed by foreigners, and contained more foreign than English monks, and sent large portions of their surplus revenues to Clugny. Hence they were often seized, during war between England and France, as alien priories. But in the fourteenth century many of them were made denizen, and Bermondsey was made an abbey, and they were all discharged from subjection to the foreign abbeys. The Clugniacs retained the Benedictine habit. At Cowfold Church, Sussex, still remains a monumental brass of Thomas Nelond, who was prior of Lewes at his death, in 1433 A.D., in which he is represented in the habit of his order.*

Carthusian Monk.

In the year 1084 A.D., the CARTHUSIAN order was founded by St. Bruno, a monk of Cologne, at Chartreux, near Grenoble. This was the most severe of all the reformed Benedictine orders. To the strictest observance of the rule of Benedict they added almost perpetual silence; flesh was forbidden even to the sick; their food was confined to one meal of pulse, bread, and water, daily. It is remarkable that this the strictest of all monastic rules has, even to the present day, been but slightly modified; and that the monks have never been accused of personally deviating from it. The order was numerous on the Continent, but only nine houses of the order were ever established in England. The principal of these was the Charterhouse (Chartreux), in London, which, at the dissolution, was rescued by Thomas Sutton to serve one at least of the purposes of its original

---

* Engraved in Boutell's "Monumental Brasses."

foundation—the training of youth in sound religious learning. There were few nunneries of the order—none in England. The Carthusian habit consisted of a white cassock and hood, over that a white scapulary—a long piece of cloth which hangs down before and behind, and is joined at the sides by a band of the same colour, about six inches wide; unlike the other orders, they shaved the head entirely.

The representation of a Carthusian monk, on previous page, is reduced from one of Hollar's well-known series of prints of monastic costumes. Another illustration may be referred to in a fifteenth century book of Hours (Add.), at f. 10, where one occurs in a group of religious, which includes also a Benedictine and a Cistercian abbot, and others.

Cistercian Monk.

In 1098 A.D., arose the CISTERCIAN order. It took the name from Citeaux (Latinised into Cistercium), the house in which the new order was founded by Robert de Thierry. Stephen Harding, an Englishman, the third abbot, brought the new order into some repute; but it is to the fame of St. Bernard, who joined it in 1113 A.D., that the speedy and widespread popularity of the new order is to be attributed. The order was introduced into England at Waverly, in Surrey, in 1128 A.D. The Cistercians professed to observe the rule of St. Benedict with rigid exactness, only that some of the hours which were devoted by the Benedictines to reading and study, the Cistercians devoted to manual labour. They affected a severe simplicity; their houses were to be simple, with no lofty towers, no carvings or representation of saints, except the crucifix; the furniture and ornaments of their establishments were to be in keeping—chasubles of fustian, candlesticks of iron, napkins of coarse cloth, the cross of wood, and only the chalice might be of precious metal. The amount of manual labour prevented the Cistercians from becoming a learned order, though they did produce a few men distinguished in literature; they were excellent farmers and horticulturists, and are said in early times to have almost monopolised the wool trade of the kingdom. They changed the colour of the Benedictine habit, wearing a white gown and hood over a white cassock; when they went beyond the walls of the monastery they also wore a black cloak. St. Bernard of Clairvaux is the great saint of the order. They had seventy-five monasteries and twenty-six nunneries in England, including some of the largest and finest in the kingdom.

The cut represents a group of Cistercian monks, from a MS. (Vitellius A. 13) in the British Museum. It shows some of them sitting with hands crossed and concealed in their sleeves—an attitude which was considered modest and respectful in the presence of superiors; some with the cowl over the head. It will. be observed that some are and some are not bearded.

Group of Cistercian Monks.

The Cistercian monk, whom we give in the opposite woodcut, is taken from Hollar's plate.

Other reformed Benedictine orders which arose in the eleventh century, viz., the order of CAMALDOLI, in 1027 A.D., and that of VALLOMBROSA, in 1073 A.D., did not extend to England. The order of the GRANDMONTINES had one or two alien priories here.

The preceding orders differ among themselves, but the rule of Benedict is the foundation of their discipline, and they are so far impressed with a common character, and actuated by a common spirit, that we may consider them all as forming the Benedictine family.

CHAPTER III.

THE AUGUSTINIAN ORDERS.

WE come next to another great monastic family which is included under the generic name of Augustinians. The Augustinians claim the great St. Augustine, Bishop of Hippo, as their founder, and relate that he established the monastic communities in Africa, and gave them a rule. That he did patronise monachism in Africa we gather from his writings, but it is not clear that he founded any distinct order; nor was any order called after his name until the middle of the ninth century. About that time all the various denominations of clergy who had not entered the ranks of monachism—priests, canons, clerks, &c.—were incorporated by a decree of Pope Leo III. and the Emperor Lothaire into one great order, and were enjoined to observe the rule which was then known under the name of St. Augustine, but which is said to have been really compiled by Ivo de Chartres from the writings of St. Augustine. It was a much milder rule than the Benedictine. The Augustinians were divided into Canons Secular and Canons Regular.

The CANONS SECULAR OF ST. AUGUSTINE were in fact the clergy of cathedral and collegiate churches, who lived in community on the monastic model; their habit was a long black cassock (the parochial clergy did not then universally wear black); over which, during divine service, they wore a surplice and a fur tippet, called an *almuce*, and a four-square black cap, called a *baret;* and at other times a black cloak and hood with a leather girdle. According to their rule they might wear their beards, but from the thirteenth century downwards we find them usually shaven. In the Canon's Yeoman's tale, from which the following extract is taken, Chaucer gives us a pen-and-ink sketch of a canon, from which it would seem that even on a journey he wore the surplice and fur hood under the black cloak :—

> "Ere we had ridden fully five mile,'
> At Brighton under Blee us gan atake [overtake]
> A man that clothed was in clothes blake,
> And underneath he wered a surplice.
> * * * *
> And in my hearte wondren I began
> What that he was, till that I understood
> How that his cloak was sewed to his hood,*
> For which when I had long avised me,
> I deemed him some chanon for to be.
> His hat hung at his back down by a lace."

The hat which hung behind may have been like that of the abbot in a subsequent woodcut; but he wore his hood; and Chaucer, with his usual humour and life-like portraiture, tells us how he had put a burdock leaf under his hood because of the heat :—

> "A clote-leaf he had laid under his hood
> For sweat, and for to keep his head from heat."

Chaucer rightly classes the canons rather with priests than monks :—

> "All be he monk or frere,
> Priest or chanon, or any other wight."

The canon whom we give in the wood-cut over-leaf, from one of Hollar's plates, is in ordinary costume. An engraving of a semi-choir of canons in their furred tippets from the MS. Domitian xvii., will be found in a subsequent chapter on the Secular Clergy.

There are numerous existing monumental brasses in which the effigies of canons are represented in choir costume, viz., surplice and amice, and often with a cope over all; they are all bareheaded and shaven. We may mention specially that of William Tannere, first master of Cobham College (died 1418 A.D.), in Cobham Church, Kent, in which the almuce, with its

---

* Probably this means that he had "clocks"—little bell-shaped ornaments—sewn to the lower margin of his tippet or hood.

fringe of bell-shaped ornaments, over the surplice, is very distinctly shown; it is fastened at the throat with a jewel. The effigy of Sir John Stodeley, canon, in Over Winchendon Church, Bucks (died 1505), is in ordinary costume, an under garment reaching to the heels, over that a shorter black cassock, girded with a leather girdle, and over all a long cloak and hood.

The CANONS REGULAR OF ST. AUGUSTINE were perhaps the least ascetic of the monastic orders. Enyol de Provins, a minstrel (and afterwards a monk) of the thirteenth century, says of them: "Among them one is well shod, well clothed, and well fed. They go out when they like, mix with the world, and talk at table." They were little known till the tenth or eleventh century, and the general opinion is, that they were first introduced into England, at Colchester, in the reign of Henry I., where the ruins of their church, of Norman style, built of Roman bricks, still remain. Their habit was like that of the secular canons—a long black cassock, cloak and hood, and leather girdle, and four-square cap; they are distinguished from the secular canons by not wearing the beard. According to Tanner, they had one hundred and seventy-four houses in England— one hundred and fifty-eight for monks, and sixteen for nuns; but the editors of the last edition of the "Monasticon" have recovered the names of additional small houses, which make up a total of two hundred and sixteen houses of the order.

Canon of St. Augustine.

The Augustinian order branches out into a number of denominations; indeed, it is considered as the parent rule of all the monastic orders and religious communities which are not included under the Benedictine order; and retrospectively it is made to include all the distinguished recluses and clerics before the institution of St. Benedict, from the fourth to the sixth century.

The most important branch of the Regular Canons is the PREMON-STRATENSIAN, founded by St. Norbert, a German nobleman, who died in 1134 A.D.; his first house, in a barren spot in the valley of Coucy, in Picardy, called Pré-montre, gave its name to the order. The rule was that of Augustine, with a severe discipline superadded; the habit was a coarse black cassock, with a white woollen cloak and a white four-square cap. Their abbots were not to use any episcopal insignia. The Premonstratensian nuns were not to sing in choir or church, and to pray in silence. They had only thirty-six houses in England, of which Welbeck was the chief; but the order was very popular on the Continent, and at length numbered one thousand abbeys and five hundred nunneries.

Under this rule are also included the GILBERTINES, who were founded by a Lincolnshire priest, Gilbert of Sempringham, in the year 1139 A.D. There were twenty-six houses of the order, most of them in Lincolnshire and Yorkshire; they were all priories dependent upon the house of Sempringham, whose head, as prior-general, appointed the priors of the other houses, and ruled absolutely the whole order. All the houses of this order were double houses, that is, monks and nuns lived in the same enclosure, though with a rigid separation between their two divisions. The monks followed the Augustinian rule; the nuns followed the rule of the Cistercian nuns. The habit was a black cassock, a white cloak, and hood lined with lambskin. The "Monasticon" gives very effective representations (after Hollar) of the Gilbertine monk and nun.

The NUNS OF FONTEVRAUD was another female order of Augustinians, of which little is known. It was founded at Fontevraud in France, and three houses of the order were established in England in the time of Henry II.; they had monks and nuns within the same enclosure, and all subject to the rule of an abbess.

The BONHOMMES were another small order of the Augustinian rule, of little repute in England; they had only two houses here, which, however, were reckoned among the greater abbeys, viz., Esserug in Bucks, and Edindon in Wilts.

The female ORDER OF OUR SAVIOUR, or, as they are usually called, the BRIGITTINES, were founded by St. Bridget of Sweden, in 1363 A.D. They were introduced into England by Henry V., who built for them the once glorious nunnery of Sion House. At the dissolution, the nuns fled to Lisbon, where their successors still exist. Some of the relics and vestments which they carried from Sion House have been carefully preserved ever since, and are now in the possession of the Earl of Shrewsbury.* Their habit was like that of the Benedictine nuns—a black tunic, white wimple and veil, but is distinguished by a black band on the veil across the forehead.

Other small offshoots of the great Augustinian tree were those which observed the rule of St. Austin according to the regulations of St. Nicholas of Arroasia, which had four houses here; and those which observed the order of St. Victor, which had three houses.

We may refer the reader to two MS. illuminations of groups of religious for further illustration of their costumes. One is in the beautiful fourteenth century MS. of Froissart in the British Museum (Harl. 4,380, at f. 18 v). It represents a dying pope surrounded by a group of representative religious, cardinals, &c. Among them are one in a brown beard, and with no appearance of tonsure (? a hermit); another in a white scapular and hood (? a Carthusian); another in a black cloak and hood over a white frock (? a Cistercian); another in a brown robe and hood, tonsured. Again, in the MS. Tiberius B iii. article 3, f. 6, the text speaks of "Convens of monkys, chanons and chartreus, celestynes, freres and prestes, palmers, pylgreymys, hermytes, and reclus," and the illuminator has illustrated it with a row of religious—first a Benedictine abbot; then a canon with red cassock and almuce over surplice; then a monk with white frock and white scapular banded at the sides, as in Hollar's cut given above, is clearly the Carthusian; then comes a man in brown, with a knotted girdle, holding a cross staff and a book, who is perhaps a friar; then one in white surplice over red cassock, who is the priest; then a hermit, in brown cloak over dark grey gown; and in the background are partly seen two pilgrims and a monk. Other illustrations of monks are frequent in the illuminated MSS.

---

* Mrs. Jameson, "Legends of the Monastic Orders," p. 137.

The HOSPITALS of the Middle Ages deserve a more extended notice than we can afford them here. Some were founded at places of pilgrimage and along the high roads, for the entertainment of poor pilgrims and travellers. Thus at St. Edmund's Bury there was St. John's Hospital, or God's House, without the south gate; and St. Nicholas Hospital, without the east gate; and St. Peter's Hospital, without the Risley gate; and St. Saviour's Hospital, without the north gate—all founded and endowed by abbots of St. Edmund. At Reading there was the Hospital of St. Mary Magdalene, for twelve leprous persons and chaplains; and the Hospital of St. Lawrence, for twenty-six poor people and for the entertainment of strangers and pilgrims—both founded by abbots of Reading; one at the gate of Fountains Abbey, for poor persons and travellers; one at Glastonbury, under the care of the almoner, for poor and infirm persons; &c., &c. Indeed, they were scattered so profusely up and down the country that the last edition of the "Monasticon" enumerates no less than three hundred and seventy of them. Those for the poor had usually a little chamber for each person, a common hall in which they took their meals, a chapel in which they attended daily service. They usually were under the care and go-

Bedesmen. Temp. Hen. VII.

vernment of one or more clergymen; sometimes in large hospitals of a prior and bretheren, who were Augustinian canons. The canons of some of these hospitals had special statutes in addition to the general rules, and were distinguished by some peculiarity of habit; for example, the canons of the Hospital of St. John Baptist at Coventry wore a cross on the breast of their black cassock, and a similar one on the shoulder of their cloak. The poor people were also under a simple rule, and were regarded as part of the community. The accompanying woodcut enables us to place a group of them before the eye of the reader. It is from one of the initial letters of the deed (Harl. 1,498) by which Henry VII.

founded a fraternity of thirteen poor men (thirteen was a favourite number for such hospitals) in Westminster Abbey, who were to be under the governance of the monks, and to repay the king's bounty by their prayers. The group represents the abbot and some of the monks, and behind them some of the bedesmen, each of whom has the royal badge—the rose and crown—on the shoulder of his habit, and holds in his hand his rosary, the symbol of his prayers. Happily some of these ancient foundations have continued to the present day, and the brethren may be seen yet in coats of antique fashion, with a cross or other badge on the sleeve. Examples of the architecture of the buildings may be seen in the Bede Houses in Higham Ferrers Churchyard, built by Archbishop Chechele in 1422; St. Thomas's Hospital, Northampton; Wyston's Hospital, Leicester; Ford's Hospital, Coventry; the Alms Houses at Sherborne; the Leicester Hospital at Warwick, &c. Mr. Turner, in the "Domestic Architecture," says that there exists a complete chronological series from the twelfth century downwards.

Hospitals were also established for the treatment of the sick, of which St. Bartholomew's Hospital is perhaps our most illustrious instance. It was founded to be an infirmary for the sick and infirm poor, a lying-in hospital for women—there were sisters on the hospital staff, and if the women happened to die in hospital their children were taken care of till seven years of age. The staff usually consisted of a community living under monastic vows and rule, viz., a prior and a number of brethren who were educated and trained to the treatment of sickness and disease, and one or more of whom were also priests; a college, in short, of clerical physicians and surgeons and hospital dressers, who devoted themselves to the service of the sick poor as an act of religion, and had always in mind our Lord's words, "Inasmuch as ye do it to one of the least of these my brethren, ye do it unto me." In the still existing church of St. Bartholomew's Hospital, in Smithfield, is a monument of the founder "Rahere, first canon and prior," which is, however, of much later date, probably of about 1410 A.D.; his recumbent effigy, and the kneeling figures of two of his canons beside him, afford good authorities for costume. They have been engraved in the "Vetusta Monumenta," vol. ii. Pl. xxxvi.

The Augustinian Orders.

The building usually consisted of a great hall in which the sick lay, a chapel for their worship, apartments for the hospital staff, and other apartments for guests. We are not aware of any examples in England so perfect as some which exist in other countries, and we shall therefore borrow some foreign examples in illustration of the subject. The commonest form of these hospitals seems to have been a great hall divided by pillars into a centre and aisles, in which rows of beds were arranged; with a chapel in a separate building at one end of the hall, and other buildings irregularly disposed in a courtyard; as at the Hôtel Dieu of Chartres, a building of 1153 A.D.,* and the Salle des Morts at Ourscamp.† At Tonerre we find a modification of the above plan. The hospital is still a vast hall, but is divided by timber partitions along the side walls into little separate cells. Above these cells, against the side walls, and projecting partly over the cells, are two galleries, along which the attendants might walk and look down into the cells. At the east end of this hall two bays were screened off for the chapel, so that they who were able might go up into the chapel, and they who could not rise from their beds could still take part in the service.‡ At Tartoine, near Laon la Fère, is a hospital on a different plan: a hall, with cells on one side of it, is placed on one side of a square courtyard, and the chapel and lodgings for the brethren on another side of the court.§

---

* Viollet le Duc's "Dictionary of Architecture," vol. vi. p. 104.
† Ibid. vi. 107.   ‡ Ibid. vi. 112.   § Ibid. vi. 112.

CHAPTER IV.

THE MILITARY ORDERS.

WE have already sketched the history of the rise of monachism in the fourth century out of the groups of Egyptian eremites, and the rapid spread of the institution, under the rule of Basil, over Christendom; the adoption in the west of the new rule of Benedict in the sixth century; the rise of the reformed orders of Benedictines in the tenth and eleventh centuries; and the institution in the eleventh and twelfth centuries of a new group of orders under the milder discipline of the Augustinian rule. We come now to a class of monastics who are included under the Augustinian rule, since that rule formed the basis of their discipline, but whose striking features of difference from all other religious orders entitle them to be reckoned as a distinct class, under the designation of the Military Orders: When the history of the mendicant orders which arose in the thirteenth century has been read, it will be seen that these military orders had anticipated the active religious spirit which formed the characteristic of the friars, as opposed to the contemplative religious spirit of the monks. But that which peculiarly characterises the military orders, is their adoption of the chivalrous crusading spirit of the age in which they arose: they were half friars, half crusaders.

The order of the KNIGHTS OF THE TEMPLE was founded at Jerusalem in 1118 A.D., during the interval between the first and second crusades, and in the reign of Baldwin I. Hugh de Payens, and eight other brave knights, in the presence of the king and his barons, and in the hands of the Patriarch, bound themselves into a fraternity which embraced the fundamental monastic vows of obedience, poverty, and chastity; and, in addition, as the special object of the fraternity, they undertook the task of escorting the companies of pilgrims from the coast up to Jerusalem, and thence on the usual tour to the Holy Places. For the open country was perpetually exposed to the incursions of irregular bands of Saracen and Turkish horsemen, and death or slavery was the fate which awaited any caravan of helpless pilgrims whom the infidel descried as they swept over the plains, or whom they could waylay in the mountain passes. The new knights undertook besides to wage a continual war in defence of the Cross against the infidel. The canons of the Temple at Jerusalem gave the new fraternity a piece of ground adjoining the Temple for the site of their home, and hence they took their name of Knights of the Temple; and they gradually acquired dependent houses, which were in fact strong castles, whose ruins may still be seen, in many a strong place in Palestine. Ten years after, when Baldwin II. sent envoys to Europe to implore the aid of the Christian powers in support of his kingdom against the Saracens, Hugh de Payens was sent as one of the envoys. His order received the approval of the Council of Troyes, and of Pope Eugene III., and the patronage of St. Bernard, who became the great preacher of the second crusade*; and when Hugh de Payens returned to Palestine, he was at the head of three hundred knights of the noblest houses of Europe, who had become members of the order. Endowments, too, for their support flowed in abundantly; and gradually the order established dependent houses on its estates in nearly every country of Europe. The order was introduced into England in the reign of King Stephen; at first its chief house, "the Temple," * was on the south side of Holborn, London, near Southampton Buildings; afterwards it was removed to Fleet Street, where the establishment still remains, long since converted to other uses; but the original church, with its round nave, after the form of the Church of the Holy Sepulchre at Jerusalem,† still continues a monument of the

---

* All its houses were called Temples, as all the Carthusian houses were called Chartereux (corrupted in England into Charterhouse).
† Of the four round churches in England, popularly supposed to have been built by the Templars, the Temple Church in London was built by them; that of Maplestead, in Essex, by the Hospitallers; that of Northampton by Simon de St. Liz, first Norman

wealth and grandeur of the ancient knights. They had only five other houses in England, which were called Preceptories, and were dependent upon the Temple in London.

The knights wore the usual armour of the period; but while other knights wore the flowing surcoat of the twelfth or thirteenth centuries, the tight-fitting jupon of the fourteenth, or the tabard of the fifteenth, of any colour which pleased their taste, and often embroidered with their armorial bearings, the Knights of the Temple were distinguished by wearing this portion of their equipment of white, with a red cross over the breast; and over all a long flowing white mantle, with a red cross on the shoulder; they also wore the monastic tonsure. In the early fourteenth century MS. in the British Museum, Royal 1,696, at f. 335, is a representation of Eracles, Prior at Jerusalem, the Prior of the Hospital, and the Master of the Temple, sent to France to ask for succour. The illumination shows us the King of France sitting on his throne, and before him is standing a religious in mitre and crozier, who is no doubt Eracles, and another in a peculiarly shaped black robe, with a cross patee on the left shoulder, who is either Hugh de Payens the Templar, or Raymond de Puy the Hospitaller, but which it is difficult to determine. Again, in the fine fourteenth

A Knight Templar.

Earl of Northampton, twice a pilgrim to the Holy Land; and that of Cambridge by some unknown individual.

century MS., Nero E. 2, at f. 345 v, is a representation of the trial of the Templars: there are three of them standing before the Pope and the King of France, dressed in a grey tunic, and over that a black mantle with a red cross on the left breast, and a pointed hood over the shoulders. Folio 350 represents the Master of the Temple being burnt to death in presence of the king and nobles. Again, in the fine MS. Royal 20, c. viii., of the time of our Richard II., at f. 42 and f. 48, are representations of the same scenes. Folio 42 is a group of Templars habited in long black coat, fitting close up to the neck, like the ordinary civil robes of the time, with a pointed hood (like that with which we are familiar in the portraits of Dante), with a cross patee on the right shoulder; the hair is tonsured. At f. 45 is the burning of a group of Templars (not tonsured), and at f. 48 the burning of the Master of the Temple and another (tonsured). Their banner was of a black and white striped cloth, called *beauseant*, which word they adopted as a war-cry. The rule allowed three horses and a servant to each knight. Married knights were admitted, but there were no sisters of the order. The order was suppressed with circumstances of gross injustice and cruelty in the fourteenth century, and the bulk of their estates was given to the Hospitallers. The knight here given, from Hollar's plate, is a prior of the order, in armour of the thirteenth century.

The KNIGHTS OF ST. JOHN OF JERUSALEM, or the Knights Hospitallers, originally were not a military order; they were founded about 1092 by the merchants of Amalfi, in Italy, for the purpose of affording hospitality to pilgrims in the Holy Land. Their chief house, which was called the Hospital, was situated at Jerusalem, over against the Church of the Holy Sepulchre; and they had independent hospitals in other places in the Holy Land, which were frequented by the pilgrims. Their kindness to the sick and wounded soldiers of the first crusade made them popular, and several of the crusading princes endowed them with estates; while many of the crusaders, instead of returning home, laid down their arms, and joined the brotherhood of the Hospital. During this period of their history their habit was a plain black robe, with a linen cross upon the left breast.

At length their endowments having become greater than the needs of their hospitals required, and incited by the example of the Templars, a little before established, Raymond de Puy, the then master of the hospital, offered to King Baldwin II. to reconstruct the order on the model of the Templars. From this time the two military orders formed a powerful standing army for the defence of the kingdom of Jerusalem. When Palestine was finally lost to the Christians, the Knights of St. John passed into the Isle of Cyprus, afterwards to the Isle of Rhodes, and, finally, to the Isle of Malta,* maintaining a constant warfare against the infidel, and doing good service in checking the westward progress of the Mohammedan arms. In the latter part of their history, and down to a recent period, they conferred great benefits by checking the ravages of the corsairs of North Africa on the commerce of the Mediterranean and the coast towns of Southern Europe. They patrolled the sea, in war-galleys, rowed by galley-slaves, each of which carried a force of armed soldiers—inferior brethren of the order, officered by its knights. They are not even now extinct.

The order was first introduced into England in the reign of Henry I., at Clerkenwell; which continued the principal house of the order in England, and was styled the Hospital. The Hospitallers had also dependent houses, called Commanderies, on many of their English estates, to the number of fifty-three in all. The houses of the military knights in England were only cells, erected on the estates with which they had been endowed, in order to cultivate those estates for the support of the order, and to form depôts for recruits; *i.e.* for novices, where they might be trained, not in learning like Benedictines, or agriculture like Cistercians, or preaching like Dominicans, but in piety and in military exercises. A plan and elevation of the Commandery of Chabburn, Northumberland, are engraved in Turner's "Domestic Architecture," vol. iii. p. 197. The superior of the order in England sat in Parliament, and was

---

* The order was divided into nations—the English knights, the French knights, &c.— each nation having a separate house, situated at different points of the island, for its defence. These houses, large and fine buildings, still remain, and many unedited records of the order are said to be still preserved on the island.

The Military Orders. 31

accounted the first lay baron. When on military duty the knights wore the ordinary armour of the period, with a red surcoat marked with a white cross on the breast, and a red mantle with a white cross on the shoulder. Some of their churches in England possibly had circular naves, like the church of the Temple in Jerusalem; out of the four "round churches," which remain, one belonged to the Knights of the Hospital. The chapel at Chabburn is a rectangular building. There were many sisters of the order, but only one house of them in England.

One of two earlier representations of knights of the order may be noted here. In a MS. in the Library at Ghent, of the date of our Edward IV., is a picture of John Lonstrother, prior of the order; he wears a long sleeveless gown over armour. It is engraved in the "Archæologia," xiii. 14. The MS. Add. 18,143 in the British Museum is said in a note at the beginning of the volume to have been the missal of Phillippe de Villiers de l'Isle Adam, the famous Grand Master of the Order of St. John of Jerusalem from 1521 to 1534.

A Knight Hospitaller.

In the frontispiece is a portrait of the Grand Master in a black robe lined with fur, and a cross patee on the breast. On the opposite page is another portrait of him in a robe of different fashion, with a cross rather differently shaped. The monument of the last English Prior, Sir Thomas Tresham, in his robes as prior of the order, still remains in Rushton Church, Northants. A fine portrait of a Knight of Malta is in the National Gallery. The Hospitaller given on the preceding page, from Hollar's plate, is a (not very good) representation of one in the armour of the early part of the fourteenth century, with the usual knight's *chapeau,* instead of the mail hood or the basinet, on his head.

It will be gathered from the authorities of the costume of the Knights of the Temple and of the Hospital here noted, that when we picture to ourselves the knights on duty in the Holy Land or elsewhere, it should be in the armour of their period with the uniform surcoat of their order; but when we desire to realise their appearance as they were to be ordinarily seen, in chapel or refectory, or about their estates, or forming part of any ordinary scene of English life, it must be in the long cassock-like gown, with the cross on the shoulder, and the tonsured head, described in the above authorities, which would make their appearance resemble that of other religious persons.

Other military orders, which never extended to England, were the order of TEUTONIC KNIGHTS, a fraternity similar to that of the Templars, but consisting entirely of Germans; and the order of OUR LADY OF MERCY, a Spanish knightly order in imitation of that of the Trinitarians.

One other order of religious—the TRINITARIANS—we have reserved for this place, because while by their rule they are classed among the Augustinian orders, the object of their foundation gives them an affinity with the military orders, and their mode of pursuing that object makes their organisation and life resemble that of friars. The moral interest of their work, and its picturesque scenes and associations, lead us to give a little larger space to them than we have been able to do to most of the other orders. It is difficult for us to realise that the Mohammedan power seemed at one time not unlikely to subjugate all Europe; and that after their career of conquest had been arrested, the Mohammedan states of North Africa continued for centuries to be a scourge to the commerce of Europe, and a terror to the inhabitants of the coasts of the Mediterranean. They scoured the Great Sea with their galleys, and captured ships; they made descents on the coasts, and plundered towns and villages; and carried off the captives into slavery, and retreated in safety with their booty, to their African harbours. It is only within quite recent times that the last of these strongholds was destroyed by an English fleet, and that the Greek and Italian feluccas have ceased to fear the Algerine pirates. We have already briefly stated how the Hospitallers, after their original service was ended by the expulsion of the Christians from the Holy Land, settled first at Cyprus, then at Rhodes, and did good service as a bulwark against the Mohammedan progress; and lastly, as Knights of Malta, acted as the police of the Mediterranean, and did their best to oppose the piracies of the Corsairs. But in spite of the vigilance and prowess of the knights, many a merchant ship was captured, many a fishing village was sacked, and many captives, men, women, and children of all ranks of society, were carried off into slavery; and their slavery was a cruel one, exaggerated by the scorn and hatred bred of antagonism in race and religion, and made ruthless by the recollection of ages of mutual injuries. The relations and friends of the unhappy captives, where they were people of wealth and influence, used every exertion to rescue those who were dear to them, and their captors were ordinarily willing to set them to ransom; but hopeless indeed was the lot of those—and they, of course, were the great majority—who had no friends rich enough to help them.

The miserable fate of these helpless ones moved the compassion of some Christ-like souls. John de Matha, born, in 1154, of noble parents in Provence, with Felix de Valois, retired to a desert place, where, at the foot of a little hill, a fountain of cold water issued forth; a white hart was accustomed to resort to this fountain, and hence it had received the name of Cervus Frigidus, represented in French by (or representing the French?) Cerfroy. There, about A.D. 1197, these two good men—the Clarkson and Wilberforce of their time—arranged the institution of a new Order for the Redemption of Captives. The new order received the approval of the Pope Innocent III., and took its place among the recognised orders of the church. This Papal approval of their institution constituted an authorisation from the head of the church to seek alms from all Christendom in furtherance of their object. Their rules directed that one-third of their income only should be reserved for their own maintenance, one-third should be given to the poor, and one-third for the special object of redeeming captives. The two philanthropists preached throughout France, collecting alms, and recruiting men who were willing to join them·in their good work. In the first year they were able to send two brethren to Africa, to negotiate the redemption of a hundred and eighty-six Christian captives; next year, John himself went, and brought back a thankful company of a hundred and ten; and on a third voyage, a hundred and twenty more; and the order continued to flourish,* and established a house of the order in Africa, as its agent with the infidel. They were introduced into England by Sir William Lucy of Charlecote, on his return from the Crusade; who built and endowed for them Thellesford Priory in Warwickshire; and subsequently they had eleven other houses in England. St. Rhadegunda was their tutelary saint. Their habit was white, with a Greek cross of red and blue on the breast—the three colours being taken to signify the three persons of the Holy Trinity, viz., the white, the Eternal Father; the blue, which was the transverse limb of the cross, the Son; and the red, the charity of the Holy Spirit.

The order were called TRINITARIANS, from their devotion to the Blessed Trinity, all their houses being so dedicated, and hence the significance of their badge; they were commonly called MATHURINS, after the name of their founder; and BRETHREN OF THE ORDER OF THE HOLY TRINITY FOR THE REDEMPTION OF CAPTIVES, from their object.

Before turning from the monks to the friars, we must devote a brief sentence to the ALIEN PRIORIES. These were cells of foreign abbeys, founded upon estates which English proprietors had given to the foreign houses. After the expenses of the establishment had been defrayed, the surplus revenue, or a fixed sum in lieu of it, was remitted to the parent house abroad. There were over one hundred and twenty of them when Edward I., on the breaking out of the war with France, seized upon them,

---

* An order, called our Lady of Mercy, was founded in Spain in 1258, by Peter Nolasco, for a similar object, including in its scope not only Christian captives to the infidel, but also all slaves, captives, and prisoners for debt.

in 1285, as belonging to the enemy. Edward II. appears to have pursued the same course; and, again, Edward III., in 1337. Henry IV. only reserved to himself, in time of war, what these houses had been accustomed to pay to the foreign abbeys in time of peace. But at length they were all dissolved by act of Parliament in the second year of Henry V., and their possessions were devoted for the most part to religious and charitable uses.

CHAPTER V.

THE ORDERS OF FRIARS.

WE have seen how for three centuries, from the beginning of the tenth to the end of the twelfth, a series of religious orders arose, each aiming at a more successful reproduction of the monastic ideal. The thirteenth century saw the rise of a new class of religious orders, actuated by a different principle from that of monachism. The principle of monachism, we have said, was seclusion from mankind, and abstraction from worldly affairs, for the sake of religious contemplation. To this end monasteries were founded in the wilds, far from the abodes of men; and he who least often suffered his feet or his thoughts to wander beyond the cloister was so far the best monk. The principle which inspired the FRIARS was that of devotion to the performance of active religious duties among mankind. Their houses were built in or near the great towns; and to the majority of the brethren the houses of the order were mere temporary resting-places, from which they issued to make their journeys through town and country, preaching in the parish churches, or from the steps of the market-crosses, and carrying their ministrations to every castle and every cottage.

> "I speke of many hundred years ago,
> For now can no man see non elves mo;
> For now the great charity and prayers
> Of lymytours and other holy freres
> That serchen every land and every stream
> As thick as motis in the sunne-beam,
> Blessing halls, chambers, kitchens, and bowers,
> Cities and burghs, castles high and towers,

> Thorps and barns, shippons and dairies,
> This maketh that there been no fairies.
> For there as wont to walken was an elf,
> There walketh now the lymytour himself
> In undermeles and in morwenings,*
> And sayeth his matins and his holy things,
> As he goeth in his lymytacioun."—*Wife of Bath's Tale.*

They were, in fact, home missionaries; and the zeal and earnestness of their early efforts, falling upon times when such an agency was greatly needed, produced very striking results. "Till the days of Martin Luther," says Sir James Stephen, " the church had never seen so great and effectual a reform as theirs . . . Nothing in the histories of Wesley or of Whitefield can be compared with the enthusiasm which everywhere welcomed them, or with the immediate visible result of their labours." In the character of St. Francis, notwithstanding its superstition and exaggerated asceticism, there is something specially attractive: in his intense sympathy with the sorrows and sufferings of the poor, his tender and respectful love for them as members of Christ, his heroic self-devotion to their service for Christ's sake, in his vivid realisation of the truth that birds, beasts, and fishes are God's creatures, and our fellow-creatures. In the work of both Francis and Dominic there is much which is worth careful study at the present day. Now, too, there is a mass of misery in our large towns huge and horrible enough to kindle the Christ-like pity of another Francis; in country as well as town there are ignorance and irreligion enough to call forth the zeal of another Dominic. In our Sisters of Mercy we see among women a wonderful rekindling of the old spirit of self-sacrifice, in a shape adapted to our time; we need not despair of seeing the same spirit rekindled among men, freed from the old superstitions and avoiding the old blunders, and setting itself to combat the gigantic evils which threaten to overwhelm both religion and social order.

Both these reformers took great pains to fit their followers for the office of preachers and teachers, sending them in large numbers to the universities, and founding colleges there for the reception of their students. With an admirable largeness of view, they did not confine

---

* Afternoons and mornings.

their studies to theology, but cultivated the whole range of Science and Art, and so successful were they, that in a short time the professional chairs of the universities of Europe were almost monopolised by the learned members of the mendicant orders.* The constitutions required that no one should be licensed as a general preacher until he had studied theology for three years; then a provincial or general chapter examined into his character and learning; and, if these were satisfactory, gave him his commission, either limiting his ministry to a certain district (whence he was called in English a *limitour*, like Chaucer's Friar Hubert), or allowing him to exercise it where he listed (when he was called a *lister*). This authority to preach, and exercise other spiritual functions, necessarily brought the friars into collision with the parochial clergy;† and while a learned and good friar would do much good in parishes which were cursed with an ignorant, or slothful, or wicked pastor, on the other hand, the inferior class of friars are accused of abusing their position by setting the people against their pastors whose pulpits they usurped, and interfering injuriously with the discipline of the parishes into which they intruded. For it was not very long before the primitive purity and zeal of the mendicant orders began to deteriorate. This was inevitable; zeal and goodness cannot be perpetuated by a system; all human societies of superior pretensions gradually deteriorate, even as the Apostolic Church itself did. But there were peculiar circumstances in the system of the mendicant orders which tended to induce rapid deterioration. The profession of mendicancy tended to encourage the use of all those little paltry arts of

---

* As an indication of their zeal in the pursuit of science it is only necessary to mention the names of Friar Roger Bacon, the Franciscan, and Friar Albert-le-Grand (Albertus Magnus), the Dominican. The Arts were cultivated with equal zeal—some of the finest paintings in the world were executed for the friars, and their own orders produced artists of the highest excellence. Fra Giacopo da Turrita, a celebrated artist in mosaic of the thirteenth century, was a Franciscan, as was Fra Antonio da Negroponti, the painter; Fra Fillippo Lippi, the painter, was a Carmelite; Fra Bartolomeo, and Fra Angelico da Fiesole—than whom no man ever conceived more heavenly visions of spiritual loveliness and purity—were Dominicans.

† " By his (*i.e.* Satan's) queyntise they comen in,
　　The curates to helpen,
　　But that harmed hem hard
　　And help them ful littel."—*Piers Ploughman's Creed.*

popularity-hunting which injure the usefulness of a minister of religion, and lower his moral tone: the fact that an increased number of friars was a source of additional wealth to a convent, since it gave an increased number of collectors of alms for it, tended to make the convents less scrupulous as to the fitness of the men whom they admitted. So that we can believe the truth of the accusations of the old satirists, that dissolute, good-for-nothing fellows sought the friar's frock and cowl, for the license which it gave to lead a vagabond life, and levy contributions on the charitable. Such men could easily appropriate to themselves a portion of what was given them for the convent; and they had ample opportunity, away from the control of their ecclesiastical superiors, to spend their peculations in dissolute living.* We may take, therefore, Chaucer's Friar John, of the Sompnour's Tale, as a type of a certain class of friars; but we must remember that at the same time there were many earnest, learned, and excellent men in the mendicant orders; even as Mawworm and John Wesley might flourish together in the same body.

The convents of friars were not independent bodies, like the Benedictine

Costumes of the Four Orders of Friars.

and Augustinian abbeys; each order was an organised body, governed by the general of the order, and under him, by provincial priors, priors of the convents, and their subordinate officials. There are usually reckoned four orders of friars—the Dominicans, Franciscans, Carmelites, and Augustines.

---

* The extract from Chaucer on p. 46, lines 4, 5, 6, seem to indicate that an individual friar sometimes "farmed" the alms of a district, paying the convent a stipulated sum, and taking the surplus for himself.

> "I found there freres,
> All the foure orders,
> Techynge the peple
> To profit of themselves."
>
> *Piers Ploughman*, l. 115.

The four orders are pictured together in the woodcut on the preceding page from the thirteenth century MS. Harl. 1,527.

They were called *Friars* because, out of humility, their founders would not have them called *Father* and *Dominus*, like the monks, but simply *Brother* (*Frater, Frère, Friar*).

The DOMINICANS and FRANCISCANS arose simultaneously at the beginning of the thirteenth century. Dominic, an Augustinian canon, a Spaniard of noble birth, was seized with a zeal for converting heretics, and having gradually associated a few ecclesiastics with himself, he at length conceived the idea of founding an order of men who should spend their lives in preaching. Simultaneously, Francis, the son of a rich Italian merchant, was inspired with a design to establish a new order of men, who should spend their lives in preaching the Gospel and doing works of charity among the people. These two men met in Rome in the year 1216 A.D., and some attempt was made to induce them to unite their institutions in one; but Francis was unwilling, and the Pope sanctioned both.

S. Dominic and S. Francis.

Both adopted the Augustinian rule, and both required not only that their followers personally should have no property, but also that they should not possess any property collectively as a body; their followers were to work for a livelihood, or to live on alms. The two orders retained something of the character of their founders: the Dominicans that of the learned, energetic, dogmatic, and stern controversialist; they were defenders of the orthodox faith, not only by argument, but by the terrors of the Inquisition, which was in their hands; even as their master is, rightly or wrongly, said to have sanctioned the cruelties which were used against the Albigenses when his preaching had failed to convince them. The Franciscans retained something of the character of the pious, ardent, fanciful enthusiast from whom they took their name.

Dominic gave to his order the name of Preaching Friars; more commonly they were styled Dominicans, or, from the colour of their habits, Black Friars*—their habit consisting of a white tunic, fastened with a white girdle, over that a white scapulary, and over all a black mantle and hood, and shoes; the lay brethren wore a black scapulary.

The woodcut which we give on the preceding page of two friars, with their names, DOMINIC and FRANCIS, inscribed over them, is taken from a representation in a MS. of the end of the thirteenth century (Sloan 346), of a legend of a vision of Dominic related in the "Legenda Aurea," in which the Virgin Mary is deprecating the wrath of Christ, about to destroy the world for its iniquity, and presenting to him Dominic and Francis, with a promise that they will convert the world from its wickedness. The next woodcut is from Hollar's print in the "Monasticon." An early fifteenth century illustration of a Dominican friar, in black mantle and brown hood over a white tunic, may be found on the last page of the Harleian MS., 1,527. A fine picture of St. Dominic, by Mario Zoppo (1471-98), in the National Gallery, shows the costume admirably; he stands preaching, with book and rosary in his left hand. The Dominican nuns wore the same dress with a white veil. They had, according to the last edition of the "Monasticon," fifty-eight houses in England.

A Dominican Friar.

---

* In France, Jacobins.

The Franciscans were styled by their founder Fratri Minori—lesser brothers, Friars Minors; they were more usually called Grey Friars, from the colour of their habits, or Cordeliers, from the knotted cord which formed their characteristic girdle. Their habit was originally a grey tunic with long loose sleeves (but not quite so loose as those of the Benedictines), a knotted cord for a girdle, and a black hood; the feet always bare, or only protected by sandals. In the fifteenth century the colour of the habit was altered to a dark brown. The woodcut is from Hollar's print. A picture of St. Francis, by Felippino Lippi (1460—1505), in the National Gallery shows the costume very clearly. Piers Ploughman describes the irregular indulgences in habit worn by less strict members of the order:—

"In cutting of his cope
Is more cloth y-folden
Than was in Frauncis' froc,
When he them first made.
And yet under that cope
A coat hath he, furred
With foyns or with fichews
Or fur of beaver,
And that is cut to the knee,
And quaintly y-buttoned
Lest any spiritual man
Espie that guile.
Fraunceys bad his brethren
Barefoot to wenden.
Now have they buckled shoon
For blenying [blistering] of ther heels,
And hosen in harde weather
Y-hamled [tied] by the ancle."

A Franciscan Friar.

A beautiful little picture of St. Francis receiving the stigmata may be found in a Book of Offices of the end of the fourteenth century (Harl. 2,897, f. 407 v.). Another fifteenth-century picture of the same subject is in a Book of Hours (Harl. 5,328, f. 123). Some fine sixteenth-century authorities for Franciscan costumes are in the MS. life of St. Francis (Harl. 3,229, f. 26). The principal picture represents St. Bonaventura, a saint of the order, in a gorgeous cope over his brown frock and hood, seated writing in his cell; through the open door is seen a corridor with doors opening off it to other cells. In the corners of the page are other pictures of St. Anthony of Padua, and St. Bernardine, and another saint, and St. Clare, foundress of the female order of Franciscans. A very good illumination of two Franciscans in grey frocks and hoods, girded with rope and barefooted, will be found in the MS. Add. 17,687 of date 1498. The Franciscan nuns, or Minoresses, or Poor Clares, as they were sometimes called, from St. Clare, the patron saint and first nun of the order, wore the same habit as the monks, only with a black veil instead of a hood. For another illustration of minoresses see MS. Royal 1,696, f. 111, v. The Franciscans were first introduced into England, at Canterbury, in the year 1223 A.D., and there were sixty-five houses of the order in England, besides four of minoresses.

While the Dominicans retained their unity of organisation to the last, the Franciscans divided into several branches, under the names of Minorites, Capuchins, Minims, Observants, Recollets, &c.

The CARMELITE FRIARS had their origin, as their name indicates, in the East. According to their own traditions, ever since the days of Elijah, whom they claim as their founder, the rocks of Carmel have been inhabited by a succession of hermits, who have lived after the pattern of the great prophet. Their institution as an order of friars, however, dates from the beginning of the thirteenth century, when Albert, Patriarch of Jerusalem, gave them a rule, founded upon, but more severe than, that of St. Basil; and gave them a habit of white and red stripes, which, according to tradition, was the fashion of the wonder-working mantle of their prophet-founder. The order immediately spread into the West, and Pope Honorius III. sanctioned it, and changed the habit to a white frock over a dark brown tunic; and very soon after, the third general of the order, an Englishman, Simon Stock, added the scapulary, of the same colour as the tunic, by which they are to be distinguished from the Premonstratensian canons, whose habit is the same, except that it wants the scapulary. From the colour of the habit the popular English name for the Carmelites was the White Friars. Sir John de Vesci, an English crusader, in the early part of the thirteenth century, made the ascent of Mount Carmel, and found these religious living there, claiming to be the successors of Elijah. The romantic incident seems to have interested him, and he brought back some of them to England, and thus introduced the order here, where it became more popular than elsewhere in Europe, but it was never an influential order. They had ultimately fifty houses in England.

The AUSTIN FRIARS were founded in the middle of the thirteenth century. There were still at that time some small communities which were not enrolled among any of the great recognised orders, and a great number of hermits and solitaries, who lived under no rule at all. Pope Innocent IV. decreed that all these hermits, solitaries, and separate communities, should be incorporated into a new order, under the rule of St. Augustine, with some stricter clauses added, under the name of Ermiti Augustini, Hermits of St. Augustine, or, as they were popularly called, Austin Friars. Their exterior habit was a black gown with broad sleeves, girded with a leather belt, and black cloth hood. There were forty-five houses of them in England.

A Carmelite Friar.

There were also some minor orders of friars, who do not need a detailed description. The Crutched (crossed) Friars, so called because they had a red cross on the back and breast of their blue habit, were introduced into England in the middle of the thirteenth century, and had ten houses here. The Friars de Pœnitentiâ, or the Friars of the Sack, were introduced a little later, and had nine houses. And there were six other friaries of obscure orders. But all these minor mendicant orders—all except the four great orders, the Franciscans, Dominicans, Augustinians, and Carmelites,—were suppressed by the Council of Lyons, A.D. 1370.

Chaucer lived in the latter half of the fourteenth century, when, after a hundred and forty years' existence, the orders of friars, or at least many individuals of the orders, had lost much of their primitive holiness and zeal. His avowed purpose is to satirise their abuses; so that, while we quote him largely for the life-like pictures of ancient customs and manners which he gives us, we must make allowance for the exaggerations of a satirist, and especially we must not take the faulty or vicious individuals, whom it suits his purpose to depict, as fair samples of the whole class. We have a nineteenth-century satirist of the failings and foibles of the clergy, to whom future generations will turn for illustrations of the life of cathedral towns and country parishes. We know how wrongly they would suppose that Dr. Proudie was a fair sample of nineteenth-century bishops, or Dr. Grantley of archdeacons "of the period," or Mr. Smylie of the evangelical clergy; we know there is no real bishop, archdeacon, or incumbent among us of whom those characters, so cleverly and amusingly, and in one sense so truthfully, drawn, are anything but exaggerated likenesses. With this caution, we do not hesitate to borrow illustrations of our subject from Chaucer and other contemporary writers.

In his description of Friar Hubert, who was one of the Canterbury pilgrims, he tells us how—

> "Full well beloved and familiar was he
> With frankelins over all in his countrie;
> And eke with worthy women of the town,*
> For he had power of confession,
> As said himself, more than a curate,
> For of his order he was licenciate.
> Full sweetely heard he confession,
> And pleasant was his absolution.
> He was an easy man to give penance
> There as he wist to have a good pittance,
> For unto a poor order for to give,
> Is signe that a man is well y-shrive.
> *   *   *   *
> His tippet was aye farsed† full of knives
> And pinnés for to give to fairé wives.
> And certainly he had a merry note,
> Well could he sing and playen on a rote.‡
> *   *   *   *

---

* Wives of burgesses.   † Stuffed.   ‡ Musical instrument so called.

> And over all there as profit should arise,
> Courteous he was, and lowly of service.
> There was no man no where so virtuous,
> He was the beste beggar in all his house,
> And gavè a certain ferme for the grant
> None of his brethren came in his haunt."

As to his costume :—

> For there was he not like a cloisterer,
> With threadbare cope, as is a poor scholar,
> But he was like a master or a pope,
> Of double worsted was his semi-cope,*
> That round was as a bell out of the press."

In the Sompnour's tale the character, here merely sketched, is worked out in detail, and gives such a wonderfully life-like picture of a friar, and of his occupation, and his intercourse with the people, that we cannot do better than lay considerable extracts from it before our readers :—

> " Lordings there is in Yorkshire, as I guess,
> A marsh country y-called Holderness,
> In which there went a limitour† about
> To preach, and eke to beg, it is no doubt.
> And so befel that on a day this frere
> Had preached at a church in his mannére,
> And specially aboven every thing
> Excited he the people in his preaching
> To trentals,‡ and to give for Goddé's sake,
> Wherewith men mighten holy houses make,
> There as divine service is honoured,
> Not there as it is wasted and devoured.§

---

* Piers Ploughman (creed 3, line 434), describing a burly Dominican friar, describes his cloak or cope in the same terms, and describes the under gown, or kirtle, also :—

> " His cope that beclypped him
> Wel clean was it folden,
> Of double worsted y-dyght
> Down to the heel.
> His kirtle of clean white,
> Cleanly y-served,
> It was good enough ground
> Grain for to beren."

† A limitour, as has been explained above, was a friar whose functions were limited to a certain district of country ; a lister might exercise his office wherever he listed.
‡ Thirty masses for the repose of a deceased person.
§ Viz., in convents of friars, not in monasteries of monks and by the secular clergy.

> 'Trentals,' said he, 'deliver from penance
> Ther friendés' soules, as well old as young,
> Yea, when that they are speedily y-sung.
> Not for to hold a priest jolly and gay,
> He singeth not but one mass* of a day,
> Deliver out,' quoth he, 'anon† the souls.
> Full hard it is, with flesh-hook or with owles
> To be y-clawed, or to burn or bake :
> Now speed you heartily, for Christé's sake.'
>   And when this frere had said all his intent,
> With *qui cum patre*‡ forth his way he went ;
> When folk in church had given him what they lest
> He went his way, no longer would he rest."

Then he takes his way through the village with his brother friar (it seems to have been the rule for them to go in couples) and a servant after them to carry their sack, begging at every house.

> "With scrippe and tipped staff, y-tucked high,
> In every house he gan to pore and pry ;
> And begged meal or cheese, or ellés corn.
> His fellow had a staff tipped with horn,
> A pair of tables all of ivory,
> And a pointel y-polished fetisly,
> And wrote always the namés, as he stood,
> Of allé folk that gave them any good,
> As though that he woulde for them pray.
> 'Give us a bushel of wheat, or malt, or rye,
> A Goddé's kichel,§ or a trippe of cheese ;
> Or ellés what you list, we may not chese ; ‖
> A Goddé's halfpenny, or a mass penny,
> Or give us of your bran, if ye have any,
> A dagon ¶ of your blanket, dearé dame,
> Our sister dear (lo ! here I write your name) :
> Bacon or beef, or such thing as you find.'
> A sturdy harlot** went them aye behind,

---

* He was forbidden to say more.

† A convent of friars used to undertake masses for the dead, and each friar saying one the whole number of masses was speedily completed, whereas a single priest saying his one mass a day would be very long completing the number, and meantime the souls were supposed to be in torment.

‡ The usual way of concluding a sermon, in those days as in these, was with an ascription of praise, " Who with the Father," &c.

§ Cake.   ‖ Choose.   ¶ Slip or piece.   ** Hired man.

That was their hosté's man, and bare a sack,
And what men gave them laid it on his back.
And when that he was out at door, anon
He planed away the names every one,
That he before had written on his tables;
He served them with triffles* and with fables."

At length he comes to a house in which, the goodwife being devôte, he has been accustomed to be hospitably received:—

" So along he went, from house to house, till he
Came to a house where he was wont to be
Refreshed more than in a hundred places.
Sick lay the husbandman whose that the place is;
Bedrid upon a couché low he lay:
'*Deus hic*,' quoth he, 'O Thomas, friend, good day'
Said this frere, all courteously and soft.
'Thomas,' quoth he, ' God yield† it you, full oft
Have I upon this bench fared full well,
Here have I eaten many a merry meal.'
And from the bench he drove away the cat,
And laid adown his potent‡ and his hat,
And eke his scrip, and set himself adown:
His fellow was y-walked into town
Forth with his knave, into that hostlery
Where as he shope him thilké night to lie
' O deré master,' quoth this sické man,
' How have ye fared since that March began?
I saw you not this fourteen night and more.'
' God wot,' quoth he, ' laboured have I full sore;
And specially for thy salvation
Have I sayd many a precious orison,
And for our other friendes, God them bless.
I have this day been at your church at messe,
And said a sermon to my simple wit.
    *   *   *   *
And there I saw our dame. Ah! where is she?'
' Yonder I trow that in the yard she be,'
Saidé this man, ' and she will come anon.'
' Eh master, welcome be ye, by St. John!'
Saide this wife; ' how fare ye heartily?'
This friar ariseth up full courteously,
And her embraceth in his armés narwe,§
And kisseth her sweet, and chirketh as a sparrow

---

* Trifles.   † Requite.   ‡ Staff.   § Closely.

With his lippes : 'Dame,' quoth he, 'right well,
As he that is your servant every deal.*
Thanked be God that you gave soul and life,
Yet saw I not this day so fair a wife
In all the churché, God so save me.'
 'Yea, God amendé defaults, sire,' quoth she;
'Algates welcome be ye, by my fay.'
 '*Graunt mercy*, dame; that have I found alway.
But of your great goodness, by your leve,
I wouldé pray you that ye not you grieve,
I will with Thomas speak a little throw;
These curates be so negligent and slow
To searchen tenderly a conscience.
In shrift, in preaching, is my diligence,
And study, on Peter's words and on Paul's,
I walk and fishen Christian menne's souls,
To yield our Lord Jesu his proper rent;
To spread his word is set all mine intent.'
 'Now, by your faith, dere sir,' quoth she,
'Chide him well for Seinté Charitee.
He is as angry as a pissemire,'" &c.

Whereupon the friar begins at once to scold the goodman :—

"'O Thomas, *je vous die*, Thomas, Thomas,
This maketh the fiend, this must be amended.
Ire is a thing that high God hath defended,†
And therefore will I speak a word or two.'
 'Now, master,' quoth the wife, 'ere that I go,
What will ye dine ? I will go thereabout.'
 'Now, dame,' quoth he, '*je vous dis sans doubte*,
Have I not of a capon but the liver,
And of your white bread but a shiver,
And after that a roasted piggé's head
(But I ne would for me no beast were dead),
Then had I with you homely suffisance;
I am a man of little sustenance,
My spirit hath his fostering in the Bible.
My body is aye so ready and so penible
To waken, that my stomach is destroyed.
I pray you, dame, that ye be not annoyed,
Though I so friendly you my counsel shew.
By God! I n'old‡ have told it but a few.'

---

* Part.   † Forbidden.   ‡ Would not.

'Now, sir,' quoth she, 'but one word ere I go.
My child is dead within these weekés two,
Soon after that ye went out of this town.' *
'His death saw I by revelation,'
Said this frere, 'at home in our dortour.†
I dare well say that ere that half an hour
After his death, I saw him borne to blisse
In mine vision, so God me wisse.
So did our sexton and our fermerere,‡
That have been trué friars fifty year;
They may now, God be thanked of his loan,
Make their jubilee and walke alone.' " §

We do not care to continue the blasphemous lies with which he plays upon the mother's tenderness for her dead babe. At length, addressing the sick goodman, he continues :—

" ' Thomas, Thomas, so might I ride or go,
And by that lord that cleped is St. Ive,
N'ere‖ thou our brother, shouldest thou not thrive,
In our chapter pray we ¶ day and night
To Christ that he thee send hele and might**
Thy body for to welden hastily.'
'God wot,' quoth he, 'I nothing thereof feel,
So help me Christ, as I in fewé years
Have spended upon divers manner freres
Full many a pound, yet fare I never the bet.'
The frere answered, 'O Thomas, dost thou so?
What need have you diverse friars to seche?
What needeth him that hath a perfect leech ††
To seeken other leches in the town?
Your inconstancy is your confusion.
Hold ye then me, or elles our convent,
To pray for you is insufficient?
Thomas, that jape is not worth a mite;
Your malady is for we have too lite.‡‡

---

* The good man also said he had not seen the friar "this fourteen nights:"—Did a limitour go round once a fortnight?
† The dormitory of the convent.
‡ Infirmarer.
§ Aged monks and friars lived in the Infirmary, and had certain privileges.
‖ Wert thou not.
¶ Implying, whether truly or not, that he had been enrolled in the fraternity of the house, and was prayed for, with other benefactors, in chapter.
** Health and strength.   †† Doctor.   ‡‡ Little.

> Ah! give that convent half a quarter of oates;
> And give that convent four and twenty groats;
> And give that friar a penny and let him go;
> Nay, nay, Thomas, it may nothing be so;
> What is a farthing worth parted in twelve?"

And so he takes up the cue the wife had given him, and reads him a long sermon on anger, quoting Seneca, and giving, for instances, Cambyses and Cyrus, and at length urges him to confession. To this—

> "'Nay,' quoth the sick man, 'by Saint Simon,
> I have been shriven this day by my curate.'
> * * * * * *
> 'Give me then of thy gold to make our cloister,'

and again he proclaims the virtues and morals of his order.

> "'For if ye lack our predication,*
> Then goth this world all to destruction.
> For whoso from this world would us bereave,
> So God me save, Thomas, by your leave,
> He would bereave out of this world the sun,' &c.

And so ends with the ever-recurring burden :—

> "'Now, Thomas, help for Sainte Charitee.'
> This sicke man wax well nigh wood for ire,†
> He woulde that the frere had been a fire.
> With his false dissimulation ;"

and proceeds to play a practical joke upon him, which will not bear even hinting at, but which sufficiently shows that superstition did not prevent men from taking great liberties, expressing the utmost contempt of these men. Moreover,—

> "His mennie which had hearden this affray,
> Came leaping in and chased out the frere."

Thus ignominiously turned out of the goodman's house, the friar goes to the court-house of the lord of the village :—

> "A sturdy pace down to the court he goth,
> Whereat there woned ‡ a man of great honour,
> To whom this friar was alway confessour ;
> This worthy man was lord of that village.

---

* Preaching; he was probably a preaching friar—*i.e.*. a Dominican.
† Waxed nearly mad. ‡ Lived.

> This frere came, as he were in a rage,
> Whereas this lord sat eating at his board.
> * * * *
> This lord gan look, and saide, *'Benedicite !*
> What, frere John ! what manner of world is this ?
> I see well that something there is amiss.' "

We need only complete the picture by adding the then actors in it :—

> " The lady of the house aye stille sat,
> Till she had herde what the friar said."

And

> "Now stood the lorde's squire at the board,
> That carved his meat, and hearde every word
> Of all the things of which I have you said."

And it needs little help of the imagination to complete this contemporary picture of an English fourteenth-century village, with its lord and its well-to-do farmer, and its villagers, its village inn, its parish church and priest, and the fortnightly visit of the itinerant friars.

We have now completed our sketch of the rise of the religious orders, and of their general character; we have only to conclude this portion of our task with a brief history of their suppression in England. Henry VIII. had resoved to break with the pope; the religious orders were great upholders of the papal supremacy; the friars especially were called " the pope's militia;" the king resolved, therefore, upon the destruction of the friars. The pretext was a reform of the religious orders. At the end of the year 1535 a royal commission undertook the visitation of all the religious houses, above one thousand three hundred in number, including their cells and hospitals. They performed their task with incredible celerity—" the king's command was exceeding urgent;" and in ten weeks they presented their report. The small houses they reported to be full of irregularity and vice; while "in the great solemne monasteries, thanks be to God, religion was right well observed and kept up." So the king's decree went forth, and parliament ratified it, that all the religious houses of less than £200 annual value should be suppressed. This just caught all the friaries, and a few of the less powerful monasteries for the sake of impartiality. Perhaps the monks were not greatly moved at the destruction which had come upon their rivals; but their turn very speedily came.

They were not suppressed forcibly; but they were induced to surrender. The patronage of most of the abbacies was in the king's hands, or under his control. He induced some of the abbots by threats or cajolery, and the offer of place and pension, to surrender their monasteries into his hand; others he induced to surrender their abbatial offices only, into which he placed creatures of his own, who completed the surrender. Some few intractable abbots—like those of Reading, Glastonbury, and St. John's, Colchester, who would do neither one nor the other—were found guilty of high treason—no difficult matter when it had been made high treason by act of Parliament to "publish in words" that the king was an "heretic, schismatic, or tyrant"—and they were disposed of by hanging, drawing, and quartering. The Hospitallers of Clerkenwell were still more difficult to deal with, and required a special act of Parliament to suppress them. Those who gave no trouble were rewarded with bishoprics, livings, and pensions; the rest were turned adrift on the wide world, to dig, or beg, or starve. We are not defending the principle of monasticism; it may be that, with the altered circumstances of the church and nation, the day of usefulness of the monasteries had passed. But we cannot restrain an expression of indignation at the shameless, reckless manner of the suppression. The commissioners suggested, and Bishop Latimer entreated in vain, that two or three monasteries should be left in every shire for religious, and learned, and charitable uses; they were all shared among the king and his courtiers. The magnificent churches were pulled down; the libraries, of inestimable value, were destroyed; the alms which the monks gave to the poor, the hospitals which they maintained for the old and impotent, the infirmaries for the sick, the schools for the people—all went in the wreck; and the tithes of parishes which were in the hands of the monasteries, were swallowed up indiscriminately—they were not men to strain at such gnats while they were swallowing camels—some three thousand parishes, including those of the most populous and important towns, were left impoverished to this day. No wonder that the fountains of religious endowment in England have been dried up ever since;—and the course of modern legislation is not calculated to set them again a-flowing.

CHAPTER VI.

THE CONVENT.

HAVING thus given a sketch of the history of the various monastic orders in England, we proceed to give some account of the constitution of a convent, taking that of a Benedictine monastery as a type, from which the other orders departed only in minor particulars.

The *convent* is the name especially appropriate to the body of individuals who composed a religious community. These were the body of cloister monks, lay and clerical; the professed brethren, who were also lay and clerical; the clerks; the novices; and the servants and artificers. The servants and artificers were of course taken from the lower ranks of society; all the rest were originally of the most various degrees of rank and social position. We constantly meet with instances of noble men and women, knights and ladies, minstrels and merchants, quitting their secular occupations at various periods of their life, and taking the religious habit; some of them continuing simply professed brethren, others rising to high offices in their order. Scions of noble houses were not infrequently entered at an early age as novices, either devoted to the religious life by the piety of their parents, or, with more worldly motives, thus provided with a calling and a maintenance; and sometimes considerable interest was used to procure the admittance of novices into the great monasteries. Again, the children of the poor were received into the monastic schools, and such as showed peculiar aptitude were sometimes at length admitted as monks,* and were eligible, and were often chosen, to the highest ecclesiastical dignities.

---

* " On the foundation," as we say now of colleges and endowed schools.

The whole convent was under the government of the *abbot*, who, however, was bound to govern according to the rule of the order. Sometimes he was elected by the convent; sometimes the king or some patron had a share in the election. Frequently there were estates attached to the office, distinct from those of the convent; sometimes the abbot had only an allowance out of the convent estates; but always he had great power over the property of the convent, and bad abbots are frequently accused of wasting the property of the house, and enriching their relatives and friends out of it. The abbots of some of the more important houses were mitred abbots, and were summoned to Parliament. In the time of Henry VIII. twenty-four abbots and the prior of Coventry had seats in the House of Peers.*

The abbot did not live in common with his monks; he had a separate establishment of his own within the precincts of the house, sometimes over the entrance gate, called the Abbot's Lodgings.† He ate in his own hall, slept in his own chamber, had a chapel, or oratory, for his private devotions, and accommodation for a retinue of chaplains and servants. His duty was to set to his monks an example of observance of the rule, to keep them to its observance, to punish breaches of it, to attend the services in church when not hindered by his other duties, to preach on holy days to the people, to attend chapter and preach on the rule, to act as confessor to the monks. But an abbot was also involved in many secular duties; there were manors of his own, and of the convent's, far and near, which required visiting; and these manors involved the abbot in all the numerous

---

* "Maysters of divinite
Her matynes to leve,
And cherliche [richly] as a cheveteyn
His chaumbre to holden,
With chymene and chaple,
And chosen whom him list,
And served as a sovereyn,
And as a lord sytten."
Piers Ploughman, l. 1,157.

† Just as heads of colleges now have their Master's, or Provost's, or Principal's Lodge. The constitution of our existing colleges will assist those who are acquainted with them in understanding many points of monastic economy.

duties which the feudal system devolved upon a lord towards his tenants, and towards his feudal superior. The greater abbots were barons, and sometimes were thus involved in such duties as those of justices in eyre, military leaders of their vassals, peers of Parliament. Hospitality was one of the great monastic virtues. The usual regulation in convents was that the abbot should entertain all guests of gentle degree, while the convent entertained all others. This again found abundance of occupation for my lord abbot in performing all the offices of a courteous host, which seems to have been done in a way becoming his character as a lord of wealth and dignity; his table was bountifully spread, even if he chose to confine himself to pulse and water; a band of wandering minstrels was always welcome to the abbot's hall to entertain his gentle and fair guests; and his falconer could furnish a cast of hawks, and his forester a leash of hounds, and the lord abbot would not decline to ride by the river or into his manor parks to witness and to share in the sport. In the Harl. MS. 1,527, at fol. 108 (?), is a picture of an abbot on horseback casting off a hawk from his fist. A pretty little illustration of this abbatial hospitality occurs in Marie's " Lay of Ywonec." * A baron and his family are travelling in obedience to the royal summons, to keep one of the high festivals at Caerleon. In the course of their journey they stop for a night at a spacious abbey, where they are received with the greatest hospitality. "The good abbot, for the sake of detaining his guests during another day, exhibited to them the whole of the apartments, the dormitory, the refectory, and the chapter-house, in which last they beheld

A Benedictine Abbot.

---

* Ellis's "Early English Romances."

a splendid tomb covered with a superb pall fringed with gold, surrounded by twenty waxen tapers in golden candlesticks, while a vast silver censer, constantly burning, filled the air with fumes of incense."

An abbot's ordinary habit was the same as that of his monks. In the processions which were made on certain great feasts he held his crosier, and, if he were a mitred abbot, he wore his mitre: this was also his parliamentary costume. We give on the opposite page a beautiful drawing of a Benedictine abbot of St. Alban's, thus habited, from the *Catalogus Benefactorum* of that abbey. When the abbot celebrated high mass on certain great festivals he wore the full episcopal costume. Thomas Delamere, abbot of St. Alban's, is so represented in his magnificent sepulchral brass in that abbey, executed in his lifetime, circa 1375 A.D. Richard Bewferest, abbot of the Augustine canons of Dorchester, Oxfordshire, has a brass in that

Benedictine Abbess and Nun.

church, date circa 1520 A.D., representing him in episcopal costume, bareheaded, with his staff; and in the same church is an incised gravestone, representing Abbot Roger, circa 1510 A.D., in full episcopal vestments. Abbesses bore the crosier in addition to the ordinary costume of their order; the sepulchral brass of Elizabeth Harvey, abbess of the Benedictine Abbey of Elstow, Bedfordshire, circa 1530 A.D., thus represents her, in the church of that place. Our representation of a Benedictine abbess on the previous page is from the fourteenth century MS. Royal, 2 B. vii.

Under the abbot were a number of officials (*obedientiarii*), the chief of whom were the Prior, Precentor, Cellarer, Sacrist, Hospitaller, Infirmarer, Almoner, Master of the Novices, Porter, Kitchener, Seneschal, &c. It was only in large monasteries that all these officers were to be found; in the smaller houses one monk would perform the duties of several offices. The officers seem to have been elected by the convent, subject to the approval of the abbot, by whom they might be deposed. Some brief notes of the duties of these obedientiaries will serve to give a considerable insight into the economy of a convent. And first for the *Prior*:—

In some orders there was only one abbey, and all the other houses were priories, as in the Clugniac, the Gilbertine, and in the Military and the Mendicant orders. In all the orders there were abbeys, which had had distant estates granted to them, on which either the donor had built a house, and made it subject to the abbey; or the abbey had built a house for the management of the estates, and the celebration of divine and charitable offices upon them. These priories varied in size, from a mere cell containing a prior and two monks, to an establishment as large as an abbey; and the dignity and power of the prior varied from that of a mere steward of the distant estate of the parent house, to that of an autocratic head, only nominally dependent on the parent house, and himself in everything but name an abbot.

The majority of the female houses of the various orders (except those which were especially female orders, like the Brigittines, &c.) were kept subject to some monastery, so that the superiors of these houses usually bore only the title of prioress, though they had the power of an abbess in the internal discipline of the house. One cannot forbear to quote at least a portion of Chaucer's very beautiful description of his prioress, among the Canterbury pilgrims:—

"That of her smiling ful simple was and coy."

She sang the divine service sweetly; she spoke French correctly, though with an accent which savoured of the Benedictine convent at Stratford-le-

Bow, where she had been educated, rather than of Paris; she behaved with lady-like delicacy at table; she was cheerful of mood, and amiable; with a pretty affectation of courtly breeding, and a care to exhibit a reverend stateliness becoming her office :—

> "But for to speken of her conscience,
> She was so charitable and so piteous,
> She would wepe if that she saw a mouse
> Caught in a trappe, if it were dead or bled;
> Of smalé houndés had she that she fed
> With rosted flesh, and milk, and wastel bread;
> But sore wept she if one of them were dead,
> Or if men smote it with a yerdé smerte;
> And all was conscience and tendre herte.
> Ful semély her wimple y-pinched was;
> Her nose tretis,* her eyen grey as glass,
> Her mouth full small, and thereto soft and red,
> And sickerly she had a fayre forehed—
> It was almost a spanné broad I trow,
> And hardily she was not undergrow."†

Her habit was becoming; her beads were of red coral gauded with green, to which was hung a jewel of gold, on which was—

> "Written a crowned A,
> And after, *Amor vincit omnia.*
> Another nun also with her had she,
> That was her chapelleine, and priestés three."

But in abbeys the chief of the obedientiaries was styled prior; and we cannot, perhaps, give a better idea of his functions than by borrowing a naval analogy, and calling him the abbot's first lieutenant; for, like that officer in a ship, the prior at all times carried on the internal discipline of the convent, and in the abbot's absence he was his vicegerent; wielding all the abbot's powers, except those of making or deposing obedientiaries and consecrating novices. He had a suite of apartments of his own, called the prior's chamber, or the prior's lodging; he could leave the house for a day or two on the business of the house, and had horses and servants appropriated to his use; whenever he entered the monks present rose out of

---

* Long and well proportioned.
† She was of tall stature.

respect; some little license in diet was allowed him in refectory, and he might also have refreshment in his own apartments; sometimes he entertained guests of a certain condition in his prior's chamber. Neither the prior, nor any of the obedientiaries, wore any distinctive dress or badge of office. In large convents he was assisted by a sub-prior.

The *Sub-prior* was the prior's deputy, sharing his duties in his residence, and fulfilling them in his absences. The especial functions appropriated to him seem to have been to say grace at dinner and supper, to see that all the doors were locked at five in the evening, and keep the keys until five next morning; and, by sleeping near the dormitory door, and by making private search, to prevent wandering about at night. In large monasteries there were additional sub-priors.

The *Chantor*, or *Precentor*, appears to come next in order and dignity, since we are told that he was censed after the abbot and prior. He was choir-master; taught music to the monks and novices; and arranged and ruled everything which related to the conduct of divine service. His place in church was in the middle of the choir on the right side; he held an instrument in his hand, as modern leaders use a bâton; and his side of the choir commenced the chant. He was besides librarian, and keeper of the archives, and keeper of the abbey seal.

He was assisted by a *Succentor*, who sat on the left side of the choir, and led that half of the choir in service. He assisted the chantor, and in his absence undertook his duties.

The *Cellarer* was in fact the steward of the house; his modern representative is the bursar of a college. He had the care of everything relating to the provision of the food and vessels of the convent. He was exempt from the observance of some of the services in church; he had the use of horses and servants for the fulfilment of his duties, and sometimes he

Adam the Cellarer.

appears to have had separate apartments. The cellarer, as we have said, wore no distinctive dress or badge; but in the *Catalogus Benefactorum* of St. Alban's there occurs a portrait of one "Adam Cellarius," who for his distinguished merit had been buried among the abbots in the chapter-house, and had his name and effigy recorded in the *Catalogus;* he is holding two keys in one hand and a purse in the other, the symbols of his office; and in his quaint features—so different from those of the dignified abbot whom we have given from the same book—the limner seems to have given us the type of a business-like and not ungenial cellarer.

The *Sacrist*, or *Sacristan* (whence our word sexton), had the care and charge of the fabric, and furniture, and ornaments of the church, and generally of all the material appliances of divine service. He, or some one in his stead, slept in a chamber built for him in the church, in order to protect it during the night. There is such a chamber in St. Alban's Abbey Church, engraved in the *Builder* for August, 1856. There was often a sub-sacrist to assist the sacrist in his duties.

The duty of the *Hospitaller* was, as his name implies, to perform the duties of hospitality on behalf of the convent. The monasteries received all travellers to food and lodging for a day and a night as of right, and for a longer period if the prior saw reason to grant it.* A special hall was provided for the entertainment of these guests, and chambers for their accommodation. The hospitaller performed the part of host on behalf of the convent, saw to the accommodation of the guests who belonged to the convent, introduced into the refectory strange priests or others who desired and had leave to dine there, and ushered guests of degree to the abbot to be entertained by him. He showed the church and house at suitable times to guests whose curiosity prompted the desire.

Every abbey had an infirmary, which was usually a detached building with its own kitchen and chapel, besides suitable apartments for the sick,

---

* "And as touching the almesse that they (the monks) delt, and the hospitality that they kept, every man knoweth that many thousands were well received of them, and might have been better, if they had not so many great men's horse to fede, and had not bin overcharged with such idle gentlemen as were never out of the abaies (abbeys)."—*A complaint made to Parliament not long after the dissolution, quoted in Coke's Institutes.*

and for aged monks, who sometimes took up their permanent residence in the infirmary, and were excused irksome duties, and allowed indulgences in food and social intercourse. Not only the sick monks, but other sick folk were received into the infirmary; it is a very common incident in mediæval romances to find a wounded knight carried to a neighbouring monastery to be healed. The officer who had charge of everything relating to this department was styled the *Infirmarer*. He slept in the infirmary, was excused from some of the "hours;" in the great houses had two brethren to assist him besides the necessary servants, and often a clerk learned in pharmacy as physician.

The *Almoner* had charge of the distribution of the alms of the house. Sometimes money was left by benefactors to be distributed to the poor annually at their obits; the distribution of this was confided to the almoner. One of his men attended in the abbot's chamber when he had guests, to receive what alms they chose to give to the poor. Moneys belonging to the convent were also devoted to this purpose; besides food and drink, the surplus of the convent meals. He had assistants allowed him to go and visit the sick and infirm folk of the neighbourhood. And at Christmas he provided cloth and shoes for widows, orphans, poor clerks, and others whom he thought to need it most.

The *Master of the Novices* was a grave and learned monk, who superintended the education of the youths in the schools of the abbey, and taught the rule to those who were candidates for the monastic profession.

The *Porter* was an officer of some importance; he was chosen for his age and gravity; he had an apartment in the gate lodge, an assistant, and a lad to run on his messages. But sometimes the porter seems to have been a layman. And, in small houses and in nunneries, his office involved other duties, which we have seen in great abbeys distributed among a number of officials. Thus, in Marie's "Lay le Fraine," we read of the porter of an abbey of nuns:—

> "The porter of the abbey arose,
> And did his office in the close;
> Rung the bells, and tapers light,
> Laid forth books and all ready dight.
> The church door he undid," &c.;

and in the sequel it appears that he had a daughter, and therefore in all probability was a layman.

The *Kitchener*, or *Cook*, was usually a monk, and, as his name implies, he ruled in the kitchen, went to market, provided the meals of the house, &c.

The *Seneschal* in great abbeys was often a layman of rank, who did the secular business which the tenure of large estates, and consequently of secular offices, devolved upon abbots and convents; such as holding manorial courts, and the like. But there was, Fosbroke tells us, another officer with the same name, but of inferior dignity, who did

Alan Middleton.

the convent business of the prior and cellarer which was to be done out of the house; and, when at home, carried a rod and acted as marshal of the guest-hall. He had horses and servants allowed for the duties of his office; and at the Benedictine Abbey of Winchcombe he had a robe of clerk's cloth once a year, with lamb's fur for a supertunic, and for a hood of budge fur; he had the same commons in hall as the cellarer, and £2 every year at Michaelmas. Probably an officer of this kind was Alan Middleton, who is recorded in the *Catalogus* of St. Alban's as "collector of rents of the obedientiaries of that monastery, and especially of those of the bursar." *Prudenter in omnibus se agebat*, and so, deserving well of the house, they put a portrait of him among their benefactors, clothed in a blue robe, of "clerk's cloth" perhaps, furred at the wrists and throat with "lamb's fur" or "budge fur;" a small tonsure shows that he had taken some minor order, the penner and inkhorn at his girdle denote the nature of his office; and he is just opening the door of one of the abbey tenants to perform his unwelcome function. They were grateful men, these Benedictines of St. Alban's; they have immortalised another of their inferior

Walter of Hamuntesham attacked by a Mob.

officers, *Walterus de Hamuntesham, fidelis minister hujus ecclesiæ*, because on one occasion he received a beating at the hands of the rabble of St. Alban's—*inter villanos Sci Albani*—while standing up for the rights and liberties of the church.

Next in dignity after the obedientiaries come the *Cloister Monks;* of these some had received holy orders at the hands of the bishop, some not. Their number was limited. A cloister monk in a rich abbey seems to have been something like in dignity to the fellow of a modern college, and a good deal of interest was sometimes employed to obtain the admission of a youth as a novice, with a view to his ultimately arriving at this dignified degree. Next in order come the *Professed Brethren*. These seem to be monks who had not been elected to the dignity of cloister monks; some of them were admitted late in life. Those monks who had been brought up in the house were called *nutriti*, those who came later in life *conversi;* the lay brothers were also sometimes called *conversi*. There were again the *Novices*, who were not all necessarily young, for a *conversus* passed through a noviciate; and even a monk of another order, or of another house of their own order, and even a monk from a cell of their own house, was reckoned among the novices. There were also the *Chaplains* of the abbot and other high officials; and frequently there were other clerics living in the monastery, who served the chantries in the abbey church, and the churches and chapels which belonged to the monastery and were in its neighbourhood. Again, there were the *Artificers and Servants* of the monastery: millers, bakers, tailors, shoemakers, smiths, and similar artificers, were often a part of a monastic establishment. And there were numerous men-servants, grooms, and the like: these were all under certain vows, and were kept under discipline. In the Cistercian abbey of Waverley there were in 1187 A.D. seventy monks and one hundred and twenty *conversi*, besides priests, clerks, servants, &c. In the great Benedictine abbey of St. Edmund's Bury, in the time of Edward I., there were eighty monks; fifteen chaplains attendant on the abbot and chief officers; about one hundred and eleven servants in the various offices, chiefly residing within the walls of the monastery; forty priests, officiating in the several chapels, chantries, and monastic appendages in the town; and an indefinite number of professed brethren. The following notes will give an idea of the occupations of the servants. In the time of William Rufus the servants at Evesham numbered—five in the church, two in the infirmary, two in the cellar, five in the kitchen, seven in the bakehouse, four brewers, four menders, two in the bath, two shoemakers, two in the orchard, three gardeners, one at the cloister gate, two at the great gate, five at the vineyard, four who served the monks when they went out, four fishermen, four in the abbot's chamber, three in the hall. At Salley Abbey, at the end of the fourteenth century, there were about thirty-five servants, among whom are mentioned the shoemaker and barber, the prior's chamberlain, the abbot's cook, the convent cook and baker's mate, the baker, brewers, tailor, cowherd, waggoners, pages of the kitchen, poultry-keeper, labourers, a keeper of animals and birds, bailiffs, foresters, shepherds, smiths: there are others mentioned by name, without a note of their office. But it was only a few of the larger houses which had such numerous establishments as these; the majority of the monasteries contained from five to twenty cloister monks. Some of the monasteries were famous as places of education, and we must add to their establishment a number of children of good family, and the learned clerks or ladies who acted as tutors; thus the abbey of St. Mary, Winchester, in 1536, contained twenty-six nuns, five priests, thirteen lay sisters, thirty-two officers and servants, and twenty-six children, daughters of lords and knights, who were brought up in the house.

Lastly, there were a number of persons of all ranks and conditions who were admitted to "fraternity." Among the Hospitallers (and probably it was the same with the other orders) they took oath to love the house and brethren, to defend the house from ill-doers, to enter that house if they did enter any, and to make an annual present to the house. In return, they were enrolled in the register of the house, they received the prayers of the brethren, and at death were buried in the cemetery. Chaucer's Dominican friar (p. 48), writes the names of those who gave him donations in his "tables." In the following extract from Piers Ploughman's Creed, an Austin friar promises more definitely to have his donors enrolled in the fraternity of his house:—

> "And gyf thou hast any good,
> And will thyself helpen,
> Help us herblich therewith.
> And here I undertake,
> Thou shalt ben brother of oure hous,
> And a book habben,
> At the next chapetre,
> Clerliche enseled.
> And then our provincial
> Hath power to assoylen

> Alle sustren and brethren
> That beth of our ordre."
>
> *Piers Ploughman's Creed*, p. 645.

In the book of St. Alban's, which we have before quoted, there is a list of many persons, knights and merchants, ladies and children, vicars and rectors, received *ad fraternitatem hujus monasterii*. In many cases portraits of them are given: they are in the ordinary costume of their time and class, without any badge of their monastic fraternisation.

Chaucer gives several sketches which enable us to fill out our realisation of the monks, as they appeared outside the cloister associating with their fellow-men. He includes one among the merry company of his Canterbury pilgrims; and first in the Monk's Prologue, makes the Host address the monk thus :—

> "'My lord, the monk,' quod he . . . .
> 'By my trothe I can not tell youre name,
> Whether shall I call you my Lord Dan John,
> Or Dan Thomas, or elles Dan Albon?
> Of what house be ye by your father kin?
> I vow to God thou hast a full fair skin;
> It is a gentle pasture ther thou goest,
> Thou art not like a penaunt* or a ghost.
> Upon my faith thou art some officer,
> Some worthy sextern or some celerer.
> For by my father's soul, as to my dome,
> Thou art a maister when thou art at home:
> No poure cloisterer, ne non novice,
> But a governor both ware and wise.'"

Chaucer himself describes the same monk in his Prologue thus :—

> "A monk there was, a fayre for the maisterie,
> An out-rider that lovered venerie,†
> A manly man to be an abbot able.
> Ful many a dainty horse had he in stable;
> And when he rode men might his bridle hear
> Gingling in a whistling wind as clear,
> And eke as loud as doth the chapel bell,
> Whereas this lord was keeper of the cell.
> The rule of Saint Maur and of Saint Benet,
> Because that it was old and somedeal strait,

---

* A person doing penance. † Hunting.

This ilke monk let olde thinges pace,
And held after the newe world the trace.
He gave not of the text a pulled hen,
That saith, that hunters been not holy men ;
Ne that a monk, when he is regneless,*
Is like a fish that is waterless ;
That is to say, a monk out of his cloister :
This ilke text he held not worth an oyster.
And I say his pinion was good.
Why should he study, and make himselven wood,
Upon a book in cloister alway to pore,
Or swinkin with his handis, and labour,
As Austin bid ? How shall the world be served ?
Therefore he was a prickasoure aright :
Greyhounds he had as swift as fowls of flight ;
Of pricking and of hunting for the hare
Was all his lust, for no cost would he spare.
I saw his sleeves purfled at the hand
With gris, and that the finest of the land.
And for to fasten his hood under his chin
He had of gold y-wrought a curious pin :
A love-knot in the greater end there was.
  * * * *
His bootis supple, his horse in great estate ;
Now certainly he was a fair prelate."

Again, in the "Shipman's Tale" we learn that such an officer had considerable freedom, so that he was able to pay very frequent visits to his friends. The whole passage is worth giving :—

"A marchant whilom dwelled at St. Denise,
That riche was, for which men held him wise.
  * * * *
This noble marchant held a worthy house,
For which he had all day so great repair
For his largesse, and for his wife was fair.
What wonder is ? but hearken to my tale.
Amonges all these guestes great and small
There was a monk, a fair man and a bold,
I trow a thirty winters he was old,
That ever anon was drawing to that place.
This youngé monk that was so fair of face,

---

* Without state.

> Acquainted was so with this goodé man,
> Sithen that their firste knowledge began,
> That in his house as familiar was he
> As it possible is any friend to be.
> And for as mochel as this goodé man,
> And eke this monk, of which that I began,
> Were bothé two y-born in one village,
> The monk him claimeth as for cosinage ;
> And he again him said not onés nay,
> But was as glad thereof, as fowl of day ;
> For to his heart it was a great plesaunce ;
> Thus ben they knit with eterne alliance,
> And eche of them gan other for to ensure
> Of brotherhood, while that life may endure."

Notwithstanding his vow of poverty, he was also able to make presents to his friends, for the tale continues :—

> "Free was Dan John, and namely of despence
> As in that house, and full of diligence
> To don plesaunce, and also great costage ;
> He not forgat to give the leaste page
> In all that house, but, after their degree,
> He gave the lord, and sithen his mennie,
> When that he came, some manner honest thing ;
> For which they were as glad of his coming
> As fowl is fain when that the sun upriseth."

Chaucer does not forget to let us know how it was that this monk came to have such liberty and such command of means :—

> "This noble monk, of which I you devise,
> Hath of his abbot, as him list, licence
> (Because he was a man of high prudence,
> And eke an officer), out for to ride
> To see their granges and their barnés wide."

CHAPTER VII.

THE MONASTERY.

WE proceed next to give some account of the buildings which compose the fabric of a monastery. And first as to the site. The orders of the Benedictine family preferred sites as secluded and remote from towns and villages as possible. The Augustinian orders did not cultivate seclusion so strictly; their houses are not unfrequently near towns and villages, and sometimes a portion of their conventual church—the nave, generally—formed the parish church. The Friaries, Colleges of secular canons, and Hospitals, were generally in or near the towns. There is a popular idea that the monks chose out the most beautiful and fertile spots in the kingdom for their abodes. A little reflection would show that the choice of the site of a new monastery must be confined within the limits of the lands which the founder was pleased to bestow upon the convent. Sometimes the founder gave a good manor, and gave money besides, to help to build the house upon it; sometimes what was given was a tract of unreclaimed land, upon which the first handful of monks squatted like settlers in a new country. Even the settled land, in those days, was only half cultivated; and on good land, unreclaimed or only half reclaimed, the skill and energy of a company of first-rate farmers would soon produce great results; barren commons would be dotted over with sheep, and rushy valleys would become rich pastures covered with cattle, and great clearings in the forest would grow green with rye and barley. The revenues of the monastic estates would rapidly augment; little of them would be required for the coarse dress and frugal fare of the monks; they did not, like the lay landowners, spend them on gilded armour and jewelled robes, and troops of armed retainers, and tournaments, and journeys to court; and so they had enough for plentiful charity and unrestricted hospitality, and the surplus they spent upon those magnificent buildings whose very ruins are among the architectural glories of the land. The Cistercians had an especial rule that their houses should be built on the lowest possible sites, in token of humility; but it was the general custom in the Middle Ages to choose low and sheltered sites for houses which were not especially intended as strongholds, and therefore it is that we find nearly all monasteries in sheltered spots. To the monks the neighbourhood of a stream was of especial importance: when headed up it supplied a pond for their fish, and water-power for their corn-mill. If, therefore, there were within the limits of their domain a quiet valley with a rivulet running through it, that was the site which the monks would select for their house. And here, beside the rivulet, in the midst of the green pasture land of the valley dotted with sheep and kine, shut in from the world by the hills, whose tops were fringed with the forest which stretched for miles around, the stately buildings of the monastery would rise year after year; the cloister court, and the great church, and the abbot's lodge, and the numerous offices, all surrounded by a stone wall with a stately gate-tower, like a goodly walled town, and a suburban hamlet of labourers' and servants' cottages sheltering beneath its walls.

There was a certain plan for the arrangement of the principal buildings of a monastery, which, with minor variations, was followed by nearly all the monastic orders, except the Carthusians. These latter differed from the other orders in this, that each monk had his separate cell, in which he lived, and ate, and slept apart from the rest, the whole community meeting only in church and chapter.* Our limits will not permit us to enter into exceptional arrangements.

---

* A plan of the Chartreuse of Clermont is given by Viollet le Duc (Dict. of Architec., vol. i. pp. 308, 309), and the arrangements of a Carthusian monastery were nearly the same in all parts of Europe. It consists of a cloister-court surrounded by about twenty square enclosures. Each enclosure, technically called a "cell," is in fact a little house and garden, the little house is in a corner of the enclosure, and consists of three apartments. In the middle of the west side of the cloister-court is the oratory, whose five-sided apsidal sanctuary projects into the court. In a small outer court on the west is the prior's

The nucleus of a monastery was the cloister court. It was a quadrangular space of green sward, around which were arranged the cloister buildings, viz., the church, the chapter-house, the refectory, and the dormitory.* The court was called the Paradise—the blessed garden in which the inmates passed their lives of holy peace. A porter was often placed at the cloister-gate, and the monks might not quit its seclusion, nor strangers enter to disturb its quiet, save under exceptional circumstances.

The cloister-court had generally, though it is doubtful whether it was always the case, a covered ambulatory round its four sides. The ambulatories of the twelfth and thirteenth centuries have usually an open arcade on the side facing the court, which supports the groined roof. In the fourteenth and fifteenth centuries, instead of an open arcade, we usually find a series of large traceried windows, tolerably close together; in many cases they were glazed, sometimes with painted glass, and formed doubtless a grand series of scriptural or historical paintings. The blank wall opposite was also sometimes painted. This covered ambulatory was not merely a promenade for the monks; it was the place in which the convent assembled regularly every day, at certain hours, for study and meditation; and in some instances (*e.g.*, at Durham) a portion of it was fitted up with little wooden closets for studies for the elder monks, with book-cupboards in the wall opposite for books. The monks were sometimes buried in the cloister, either under the turf in the open square, or beneath the pavement of the ambulatory. There was sometimes a fountain at the corner of the cloister, or on its south side near the entrance to the refectory, at which the monks washed before meals.

---

lodgings, which is a "cell" like the others, and a building for the entertainment of guests. See also a paper on the Carthusian priory of Mount Grace, near Thirsk, read by Archdeacon Churton before the Yorkshire Architectural Society, in the year 1850.

* A bird's-eye view of Citeaux, given in Viollet le Duc's " Dictionary of Architecture," vol. i. p. 271, will give a very good notion of a thirteenth-century monastery. Of the English monasteries Fountains was perhaps one of the finest, and its existing remains are the most extensive of any which are left in England. A plan of it will be found in Mr. Walbran's " Guide to Ripon." See also plan of Furness, *Journal of the Archæological Association*, vi. 309; of Newstead (an Augustinian house), ibid. ix. p. 30; and of Durham (Benedictine), ibid. xxii. 201.

The church was always the principal building of a monastery. Many of them remain entire, though despoiled of their shrines, and tombs, and altars, and costly furniture, and many more remain in ruins, and they fill us with astonishment at their magnitude and splendour. Our existing cathedrals were, in fact, abbey churches; nine or ten of them were the churches of Benedictine monasteries, the remainder of secular Augustines. But these, the reader may imagine, had the wealth of bishops and the offerings of dioceses lavished upon them, and may not be therefore fair examples of ordinary abbey churches. But some of them originally were ordinary abbey churches, and were subsequently made Episcopal sees, such as Beverley, Gloucester, Christ Church Oxford, and Peterborough, which were originally Benedictine abbey churches; Bristol was the church of a house of regular canons; Ripon was the church of a college of secular canons. The Benedictine churches of Westminster and St. Alban's, and the collegiate church of Southwell, are equal in magnitude and splendour to any of the cathedrals; and the ruins of Fountains, and Tintern, and Netley, show that the Cistercians equalled any of the other orders in the magnitude and beauty of their churches.

It is indeed hard to conceive that communities of a score or two of monks should have built such edifices as Westminster and Southwell as private chapels attached to their monasteries. And this, though it is one aspect of the fact, is not the true one. They did not build them for private chapels to say their daily prayers in; they built them for temples in which they believed that the Eternal and Almighty condescended to dwell; to whose contemplation and worship they devoted their lives. They did not think of the church as an appendage to their monastery, but of their monastery as an appendage to the church. The cloister, under the shadow and protection of the church, was the court of the Temple, in which its priests and Levites dwelt.

The church of a monastery was almost always a cross church, with a nave and aisles; a central tower (in Cistercian churches the tower was only to rise one story above the roof); transepts, which usually have three chapels on the north side of each transept, or an aisle divided into three chapels by parclose screens; a choir with or without aisles; a retro-choir or presbytery; and often a Lady chapel, east of the presbytery, or in some instances parallel with the choir.

The entrance for the monks was usually on the south side opposite to the eastern alley of the cloisters; there was also in Cistercian churches, and in some others, a newel stair in the south transept, by means of which the monks could descend from their dormitory (which was in the upper story of the east side of the cloister court) into the church for the night services, without going into the open air. The principal entrance for the laity was on the north side, and was usually provided with a porch. The great western

A Semi-choir of Franciscan Friars.

entrance was chiefly used for processions; the great entrance gate in the enclosure wall of the abbey being usually opposite to it or nearly so. In several instances stones have been found, set in the pavements of the naves of conventual churches, to mark the places where the different members of the convent were to stand before they issued forth in procession, amidst the tolling of the great bell, with cross and banner, and chanted psalms, to meet the abbot at the abbey-gate, on his return from an absence, or any person to whom it was fitting that the convent should show such honour.

The Minster Church. 75

The internal arrangements of an abbey-church were very nearly like those of our cathedrals. The convent occupied the stalls in the choir; the place of the abbot was in the first stall on the right-hand (south) side to one entering from the west—it is still appropriated to the dean in cathedrals; in the corresponding stall on the other side sat the prior; the precentor sat in the middle stall on the right or south side; the succentor in the middle stall on the north side.

The beautiful little picture of a semi-choir of Franciscan friars on the opposite page is from a fourteenth-century psalter in the British Museum (Domitian, A. 17). It is from a large picture, which gives a beautiful

A Semi-choir of Minoresses.

representation of the interior of the choir of the church. The picture is worth careful examination for the costume of the friars—grey frock and cowl, with knotted cord girdle and sandalled feet; some wearing the hood drawn over the head, some leaving it thrown back on the neck and shoulders; one with his hands folded under his sleeves like the Cistercians at p. 17. The precentor may be easily distinguished in the middle stall beating time, with an air of leadership. There is much character in all the faces and attitudes—*e.g.*, in the withered old face on the left, with his cowl pulled over his ears to keep off the draughts, or the one on the precentor's left, a rather burly friar, evidently singing bass.* On the next page is an engraving from the same MS. of a similar semi-choir of minoresses, which also is only a portion of a large church interior.

When there was a shrine of a noted saint† it was placed in the presbytery, behind the high-altar; and here, and in the choir aisles, were frequently placed the monuments of the abbots, and of founders and distinguished benefactors of the house; sometimes heads of the house and founders were buried in the chapter-house.

It would require a more elaborate description than our plan will admit to endeavour to bring before the mind's-eye of the reader one of these abbey churches before its spoliation;—when the sculptures were unmutilated and the paintings fresh, and the windows filled with their stained glass, and the choir hung with hangings, and banners and tapestries waved from the arches of the triforium, and the altar shone gloriously with jewelled plate, and the monuments‡ of abbots and nobles were still perfect, and the wax tapers burned night and day§ in the hearses, throwing a flickering light on the solemn effigies below, and glancing upon the tarnished armour and

---

* A double choir of the fifteenth century is in King René's Book of Hours (Egerton, 1,070), at folio 54. Another semi-choir of Religious of late fifteenth and early sixteenth century date, very well drawn, may be found in Egerton, 2,125, f. 117, v.

† Lydgate's Life of St. Edmund, a MS. executed in 1473 A.D., preserved in the British Museum (Harl. 2,278), gives several very good representations of the shrine of that saint at St. Edmund's Bury, with the attendant monks, pilgrims worshipping, &c.

‡ "Tombes upon tabernacles, tiled aloft,
* * *
Made of marble in many manner wise,
Knights in their conisantes clad for the nonce,
All it seemed saints y-sacred upon earth,
And lovely ladies y-wrought lyen by their sides
In many gay garments that were gold-beaten."
Piers Ploughman's Creed.

§ Henry VII. agreed with the Abbot and Convent of Westminster that there should be four tapers burning continually at his tomb—two at the sides, and two at the ends, each eleven feet long, and twelve pounds n weight; thirty tapers, &c., in the hearse; and four torches to be held about it at his weekly obit; and one hundred tapers nine feet long, and twenty-four torches of twice the weight, to be lighted at his anniversary.

the dusty banners * which hung over the tombs, while the cowled monks sat in their stalls and prayed. Or when, on some high festival, the convent walked round the lofty aisles in procession, two and two, clad in rich copes over their coarse frocks, preceded by cross and banner, with swinging censers pouring forth clouds of incense, while one of those angelic boy's voices which we still sometimes hear in cathedrals chanted the solemn litany—the pure sweet ringing voice floating along the vaulted aisles, until it was lost in the swell of the chorus of the whole procession— *Ora! Ora! Ora! pro nobis!*

The Cloister was usually situated on the south side of the nave of the church, so that the nave formed its north side, and the south transept a part of its eastern side; but sometimes, from reasons of local convenience, the cloister was on the north side of the nave, and then the relative positions of the other buildings were similarly transposed.

The Chapter-house was always on the east side of the court. In establishments of secular canons it seems to have been always multi-sided † with a central pillar to support its groining, and a lofty, conical, lead-covered roof. In these instances it is placed in the open space eastward of the cloister, and is usually approached by a passage from the east side of the cloister court. In the houses of all the other orders ‡ the chapter-house is rectangular, even where the church is a cathedral. Usually, then, the chapter-house is a rectangular building on the east side of the cloister, and its longest axis is east and west; at Durham it has an

---

* "For though a man in their mynster a masse wolde heren,
His sight shal so be set on sundrye werkes,
The penons and the pornels and poyntes of sheldes
Withdrawen his devotion and dusken his heart."
Piers Ploughman's Vision.

† The chapter-houses attached to the cathedrals of York, Salisbury, and Wells, are octagonal; those of Hereford and Lincoln, decagonal; Lichfield, polygonal; Worcester is circular. All these were built by secular canons.

‡ There are only two exceptions hitherto observed: that of the Benedictine Abbey of Westminster, which is polygonal, and that of Thornton Abbey, of regular canons, which is octagonal.

eastern apse.* It was a large and handsome room, with a good deal of architectural ornament;† often the western end of it is divided off as a vestibule or ante-room; and generally it is so large as to be divided into two or three aisles by rows of pillars. Internally, rows of stalls or benches

Monks and Lawyers in Chapter-house.

were arranged round the walls for the convent; there was a higher seat at the east end for the abbot or prior, and a desk in the middle from which certain things were read. Every day after the service called Terce, the convent walked in procession from the choir to the chapter-house, and took their proper places. When the abbot had taken his place, the monks

---

* And at Norwich it appears to have had an eastern apse. See ground-plan in Mr. Mackenzie E. C. Walcott's " Church and Conventual Arrangement," p. 85.
† Piers Ploughman describes the chapter-house of a Benedictine convent:—
"There was the chapter-house, wrought as a great church,
Carved and covered and quaintly entayled [sculptured];
With seemly selure [ceiling] y-set aloft,
As a parliament house y-painted about."

The Cloister Buildings. 79

descended one step and bowed; he returned their salutation, and all took their seats. A sentence of the rule of the order was read by one of the novices from the desk, and the abbot, or in his absence the prior, delivered an explanatory or hortatory sermon upon it; then from another portion of the book was read the names of brethren, and benefactors, and persons who had been received into fraternity, whose decease had happened on that day of the year; and the convent prayed a *requiescant in pace* for their souls, and the souls of all the faithful departed this life. Then members of the convent who had been guilty of slight breaches of discipline confessed them, kneeling upon a low stool in the middle, and on a bow from the abbot, intimating his remission of the breach, they resumed their seats. If any had a complaint to make against any brother, it was here made and adjudged.* Convent business was also transacted. The woodcut gives an example of the kind. Henry VII. had made grants to Westminster Abbey, on condition that the convent should perform certain religious services on his behalf;† and in order that the services should not fall into disuse, he directed that yearly, at a certain period, the chief-justice, or the king's attorney, or the recorder of London, should attend in chapter, and the abstract of the grant and agreement between the king and the convent should be read. The grant which was thus to be read still exists in the British Museum; it is written in a volume superbly bound, with the royal seals attached in silver cases; it is from the illuminated letter at the head of one of the deeds in this book ‡ that our woodcut is taken. It rudely represents the chapter-house, with the chief-justice and a group of lawyers on one side, the abbot and convent on the other, and a monk reading the grant from the desk in the middle.

Lydgate's "Life of St. Edmund" (Harl. 2,278) was written A.D. 1433, by

---

* In the "Vision of Piers Ploughman" one of the characters complains that if he commits any fault—
"They do me fast fridays to bread and water,
And am challenged in the chapitel-house as I a child were;"
and he is punished in a childish way, which is too plainly spoken to bear quotation.
† See note on p. 76.
‡ The woodcut on a preceding page (23) is from another initial letter of the same book.

command of his abbot—he was a monk of St. Edmund's Bury—on the occasion of King Henry VI. being received—

" Of their chapter a brother for to be;"

that is, to the fraternity of the house. An illumination on f. 6 seems to represent the king sitting in the abbot's place in the chapter-house, with royal officers behind him, monks in their places on each side of the chapter-house, the lectern in the middle, and a group of clerks at the west end. It is probably intended as a picture of the scene of the king's being received to fraternity.

Adjoining the south transept is usually a narrow apartment; the description of Durham, drawn up soon after the Dissolution, says that it was the " Locutory." Another conjecture is that it may have been the vestry. At Netley it has a door at the west, with a trefoil light over it, a two-light window at the east, two niches, like monumental niches, in its north and south walls, and a piscina at the east end of its south wall.

Again, between this and the chapter-house is often found a small apartment, which some have conjectured to be the penitential cell. In other cases it seems to be merely a passage from the cloister-court to the space beyond; in which space the abbot's lodging is often situated, so that it may have been the abbot's entrance to the church and chapter.

In Cistercian houses there is usually another long building south of the chapter-house, its axis running north and south. This was perhaps in its lower story the Frater-house, a room to which the monks retired after refection to converse, and to take their allowance of wine, or other indulgences in diet which were allowed to them; and some quotations in Fosbroke would lead us to imagine that the monks dined here on feast days. It would answer to the great chamber of mediæval houses, and in some respects to the Combination-room * of modern colleges. The upper story of this building was probably the Dormitory. This was a long room, with a vaulted or open timber roof, in which the pallets were arranged in rows on each side against the wall. The prior or sub-prior usually slept in the

---

* A room adjoining the hall, to which the fellows retire after dinner to take their wine and converse.

dormitory, with a light burning near him, in order to maintain order. The monks slept in the same habits * which they wore in the day-time.

About the middle of the south side of the court, in Cistercian houses, there is a long room, whose longer axis lies north and south, with a smaller room on each side of it, which was probably the Refectory. In other houses, the refectory forms the south side of the cloister court, lying parallel with the nave of the church. Very commonly it has a row of pillars down the centre, to support the groined roof. It was arranged, like all mediæval halls, with a dais at the upper end and a screen at the lower. In place of the oriel window of mediæval halls, there was a pulpit, which was often in the embrasure of a quasi-oriel window, in which one of the brethren read some edifying book during meals.

The remaining apartments of the cloister-court it is more difficult to appropriate. In some of the great Cistercian houses whose ground-plan can be traced—as Fountains, Salley, Netley, &c.—possibly the long apartment which is found on the west side of the cloister was the hall of the Hospitium, with chambers over it. Another conjecture is, that it was the house of the lay brethren.

In the uncertainty which at present exists on these points of monastic arrangement, we cannot speak with any degree of certainty; but we throw together some data on the subject in the subjoined note.†

---

* The ordinary fashion of the time was to sleep without any clothing whatever.

† In the plan of the ninth-century Benedictine monastery of St. Gall, published in the *Archæological Journal* for June, 1848, the dormitory is on the east, with the calefactory under it; the refectory on the south, with the clothes-store above; the cellar on the west, with the larders above. In the plan of Canterbury Cathedral, a Benedictine house, as it existed in the latter half of the twelfth century, the church was on the south, the chapter-house and dormitory on the east, the refectory, parallel with the church, on the north, and the cellar on the west. At the Benedictine monastery at Durham, the church was on the north, the chapter-house and locutory on the east, the refectory on the south, and the dormitory on the west. At the Augustinian Regular Priory of Bridlington, the church was on the north, the fratry (refectory) on the south, the chapter-house on the east, the dortor also on the east, up a stair twenty steps high, and the west side was occupied by the prior's lodgings.

At the Premonstratensian Abbey of Easby, the church is on the north, the transept, passage, chapter-house, and small apartments on the east, the refectory on the south, and on the west two large apartments, with a passage between them. The Rev. J. F. Turner,

The Scriptorium is said to have been usually over the chapter-house. It was therefore a large apartment, capable of containing many persons, and, in fact, many persons did work together in it in a very business-like manner at the transcription of books. For example, William, Abbot of Herschau, in the eleventh century, as stated by his biographer: "Knowing, what he had learned by laudable experience, that sacred reading is the necessary food of the mind, made twelve of his monks very excellent writers, to whom he committed the office of transcribing the holy Scriptures, and the treatises of the Fathers. Besides these, there were an indefinite number of other scribes, who wrought with equal diligence on the transcription of other books. Over them was a monk well versed in all kinds of knowledge, whose business it was to appoint some good work as a task for each, and to correct the mistakes of those who wrote negligently."* The general chapter of the Cistercian order, held in A.D. 1134, directs that the same silence should be maintained in the scriptorium as in the cloister. Sometimes perhaps little separate studies of wainscot were made round this large apartment, in which the writers sat at their desks. Sometimes this literary work was carried on in the cloister, which, being glazed, would be a not uncomfortable place in temperate weather, and a very comfortable place in summer, with its coolness and quiet, and the peep through its windows on the green court and the fountain in the centre, and the grey walls of the monastic buildings beyond; the slow footfall of a brother going to and fro, and the cawing of the rooks in the minster tower, would add to the dreamy charm of such a library.†

Odo, Abbot of St. Martin's, at Tournay, about 1093, "used to exult in the number of writers the Lord had given him; for if you had gone into the cloister you might in general have seen a dozen young monks sitting on chairs in perfect silence, writing at tables carefully and artificially

---

Chaplain of Bishop Cozin's Hall, Durham, describes these as the common house and kitchen, and places the dormitory in a building west of them, at a very inconvenient distance from the church.

* Maitland's "Dark Ages."
† At Winchester School, until a comparatively recent period, the scholars in the summer time studied in the cloisters.

constructed. All Jerome's commentaries on the Prophets, all the works of St. Gregory, and everything that he could find of St. Augustine, Ambrose, Isodore, Bede, and the Lord Anselm, then Abbot of Bec, and afterwards Archbishop of Canterbury, he caused to be transcribed. So that you would scarcely have found such a monastery in that part of the country, and everybody was begging for our copies to correct their own." Sometimes little studies of wainscot were erected in the cloisters for the monks to study or transcribe in. At Gloucester Cathedral, at Beaulieu, and at Melrose, for example, there are traces of the way in which the windows of the cloisters were enclosed and turned into such studies.*

Monk in Scriptorium.

There are numerous illuminations representing monks and ecclesiastics writing; they sit in chairs of various kinds, some faldstools, some armed chairs, some armed backed; and they have desks and bookstands before them of various shapes, commonly a stand with sloping desk like a Bible lectern, not unfrequently a kind of dumb-waiter besides on which are several books. We see also in these illuminations the forms of the

---

* For much curious information about scriptoria and monastic libraries, see Maitland': "Dark Ages," quoted above.

pens, knives, inkstands, &c., which were used. We will only mention two of unusual interest. One is in a late fourteenth-century Psalter, Harl. 2,897, at p. 186, v., where St. Jude sits writing his Epistle in a canopied chair, with a shelf across the front of the chair to serve as a desk; a string with a weight at the end holds his parchment down, and there is a bench beside, on which lies a book. A chair with a similar shelf is at f. 12 of the MS. Egerton, 1,070. Our woodcut on the preceding page is from a MS. in the Library of Soissons. We also find representations of ecclesiastics writing in a small cell which may represent the enclosed scriptoria—*e.g.* St. Bonaventine writing, in the MS. Harl. 3,229; St. John painting, in the late fifteenth-century MS. Add. 15,677, f. 35.

The Abbot's Lodging sometimes formed a portion of one of the monastic courts, as at St. Mary, Bridlington, where it formed the western side of the cloister-court; but more usually it was a detached house, precisely similar to the contemporary unfortified houses of laymen of similar rank and wealth. No particular site relative to the monastic buildings was appropriated to it; it was erected wherever was most convenient within the abbey enclosure. The principal rooms of an abbot's house are the Hall, the Great Chamber, the Kitchen, Buttery, Cellars, &c., the Chambers, and the Chapel. We must remember that the abbots of the greater houses were powerful noblemen; the abbots of the smaller houses were equal in rank and wealth to country gentlemen. They had a very constant succession of noble and gentle guests, whose entertainment was such as their rank and habits required. This involved a suitable habitation and establishment; and all this must be borne in mind when we endeavour to picture to ourselves an abbot's lodging. To give an idea of the magnitude of some of the abbots' houses, we may record that the hall of the Abbot of Fountains was divided by two rows of pillars into a centre and aisles, and that it was 170 feet long by 70 feet wide.* Half a dozen noble guests, with their retinues of knights and squires, and men-at-arms and lacqueys, and all the abbot's men to boot, would be lost in

---

* The hall of the Royal Palace of Winchester, erected at the same period, was 111 feet by 55 feet 9 inches.

such a hall. On the great feast-days it might, perhaps, be comfortably filled. But even such a hall would hardly contain the companies who were sometimes entertained, on such great days for instance as an abbot's installation-day, when it is on record that an abbot of one of the greater houses would give a feast to three or four thousand people.

Of the lodgings of the superiors of smaller houses, we may take that of the Prior of St. Mary's, Bridlington, as an example. It is very accurately described by King Henry's commissioners; it formed the west side of the cloister-court; it contained a hall with an undercroft, eighteen paces long from the screen to the dais,* and ten paces wide; on its north side a great chamber, twenty paces long and nineteen wide; at the west end of the great chamber the prior's sleeping-chamber, and over that a garret; on the east side of the same chamber a little chamber and a closet; at the south end of the hall the buttery and pantry, and a chamber called the Auditor's Chamber; at the same end of the hall a fair parlour, called the Low Summer Parlour; and over it another fair chamber; and adjoining that three little chambers for servants; at the south end of the hall the Prior's Kitchen, with three houses covered with lead, and adjoining it a chamber called the South Cellarer's Chamber.†

A Present of Fish.

There were several other buildings of a monastery, which were sometimes detached, and placed as convenience dictated. The Infirmary especially seems to have been more commonly detached; in many cases it had its own kitchen, and refectory, and chapel, and chambers, which sometimes were arranged round a court, and formed a complete little separate establishment.

The Hospitium, or Guest-house, was sometimes detached; but more

---

* Its total length would perhaps be about twenty-four paces.

† The above woodcut, from the Harleian MS. 1,527, represents, probably, the cellarer of a Dominican convent receiving a donation of a fish. It curiously suggests the scene depicted in Sir Edwin Landseer's "Bolton Abbey in the Olden Time."

usually it seems to have formed a portion of an outer court, westward of the cloister-court, which court was entered from the great gates, or from one of the outer gates of the abbey. In Cistercian houses, as we have said, the guest-house, with its hall below and its chambers above, perhaps occupied the west side of the cloister-court, and would therefore form the eastern range of buildings of this outer court. At St. Mary's, Bridlington, where the prior's lodging occupied this position, the "lodgings and stables for strangers" were on the north side of this outer court. The guest-houses were often of great extent and magnificence. The Guesten-hall of St. Augustine's, Canterbury, still remains, and is a very noble building, 150 feet long by 50 broad, of Norman date, raised on an undercroft. The Guesten-hall of Worcester also remains, a very noble building on an undercroft, with a fine carved timber roof, and portions of the painting which decorated the wall behind the dais still visible.* Besides the hall, the guest-house contained often a great-chamber (answering to our modern drawing-room) and sleeping-chambers, and a chapel, in which service was performed for guests—for in those days it was the custom always to hear prayers before dinner and supper.

Thus, at Durham, we are told that "a famous house of hospitality was kept within the abbey garth, called the Guest-hall, and was situate in the west side, towards the water. The sub-prior of the house was the master thereof, as one appointed to give entertainment to all estates, noble, gentle, or what other degree soever, came thither as strangers. Their entertainment was not inferior to that of any place in England, both for the goodness of their diet, the clean and neat furniture of their lodgings, and generally all things necessary for travellers; and, with this entertainment, no man was required to depart while he continued honest and of good behaviour. This hall was a stately place, not unlike the body of a church, supported on each side by very fine pillars, and in the midst of the hall a long range for the fire. The chambers and lodgings belonging to it were kept very clean and richly furnished." At St. Albans, the Guest-

---

* See an account of this hall, with pen-and-ink sketches by Mr. Street, in the volume of the Worcester Architectural Society for 1854.

house was an enormous range of rooms, with stabling for three hundred horses.

There is a passage in the correspondence of Coldingham Priory (published by the Surties Society, 1841, p. 52) which gives us a graphic sketch of the arrival of guests at a monastery :—" On St. Alban's-day, June 17 [year not given—it was towards the end of Edward III.], two monks, with a company of certain secular persons, came riding into the gateway of the monastery about nine o'clock in the morning. This day happened to be Sunday, but they were hospitably and reverently received, had lodgings assigned them, a special mass service performed for them, and after a refection and washing their feet, it being supposed that they were about to pursue their journey to London the next morning, they were left at an early hour to take repose. While the bell was summoning the rest of the brotherhood to vespers, the monk who had been in attendance upon them (the hospitaller) having gone with the rest to sing his chant in the choir, the secular persons appear to have asked the two monks to take a walk with them to look at the Castle of Durham," &c.*

There could hardly have been any place in the Middle Ages which could have presented such a constant succession of picturesque scenes as the Hospitium of a monastery. And what a contrast must often have existed between the Hospitium and the Cloister. Here a crowd of people of every degree—nobles and ladies, knights and dames, traders with their wares, minstrels with their songs and juggling tricks, monks and clerks, palmers, friars, beggars—bustling about the court or crowding the long tables of the hall; and, a few paces off, the dark-frocked monks, with faces buried in their cowls, pacing the ambulatory in silent meditation, or sitting at their meagre refection, enlivened only by the monotonous sound of the novice's voice reading a homily from the pulpit!

Many of the remaining buildings of the monastery were arranged around this outer court. Ingulphus tells us that the second court of the Saxon monastery of Croyland (about 875 A.D.) had the gate on the north, and

---

* Quoted by Archdeacon Churton in a paper read before the Yorkshire Architectural Society in 1853.

the almonry near it—a very usual position for it; the shops of the tailors and shoe-makers, the hall of the novices, and the abbot's lodgings on the east; the guest-hall and its chambers on the south; and the stable-house, and granary, and bake-house on the west. The Gate-house was usually a large and handsome tower, with the porter's lodge on one side of the arched entrance; and often a strong room on the other, which served as the prison of the manor-court of the convent; and often a handsome room over the entrance, in which the manorial court was held. ·In the middle of the court was often a stone cross, round which markets and fairs were often held.

In the "Vision of Piers Ploughman" an interesting description is given of a Dominican convent of the fourteenth century. We will not trouble the reader with the very archaic original, but will give him a paraphrase of it. The writer says that, on approaching, he was so bewildered by their magnitude and beauty, that for a long time he could distinguish nothing certainly but stately buildings of stone, pillars carved and painted, and great windows well wrought. In the quadrangle he notices the cross standing in the centre, surrounded with tabernacle-work: he enters the minster (church), and describes the arches carved and gilded, the wide windows full of shields of arms and merchants' marks on stained glass, the high tombs under canopies, with armed effigies in alabaster, and lovely ladies lying by their sides in many gay garments. He passes into the cloister and sees it pillared and painted, and covered with lead and paved with tiles, and conduits of white metal pouring their water into latten (bronze) lavatories beautifully wrought. The chapter-house he says was wrought like a great church, carved and painted like a parliament-house. Then he went into the fratry, and found it a hall fit for a knight and his household, with broad boards (tables) and clean benches, and windows wrought as in a church. Then he wandered all about—

"And seigh halles ful heigh, and houses ful noble,
Chambres with chymneys, and chapeles gaye,
And kychenes for an high kynge in castels to holden,
And their dortoure ydight with dores ful stronge,
Fermerye, and fraitur, with fele more houses,

And all strong stone wall, sterne opon heithe,
With gay garites and grete, and ich whole yglazed,
And other houses ynowe to herberwe the queene."

The churches of the friars differed from those of monks. They were frequently composed either of a nave only or a nave and two (often very narrow) aisles, without transepts, or chapels, or towers; they were adapted especially for preaching to large congregations—*e.g.* the Austin Friars' Church in the City of London, lately restored; St. Andrew's Hall, Norwich. In Viollet le Duc's "Dictionary of Architecture" is given a bird's-eye view of the monastery of the Augustine Friars of St. Marie des Vaux Verts, near Brussels, which is a complete example of one of these houses.*

Every monastery had a number of dependent establishments of greater or less size: cells on its distant estates; granges on its manors; chapels in places where the abbey tenants were at a distance from a church; and often hermitages under its protection. A ground-plan and view of one of these cells, the Priory of St. Jean-les-Bons-hommes, of the end of the twelfth century, still remaining in a tolerably perfect state, is given by Viollet le Duc (Dict. Arch., i. 276, 277). It is a miniature monastery, with a little cloistered court, surrounded by the usual buildings: an oratory on the north side; on the east a sacristy, and chapter-house, and long range of buildings, with dormitory over; on the south side the refectory and kitchen; and another exterior court, with stables and offices. The preceptory of Hospitallers at Chibburn, Northumberland, which remains almost as the knights left it, is another example of these small rural houses. It is engraved in Turner's "Domestic Architecture," vol. ii. p. 197. It also consists of a small court, with a chapel about forty-five feet long, on the west side; and other buildings, which we cannot appropriate, on the remaining sides. Of the monastic cells we have already spoken in describing the office of prior. The one or two brethren who were placed in a cell to manage the distant estates of the monastery would probably be

---

* Ground-plans of the Dominican Friary at Norwich, the Carmelite Friary at Hulne and the Franciscan Friary at Kilconnel, may be found in Walcott's "Church and Conventual Arrangement."

chosen rather for their qualities as prudent stewards than for their piety.
The command of money which their office gave them, and their distance
from the supervision of their ecclesiastical superiors, brought them under
temptation, and it is probably in these cells, and among the brethren who
superintended the granges, and the officials who could leave the monastery
at pleasure on the plea of convent business, that we are to look for the
irregularities of which the Middle-Age satirists speak. The monk among
Chaucer's " Canterbury Pilgrims " was prior of a cell, for we read that—

> " When he rode, men might his bridel here
> Gingeling in a whistling sound, as clere
> And eke as loud *as doth the chapelle belle,*
> *Ther as this lord was keeper of the celle.*"

The monk on whose intrigue "The Shipman's Tale" is founded, was
probably the ce'larer of his convent :—

> " This noble monk of which I you devise,
> Had of his abbot, as him list, licence ;
> Because he was a man of high prudence,
> And eke an officer, out for to ride
> To seen his granges and his bernes wide."

An Abbot travelling.

The abbot, too, sometimes gave license to the monks to go and see their
friends, or to pass two or three days at one or other of the manors of the

house for recreation; and sometimes he took a monk with him on his own journeys. In a MS. romance, in the British Museum (Add. 10,293, f. 11), is a representation of a monk with his hood on, journeying on horseback. We give here, from the St. Alban's Book (Nero, D. vii.), a woodcut of an abbot on horseback, with a hat over his hood—" an abbot on an ambling pad;" he is giving his benediction in return to the salute of some passing traveller.

Hermitages or anchorages sometimes depended on a monastery, and were not necessarily occupied by brethren of the monastery, but by any one desirous to embrace this mode of life whom the convent might choose. The hermit, however, probably, usually wore the habit of the order. The monastery often supplied the hermit with his food. In a picture in the MS. romance, before quoted (Add. 10,292, f. 98), is a representation of a knight-errant on horseback, conversing by the way with a clerk, who is carrying bread and wine to a hermitage.

The woodcut with which we conclude, from the Harleian MS., 1,527, represents the characteristic costume of three orders of religious with whom we have been concerned—a bishop, an abbot, and a clerk.

Bishop, Abbot, and Clerk.

THE HERMITS AND RECLUSES OF THE MIDDLE AGES.

CHAPTER I.

THE HERMITS.

WE have already related, in a former chapter (p. 3), that the ascetics who abandoned the stirring world of the Ægypto-Greek cities, and resorted to the Theban desert to lead a life of self-mortification and contemplation, frequently associated themselves into communities, and thus gave rise to the cœnobitical orders of Christendom. But there were others who still preferred the solitary life; and they had their imitators in every age and country of the Christian world. We have not the same fulness of information respecting these solitaries that we have respecting the great orders of monks and friars; but the scattered notices which remain of them, when brought together, form a very curious chapter in the history of human nature, well worthy of being written out in full. The business of the present paper, however, is not to write the whole chapter, but only to select that page of it which relates to the English solitaries, and to give as distinct a picture as we can of the part which the Hermits and Recluses played on the picturesque stage of the England of the Middle Ages.

We have to remember, at the outset, that it was not all who bore the name of Eremite who lived a solitary life. We have already had occasion to mention that Innocent IV., in the middle of the thirteenth century, found a number of small religious communities and solitaries, who were not in any of the recognised religious orders, and observed no authorised rule; and that he enrolled them all into a new order, with the rule of St. Augustine, under the name of Eremiti Augustini. The new order took root, and flourished, and gave rise to a considerable number of large communities, very similar in every respect to the communities of friars of the three orders previously existing. The members of these new communities did not affect seclusion, but went about among the people, as the Dominicans, and Franciscans, and Carmelites did. The popular tongue seems to have divided the formal title of the new order, and to have applied the name of *Augustine*, or, popularly, *Austin Friars*, to these new communities of friars; while it reserved the distinctive name of *Eremites*, or Hermits, for the religious, who, whether they lived absolutely alone, or in little aggregations of solitaries, still professed the old eremitical principle of seclusion from the world. These hermits may again be subdivided into Hermits proper, and Recluses. The difference between them was this: that the hermit, though he professed a general seclusion from the world, yet, in fact, held communication with his fellow-men as freely as he pleased, and might go in and out of his hermitage as inclination prompted, or need required; the recluse was understood to maintain a more strict abstinence from unnecessary intercourse with others, and had entered into a formal obligation not to go outside the doors of his hermitage. In the imperfect notices which we have of them, it is often impossible to determine whether a particular individual was a hermit or a recluse; but we incline to the opinion that of the male solitaries few had taken the vows of reclusion; while the female solitaries appear to have been all recluses. So that, practically, the distinction almost amounts to this—that the male solitaries were hermits, and the females recluses.

Very much of what we have to say of the mediæval solitaries, of their abodes, and of their domestic economy, applies both to those who had, and to those who had not, made the further vow of reclusion. We shall, therefore, treat first of those points which are common to them, and then devote a further paper to those things which are peculiar to the recluses.

The popular idea of a hermit is that of a man who was either a half-crazed enthusiast, or a misanthrope—a kind of Christian Timon—who abandoned the abodes of men, and scooped out for himself a cave in the rocks, or built himself a rude hut in the forest; and lived there a half-savage life, clad in sackcloth or skins,* eating roots and wild fruits, and drinking of the neighbouring spring; visited occasionally by superstitious people, who gazed and listened in fear at the mystic ravings, or wild denunciations, of the gaunt and haggard prophet. This ideal has probably been derived from the traditional histories, once so popular,† of the early hermit-saints; and there may have been, perhaps, always an individual or two of whom this traditional picture was a more or less exaggerated representation. But the ordinary English hermit of the Middle Ages was a totally different type of man. He was a sober-minded and civilised person, who

---

* In the National Gallery is a painting by Fra Angelico, in which is a hermit clad in a dress woven of rushes or flags.

† "The Wonderful and Godly History of the Holy Fathers Hermits," is among Caxton's earliest-printed books. Piers Ploughman (" Vision ") speaks of—

"Anthony and Egidius and other holy fathers
  Woneden in wilderness amonge wilde bestes
  In spekes and in spelonkes, seldom spoke together.
  Ac nobler Antony ne Egedy ne hermit of that time
  Of lions ne of leopards no livelihood ne took,
  But of fowles that fly, thus find men in books."
And again—
  "In prayers and in penance putten them many,
  All for love of our Lord liveden full strait,
  In hope for to have heavenly blisse
  As ancres and heremites that holden them in their cells
  And coveten not in country to kairen [walk] about
  For no likerous lifelihood, their liking to please."
And yet again—
  "Ac ancres and heremites that eaten not but at nones
  And no more ere morrow, mine almesse shall they have,
  And of my cattle to keep them with, that have cloisters and churches,
  Ac Robert Run-about shall nought have of mine."
                                            Piers Ploughman's Vision.

dressed in a robe very much like the robes of the other religious orders; lived in a comfortable little house of stone or timber; often had estates, or a pension, for his maintenance, besides what charitable people were pleased to leave him in their wills, or to offer in their lifetime; he lived on bread and meat, and beer and wine, and had a chaplain to say daily prayers for him, and a servant or two to wait upon him; his hermitage was not always up in the lonely hills, or deep-buried in the shady forests—very often it was by the great high roads, and sometimes in the heart of great towns and cities.

This summary description is so utterly opposed to all the popular notions, that we shall take pains to fortify our assertions with sufficient proofs; indeed, the whole subject is so little known that we shall illustrate it freely from all the sources at our command. And first, as it is one of our especial objects to furnish authorities for the pictorial representation of these old hermits, we shall inquire what kind of dress they did actually wear in place of the skins, or the sackcloth, with which the popular imagination has clothed them.

We should be inclined to assume *a priori* that the hermits would wear the habit prescribed by Papal authority for the Eremiti Augustini, which, according to Stevens, consisted of "a white garment, and a white scapular over it, when they are in the house; but in the choir, and when they go abroad, they put on, over all, a sort of cowl and a large hood, both black, the hood round before, and hanging down to the waist in a point, being girt with a black leather thong." And in the rude woodcuts which adorn Caxton's "Vitas Patrum," or "Lives of the Hermits," we do find some of the religious men in a habit which looks like a gown, with the arms coming through slits, which may be intended to represent a scapular, and with hoods and cowls of the fashion described; while others, in the same book, are in a loose gown, in shape more like that of a Benedictine. Again, in Albert Durer's "St. Christopher," as engraved by Mrs. Jameson, in her "Sacred and Legendary Art," p. 445, the hermit is represented in a frock and scapular, with a cowl and hood. But in the majority of the representations of hermits which we meet with in mediæval paintings and illuminated manuscripts, the costume consists of a frock, sometimes girded, sometimes not.

and over it an ample gown, like a cloak, with a hood; and in the cases where the colour of the robe is indicated, it is almost always indicated by a light brown tint.* It is not unlikely that there were varieties of costume among the hermits. Perhaps those who were attached to the monasteries of monks and friars, and who seem to have been usually admitted to the fraternity of the house,† may have worn the costume of the order to which they were attached; while priest-hermits serving chantries may have worn the usual costume of a secular priest. Bishop Poore, who died 1237, in his "Ancren Riewle," speaks of the fashion of the dress to be worn, at least by female recluses, as indifferent. Bilney, speaking especially of the recluses in his day, just before the Reformation, says, "their apparell is indifferent, so it be dissonant from the laity." In the woodcuts, from various sources, which illustrate this paper, the reader will see for himself how the hermits are represented by the mediæval artists, who had them constantly under their observation, and who at least tried their best to represent faithfully what they saw. The best and clearest illustration which we have been able to find of the usual costume in which the hermits are represented, we here give to the reader. It is from the figure of St. Damasus, one of the group in the fine picture of "St. Jerome," by

St. Damasus, Hermit.

---

* Piers Ploughman ("Vision") describes himself at the beginning of the poem as assuming the habit of a hermit—

"In a summer season when soft was the sun
In habit as a hermit unholy of works,
Went wild in this world, wonders to hear,
All on a May morning on Malvern Hills," &c.

And at the beginning of the eighth part he says—

"Thus robed in *russet* I roamed about
All a summer season."

† For the custom of admitting to the fraternity of a religious house, see p. 66.

Cosimo Roselli (who lived from 1439 to 1506), now in the National Gallery. The hermit-saint wears a light-brown frock, and scapular, with no girdle, and, over all, a cloak and hood of the same colour, and his naked feet are protected by wooden clogs.

Other illustrations of hermits may be found in the early fourteenth century MS. Romances Additional 10,293 f. 335, and 10,294 f. 95. In the latter case there are two hermits in one hermitage; also in Royal 16 G. vi. Illustrations of St. Anthony, which give authorities for hermit costume, and indications of what hermitages were, abound in the later MSS.; for example, in King René's "Book of Hours" (Egerton 1,070), at f. 108, the hermit-saint is habited in a grey frock and black cloak with a T-cross on the breast; he holds bell and book and staff in his hands. In Egerton 1,149, of the middle of the fifteenth century. In Add. 15,677, of the latter part of the fifteenth century, at f. 150, is St. Anthony in brown frock and narrow scapulary, with a grey cloak and hood and a red skull cap; he holds a staff and book; his hermitage, in the background, is a building like a little chapel with a bell-cot on the gable, within a grassy enclosure fenced with a low wattled fence. Add. 18,854, of date 1525 A.D., f. 146, represents St. Anthony in a blue-grey gown and hood, holding bell, rosary, and staff, entering his hermitage, a little building with a bell-cot on the gable.

A man could not take upon himself the character of a hermit at his own pleasure. It was a regular order of religion, into which a man could not enter without the consent of the bishop of the diocese, and into which he was admitted by a formal religious service. And just as bishops do not ordain men to holy orders until they have obtained a "title," a place in which to exercise their ministry, so bishops did not admit men to the order of Hermits until they had obtained a hermitage in which to exercise their vocation.

The form of the vow made by a hermit is here given, from the Institution Books of Norwich, lib. xiv. fo. 27a ("East Anglian," No. 9, p. 107). "I, John Fferys, nott maridd, promyt and avowe to God, o[r] Lady Sent Mary, and to all the seynts in heven, in the p'sence of you reverend fadre in God, Richard bishop of Norwich, the wowe of chastite, after the rule of sent

paule the heremite. In the name of the fadre, sone, and holy gost. JOHN
FFERERE. xiij. meii, anno dni. MLVCIIIJ. in capella de Thorpe."

We summarize the service for habiting and blessing a hermit* from the pontifical of Bishop Lacy of Exeter, of the fourteenth century.† It begins with several psalms; then several short prayers for the incepting hermit, mentioning him by name.‡ Then follow two prayers for the benediction of his vestments, apparently for different parts of his habit; the first mentioning "hec indumenta humilitatem cordis et mundi contemptum significancia,"—these garments signifying humility of heart, and contempt of the world; the second blesses "hanc vestem pro conservande castitatis signo,"—this vestment the sign of chastity. The priest then delivers the vestments to the hermit kneeling before him, with these words, "Brother, behold we give to thee the eremitical habit (*habitum heremiticum*), with which we admonish thee to live henceforth chastely, soberly, and holily; in holy watchings, in fastings, in labours, in prayers, in works of mercy, that thou mayest have eternal life, and live for ever and ever." And he receives them saying, "Behold, I receive them in the name of the Lord; and promise myself so to do according to my power, the grace of God, and of the saints, helping me." Then he puts off his secular habit, the priest saying to him, "The Lord put off from thee the old man with his deeds;" and while he puts on his hermit's habit, the priest says, "The Lord put on thee the new man, which, after God, is created in righteousness and true holiness." Then follow a collect and certain psalms, and finally the priest sprinkles him with holy water, and blesses him.

Men of all ranks took upon them the hermit life, and we find the popular writers of the time sometimes distinguishing among them; one is a "hermit-priest,"§ another is a "gentle hermit," not in the sense of the

---

* "Officium induendi et benedicendi heremitam."
† We are indebted to Mr. M. H. Bloxam for a copy of it.
‡ "*Famulus tuus N.*" It is noticeable that the masculine gender is used all through, without any such note as we find in the Service for Inclosing (which we shall have to notice hereafter), that this service shall serve for both sexes.
§ The hermit who interposed between Sir Lionel and Sir Bors, and who was killed by Sir Lionel for his interference (Malory's "Prince Arthur," III., lxxix.), is called a

"gentle hermit of the dale," but meaning that he was a man of gentle birth. The hermit in whose hermitage Sir Launcelot passed long time is described as a "gentle hermit, which sometime was a noble knight and a great lord of possessions, and for great goodness he hath taken him unto wilful poverty, and hath forsaken his possessions, and his name is Sir Baldwin of Britain, and he is a full noble surgeon, and a right good leech." This was the type of hermit who was venerated by the popular superstition of the day: a great and rich man who had taken to wilful poverty, or a man who lived wild in the woods—a St. Julian, or a St. Anthony. A poor man who turned hermit, and lived a prosaic, pious, useful life, showing travellers the way through a forest, or over a bog, or across a ferry, and humbly taking their alms in return, presented nothing dramatic and striking to the popular mind; very likely, too, many men adopted the hermit life for the sake of the idleness and the alms,* and deserved the small repute they had.

It is *àpropos* of Sir Launcelot's hermit above-mentioned that the romancer complains "for in those days it was not with the guise of hermits as it now is in these days. For there were no hermits in those days, but that they have been men of worship and prowess, and those hermits held great households, and refreshed people that were in distress." We find the author of "Piers Ploughman" making the same complaint. We have, as in other cases, a little modernised his language:—

> "But eremites that inhabit them by the highways,
> And in boroughs among brewers, and beg in churches,
> All that holy eremites hated and despised,
> (As riches, and reverences, and rich men's alms),
> These lollers,† latche drawers,‡ lewd eremites,

"hermit-priest." Also, in the Episcopal Registry of Lichfield, we find the bishop, date 10th February, 1409, giving to Brother Richard Goldeston, late Canon of Wombrugge, now recluse at Prior's Lee, near Shiffenall, license to hear confessions.

* "Great loobies and long, that loath were to swink [work],
 Clothed them in copes to be known from others,
 And shaped them hermits their ease to have."

† Wanderers.   ‡ Breakers out of their cells.

>   Covet on the contrary. Nor live holy as eremites,
>   That lived wild in woods, with bears and lions.
>   Some had livelihood from their lineage* and of no life else;
>   And some lived by their learning, and the labour of their hands.
>   Some had foreigners for friends, that their food sent;
>   And birds brought to some bread, whereby they lived.
>   All these holy eremites were of high kin,
>   Forsook land and lordship, and likings of the body.
>   But these eremites that edify by the highways
>   Whilome were workmen—webbers, and tailors,
>   And carter's knaves, and clerks without grace.
>   They held a hungry house, And had much want,
>   Long labour, and light winnings. And at last espied
>   That lazy fellows in friar's clothing had fat cheeks.
>   Forthwith left they their labour, these lewd knaves,
>   And clothed them in copes as they were clerks,
>   Or one of some order [of monks or friars], or else prophets [eremites]."

This curious extract from "Piers Ploughman" leads us to notice the localities in which hermitages were situated. Sometimes, no doubt, they were in lonely and retired places among the hills, or hidden in the depths of the forests which then covered so large a portion of the land. On the next page is a very interesting little picture of hermit life, from a MS. Book of Hours, executed for Richard II. (British Museum, Domitian, A. xvii., folio 4 v.) The artist probably intended to represent the old hermits of the Egyptian desert, Piers Poughman's—

>   " Holy eremites,
>   That lived wild in woods
>   With bears and lions;"

but, after the custom of mediæval art, he has introduced the scenery, costume, and architecture of his own time. Erase the bears, which stand for the whole tribe of outlandish beasts, and we have a very pretty bit of English mountain scenery. The stags are characteristic enough of the scenery of mediæval England. The hermitage on the right seems to be of the ruder sort, made in part of wattled work. On the left we have the more usual hermitage of stone, with its little chapel bell in a bell-cot on the gable. The venerable old hermit, coming out of the doorway, is a charming illus-

---

* Kindred.

tration of the typical hermit, with his venerable beard, and his form bowed by age, leaning with one hand on his cross-staff, and carrying his rosary in the other. The hermit in the illustration hereafter given from the "History of Launcelot," on page 114, leans on a similar staff; it would seem as if such a staff was a usual part of the hermit's equipment.* The hermit in Albert Dürer's "St. Christopher." already

Hermits and Hermitages.

mentioned, also leans on a staff, but of rather different shape. Here is a companion-picture, in pen and ink, from the "Morte d'Arthur:"—"Then he departed from the cross [a stone cross which parted two ways in waste land, under which he had been sleeping], on foot, into a wild forest. And so by prime he came unto an high mountain, and there he found an hermitage,

---

* In "Piers Ploughman" we read that—
"Hermits with hoked staves
Wenden to Walsingham;"

These hooked staves may, however, have been pilgrim staves, not hermit staves. The pastoral staff on the official seal of Odo, Bishop of Bayeux, was of the same shape as the staff above represented. A staff of similar shape occurs on an early grave-stone at Welbeck Priory, engraved in the Rev. E. L. Cutts's "Manual of Sepulchral Slabs and Crosses," plate xxxv.

and an hermit therein, which was going to mass. And then Sir Launcelot kneeled down upon both his knees, and cried out, 'Lord, mercy!' for his wicked works that he had done. So when mass was done, Sir Launcelot called the hermit to him, and prayed him for charity to hear his confession. 'With a good will,' said the good man."

But many of the hermitages were erected along the great highways of the country, and especially at bridges and fords,* apparently with the express view of their being serviceable to travellers. One of the hermit-saints set up as a pattern for their imitation was St. Julian, who, with his wife, devoted his property and life to showing hospitality to travellers; and the hermit who is always associated in the legends and pictures with St. Christopher, is represented as holding out his torch or lantern to light the giant ferryman, as he transports his passengers across the dangerous ford by which the hermitage was built. When hostelries, where the traveller could command entertainment for hire, were to be found only in the great towns, the religious houses were the chief resting-places of the traveller; not only the conventual establishments, but the country clergy also were expected to be given to hospitality.† But both monasteries and country parsonages often lay at a distance of miles of miry and intricate by-road off the highway. We must picture this state of the country and of society to ourselves, before we can appreciate the intentions of those who founded these hospitable establishments; we must try to imagine ourselves travellers, getting belated in a dreary part of the road, where it ran over a bleak wold, or dived through a dark forest, or approached an unknown ford, before we can appreciate the gratitude of those who suddenly caught

---

* Blomfield, in his "History of Norfolk," 1532, says, "It is to be observed that hermitages were erected, for the most part, near great bridges (see *Mag. Brit.*, On Warwickshire, p. 597, Dugdale, &c., and Badwell's 'Description of Tottenham') and high roads, as appears from this, and those at Brandon, Downham, Stow Bardolph, in Norfolk, and Erith, in the Isle of Ely, &c."

† In the settlement of the vicarage of Kelvedon, Essex, when the rectory was impropriated to the abbot and convent of Westminster, in the fourteenth century, it was expressly ordered that the convent, besides providing the vicar a suitable house, should also provide a hall for receiving guests. See subsequent chapter on the Secular Clergy.

the light from the hermit's window, or heard the faint tinkle of his chapel bell ringing for vespers.

Such incidents occur frequently in the romances. Here is an example:— "Sir Launcelot rode all that day and all that night in a forest; and at the last, he was ware of an hermitage and a chapel that stood between two cliffs; and then he heard a little bell ring to mass, and thither he rode, and alighted, and tied his horse to the gate, and heard mass." Again: "Sir Gawayne rode till he came to an hermitage, and there he found the good man saying his even-song of our Lady. And there Sir Gawayne asked harbour for charity, and the good man granted it him gladly."

We shall, perhaps, most outrage the popular idea of a hermit, when we assert that hermits sometimes lived in towns. The extract from "Piers Ploughman's Vision," already quoted, tells us of—

"Eremites that inhabit them
In boroughs among brewers."

The difficulty of distinguishing between hermits proper and recluses becomes very perplexing in this part of our subject. There is abundant proof, which we shall have occasion to give later, that recluses, both male and female, usually lived in towns and villages, and these recluses are sometimes called hermits, as well as by their more usual and peculiar name of anchorites and anchoresses. But we are inclined to the opinion, that not all the male solitaries who lived in towns were recluses. The author of "Piers Ploughman's Vision" speaks of the eremites who inhabited in boroughs as if they were of the same class as those who lived by the highways, and who ought to have lived in the wildernesses, like St. Anthony. The theory under which it was made possible for a solitary, an eremite, a man of the desert, to live in a town, was, that a churchyard formed a solitary place —a desert—within the town. The curious history which we are going to relate, seems to refer to hermits, not to recluses. The Mayor of Sudbury, under date January 28, 1433, petitioned the Bishop of Norwich, setting forth that the bishop had refused to admit "Richard Appleby, of Sudbury, conversant with John Levynton, of the same town, heremyte, to the order of Hermits, unless he was sure to be inhabited in a solitary place where virtues might be increased, and vice exiled;" and that therefore " we have granted hym, be the assent of all the sayd parish and cherch reves, to be inhabited with the sayd John Levynton in his solitary place and hermytage, whych y^t is made at the cost of the parysh, in the cherchyard of St. Gregory Cherche, to dwellen togedyr as (long as) yey liven, or whiche of them longest liveth;" and thereupon the mayor prays the bishop to admit Richard Appleby to the order.

This curious incident of two solitaries living together has a parallel in the romance of " King Arthur." When the bold Sir Bedivere had lost his lord King Arthur, he rode away, and, after some adventures, came to a chapel and an hermitage between two hills, "and he prayed the hermit that he might abide there still with him, to live with fasting and prayers. So Sir Bedivere abode there still with the hermit; and there Sir Bedivere put upon him poor clothes, and served the hermit full lowly in fasting and in prayers." And afterwards (as we have already related) Sir Launcelot " rode all that day and all that night in a forest. And at the last he was ware of an hermitage and a chapel that stood between two cliffs, and then he heard a little bell ring to mass; and thither he rode, and alighted, and tied his horse to the gate and heard mass." He had stumbled upon the hermitage in which Sir Bedivere was living. And when Sir Bedivere had made himself known, and had "told him his tale all whole," " Sir Launcelot's heart almost burst for sorrow, and Sir Launcelot threw abroad his armour, and said,—' Alas! who may trust this world?' And then he kneeled down on his knees, and prayed the hermit for to shrive him and assoil him. And then he besought the hermit that he might be his brother. And he put an habit upon Sir Launcelot, and there he served God day and night with prayers and fastings." And afterwards Sir Bors came in the same way. And within half a year there was come Sir Galahad, Sir Galiodin, Sir Bleoberis, Sir Villiers, Sir Clarus, and Sir Gahalatine. " So these seven noble knights abode there still: and when they saw that Sir Launcelot had taken him unto such perfection, they had no list to depart, but took such an habit as he had. Thus they endured in great penance six years, and then Sir Launcelot took the habit of priesthood, and twelve months he sung the mass; and there was none of these other knights but that they read in books, and helped for to sing mass, and ring bells, and did lowly all manner of service. And so their horses went where they would, for they took no regard in worldly riches." And after a little time Sir Launcelot died at the hermitage: "then was there weeping and wringing of hands, and the greatest dole they made that ever made man. And on the morrow the bishop-hermit sung his mass of requiem." The accompanying wood-cut, from one of the small compartments at the bottom of Cosimo Roselli's picture of St. Jerome, from which we have already taken the figure of St. Damasus, may serve to illustrate this

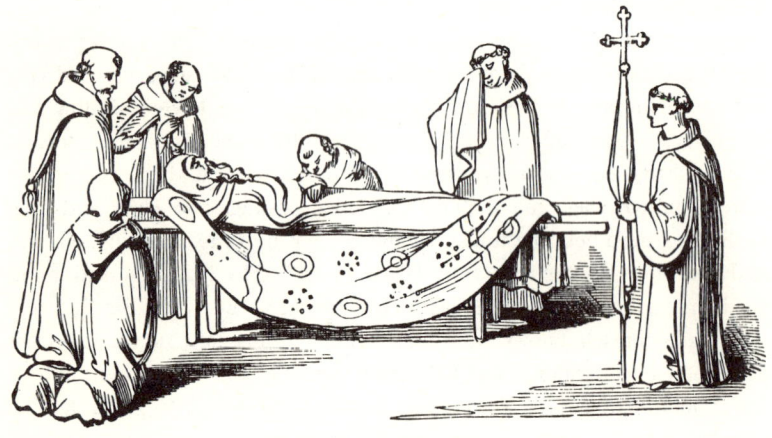

Funeral Service of a Hermit.

incident. It represents a number of hermits mourning over one of their brethren, while a priest, in the robes proper to his office, stands at the head of the bier and says prayers, and his deacon stands at the foot, holding a processional cross. The contrast between the robes of the priest and those of the hermits is lost in the woodcut; in the original the priest's cope and amys are coloured red, while those of the hermits are tinted with light brown.

If the reader has wondered how the one hermitage could accommodate these seven additional habitants, the romancer does not forget to satisfy his curiosity: a few pages farther we read—"So at the season of the night they went all to their beds, for they all lay in one chamber." It was not very unusual for hermitages to be built for more than one occupant; but probably, in all such cases, each hermit had his own cell, adjoining their common chapel. This was the original arrangement of the hermits of the Thebais in their laura. The great difference between a hermitage with more than one hermit, and a small cell of one of the other religious orders, was that in such a cell one monk or friar would have been the prior, and the others subject to him; but each hermit was independent of any authority on the part of the other; he was subject only to the obligation of his rule, and the visitation of his bishop.

The life [*] of the famous hermit, Richard of Hampole, which has lately been published for the first time by the Early English Text Society, will enable us to realise in some detail the character and life of a mediæval hermit of the highest type. Saint Richard was born [†] in the village of Thornton, in Yorkshire. At a suitable age he was sent to school by the care of his parents, and afterwards was sent by Richard Neville, Archdeacon of Durham, to Oxford, where he gave himself specially to theological study. At the age of nineteen, considering the uncertainty of life and the awfulness of judgment, especially to those who waste life in pleasure or spend it in acquiring wealth, and fearing lest he should fall into such courses, he left Oxford and returned to his father's house. One day he asked of his sister two of her gowns (tunicas), one white, the other grey, and a cloak and hood of his father's. He cut up the two gowns, and fashioned out of them and of the hooded cloak an imitation of a hermit's habit, and next day he went off into a neighbouring wood bent upon living a hermit life. Soon after, on the vigil of the Assumption of the Blessed Virgin, he went to a certain church, and knelt down to pray in the place which the wife of a certain worthy knight, John de Dalton, was accustomed to occupy. When the lady came to church, her servants would have turned out the intruder, but she would not permit it. When vespers were over and he rose from his

---

[*] From the "Officium et Legenda de Vita Ricardi Rolle."
[†] When is not stated; he died in 1349.

knees, the sons of Sir John, who were students at Oxford, recognised him as the son of William Rolle, whom they had known at Oxford. Next day Richard again went to the same church, and without any bidding put on a surplice and sang mattins and the office of the mass with the rest. And when the gospel was to be read at mass, he sought the blessing of the priest, and then entered the pulpit and preached a sermon to the people of such wonderful edification that many were touched with compunction even to tears, and all said they had never heard before a sermon of such power and efficacy. After mass Sir John Dalton invited him to dinner. When he entered into the manor he took his place in a ruined building, and would not enter the hall, according to the evangelical precept, "When thou art bidden to a wedding sit down in the lowest room, and when he that hath bidden thee shall see it he will say to thee, Friend, go up higher;" which was fulfilled in him, for the knight made him sit at table with his own sons. But he kept such silence at dinner that he did not speak one word; and when he had eaten sufficiently he rose before they took away the table and would have departed, but the knight told him this was contrary to custom, and made him sit down again. After dinner the knight had some private conversation with him, and being satisfied that he was not a madman, but really seemed to have the vocation to a hermit's life, he clothed him at his own cost in a hermit's habit, and retained him a long time in his own house, giving him a solitary chamber (*locum mansionis solitariæ*)* and providing him with all necessaries. Our hermit then gave himself up to ascetic discipline and a contemplative life. He wrote books; he counselled those who came to him. He did both at the same time; for one afternoon the lady of the house

---

* Afterwards it is described as a cell at a distance from the family, where he was accustomed to sit solitary and to pass his time in contemplation. In doing this Sir John Dalton and his wife were, according to the sentiment of the time, following the example of the Shunammite and her husband, who made for Elisha a little chamber on the wall, and set for him there a bed, and a table, and a stool, and a candlestick (2 Kings iv. 10). The Knight of La Tour Landry illustrates this when in one of his tales (ch. xcv.) he describes the Shunammite's act in the language of mediæval custom: "This good woman had gret devocion unto this holy man, and required and praied hym for to come to her burghe and loged in her hous, and her husbonde and she made a chambre solitaire for this holy man, where as he might use his devocions and serve God."

came to him with many other persons and found him writing very rapidly, and begged him to stop writing and speak some words of edification to them; and he began at once and continued to address them for two hours with admirable exhortations to cultivate virtue and to put away worldly vanities, and to increase the love of their hearts for God; but at the same time he went on writing as fast as before. He used to be so absorbed in prayer that his friends took off his torn cloak, and when it had been mended put it on him again, without his knowing it. Soon we hear of his having temptations like those which assailed St. Anthony, the devil tempting him in the form of a beautiful woman. He was specially desirous to help recluses and those who required spiritual consolation, and who were vexed by evil spirits.

At length Lady Dalton died, and (whether as a result of this is not stated) the hermit left his cell and began to move from place to place. One time he came near the cell of Dame Margaret, the recluse of Anderby in Richmondshire, and was told that she was dumb and suffering from some strange disease, and went to her. And he sat down at the window of the house of the recluse,* and when they had eaten, the recluse felt a desire to sleep; and being oppressed with sleep her head fell towards the window at which St. Richard was reclined. And when she had slept a little, leaning somewhat on Richard, suddenly she was seized with a convulsion, and awoke with her power of speech restored.

He wrote many works of ascetic and mystical divinity which were greatly esteemed. The Early English Text Society has published some specimens in the work from which these notices are gathered, which show that his reputation as a devotional writer was not undeserved. At length he settled at Hampole, where was a Cistercian nunnery. Here he died, and in the church of the nunnery he was buried. We are indebted for the Officium and Legenda from which we have gathered this outline of his life to the pious care of the nuns of Hampole, to whom the fame of Richard's sanctity was a source of great profit and honour. That he had a line of

---

* Either the little window through which she communicated with the outer world, or perhaps (as suggested further on) a window between her cell and a guest-chamber in which she received visitors.

successors in his anchorage is indicated by the fact hereafter stated (p. 128), that in 1415 A.D., Lord Scrope left by will a bequest to Elizabeth, late servant to the anchoret of Hampole.

There are indications that these hermitages were sometimes mere bothies of branches; there is a representation of one, from which we here give a woodcut, in an illuminated MS. romance of Sir Launcelot, of early fourteenth-century date (British Museum, Add. 10,293, folio 118 v., date 1316) : we have already noticed another of wattled work.* There are also

Sir Launcelot and a Hermit.

caves † here and there in the country which are said by tradition to have been hermitages: one is described in the *Archæological Journal*, vol. iv., p. 150. It is a small cave, not easy of access, in the side of a hill called Carcliff Tor, near Rowsley, a little miserable village not far from Haddon Hall. In a recess, on the right side as you enter the cave, is a crucifix about four feet high, sculptured in bold relief in the red grit rock out of

---

* A hermitage, partly of stone, partly of timber, may be seen in the beautiful MS. Egerton 1,147, f. 218 v.

† A very good representation of a cave hermitage may be found in the late MS. Egerton, 2,125, f. 206 v. Also in the Harl. MS. 1,527, at f. 14 v., is a hermit in a cave; and in Royal 10 E IV. f. 130, here a man is bringing the hermit food and drink.

which the cave is hollowed; and close to it, on the right, is a rude niche, perhaps to hold a lamp.

St. Robert's Chapel, at Knaresborough, Yorkshire, is a very excellent example of a hermitage.* It is hewn out of the rock, at the bottom of a cliff, in the corner of a sequestered dell. The exterior, a view of which is given below, presents us with a simply arched doorway at the bottom of

Exterior View of St. Robert's Chapel, Knaresborough.

the rough cliff, with an arched window on the left, and a little square opening between, which looks like the little square window of a recluse. Internally we find the cell sculptured into the fashion of a little chapel, with a groined ceiling, the groining shafts and ribs well enough designed, but rather rudely executed. There is a semi-octagonal apsidal recess at the east end, in which the altar stands; a piscina and a credence and stone seat in the north wall; a row of sculptured heads in the south wall, and a grave-stone in the middle of the floor. This chapel appears to have been

---

* Eugene Aram's famous murder was perpetrated within it. See Sir E. L. Bulwer's description of the scene in his "Eugene Aram."

also the hermit's living room. The view of the exterior, and of the interior and ground-plan, are from Carter's "Ancient Architecture," pl. lxvii. Another hermitage, whose chapel is very similar to this, is at Warkworth. It is half-way up the cliff, on one side of a deep, romantic valley, through which runs the river Coquet, overhung with woods. The chapel is hewn out of the rock, 18 feet long by 7½ wide, with a little entrance-porch on the south, also hewn in the rock; and, on the farther side, a long, narrow

Interior View of St. Robert's Chapel.

apartment, with a small altar at the east end, and a window looking upon the chapel altar. This long apartment was probably the hermit's living room; but when the Earls of Northumberland endowed the hermitage for a chantry priest, the priest seems to have lived in a small house, with a garden attached, at the foot of the cliff. The chapel is groined, and has Gothic windows, very like that of Knaresborough. A minute description of this hermitage, and of the legend connected with it, is given in a poem called "The History of Warkworth" (4to, 1775), and in a letter in Grose's "Antiquities," vol. iii., is a ground-plan of the chapel and its appurtenances.

Hermitages. 113

A view of the exterior, showing its picturesque situation, will be found in Herne's "Antiquities of Great Britain," pl. 9.

There is a little cell, or oratory, called the hermitage, cut out of the face of a rock near Dale Abbey, Derbyshire. On the south side are the door and three windows; at the east end, an altar standing upon a raised platform, both cut out of the rock; there are little niches in the walls, and a stone seat all round.*

There is another hermitage of three cells at Wetheral, near Carlisle, called Wetheral Safeguard, or St. Constantine's Cells—Wetheral Priory was dedicated to St. Constantine, and this hermitage seems to have belonged to the priory. It is not far from Wetheral Priory, in the face of a rock standing 100 feet perpendicularly out of the river Eden, which washes its base; the hill rising several hundred feet higher still above this rocky escarpment. The hermitage is at a height of 40 feet from the river, and can only be approached from above by a narrow and difficult path down the face of the precipice. It consists of three square cells, close together, about 10 feet square and 8 feet high; each with

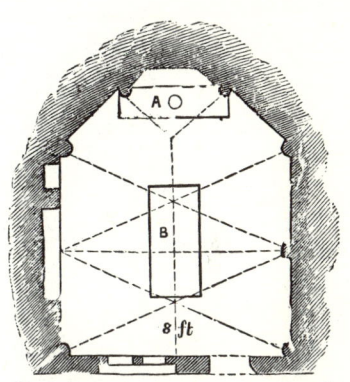

Ground-Plan of St. Robert's Chapel.

a short passage leading to it, which increases its total length to about 20 feet. These passages communicate with a little platform of rock in front of the cells. At a lower level than this platform, by about 7 feet, there is a narrow gallery built up of masonry; the door to the hermitage is at one end of it, so that access to the cells can only be obtained by means of a ladder from this gallery to the platform of rock 7 feet above it. In the front of the gallery are three windows, opposite to the three cells, to give them light, and one chimney. An engraving will be found in Hutchinson's "History of Cumberland," vol. i. p. 160, which

---

* See view in Stukeley's "Itin. Curios.," pl. 14.

shows the picturesque scene—the rocky hill-side, with the river washing round its base, and the three windows of the hermitage, half-way up, peeping through the foliage; there is also a careful plan of the cells in the letterpress.

A chapel, and a range of rooms—which communicate with one another, and form a tolerably commodious house of two floors, are excavated out of a rocky hill-side, called Blackstone Rock, which forms the bank of the Severn, near Bewdley, Worcestershire. A view of the exterior of the rock, and a plan and section of the chambers, are given both in Stukeley's

"Itinerarium Curiosum," pls. 13 and 14, and in Nash's "History of Worcestershire," vol. ii. p. 48.

At Lenton, near Nottingham, there is a chapel and a range of cells excavated out of the face of a semicircular sweep of rock, which crops out on the bank of the river Leen. The river winds round the other semicircle, leaving a space of greensward between the rock and the river, upon which the cells open. Now, the whole place is enclosed, and used as a public garden and bowling-green, its original features being, however, preserved with a praiseworthy appreciation of their interest. In former days this hermitage was just within the verge of the park of the royal castle of Nottingham; it was doubtless screened by the trees of the park; and its inmates might pace to and fro on their secluded grass-plot, fenced in by the rock and the river from every intruding foot, and yet in full view of the walls and towers of the castle, with the royal banner waving from its keep, and catch a glimpse of the populous borough, and see the parties of knights and ladies prance over the level meadows which stretched out to the neighbouring Trent like a green carpet, embroidered in spring and autumn by the purple crocus, which grows wild there in myriads. Stukeley, in his " Itinerarium Curiosum," pl. 39, gives a view and ground-plan of these curious cells. Carter also figures them in his " Ancient Architecture," pl. 12, and gives details of a Norman shaft and arch in the chapel.

But nearly all the hermitages which we read of in the romances, or see depicted in the illuminations and paintings, or find noticed in ancient historical documents, are substantial buildings of stone or timber. Here is one from folio 56 of the " History of Launcelot " (Add. 10,293): the hermit stands at the door of his house, giving his parting benediction to Sir Launcelot, who, with his attendant physician, is taking his leave after a night's sojourn at the hermitage. In the paintings of the Campo Santo, at Pisa (engraved in Mrs. Jameson's " Sacred and Legendary Art "), which represent the hermits of the Egyptian desert, some of the hermitages are caves, some are little houses of stone. In Caxton's " Vitas Patrum " the hermitages are little houses; one has a stepped gable; another is like a gateway, with a room over it.* They were founded and built, and often endowed, by the same men who founded chantries, and built churches, and endowed monasteries; and from the same motives of piety, charity, or superstition. And the founders seem often to have retained the patronage of the hermitages, as of valuable benefices, in their own hands.† A hermit-

---

* Suggesting the room so often found over a church porch.

† In the year 1499, a dispute having arisen between the abbot and convent of Easby and the Grey Friars of Richmond, on the one part, and the burgesses of Richmond, on the other part, respecting the disposition of the goods of Margaret Richmond, late anchoress of the same town, it was at length settled that the goods should remain with the warden and brethren of the friars, after that her debts and the repair of the anchorage were defrayed, " because the said anchoress took her habit of the said friars," and that the abbot and convent should have the disposition of the then anchoress, Alison

age was, in fact, a miniature monastery, inhabited by one religious, who was abbot, and prior, and convent, all in one: sometimes also by a chaplain,* where the hermit was not a priest, and by several lay brethren, *i.e.* servants. It had a chapel of its own, in which divine service was performed daily. It had also the apartments necessary for the accommodation of the hermit, and his chaplain—when one lived in the hermitage—and his servants, and the necessary accommodation for travellers besides; and it had often, perhaps generally, its court-yard and garden.

The chapel of the hermitage seems not to have been appropriated solely to the performance of divine offices, but to have been made useful for other more secular purposes also. Indeed, the churches and chapels in the Middle Ages seem often to have been used for great occasions of a semi-religious character, when a large apartment was requisite, *e.g.* for holding councils, for judicial proceedings, and the like. Godric of Finchale, a hermit who lived about the time of Henry II.,† had two chapels adjoining his cell; one he called by the name of St. John Baptist, the other after the Blessed Virgin. He had a kind of common room, "communis domus," in which he cooked his food and saw visitors; but he lived chiefly, day and night, in the chapel of St. John, removing his bed to the chapel of St. Mary at times of more solemn devotion.

In an illumination on folio 153 of the "History of Launcelot," already quoted (British Mus., Add. 10,293), is a picture of King Arthur taking

---

Comeston, after her decease; and so to continue for evermore between the said abbot and warden, as it happens that the anchoress took her habit of religion. And that the burgesses shall have the nomination and free election of the said anchoress for evermore from time to time when it happens to be void, as they have had without time of mind. (Test. Ebor. ii. 115.)

* In June 5, 1356, Edward III. granted to brother Regnier, hermit of the Chapel of St. Mary Magdalen, without Salop, a certain plot of waste called Shelcrosse, contiguous to the chapel, containing one acre, to hold the same to him and his successors, hermits there, for their habitation, and to find a chaplain to pray in the chapel for the king's soul, &c. (Owen and Blakeway's "History of Shrewsbury," vol. ii. p. 165). "Perhaps," say our authors, "this was the eremitical habitation in the wood of Suttona (Sutton being a village just without Salop), which is recorded elsewhere to have been given by Richard, the Dapifer of Chester, to the monks of Salop."

† "Vita S. Godrici," published by the Surtees Society.

counsel with a hermit in his hermitage. The building in which they are seated has a nave and aisles, a rose-window in its gable, and a bell-turret, and seems intended to represent the chapel of the hermitage. Again, at folio 107 of the same MS. is a picture of a hermit talking to a man, with the title,—"Ensi y come une hermites prole en une chapele de son hermitage,"—" How a hermit conversed in the chapel of his hermitage." It may, perhaps, have been in the chapel that the hermit received those who sought his counsel on spiritual or on secular affairs.

In addition to the references which have already been given to illustrations of the subject in the illuminations of MSS., we call the special attention of the student to a series of pictures illustrating a mediæval story of which a hermit is the hero, in the late thirteenth century MS. Royal 10 E IV.; it begins at folio 113 v., and runs on for many pages, and is full of interesting passages.

We also add a few lines from Lydgate's unpublished "Life of St. Edmund," as a typical picture of a hermit, drawn in the second quarter of the fifteenth century:—

> " — holy Ffremund though he were yonge of age,
> And ther he bilte a litel hermitage
> Be side a ryver with al his besy peyne,
> He and his fellawis that were in nombre tweyne.
>
> " A litel chapel he dide ther edifie,
> Day be day to make in his praiere,
> In the reverence only off Marie
> And in the worshipe of her Sone deere,
> And the space fully off sevene yeere
> Hooly Ffremund, lik as it is founde,
> Leved be frut and rootes off the grounde.
>
> " Off frutes wilde, his story doth us telle,
> Was his repast penance for t' endure,
> To stanch his thurst drank water off the welle
> And eet acorns to sustene his nature,
> Kernelles off notis [nuts] when he myhte hem recure.
> To God alway doying reverence,
> What ever he sent took it in patience."

And in concluding this chapter let us call to mind Spenser's description of a typical hermit and hermitage, while the originals still lingered in the living memory of the people :—

"At length they chaunst to meet upon the way
An aged sire, in long blacke weedes yclad,
His feet all bare, his head all hoarie gray,
And by his belt his booke he hanging had ;
Sober he seemde, and very sagely sad,
And to the ground his eyes were lowly bent,
Simple in shew, and voide of malice bad ;
And all the way he prayed as he went,
And often knockt his brest as one that did repent.

"He faire the knight saluted, louting low,
Who faire him quited, as that courteous was ;
And after asked him if he did know
Of strange adventures which abroad did pas.
'Ah ! my dear sonne,' quoth he, ' how should, alas !
Silly* old man, that lives in hidden cell,
Bidding his beades all day for his trespas,
Tidings of war and worldly trouble tell ?
With holy father sits not with such things to mell.'†
     *   *   *   *   *
Quoth then that aged man, ' The way to win
Is wisely to advise. Now day is spent,
Therefore with me ye may take up your in
For this same night.' The knight was well content;
So with that godly father to his home he went.

"A little lowly hermitage it was,
Down in a dale, hard by a forest's side,
Far from resort of people that did pass
In traveill to and froe ; a little wyde
There was an holy chappell edifyde,
Wherein the hermite dewly wont to say
His holy things, each morne and eventyde ;
Hereby a chrystall streame did gently play,
Which from a sacred fountaine welled forth alway.

"Arrived there, the little house they fill ;
Ne look for entertainment where none was ;
Rest is their feast, and all things at their will ;
The noblest mind the best contentment has.
With fair discourse the evening so they pas ;
For that old man of pleasing words had store,
And well could file his tongue as smooth as glas ;

---

* Simple.   † Meddle.

> He told of saintes and popes, and evermore
> He strowd an Ave-Mary after and before."*
> *Faery Queen*, i. 1, 29, 33, 34, 35.

* Since the above was written, the writer has had an opportunity of visiting a hermitage very like those at Warkworth, Wetheral, Bewdley, and Lenton, still in use and habitation. It is in the parish of Limay, near Mantes, a pretty little town on the railway between Rouen and Paris. Nearly at the top of a vine-clad hill, on the north of the valley of the Seine, in which Mantes is situated, a low face of rock crops out. In this rock have been excavated a chapel, a sacristy, and a living-room for the hermit; and the present hermit has had a long refectory added to his establishment, in which to give his annual dinner to the people who come here, one day in the year, in considerable numbers, on pilgrimage. The chapel differs from those which we have described in the text in being larger and ruder; it is so wide that its rocky roof is supported by two rows of rude pillars, left standing for that purpose by the excavators. There is an altar at the east end. At the west end is a representation of the Entombment; the figure of our Lord, lying as if it had become rigid in the midst of the writhing of his agony, is not without a rude force of expression. One of the group of figures standing about the tomb has a late thirteenth-century head of a saint placed upon the body of a Roman soldier of the Renaissance period. There is a grave-stone with an incised cross and inscription beside the tomb; and in the niche on the north side is a recumbent monumental effigy of stone, with the head and hands in white glazed pottery. But whether these things were originally placed in the hermitage, or whether they are waifs and strays from neighbouring churches, brought here as to an ecclesiastical peep-show, it is hard to determine; the profusion of other incongruous odds and ends of ecclesiastical relics and fineries, with which the whole place is furnished, inclines one to the latter conjecture. There is a bell-turret built on the rock over the chapel, and a chimney peeps through the hill-side, over the sacristy fireplace. The platform in front of the hermitage is walled in, and there is a little garden on the hill above. The curé of Limay performs service here on certain days in the year. The hermit will disappoint those who desire to see a modern example of

> " An aged sire, in long black weedes yclad,
> His feet all bare, his beard all hoarie gray."

He is an aged sire, seventy-four years old; but for the rest, he is simply a little, withered, old French peasant, in a blue blouse and wooden sabots. He passes his days here in solitude, unless when a rare party of visitors ring at his little bell, and, after due inspection through his *grille*, are admitted to peep about his chapel and his grotto, and to share his fine view of the valley shut in by vine-clad hills, and the Seine winding through the flat meadows, and the clean, pretty town of Mantes *le jolie* in the middle, with its long bridge and its cathedral-like church. Whether he spends his time

> " Bidding his beades all day for his trespas,"

we did not inquire; but he finds the hours lonely. The good curé of Limay wishes him to sleep in his hermitage, but, like the hermit-priest of Warkworth, he prefers sleeping in the village at the foot of the hill.

CHAPTER II.

ANCHORESSES, OR FEMALE RECLUSES.

AND now we proceed to speak more particularly of the recluses. The old legend tells us that John the Hermit, the contemporary of St. Anthony, would hold communication with no man except through the window of his cell.* But the recluses of more modern days were not content to quote John the Egyptian as their founder. As the Carmelite friars claimed Elijah, so the recluses, at least the female recluses, looked up to Judith as the foundress of their mode of life, and patroness of their order.

Mabillon tells us that the first who made any formal rule for recluses was one Grimlac, who lived about 900 A.D. The principal regulations of his rule are, that the candidate for reclusion, if a monk, should signify his intention a year beforehand, and during the interval should continue to live among his brethren. If not already a monk, the period of probation was doubled. The leave of the bishop of the diocese was to be first obtained, and if the candidate were a monk, the leave of his abbot and convent also. When he had entered his cell, the bishop was to put his seal upon the door, which was never again to be opened,† unless for the

---

* One of the little hermitages represented in the Campo Santo series of paintings of the old Egyptian hermit-saints (engraved in Mrs. Jameson's "Legends of the Monastic Orders") has a little grated window, through which the hermit within (probably this John) is talking with another outside.

† That recluses did, however, sometimes quit their cells on a great emergency, we learn from the Legenda of Richard of Hampole already quoted, where we are told that at his death Dame Margaret Kyrkley, the recluse of Anderby, on hearing of the saint's death, hastened to Hampole to be present at his funeral.

help of the recluse in time of sickness or on the approach of death. Successive councils published canons to regulate this kind of life. That of Millo, in 692, repeats in substance the rule of Grimlac. That of Frankfort, in 787, refers to the recluses. The synod of Richard de la Wich, Bishop of Chichester, A.D. 1246, makes some canons concerning them : " Also we ordain to recluses that they shall not receive or keep any person in their houses concerning whom any sinister suspicion might arise. Also that they have narrow and proper windows; and we permit them to have secret communication with those persons only whose gravity and honesty do not admit of suspicion." *

Towards the end of the twelfth century a rule for anchorites was written by Bishop Richard Poore† of Chichester, and afterwards of Salisbury, who died A.D. 1237, which throws abundant light upon their mode of life; for it is not merely a brief code of the regulations obligatory upon them, but it is a book of paternal counsels, which enters at great length, and in minute detail, into the circumstances of the recluse life, and will be of great use to us in the subsequent part of this chapter.

There were doubtless different degrees of austerity among the recluses; but, on the whole, we must banish from our minds the popular ‡ idea that they inhabited a living grave, and lived a life of the extremest mortification. Doubtless there were instances in which religious enthusiasm led the

---

* Wilkins's "Concilia," i. 693.

† Several MSS. of this rule are known under different names. Fosbroke quotes one as the rule of Simon de Gandavo (or Simon of Ghent), in Cott. MS. Nero A xiv.; another in Bennet College, Cambridge; and another under the name of Alfred Reevesley. See Fosbroke's " British Monachism," pp. 374-5. The various copies, indeed, seem to differ considerably, but to be all derived from the work ascribed to Bishop Poore. All these books are addressed to female recluses, which is a confirmation of the opinion which we have before expressed, that the majority of the recluses were women.

‡ Thus the player-queen in *Hamlet*, iii. 2 :—

 " Nor earth to me give food, nor heaven light !
 Sport and repose lock from me, day, and night !
 To desperation turn my trust and hope !
 An anchor's cheer in prison be my scope !
 Each opposite, that blanks the face of joy,
 Meet what I would have well, and it destroy," &c.

recluse into frightful and inhuman self-torture, like that of Thaysis, in the "Golden Legend:" "She went to the place whiche th' abbot had assygned to her, and there was a monasterye of vyrgyns; and there he closed her in a celle, and sealed the door with led. And the celle was lytyll and strayte, and but one lytell wyndowe open, by whyche was mynistred to her poor lyvinge; for the abbot commanded that they shold gyve to her a lytell brede and water."* Thaysis submitted to it at the command of Abbot Pafnucius, as penance for a sinful life, in the early days of Egyptian austerity; and now and then throughout the subsequent ages the self-hatred of an earnest, impassioned nature, suddenly roused to a feeling of exceeding sinfulness; the remorse of a wild, strong spirit, conscious of great crimes; or the enthusiasm of a weak mind and morbid conscience, might urge men and women to such self-revenges, to such penances, as these. Bishop Poore gives us episodically a pathetic example, which our readers will thank us for repeating here. "Nothing is ever so hard that love doth not make tender, and soft, and sweet. Love maketh all things easy. What do men and women endure for false love, and would endure more! And what is more to be wondered at is, that love which is faithful and true, and sweeter than any other love, doth not overmaster us as doth sinful love! Yet I know a man who weareth at the same time both a heavy cuirass† and haircloth, bound with iron round the middle too, and his arms with broad and thick bands, so that to bear the sweat of it is severe suffering. He fasteth, he watcheth, he laboureth, and, Christ knoweth, he complaineth, and saith that it doth not oppress him; and often asks me to teach him something wherewith he might give his body pain. God knoweth that he, the most sorrowful of men, weepeth to me, and saith that God hath quite forgotten him, because He sendeth him no great sickness; whatever is bitter seems sweet to him for our Lord's sake. God knoweth love doth this, because, as he often saith to me, he could never love God the less for any evil thing that He might do to him, even

---

* A cell in the north-west angle of Edington Abbey Church, Wilts, seems to be of this kind.

† The wearing a cuirass, or hauberk of chain mail, next the skin became a noted form of self-torture; those who undertook it were called *Loricati*.

were He to cast him into hell with those that perish. And if any believe any such thing of him, he is more confounded than a thief taken with his theft. I know also a woman of like mind that suffereth little less. And what remaineth but to thank God for the strength that He giveth them; and let us humbly acknowledge our own weakness, and love their merit, and thus it becomes our own. For as St. Gregory says, love is of so great power that it maketh the merit of others our own, without labour." But though powerful motives and great force of character might enable an individual here and there to persevere with such austerities, when the severities of the recluse life had to be reduced to rule and system, and when a succession of occupants had to be found for the vacant anchor-holds, ordinary human nature revolted from these unnatural austerities, and the common sense of mankind easily granted a tacit dispensation from them; and the recluse life was speedily toned down in practice, to a life which a religiously-minded person, especially one who had been wounded and worsted in the battle of life, might gladly embrace and easily endure.

Usually, even where the cell consisted of a single room, it was large enough for the comfortable abode of a single inmate, and it was not destitute of such furnishing as comfort required. But it was not unusual for the cell to be in fact a house of several apartments, with a garden attached; and it would seem that the technical "cell" within which the recluse was immured, included house and garden, and everything within the boundary wall.* It is true that many of the recluses lived entirely, and perhaps all partly, upon the alms of pious and charitable people. An alms-box was hung up to receive contributions, as appears from "Piers Ploughman,"—

"In ancres there a box hangeth."

And in the extracts hereafter given from the "Ancren Riewle," we shall find several allusions to the giving of alms to recluses as a usual custom. But it was the bishop's duty, before giving license for the building of a reclusorium, to satisfy himself that there would be, either from alms or from an endowment, a sufficient maintenance for the recluse. Practically, they

---

* The cell of a Carthusian monk, as we have stated, consisted of a little house of three apartments and a little garden within an inclosure wall.

do not seem often to have been in want; they were restricted as to the times when they might eat flesh-meat, but otherwise their abstemiousness depended upon their own religious feeling on the subject; and the only check upon excess was in their own moderation. They occupied themselves, besides their frequent devotions, in reading, writing, illuminating, and needlework; and though the recluses attached to some monasteries seem to have been under an obligation of silence, yet in the usual case the recluse held a perpetual levee at the open window, and gossiping and scandal

Sir Percival at the Reclusorium.

appear to have been among her besetting sins. It will be our business to verify and further to illustrate this general sketch of the recluse life.

And, first, let us speak more in detail of their habitations. The reclusorium, or anchorhold, seems sometimes to have been, like the hermitage, a house of timber or stone, or a grotto in a solitary place. In Sir T. Mallory's "Prince Arthur" we are introduced to one of these, which afforded all the appliances for lodging and entertaining even male guests. We read:—" Sir Percival returned again unto the recluse, where he deemed to have tidings of that knight which Sir Launcelot followed. And so he kneeled at her window, and anon the recluse opened it, and asked Sir Percival what he would. 'Madam,' said he, 'I am a knight of King

The Reclusorium.

Arthur's court, and my name is Sir Percival de Gális.' So when the recluse heard his name, she made passing great joy of him, for greatly she loved him before all other knights of the world; and so of right she ought to do, for she was his aunt. And then she commanded that the gates should be opened to him, and then Sir Percival had all the cheer that she might make him, and all that was in her power was at his commandment." But it does not seem that she entertained him in person; for the story continues that "on the morrow Sir Percival went unto the recluse," *i.e.*, to her little audience-window, to propound his question, "if she knew that knight with the white shield." Opposite is a woodcut of a picture in the MS. "History of Sir Launcelot" (Royal 14, E. III. folio 101 v.), entitled, " Ensi q Percheva retourna à la recluse qui estait en son hermitage."*

In the case of these large remote anchorholds, the recluse must have had a chaplain to come and say mass for her every day in the chapel of her hermitage.† But in the vast majority of cases, anchorholds were attached to a church either of a religious house, or of a town, or of a village; and in these situations they appear to have been much more numerous than is at all suspected by those who have not inquired into this little-known portion of our mediæval antiquities. Very many of our village churches had a recluse living within or beside them, and it will, perhaps, especially surprise the majority of our readers to learn that these recluses were specially numerous in the mediæval towns.‡ The proofs of this fact are abundant; here are some. Henry, Lord Scrope, of Masham, by will, dated 23rd June, 1415, bequeathed to every anchoret§ and recluse dwelling in London or its suburbs 6*s.* 8*d.*; also to every anchoret and recluse dwelling in York and its suburbs 6*s.* 8*d.* From other sources we learn more about

---

* This very same picture is given also in another MS. of about the same date, marked Add. 10,294, at folio 14.

† As was probably the case at Warkworth, the hermit living in the hermitage, while the chantry priest lived in the house at the foot of the hill.

‡ " Eremites that inhabiten
   By the highways,
   And in boroughs among brewers."
   Piers Ploughman's Vision.

§ Probably " anchoret " means male, and "recluse" female recluse.

these York anchorets and recluses. The will of Adam Wigan, rector of St. Saviour, York (April 20, 1433, A.D.)*, leaves 3s. 4d. to Dan John, who dwelt in the Chapel of St. Martin, within the parish of St. Saviour. The female recluses of York were three in number in the year 1433, as we learn from the will of Margaret, relict of Nicholas Blackburne:† "Lego tribus reclusis Ebor.," ijs. Where their cells were situated we learn from the will of Richard Rupell (A.D. 1435 ‡), who bequeaths to the recluse in the cemetery of the Church of St. Margaret, York, five marks; and to the recluse in the cemetery of St. Helen, in Fishergate, five marks; and to the recluse in the cemetery of All Saints, in North Street, York, five marks. They are also all three mentioned in the will of Adam Wigan, who leaves to the anchorite enclosed in Fishergate 2s.; to her enclosed near the church of St. Margaret 2s.; to her enclosed in North Street, near the Church of All Saints, 2s. The will of Lady Margaret Stapelton, 1465 A.D.,§ mentions anchorites in Watergate and Fishergate, in the suburbs of York, and in another place the anchorite of the nunnery of St. Clement, York. At Lincoln, also, we are able to trace a similar succession of anchoresses. In 1383 A.D., William de Belay, of Lincoln, left to an anchoress named Isabella, who dwelt in the Church of the Holy Trinity, in Wigford, within the city of Lincoln, 13s. 4d. In 1391, John de Sutton left her 20s.; in 1374, John de Ramsay left her 12d. Besides these she had numerous other legacies from citizens. In 1453, an anchoress named Matilda supplied the place of Isabella, who we may suppose had long since gone to her reward. In that year John Tilney—one of the Tilneys of Boston—left "Domine Matilde incluse infra ecclesiam sanctæ Trinitatis ad gressus in civitate Lincoln, vjs. viijd." In 1502, Master John Watson, a chaplain in Master Robert Flemyng's chantry, left xijd. to the "ankers" at the Greese foot. This Church of the Holy Trinity "ad gressus" seems to have been for a long period the abode of a female recluse.‖ The will of Roger Eston, rector of Richmond, Yorkshire, A.D. 1446, also mentions the recluses in the city of York and its suburbs. The

---

* Test. Vetust., ii. 25.   † Ibid. ii. 47.   ‡ Ibid. ii. 56.   § Ibid. ii. 271.
‖ Note p. 87 to "Instructions for Parish Priests," Early English Text Society.

will of Adam Wilson also mentions Lady Agnes, enclosed at (*apud*) the parish church of Thorganby, and anchorites (female) at Beston and Pontefract. Sir Hugh Willoughby, of Wollaton, in 1463 bequeathed 6*s.* 5*d.* to the anchoress of Nottingham.* The will of Lady Joan Wombewell, A.D. 1454,† also mentions the anchoress of Beyston. The will of John Brompton, of Beverley, A.D. 1444,‡ bequeaths 3*s.* 4*d.* to the recluse by the Church of St. Giles, and 1*s.* 6*d.* to anchorite at the friary of St. Nicholas of Beverley. Roger Eston also leaves a bequest to the anchorite of his parish of Richmond, respecting whom the editor gives a note whose substance is given elsewhere. In a will of the fifteenth century § we have a bequest "to the ancher in the wall beside Bishopsgate, London." ‖ In the will of St. Richard, Bishop of Chichester,¶ we have bequests to Friar Humphrey, the recluse of Pageham, to the recluse of Hogton, to the recluse of Stopeham, to the recluse of Herringham; and in the will of Walter de Suffield, Bishop of Norwich, bequests to " anchers" and recluses in his diocese, and especially to his niece Ela, *in reclusorio* at Massingham.**

Among the other notices which we have of solitaries living in towns, Lydgate mentions one in the town of Wakefield. Morant says there was one in Holy Trinity churchyard, Colchester. The episcopal registers of Lichfield show that there was an anchorage for several female recluses in the churchyard of St. George's Chapel, Shrewsbury. The will of Henry, Lord Scrope, already quoted, leaves 100*s.* and the pair of beads which the testator was accustomed to use to the anchorite of Westminster: it was his predecessor, doubtless, who is mentioned in the time of Richard II.: when the young king was going to meet Wat Tyler in Smithfield, he went to Westminster Abbey, "then to the church, and so to the high altar, where he devoutedly prayed and offered; after which he spake with the

---

* Test. Vetust., ii. 131. † Ibid. 178. ‡ Ibid. ii. 98. § Ibid. 356.
‖ Other bequests to recluses occur in the will of Henry II., to the recluses (*incluses*) of Jerusalem, England, and Normandy.
¶ Sussex Archæol. Coll., i. p. 174.
** Blomfield's "Norfolk," ii. pp. 347-8. See also the bequests to the Norwich recluses, *infra*.

128   *The Hermits and Recluses of the Middle Ages.*

anchore, to whom he confessed himself."* Lord Scrope's will goes on to bequeath 40*s*. to Robert, the recluse of Beverley; 13*s*. 4*d*. each to the anchorets of Stafford, of Kurkebeck, of Wath, of Peasholme, near York, of Kirby, Thorganby, near Colingworth, of Leek, near Upsale, of Gainsburgh, of Kneesall, near South Well, of Dartford, of Stamford, living in the parish church there; to Thomas, the chaplain dwelling continually in the church of St. Nicholas, Gloucester; to Elizabeth, late servant to the anchoret of Hamphole; and to the recluse in the house of the Dominicans at Newcastle; and also 6*s*. 8*d*. to every other anchorite and anchoritess that could be easily found within three months of his decease.

We have already had occasion to mention that there were several female recluses, in addition to the male solitaries, in the churchyards of the then great city of Norwich. The particulars which that laborious antiquary, Blomfield, has collected together respecting several of them will throw a little additional light upon our subject, and fill up still further the outlines of the picture which we are engaged in painting.

There was a hermitage in the churchyard of St. Julian, Norwich, which was inhabited by a succession of anchoresses, some of whose names Blomfield records :—Dame Agnes, in 1472; Dame Elizabeth Scot, in 1481; Lady Elizabeth, in 1510; Dame Agnes Edrigge, in 1524. The Lady Julian, who was the anchoress in 1393, is said to have had two servants to attend her in her old age. "She was esteemed of great holiness. Mr. Francis Peck had a vellum MS. containing an account of her visions." Blomfield says that the foundations of the anchorage might still be seen in his time, on the east side of St. Julian's churchyard. There was also an anchorage in St. Ethelred's churchyard, which was rebuilt in 1305, and an anchor continually dwelt there till the Reformation, when it was pulled down, and the grange, or tithe-barn, at Brakendale was built with its timber; so that it must have been a timber house of some magnitude. Also in St. Edward's churchyard, joining to the church on the north side, was a cell, whose ruins were still visible in Blomfield's time, and most persons who died in Norwich left small sums towards its maintenance. In

---

* Stow's Chronicle, p. 559.

1428 Lady Joan was anchoress here, to whom Walter Ledman left 20*s.*, and 40*d.* to each of her servants. In 1458, Dame Anneys Kite was the recluse here; in 1516, Margaret Norman, widow, was buried here, and gave a legacy to the lady anchoress by the church. St. John the Evangelist's Church, in Southgate, was, about A.D. 1300, annexed to the parish of St. Peter per Montergate, and the Grey Friars bought the site; they pulled down the whole building, except a small part left for an anchorage, in which they placed an anchor, to whom they assigned part of the churchyard for his garden. Also there used anciently to be a recluse dwelling in a little cell joining to the north side of the tower of St. John the Baptist's Church, Timber Hill, but it was down before the Dissolution. Also there was an anchor, or hermit, who had an anchorage in or adjoining to All Saints' Church. Also in Henry III.'s time a recluse dwelt in the churchyard of St. John the Baptist, and the Holy Sepulchre, in Ber Street. In the monastery of the Carmelites, or White Friars, at Norwich, there were two anchorages—one for a man, who was admitted brother of the house, and another for a woman, who was admitted sister thereof. The latter was under the chapel of the Holy Cross, which was still standing in Blomfield's time, though converted into dwelling-houses. The former stood by St. Martin's Bridge, on the east side of the street, and had a small garden to it, which ran down to the river. In 1442, December 2nd, the Lady Emma, recluse, or anchoress, and religious sister of the Carmelite order, was buried in their church. In 1443, Thomas Scroope was anchorite in this house. In 1465, Brother John Castleacre, a priest, was anchorite. In 1494 there were legacies given to the anchor of the White Friars. This Thomas Scroope was originally a Benedictine monk; in 1430 he became anchorite here (being received a brother of the Carmelite order), and led an anchorite's life for many years, seldom going out of his cell but when he preached; about 1446 Pope Eugenius made him Bishop of Down, which see he afterwards resigned, and came again to his convent, and became suffragan to the Bishop of Norwich. He died, and was buried at Lowestoft, being near a hundred years old.

The document which we are about to quote from Whittaker's "History of Whalley" (pp. 72 and 77), illustrates many points in the history of these anchorholds. The anchorage therein mentioned was built in a parish churchyard, it depended upon a monastery, and was endowed with an allowance in money and kind from the monastery; it was founded for two recluses; they had a chaplain and servants; and the patronage was retained by the founder. The document will also give us some very curious and minute details of the domestic economy of the recluse life; and, lastly, it will give us an historical proof that the assertions of the contemporary satirists, of the laxity* with which the vows were sometimes kept, were not without foundation.

"In 1349, Henry, Duke of Lancaster, granted in trust to the abbot and convent of Whalley rather large endowments to support two recluses (women) in a certain place within the churchyard of the parish church of Whalley, and two women servants to attend them, there to pray for the soul of the duke, &c.; to find them seventeen ordinary loaves, and seven inferior loaves, eight gallons of better beer, and 3*d*. per week; and yearly ten large stock-fish, one bushel of oatmeal, one of rye, two gallons of oil for lamps, one pound of tallow for candles, six loads of turf, and one load of faggots; also to repair their habitations; and to find a chaplain to say mass in the chapel of these recluses daily; their successors to be nominated by the duke and his heirs. On July 6, 15th Henry VI., the king nominated Isole de Heton, widow, to be an *anachorita* for life, *in loco ad hoc ordinato juxta ecclesiam parochialem de Whalley*. Isole, however, grew tired of the solitary life, and quitted it; for afterwards a representation was made to the king that 'divers that had been anchores and recluses in the seyd place aforetyme, have broken oute of the seyd place wherein they were reclusyd, and departyd therefrom wythout any reconsilyation;' and that Isole de Heton had broken out two years before, and was not willing to return; and that divers of the women that had been servants there had been with child. So Henry VI. dissolved the hermitage, and appointed instead two chaplains to say mass daily, &c." Whittaker thinks that the hermitage occupied the site of some cottages on the west side of the church-

---

* In the "Ancren Riewle," p. 129, we read, "Who can with more facility commit sin than the false recluse?"

yard, which opened into the churchyard until he had the doors walled up.

There was a similar hermitage for several female recluses in the churchyard of St. Romauld, Shrewsbury, as we learn from a document among the Bishop of Lichfield's registers,* in which he directs the Dean of St. Chadd, or his procurator, to enclose Isolda de Hungerford an anchorite in the houses of the churchyard of St. Romauld, where the other anchorites dwell. Also in the same registry there is a precept, dated Feb. 1, 1310, from Walter de Langton, Bishop, to Emma Sprenghose, admitting her an anchorite in the houses of the churchyard of St. George's Chapel, Salop, and he appoints the archdeacon to enclose her. Another license from Roger, Bishop of Lichfield, dated 1362, to Robert de Worthin, permitting him, on the nomination of Queen Isabella, to serve God in the reclusorium built adjoining (*juxta*) the chapel of St. John Baptist in the city of Coventry, has been published *in extenso* by Dugdale, and we transcribe it for the benefit of the curious.† Thomas Hearne has printed an Episcopal Commission, dated 1402, for enclosing John Cherde, a monk of Ford Abbey. Burnett's "History of Bristol" mentions a commission opened by Bishop William of Wykham, in August, 1403, for enclosing Lucy de Newchurch, an anchoritess in the hermitage of St. Brendon in Bristol. Richard Francis, an ankret, is spoken of as *inter quatuor parietes pro christi inclusus* in Langtoft's "Chronicle," ij. 625.

---

* Owen and Blakeway's "History of Shrewsbury."
† "Rogerus, &c., delecto in Christo filio Roberto de Worthin, cap. salutem, &c. Precipue devotionis affectum, quem ad serviendum Deo in reclusorio juxta capellam Sancti Joh. Babtiste in civitate Coventriensi constructo, et spretis mundi deliciis et ipsius vagis discurribus contemptis, habere te asseres, propensius intuentes, ac volentes te, consideratione nobilis domine, domine Isabelle Regine Anglie nobis pro te supplicante in hujus laudabili proposito confovere, ut in prefato reclusorio morari possis, et recludi et vitam tuam in eodam ducere in tui laudibus Redemptoris, licentiam tibi quantum in nobis est concedi per presentes, quibus sigillum nostrum duximus apponendum. Dat apud Heywood, 5 Kal. Dec. M.D. A.D. MCCCLXII, et consecrationis nostræ tricessimo sexto."— DUGDALE'S *Warwickshire*, 2nd Edit., p. 193.

CHAPTER III.

ANCHORAGES.

JUST as in a monastery, though it might be large or small in magnitude, simple or gorgeous in style, with more or fewer offices and appendages, according to the number and wealth of the establishment, yet there was always a certain suite of conventual buildings, church, chapter refectory, dormitory, &c., arranged in a certain order, which formed the cloister; and this cloister was the nucleus of all the rest of the buildings of the establishment; so, in a reclusorium, or anchorhold, there was always a "cell" of a certain construction, to which all things else, parlours or chapels, apartments for servants and guests, yards and gardens, were accidental appendages. Bader's rule for recluses in Bavaria* describes the dimensions and plan of the cell minutely; the *domus inclusi* was to be 12 feet long by as many broad, and was to have three windows—one towards the choir (of the church to which it was attached), through which he might receive the Holy Sacrament; another on the opposite side, through which he might receive his victuals; and a third to give light, which last ought always to be closed with glass or horn.

The reader will have already gathered from the preceding extracts that the reclusorium was sometimes a house of timber or stone within the churchyard, and most usually adjoining the church itself. At the west end of Laindon Church, Essex, there is a unique erection of timber, of which we here give a representation. It has been modernised in appearance by

---

* Fosbroke's "British Monachism," p. 372.

the insertion of windows and doors; and there are no architectural details of a character to reveal with certainty its date, but in its mode of construction—the massive timbers being placed close together—and in its general appearance, there is an air of considerable antiquity. It is improbable that a house would be erected in such a situation after the Reformation, and it accords generally with the descriptions of a recluse house. Probably, however, many of the anchorholds attached to churches were of smaller dimensions; sometimes, perhaps, only a single little timber

Laindon Church, Essex.

apartment on the ground floor, or sometimes probably raised upon an under croft, according to a common custom in mediæval domestic buildings. Very probably some of those little windows which occur in many of our churches, in various situations, at various heights, and which, under the name of "low side windows," have formed the subject of so much discussion among ecclesiologists, may have been the windows of such anchorholds. The peculiarity of these windows is that they are sometimes merely a square opening, which originally was not glazed, but closed with a shutter; sometimes a small glazed window, in a position where it was clearly not intended to light the church generally; sometimes a window has a stone transom across, and the upper part is glazed, while the lower part is closed only by a shutter. It is clear that some of these may have served to enable the anchorite, living in a cell *outside* the church, to see the altar. It seems to have been such a window which is alluded to in the following incident from Mallory's "Prince Arthur:"—"Then Sir Launcelot armed him and took his horse, and as he rode that way he saw a chapel where was a recluse, which had a window that she might see

Reclusorium, or Anchorhold, at Rettenden, Essex.

up to the altar; and all aloud she called Sir Launcelot, because he seemed a knight arrant. . . . . . And (after a long conversation) she commanded Launcelot to dinner." In the late thirteenth-century MS., Royal 10 E. IV. at f. 181, is a representation of a recluse-house, in which, besides two two-light arched windows high up in the wall, there is a smaller square "low side window" very distinctly shown. Others of these low side windows may have been for the use of wooden anchorholds built *within* the church, combining two of the usual three windows of the cell, viz., the one to give light, and the one through which to receive food and communicate with the outer world. There is an anchorhold still remaining in a tolerably unmutilated state at Rettenden, Essex. It is a stone building of fifteenth-century date, of two stories, adjoining the north side of the chancel. It is entered by a rather elaborately moulded doorway from the chancel. The lower story is now used as a vestry, and is lighted by a modern window broken through its east wall; but it is described as having been a dark room, and there is no trace of any original window. In the north wall, and towards the east, is a bracket, such as would hold a small statue or a lamp. In the west side of this room, on the left immediately on entering it from the chancel, is the door of a stone winding stair (built up in the nave aisle, but now screened towards the aisle by a very large monument), which gives access to the upper story. This story consists of a room which very exactly agrees with the description of a recluse's cell (see opposite woodcut). On the south side are two arched niches, in which are stone benches, and the back of the easternmost of these niches is pierced by a small arched window, now blocked up, which looked down upon the altar. On the north side is a chimney, now filled with a modern fireplace, but the chimney is a part of the original building; and westward of the chimney is a small square opening, now filled with modern glazing, but the hook upon which the original shutter hung still remains. This window is not splayed in the usual mediæval manner, but is recessed in such a way as to allow the head of a person to look out, and especially down, with facility. On the exterior this window is about 10 feet from the ground. In this respect it resembles the situation of a low side window in Prior Crawden's Chapel, Ely Cathedral,* which is on the first floor, having a room, lighted only by narrow slits, beneath it; and at the Sainte Chapelle, in Paris, which also has an undercroft, there is a similar example of a side window, at a still greater height from the ground. The east side of the Rettenden reclusorium has now a modern window, probably occupying the place of the original window which gave light to the cell. The stair-turret at the top of the winding staircase, seems to have been intended to serve

---

* Engraved in the *Archæological Journal*, iv. p. 320.

for a little closet: it obtained some light through a small loop which looked out into the north aisle of the church; the wall on the north side of it is recessed so as to form a shelf, and a square slab of stone, which looks like a portion of a thirteenth-century coffin-stone, is laid upon the top of the newel, and fitted into the wall, so as to form another shelf or little table.

At East Horndon Church, Essex, there are two transept-like projections from the nave. In the one on the south there is a monumental niche in the south wall, upon the back of which are the indents of the brasses of a man and wife and several children; and there is a tradition, with which these indents are altogether inconsistent, that the heart of the unfortunate Queen Anne Bullen is interred therein. Over this is a chamber, open to the nave, and now used as a gallery, approached by a modern wooden stair; and there is a projection outside which looks like a chimney, carried out from this floor upwards. The transeptal projection on the north side is very similar in plan. On the ground floor there is a wide, shallow, cinque-foil headed niche (partly blocked) in the east wall; and there is a wainscot ceiling, very neatly divided into rectangular panels by moulded ribs of the date of about Henry VIII. The existence of the chamber above was unknown until the present rector discovered a doorway in the east wall of the ground floor, which, on being opened, gave access to a stone staircase behind the east wall, which led up into a first-floor chamber, about 12 feet from east to west, and 8 feet from north to south: the birds had had access to it through an unglazed window in the north wall for an unknown period, and it was half filled with their nests; the floor planks were quite decayed. There is no trace of a chimney here. It is now opened out to the nave to form a gallery. Though we do not find in these two first-floor chambers the arrangements which could satisfy us that they were recluse cells, yet it is very probable that they were habitable chambers, inhabited, if not by recluses, perhaps by chantry priests, serving chantry chapels of the Tyrrells.

Mr. M. H. Bloxam, in an interesting paper in the Transactions of the Lincoln Diocesan Architectural Society, mentions several other anchor-holds:—"Adjoining the little mountain church of S. Patricio, about five miles from Crickhowel, South Wales, is an attached building or cell. It contains on the east side a stone altar, above which is a small window, now blocked up, which looked towards the altar of the church; but there was no other internal communication between this cell and the church, to the west end of which it is annexed; it appears as if destined for a recluse who was also a priest." Mr. Bloxam mentions some other examples, very much resembling the one described at Rettenden. The north transept of Clifton Campville Church, Staffordshire, a structure of the fourteenth century, is vaulted and groined with stone; it measures 17 feet from north to south, and 12 feet from east to west. Over this is a loft or chamber, apparently an anchorhold or *domus inclusi*, access to which is obtained by means of a newell staircase in the south-east angle, from a doorway at the north-east angle of the chancel. A small window on the south side of this chamber, now blocked up, afforded a view into the interior of the church. The roof of this chamber has been lowered, and all the windows blocked up.

" On the north side of the chancel of Chipping Norton Church, Oxfordshire, is a revestry which still contains an ancient stone altar, with its appurtenances, viz., a piscina in the wall on the north side, and a bracket for an image projecting from the east wall, north of the altar. Over this revestry is a loft or chamber, to which access is obtained by means of a staircase in the north-west angle. Apertures in the wall enabled the recluse, probably a priest, here dwelling, to overlook the chancel and north aisle of the church.

" Adjoining the north side of the chancel of Warmington Church, Warwickshire, is a revestry, entered through an ogee-headed doorway in the north wall of the chancel, down a descent of three steps. This revestry contains an ancient stone altar, projecting from a square-headed window in the east wall, and near the altar, in the same wall, is a piscina. In the south-west angle of this revestry is a flight of stone steps, leading up to a chamber or loft. This chamber contains, in the west wall, a fire-place, in the north-west angle a retiring-closet, or jakes, and in the south wall a small pointed window, of decorated character, through which the high-altar in the chancel might be viewed. In the north wall there appears to have been a pointed window, filled with decorated tracery, and in the east wall is another decorated window. This is one of the most interesting and complete specimens of the *domus inclusi* I have met with."*

The chamber which is so frequently found over the porch of our churches, often with a fireplace, and sometimes with a closet within it, may probably have sometimes been inhabited by a recluse. Chambers are also sometimes found in the towers of churches.† Mr. Bloxam mentions a room, with a fire-place, in the tower of Upton Church, Nottinghamshire. Again, at Boyton Church, Wiltshire, the tower is on the north side of the church, "and adjoining the tower on the west side, and communicating with it, is a room which appears to have been once permanently inhabited, and in the north-east angle of this room is a fire-place." At Newport, Salop, the first floor of the tower seems to have been a habitable chamber, and has a little inner chamber corbelled out at the north-west angle of the tower.

We have already hinted that it is not improbable that timber anchor-holds were sometimes erected inside our churches. Or perhaps the recluse lived in the church itself, or, more definitely, in a par-closed chantry chapel, without any chamber being purposely built for him. The indications which lead us to this supposition are these: there is sometimes an ordinary domestic fire-place to be found inside the church. For instance, in the north aisle of Layer Marney Church, Essex, the western part of the aisle is screened off for the chantry of Lord Marney, whose tomb has the chantry altar still remaining, set crosswise at the west end of the tomb; in the eastern division of the aisle there is an ordinary domestic fire-place in the north wall. There is a similar fire-place, of about the same date, in Sir Thomas Bullen's church of Hever, in Kent.

Again, we sometimes find beside the low side-windows already spoken of, an arrangement which shows that it was intended for some one

---

* Reports of the Lincoln Diocesan Archæological Society for 1853, pp. 359-60.
† Peter, Abbot of Clugny, tells us of a monk and priest of that abbey who had for a cell an oratory in a very high and remote steeple-tower, consecrated to the honour of St. Michael the archangel. "Here, devoting himself to divine meditation night and day, he mounted high above mortal things, and seemed with the angels to be present at the nearer vision of his Maker."

habitually to sit there. Thus, at Somerton, Oxfordshire, on the north side of the chancel, is a long and narrow window, with decorated tracery in the head; the lower part is divided by a thick transom, and does not appear to have been glazed. In the interior the wall is recessed beside the window, with a sort of shoulder, exactly adapted to give room for a seat, in such a position that its occupant would get the full benefit of the light through the glazed upper part of the little window, and would be in a convenient position for conversing through the unglazed lower portion of it.

At Elsfield Church, Oxfordshire, there is an early English lancet window, similarly divided by a transom, the lower part, now blocked up, having been originally unglazed, and the sill of the window in the interior has been formed into a stone seat and desk. We reproduce here a view of the latter from the "Oxford Architectural Society's Guide to the Neighbourhood of Oxford." Perhaps in such instances as these, the recluse may have been a priest serving a chantry altar, and licensed, perhaps, to hear confessions,* for which the seat beside the little open window would be a convenient arrangement.

Window, Elsfield Church.

Lord Scrope's will has already told us of a chaplain dwelling continually (*commoranti continuo*) in the Church of St. Nicholas, Gloucester, and of an anchorite living in the parish church of Stamford. There is a low side-window at Mawgan Church, Cornwall. In the south-east angle between the south transept and the chancel, the inner angle at the junction of the transept and chancel walls is cut away, from the floor upwards, to the

---

* In the Lichfield Registers we find that, on February 10, 1409, the bishop granted to Brother Richard Goldestone, late canon of Wombrugge, now recluse at Prior's Lee, near Shiffenale, license to hear confessions. (History of Whalley, p. 55.)

height of six feet, and laterally about five feet in south and east directions from the angle. A short octagonal pillar, six feet high, supports all that remains of the angle of these walls, whilst the walls themselves rest on two flat segmental arches of three feet span. A low diagonal wall is built across the angle thus exposed, and a small lean-to roof is run up from it into the external angle enclosing a triangular space within. In this wall the low side-window is inserted. The sill of the window is four feet from the pavement. Further eastward a priest's door seems to have formed part of the arrangement. The west jamb of the doorway is cut away so that from this triangular space and from the transept beyond a view is obtained of the east window.

The position of the low side-windows at Grade, Cury, and Landewednack is the same as that of Mawgan, but the window itself is different in form, those at Grade and at Cury being small oblong openings, the former 1 ft. 9 in. by 1 ft. 4 in., the sill only 1 ft. 9 in. from the ground; the latter is 1 ft. by 11 in., the sill 3 ft. 4 in. from ground. At Landewednack the window has two lights, square headed, 2 ft. 6 in. by 1 ft. 4 in., sill 4 ft. 3½ in. from ground. A large block of serpentine rock is fixed in the ground beneath the window in a position convenient for a person standing but not kneeling at the window.*

Knighton gives us some particulars of a recluse priest who lived at Leicester. "There was," he says, "in those days at Leicester, a certain priest, hight William of Swynderby, whom they commonly called William the Hermit, because, for a long time, he had lived the hermitical life there; they received him into a certain chamber within the church, because of the holiness they believed to be in him, and they procured for him victuals and a pension, after the manner of other priests." †

In the "Test. Ebor.," p. 244, we find a testator leaving "to the chantry chapel of Kenby my red vestment, ... also the great missal and the great portifer, which I bought of Dominus Thomas Cope, priest and anchorite in that chapel." Blomfield also (ii. 75) tells us of a hermit, who

---

* Paper by J. J. Rogers, *Archæological Journal*, xi. 33.
† Twysden's "Henry de Knighton," vol. ii. p. 2665.

lived in St. Cuthbert's Church, Thetford, and performed divine service therein.

Who has not, at some time, been deeply impressed by the solemn stillness, the holy calm, of an empty church? Earthly passions, and cares, and ambitions, seemed to have died away; one's soul was filled with a spiritual peace. One stood and listened to the wind surging against the walls outside, as the waves of the sea may beat against the walls of an ingulfed temple; and one felt as effectually secluded from the surge and roar of the worldly life outside the sacred walls, as if in such a temple at the bottom of the sea. One gazed upon the monumental effigies, with their hands clasped in an endless prayer, and their passionless marble faces turned for ages heavenward, and read their mouldering epitaphs, and moralized on the royal preacher's text—" All is vanity and vexation of spirit." And then one felt the disposition—and, perhaps, indulged it—to kneel before the altar, all alone with God, in that still and solemn church, and pour out one's high-wrought thoughts before Him. At such times one has probably tasted something of the transcendental charm of the life of a recluse priest. One could not sustain the tension long. Perhaps the old recluse, with his experience and his aids, could maintain it for a longer period. But to him, too, the natural reaction must have come in time; and then he had his mechanical occupations to fall back upon—trimming the lamps before the shrines, copying his manuscript, or illuminating its initial letters; perhaps, for health's sake, he took a daily walk up and down the aisle of the church, whose walls re-echoed his measured footfalls; then he had his oft-recurring "hours" to sing, and his books to read; and, to prevent the long hours which were still left him in his little par-closed chapel from growing too wearily monotonous, there came, now and then, a tap at the shutter of his "parlour" window, which heralded the visit of some poor soul, seeking counsel or comfort in his difficulties of this world or the next, or some pilgrim bringing news of distant lands, or some errant knight seeking news of adventures, or some parishioner come honestly to have a dish of gossip with the holy man, about the good and evil doings of his neighbours.

There is a pathetic anecdote in Blomfield's "Norfolk," which will show that the spirit and the tradition of the old recluse priests survived the Reformation. The Rev. Mr. John Gibbs, formerly rector of Gessing, in that county, was ejected from his rectory in 1690 as a non-juror. "He was an odd but harmless man, both in life and conversation. After his ejection he dwelt in the north porch chamber, and laid on the stairs that led up to the rood-loft, between the church and chancel, having a window at his head, so that he could lie in his couch, and see the altar. He lived to be very old, and was buried at Frenze."

Let us turn again to the female recluse, in her anchor-house outside the church. How was her cell furnished? It had always a little altar at the east end, before which the recluse paid her frequent devotions, hearing, besides, the daily mass in church through her window, and receiving the Holy Sacrament at stated times. Bishop Poore advises his recluses to receive it only fifteen times a year. The little square unglazed window was closed with a shutter, and a black curtain with a white cross upon it also hung before the opening, through which the recluse could converse without being seen. The walls appear to have been sometimes painted —of course with devotional subjects. To complete the scene add a comfortable carved oak chair, and a little table, an embroidery frame, and such like appliances for needlework; a book of prayers, and another of saintly legends, not forgetting Bishop Poore's "Ancren Riewle;" a fire on the hearth in cold weather, and the cat, which Bishop Poore expressly allows, purring beside it; and lastly paint in the recluse, in her black habit and veil, seated in her chair; or prostrate before her little altar; or on her knees beside her church window listening to the chanted mass; or receiving her basket of food from her servant, through the open parlour window; or standing before its black curtain, conversing with a stray knight-errant; or putting her white hand through it, to give an alms to some village crone or wandering beggar.

A few extracts from Bishop Poore's "Ancren Riewle," already several times alluded to, will give life to the picture we have painted. Though intended for the general use of recluses, it seems to have been specially addressed, in the first instance, to three sisters, who, in the bloom of youth, forsook the world, and became the tenants of a reclusorium. It would seem that in such cases each recluse had a separate cell, and did not communicate, except on rare occasions, with her fellow inmates; and each had her own separate servant to wait upon her. Here are some particulars as to their communication with the outer world. "Hold no conversation with any man out of a church window, but respect it for the sake of the Holy Sacrament which ye see there through;* and at other times (other whiles) take your women to the window of the house (huses thurle), other men and women to the parlour-window to speak when necessary; nor ought ye (to converse) but at these two windows." Here we have three windows; we have no difficulty in understanding which was the church-window, and the parlour-window—the window *pour parler;* but what was the house-window, through which the recluse might speak to her servant? Was it merely the third glazed window, through which she might, if it were convenient, talk with her maid, but not with strangers, because she would be seen through it? or was it a window in the larger anchorholds, between the recluse cell, and the other apartment in which her maid lived, and in which, perhaps, guests were entertained? The latter seems the more probable explanation, and will receive further confirmation when we come to the directions about the entertainment of guests. The recluse was not to give way to the very natural temptation to put her head out of the open window, to get sometimes a wider view of the world about her. "A peering anchoress, who is always thrusting her head outward," he compares to "an untamed bird in a cage"—poor human bird! In another place he gives a more serious exhortation on the same subject. " Is not she too forward and foolhardy who holds her head boldly forth on the open battlements while men with crossbow bolts without assail the castle? Surely our foe, the warrior of hell, shoots, as I ween, more bolts at one anchoress than at seventy and seven secular ladies. The battlements of the castle are the windows of their houses; let her not look out at them, lest she

---

* The translator of this book for the Camden Society's edition of it, says "therein," but the word in the original Saxon English is "ther thurgh." It refers to the window looking into the church, through which the recluse looked down daily upon the celebration of the mass.

have the devil's bolts between her eyes before she even thinks of it." Here are directions how to carry on her "parlements":—" First of all, when you have to go to your parlour-window, learn from your maid who it is that is come; . . . . . and when you must needs go forth, go forth in the fear of God to a priest, ... and sit and listen, and not cackle." They were to be on their guard even with religious men, and not even confess, except in presence of a witness. " If any man requests to see you (*i.e.* to have the black curtain drawn aside), ask him what good might come of it. . . . If any one become so mad and unreasonable that he puts forth his hand toward the window-cloth (curtain), shut the window (*i.e.* close the shutter) quickly, and leave him; . . . . and as soon as any man falls into evil discourse, close the window, and go away with this verse, that he may hear it, 'The wicked have told me foolish tales, but not according to thy law;' and go forth before your altar, and say the 'Miserere.'" Again, "Keep your hands within your windows, for handling or touching between a man and an anchoress is a thing unnatural, shameful, wicked," &c.

The bishop adds a characteristic piece of detail to our picture when he speaks of the fair complexions of the recluses because not sunburnt, and their white hands through not working, both set in strong relief by the black colour of the habit and veil. He says, indeed, that " since no man seeth you, nor ye see any man, ye may be content with your clothes white or black." But in practice they seem usually to have worn black habits, unless, when attached to the church of any monastery, they may have worn the habit of the order. They were not to wear rings, brooches, ornamented girdles, or gloves. "An anchoress," he says, " ought to take sparingly (of alms), only that which is necessary (*i.e.* she ought not to take alms to give away again). If she can spare any fragments of her food, let her send them away (to some poor person) privately out of her dwelling. For the devil," he says elsewhere, "tempts anchoresses, through their charity, to collect to give to the poor, then to a friend, then to make a feast." "There are anchoresses," he says, "who make their meals with their friends without; that is too much friendship." The editor thinks this to mean that some anchoresses left their cells, and went to dine at the houses of their friends; but the word is *gistes* (guests), and, more probably, it only means that the recluse ate her dinner in her cell while a guest ate hers in the guest-room of the reclusorium, with an open window between, so that they could see and converse with one another. For we find in another place that she was to maintain "silence always at meals; . . . . . and if any one hath a guest whom she holds dear, she may cause her maid, as in her stead, to entertain her friend with glad cheer, and she shall have leave to open her window once or twice, and make signs to her of gladness." But "let no *man* eat in your presence, except he be in great need. The narrative already given at p. 109, of the visit of St. Richard the hermit to Dame Margaret the recluse of Anderby, also shows that in exceptional cases a recluse ate with men. The incident of the head of the recluse, in her convulsive sleep, falling at the window at which the hermit was reclining, and leaning partly upon him,* is explained by the theory that they were sitting in separate apartments, each close by this house window, which was open between them. As we have already seen, in the case of Sir Percival, a man might even sleep in the reclusorium; and so the Rule says, "let no man sleep within your walls" as a general rule; "if however, great necessity should cause your house to be used" by travellers, "see that ye have a woman of unspotted life with you day and night."

As to their occupations, he advises them to make "no purses and blodbendes of silk, but shape and sew and mend church vestments, and poor people's clothes, and help to clothe yourselves and your domestics." "An anchoress must not become a school-mistress, nor turn her house into a school for children. Her maiden may, however, teach any little girl concerning whom it might be doubtful whether she should learn among the boys."†

Doubtless, we are right in inferring from the bishop's advice not to do certain things, that anchoresses were in the habit of doing them. From this kind of evidence we glean still further traits. He suggests to them that in confession they will perhaps have to mention such faults as these,

---

* "Caput suum decidit ad fenestram ad quam se reclinabit sanctus Dei Ricardus."
† In one of the stories of Reginald of Durham we learn that a school, according to a custom then "common enough," was kept in the church of Norham on Tweed, the parish priest being the teacher. (Wright's "Domestic Manners of the Middle Ages," p. 117.)

"I played or spoke thus in the church; went to the play in the churchyard;* looked on at this, or at the wrestling, or other foolish sports; spoke thus, or played, in the presence of secular men, or of religious men, in a house of anchorites, and at a different window than I ought; or, being alone in the church, I thought thus." Again he mentions, "Sitting too long at the parlour-window, spilling ale, dropping crumbs." Again we find, "Make no banquetings, nor encourage any strange vagabonds about the gate." But of all their failings, gossiping seems to have been the besetting sin of anchoresses. "People say of anchoresses that almost every one hath an old woman to feed her ears, a prating gossip, who tells her all the tales of the land, a magpie that chatters to her of everything that she sees or hears; so that it is a common saying, from mill and from market, from smithy and from anchor-house, men bring tidings."

Let us add the sketch drawn of them by the unfavourable hand of Bilney the Reformer, in his "Reliques of Rome," published in 1563, and we have done:—"As touching the monastical sect of recluses, and such as be shutte up within walls, there unto death continuall 'to remayne, giving themselves to the mortification of carnal effects, to the contemplation of heavenly and spirituall thinges, to abstinence, to prayer, and to such other ghostly exercises, as men dead to the world, and havyng their lyfe hidden with Christ, I have not to write. Forasmuch as I cannot fynde probably in any author whence the profession of anckers and anckresses had the beginning and foundation, although in this behalf I have talked with men of that profession which could very little or nothing say of the matter. Notwithstanding, as the Whyte Fryers father that order on Helias the prophet (but falsely), so likewise do the ankers and ankresses make that holy and virtuous matrone Judith their patroness and foundress; but how unaptly who seeth not? Their profession and religion differeth as far

---

* These two expressions seem to imply that recluses sometimes went out of their cell, not only into the church, but also into the churchyard. We have already noticed that the technical word "cell" seems to have included everything within the enclosure wall of the whole establishment. Is it possible that in the case of anchorages adjoining churches, the churchyard wall represented this enclosure, and the "cell" included both church and churchyard?

from the manners of Judith as light from darknesse, or God from the devill, as shall manifestly appere to them that will diligentlye conferre the history of Judith with their life and conversation. Judith made herself a privy chamber where she dwelt (sayth the scripture), being closed in with her maydens. Our recluses also close themselves within the walls, but they suffer no man to be there with them. Judith ware a smoche of heare, but our recluses are both softly and finely apparalled. Judith fasted all the days of her lyfe, few excepted. Our recluses eate and drinke at all tymes of the beste, being of the number of them *qui curios simulant et Bacchanalia vivunt.* Judith was a woman of a very good report. Our recluses are reported to be superstitious and idolatrous persons, and such as all good men flye their company. Judith feared the Lord greatly, and lyved according to His holy word. Our recluses fear the pope, and gladly doe what his pleasure is to command them. Judith lyved of her own substance and goods, putting no man to charge. Our recluses, as persons only borne to consume the good fruits of the erth, lyve idely of the labour of other men's handes. Judith, when tyme required, came out of her closet, to do good unto other. Our recluses never come out of their lobbies, sincke or swimme the people. Judith put herself in jeopardy for to do good to the common countrye. Our recluses are unprofitable clods of the earth, doing good to no man. Who seeth not how farre our ankers and ankresses differe from the manners and life of this vertuous and godly woman Judith, so that they cannot justly claime her to be their patronesse? Of some idle and superstitious heremite borrowed they their idle and superstitious religion. For who knoweth not that our recluses have grates of yron in theyr spelunckes, and dennes out of the which they looke, as owles out of an yvye todde, when they will vouchsafe to speake with any man at whose hand they hope for advantage? So reade we in 'Vitis Patrum,' that John the Heremite so enclosed himself in his hermitage that no person came in unto him; to them that came to visit him he spoke through a window onely. Our ankers and ankresses professe nothing but a solitary lyfe in their hallowed house, wherein they are inclosed wyth the vowe of obedience to the pope, and to their ordinary bishop. Their apparel is indifferent, so it be dissonant from the laity. No kind of meates they are forbidden to eat. At midnight they are bound to say certain prayers. Their profession is counted to be among other professions so hardye and so streight that they may by no means be suffered to come out of their houses except it be to take on them an harder and streighter, which is to be made a bishop."

It is not to be expected that mediæval paintings should give illustrations of persons who were thus never visible in the world. In the pictures of the hermits of the Egyptian desert, on the walls of the Campo Santo at Pisa, we see a representation of St. Anthony holding a conversation with St. John the Hermit, who is just visible through his grated window, "like an owl in an ivy tod," as Bilney says; and we have already given a picture of Sir Percival knocking at the door of a female recluse. Bilney says, that they wore any costume, "so it were dissonant from the laity;" but in all probability they commonly wore a costume similar in colour to that of the male hermits. The picture which we here give of an anchoress, is taken from a figure of St. Paula, one of the anchorite saints of the desert, in the same picture of St. Jerome, which has already supplied us, in the figure of St. Damasus, with our best picture of the hermit's costume.

St. Paula.

The service for enclosing a recluse * may be found in some of the old Service Books. We derive the following account of it from an old black-letter *Manuale ad usum percelebris ecclesie Sarisburiensis* (London, 1554), in the British Museum. The rubric before the service orders that no

---

* A commission given by William of Wykham, Bishop of Winchester, for enclosing Lucy de Newchurch as an anchoritess in the hermitage of St. Brendun, at Bristol, is given in Burnett's "History and Antiquities of Bristol," p. 61.

one shall be enclosed without the bishop's leave; that the candidate shall be closely questioned as to his motives; that he shall be taught not to entertain proud thoughts, as if he merited to be set apart from intercourse with common men, but rather on account of his own infirmity it was good that he should be removed from contact with others, that he might be kept out of sin himself, and not contaminate ·them. So that the recluse should esteem himself to be condemned for his sins, and shut up in his solitary cell as in a prison, and unworthy, for his sins, of the society of men. There is a note, that this office shall serve for both sexes. On the day before the ceremony of inclusion, the *Includendus*—the person about to be inclosed—was to confess, and to fast that day on bread and water; and all that night he was to watch and pray, having his wax taper burning, in the monastery,* near his inclusorium. On the morrow, all being assembled in church, the bishop, or priest appointed by him, first addressed an exhortation to the people who had come to see the ceremony, and to the includendus himself, and then began the service with a response, and several appropriate psalms and collects. After that, the priest put on his chasuble, and began mass, a special prayer being introduced for the includendus. After the reading of the gospel, the includendus stood before the altar, and offered his taper, which was to remain burning on the altar throughout the mass; and then, standing before the altar-step, he read his profession, or if he were a layman (and unable to read), one of the chorister boys read it for him. And this was the form of his profession:—" I, brother (or sister) N, offer and present myself to serve the Divine Goodness in the order of Anchorites, and I promise to remain, according to the rule of that order, in the service of God, from henceforth, by the grace of God, and the counsel of the Church." Then he signed the document in which his profession was written with the sign of the cross, and laid it upon the altar on bended knees. Then the bishop or priest said a prayer, and asperged with holy water the habit of the includendus; and he put on the habit, and prostrated himself before the altar, and so remained, while the

---

* " In monasterio inclusorio suo vicino;" it seems as if the writer of the rubric were specially thinking of the inclusoria within monasteries.

priest and choir sang over him the hymn *Veni Creator Spiritus*, and then proceeded with the mass. First the priest communicated, then the includendus, and then the rest of the congregation; and the mass was concluded. Next his wax taper, which had all this time been burning on the altar, was given to the includendus, and a procession was formed; first the choir; then the includendus, clad in his proper habit, and carrying his lighted taper; then the bishop or priest, in his mass robes; and then the people following; and so they proceeded, singing a solemn litany, to the cell. And first the priest entered alone into the cell, and asperged it with holy water, saying appropriate sentences; then he consecrated and blessed the cell, with prayers offered before the altar of its chapel. The third of these short prayers may be transcribed: "Benedic domine domum istam et locum istum, ut sit in eo sanitas, sanctitas, castitas, virtus, victoria, sanctimonia, humilitas, lenitas, mansuetudo, plenitudo, legis et obedientæ Deo Patre et Filio et Spiritui Sancto et sit super locum istum et super omnes habitantes in eo tua larga benedictio, ut in his manufactis habitaculis cum solemtate manentes ipsi tuum sit semper habitaculum. Per dominum," &c. Then the bishop or priest came out, and led in the includendus, still carrying his lighted taper, and solemnly blessed him. And then—a mere change in the tense of the rubric has an effect which is quite pathetic; it is no longer the *includendus*, the person to be enclosed, but the *inclusus*, the enclosed one, he or she upon whom the doors of the cell have closed for ever in this life—then the enclosed is to maintain total and solemn silence throughout, while the doors are securely closed, the choir chanting appropriate psalms. Then the celebrant causes all the people to pray for the inclusus privately, in solemn silence, to God, for whose love he has left the world, and caused himself to be inclosed in that strait prison. And after some concluding prayers, the procession left the inclusus to his solitary life, and returned, chanting, to the church, finishing at the step of the choir.

One cannot read this solemn—albeit superstitious—service, in the quaint old mediæval character, out of the very book which has, perhaps, been used in the actual enclosing of some recluse, without being moved. Was it some frail woman, with all the affections of her heart and the hopes of her earthly life shattered, who sought the refuge of this living tomb? was it some man of strong passions, wild and fierce in his crimes, as wild and fierce in his penitence? or was it some enthusiast, with the over-excited religious sensibility, of which we have instances enough in these days? We can see them still, in imagination, prostrate, "in total and solemn silence," before the wax taper placed upon the altar of the little chapel, and listening while the chant of the returning procession grows fainter and fainter in the distance. Ah! we may scornfully smile at it all as a wild superstition, or treat it coldly as a question of mere antiquarian interest; but what broken hearts, what burning passions, have been shrouded under that recluse's robe, and what wild cries of human agony have been stifled under that "total and solemn silence!" When the processional chant had died away in the distance, and the recluse's taper had burnt out on his little altar, was that the end of the tragedy, or only the end of the first act? Did the broken heart find repose? Did the wild spirit grow tame? Or did the one pine away and die like a flower in a dungeon, and the other beat itself to death against the bars of its self-made cage?

CHAPTER IV.

CONSECRATED WIDOWS OF THE MIDDLE AGES.

BESIDES all other religious people living under vows, in community in monasteries, or as solitaries in their anchorages, there were also a number of Widows vowed to that life and devoted to the service of God, who lived at home in their own houses or with their families. This was manifestly a continuation, or imitation, of the primitive Order of Widows, of whom St. Paul speaks in his first Epistle to Timothy (ch. v.). For although religious women, from an early period (fourth century), were usually nuns, the primitive Orders of Deaconesses and Widows did not altogether cease to exist in the Church. The Service Books [*] contain offices for their benediction; and though it is probable that in fact a deaconess was very rarely consecrated in the Western Church, yet the number of allusions to widows throughout the Middle Ages leads us to suspect that there may have been no inconsiderable number of them. A common form of commission[†] to a suffragan bishop includes the consecrating of widows. From the Pontifical of Edmund Lacey, Bishop of Exeter, of the fourteenth century, we give a sketch of the service.[‡] It is the same in substance as those in the earlier books. First, a rubric states that though a widow may be blessed on any day, it is more fitting that she be blessed on a holy day, and especially on the Lord's day. Between the

---

[*] The Ordo Romanus. The Pontifical of Egbert. The Pontifical of Bishop Lacey.
[†] *Guardian* newspaper, Feb. 7, 1870.
[‡] Surrey Society's Transactions, vol. iii. p. 218.

Epistle and the Gospel, the bishop sitting on a faldstool facing the people, the widow kneeling before the bishop is to be interrogated if she desires, putting away all carnal affections, to be joined as a spouse to Christ. Then she shall publicly in the vulgar tongue profess herself, in the bishop's hands, resolved to observe perpetual continence. Then the bishop blesses her habit (clamidem), saying a collect. Then the bishop, genuflecting, begins the hymn *Veni Creator Spiritus;* the widow puts on the habit and veil, and the bishop blesses and gives her the ring; and with a final prayer for appropriate virtues and blessings, the ordinary service of Holy Communion is resumed, special mention of the widow being made therein.

These collects are of venerable age, and have much beauty of thought and expression. The reader may be glad to see one of them as an example, and as an indication of the spirit in which people entered into these religious vows: "O God, the gracious inhabiter of chaste bodies and lover of uncorrupt souls, look we pray Thee, O Lord, upon this Thy servant, who humbly offers her devotion to Thee. May there be in her, O Lord, the gift of Thy spirit, a prudent modesty, a wise graciousness, a grave gentleness, a chaste freedom; may she be fervent in charity and love nothing beside Thee (*extra te*); may she live praiseworthy and not desire praise; may she fear Thee and serve Thee with a chaste love; be Thou to her, O Lord, honour, Thou delight; be Thou in sorrow her comfort, in doubt her counsellor; be Thou to her defence in injury, in tribulation patience, in poverty abundance, in fasting food, in sickness medicine. By Thee, whom she desires to love above all things, may she keep what she has vowed; so that by Thy help she may conquer the old enemy, and cast out the defilements of sin; that she may be decorated with the gift of fruit sixty fold,[*] and adorned with the lamps of all virtues, and by Thy grace may be worthy to join the company of the elect widows. This we humbly ask through Jesus Christ our Lord."

---

[*] The same collect, with a few variations, was used also in the consecration of nuns. Virgin chastity was held to bring forth fruit a hundred fold; widowed chastity, sixty fold; married chastity, thirty fold.

In a paper in the "Surrey Transactions," vol. iii. p. 208, Mr. Baigent, the writer of it, finds two, and only two, entries of the consecration of widows in the Episcopal Registers of Winchester, which go back to the early part of the reign of Edward I. The first of these is on May 4, 1348, of the Lady Aleanor Giffard, probably, says Mr. Baigent, the widow of John Giffard, of Bowers Giffard, in Essex. The other entry, on October 18, 1379, is of the Benediction of Isabella Burgh, the widow of a citizen of London (whose will is given by Mr. Baigent), and of Isabella Golafre, widow of Sir John Golafre.

The profession of the widow is given in old French, and a translation of it in old English, as follows: " In ye name of God, Fader and Sone and Holy Ghost. Iche Isabelle Burghe, that was sometyme wyfe of Thomas Burghe, wyche that is God be taught helpynge the grace of God [the parallel French is, Quest à Dieu commande ottriaunte la grace de Dieu] behote [promise] conversione of myn maners, and make myn avows to God, and to is swete moder Seynte Marie and to alle seintz, into youre handes leve [dear] fader in God, William be ye grace of God Bisshope of Wynchestre, that fro this day forward I schal ben chaste of myn body and in holy chastite kepe me treweliche and devouteliche all ye dayes of myn life." Another form of profession is written on the lower margin of the Exeter Pontifical, and probably in the handwriting of Bishop Lacy : " I, N., wedowe, avowe to God perpetuall chastite of my body from henceforward, and in the presence of the honorable fadyr in God, my Lord N., by the grace of God, Bishop of N., I promyth sabilly to leve in the Church, a wedowe. And this to do, of myne own hand I subscribe this writing : *Et postea faciat signum crucis."*

Another example of a widow in the Winchester registers is that of Elizabeth de Julien, widow of John Plantagenet, Earl of Kent, who made that vow to Bishop William de Edyndon, but afterwards married Sir Eustache Dabrichecourt, September 29, 1360, whereupon proceedings were commenced against her by the Archbishop of Canterbury, who imposed on her a severe and life-long penance. She survived her second husband many years, and dying in 1411, was buried in the choir of the Friars Minor at Winchester, near the tomb of her first husband.

Vidua ac Deo devota.

The epitaph on the monumental brass of Joanna Braham, A.D. 1519, at Frenze, in Norfolk, describes her as "Vidua ac Deo devota."

In the Book of the Knight of La Tour-Landry is a description of a lady who, if she had not actually taken the vows of widowhood, lived the life we should suppose to be that of a vowess. "It is of a good lady whiche longe tyme was in wydowhode. She was of a holy lyf, and moste humble and honourable, as the whiche every yere kepte and held a feste upon Crystemasse-day of her neyghbours bothe farre and nere, tyll her halle was ful of them. She served and honoured eche one after his degree, and specially she bare grete reverence to the good and trewe wymmen, and to them whiche has deservyd to be worshipped. Also she was of suche custome that yf she knewe any poure gentyll woman that shold be wedded she arayed her with her jewels. Also she wente to the obsequye of the poure gentyll wymmen, and gaf there torches, and all such other lumynary as it neded thereto. Her dayly ordenaunce was that she rose erly ynough, and had ever freres, and two or three chappellayns whiche sayd matyns before her within her oratorye; and after she herd a hyhe masse and two lowe, and sayd her servyse full devoutely; and after this she wente and arayed herself, and walked in her gardyn, or else aboute her plase, sayenge her other devocions and prayers. And as tyme was she wente to dyner; and after dyner, if she wyste and knewe ony seke folke or wymmen in theyr childbedde, she went to see and vysited them, and made to be brought to them of her best mete. And then, as she myght not go herself, she had a servant propyer therefore, whiche rode upon a lytell hors, and bare with him grete plente of good mete and drynke for to gyve to the poure and seke folk there as they were. And after she had herd evensonge she went to her souper, yf she fasted not. And tymely she wente to bedde; made her styward to come to her to wete what mete sholde be had the next daye, and lyved by good ordenaunce, and wold be purveyed byfore of alle such thynge that was nedefull for her household. She made grete abstynence, and wered the hayre * upon the Wednesday and upon the Fryday. . . . . And she rose

---

* Hair-cloth garment worn next the skin for mortification.

everye night thre tymes, and kneled downe to the ground by her bedde, and redryd thankynges to God, and prayd for al Crysten soules, and dyd grete almes to the poure. This good lady, that wel is worthy to be named and preysed, had to name my lady Cecyle of Ballavylle. . . . . She was the most good and curtoys lady that ever I knewe or wyste in ony countrey, and that lesse was envious, and never she wold here say ony evyll of no body, but excused them, and prayd to God that they myght amende them, and that none was that knewe what to hym shold happe. . . . . She had a ryhte noble ende, and as I wene ryht agreable to God; and as men say commonely, of honest and good lyf cometh ever a good ende."

In post-Reformation times there are biographies of holy women which show that the idea of consecrated widowhood was still living in the minds of the people. Probably the dress commonly worn by widows throughout their widowhood is a remnant of the mediæval custom.

THE PILGRIMS OF THE MIDDLE AGES.

CHAPTER I.

THE fashion of going on pilgrimage seems to have sprung up in the fourth century. The first object of pilgrimage was the Holy Land. Jerome said, at the outset, the most powerful thing which can be said against it; viz., that the way to heaven is as short from Britain as from Jerusalem—a consolatory reflection to those who were obliged, or who preferred, to stay at home; but it did not succeed in quenching the zeal of those many thousands who desired to see, with their own eyes, the places which had been hallowed by the presence and the deeds of their Lord—to tread, with their own footsteps,

> "Those holy fields
> Over whose acres walked those blessed feet,
> Which " eighteen " hundred years ago were nailed
> For our advantage on the bitter cross;"*

to kneel down and pray for pardon for their sins upon that very spot where the Great Sacrifice for sin was actually offered up; to stand upon the summit of Mount Olivet, and gaze up into that very pathway through the sky by which He ascended to His kingdom in Heaven.

We should, however, open up too wide a field if we were to enter into

---

* King Henry IV., Pt. I., Act i. Sc. 1.

the subject of the early pilgrims to the Holy Land;* to trace their route from Britain, usually *viâ* Rome, by sea and land; to describe how a pilgrim passenger-traffic sprung up, of which adventurous ship-owners took advantage; how hospitals† were founded here and there along the road, to give refuge to the weary pilgrims, until they reached the Hospital *par*

Thirteenth Century Pilgrims (the two Disciples at Emmaus).

excellence, which stood beside the Church of the Holy Sepulchre; how Saxon kings made treaties to secure their safe conduct through foreign

---

* There have come down to us a series of narratives of pilgrimages to the Holy Land. One of a Christian of Bordeaux as early as 333 A.D.; that of S. Paula and her daughter, about 386 A.D., given by St. Jerome; of Bishop Arculf, 700 A.D.; of Willebald, 725 A.D.; of Sæwulf, 1102 A.D.; of Sigurd the Crusader, 1107 A.D.; of Sir John de Mandeville, 1322—1356.—*Early Travels in Palestine* (Bohn's Antiq. Lib.).

† At the present day, the Hospital of the Pellegrini at Rome is capable of entertaining seven thousand guests, women as well as men; to be entitled to the hospitality of the institution, they must have walked at least sixty miles, and be provided with a certificate from a bishop or priest to the effect that they are *bonâ-fide* pilgrims. (Wild's "Last Winter in Rome." Longmans: 1865.)

countries;* how the Order of the Knights of the Temple was founded to escort the caravans of pilgrims from one to another of the holy places, and protect them from marauding Saracens and Arabs; how the Crusades were organised partly, no doubt, to stem the course of Mahommedan conquest, but ostensibly to wrest the holy places from the hands of the infidel: this part of the subject of pilgrimage would occupy too much of our space here. Our design is to give a sketch of the less known portion of the subject, which relates to the pilgrimages which sprung up in after-times, when the veneration for the holy places had extended to the shrines of saints; and when, still later, veneration had run wild into the grossest superstition, and crowds of sane men and women flocked to relic-worships, which would be ludicrous if they were not so pitiable and humiliating. This part of the subject forms a chapter in the history of the manners of the Middle Ages, which is little known to any but the antiquarian student; but it is an important chapter to all who desire thoroughly to understand what were the modes of thought and habits of life of our English forefathers in the Middle Ages.

The most usual foreign pilgrimages were to the Holy Land, the scene of our Lord's earthly life; to Rome, the centre of western Christianity; and to the shrine of St. James at Compostella.†

The number of pilgrims to these places must have been comparatively limited; for a man who had any regular business or profession could not

---

* In the latter part of the Saxon period of our history there was a great rage for foreign pilgrimage; thousands of persons were continually coming and going between England and the principal shrines of Europe, especially the threshold of the Apostles at Rome. They were the subject of a letter from Charlemagne to King Offa:—"Concerning the strangers who, for the love of God and the salvation of their souls, wish to repair to the thresholds of the blessed Apostles, let them travel in peace without any trouble." Again, in the year 1031 A.D., King Canute made a pilgrimage to Rome (as other Saxon kings had done before him) and met the Emperor Conrad and other princes, from whom he obtained for all his subjects, whether merchants or pilgrims, exemptions from the heavy tolls usually exacted on the journey to Rome.

† At the marriage of our Edward I., in 1254, with Leonora, sister of Alonzo of Castile, a protection to English pilgrims was stipulated for; but they came in such numbers as to alarm the French, and difficulties were thrown in the way. In the fifteenth century, Rymer mentions 916 licences to make the pilgrimage to Santiago granted in 1428, and 2,460 in 1434.

well undertake so long an absence from home. The rich of no occupation could afford the leisure and the cost; and the poor who chose to abandon their lawful occupation could make these pilgrimages at the cost of others ; for the pilgrim was sure of entertainment at every hospital, or monastery, or priory, probably at every parish priest's rectory and every gentleman's hall,* on his way; and there were not a few poor men and women who indulged a vagabond humour in a pilgrim's life. The poor pilgrim repaid his entertainer's hospitality by bringing the news of the countries† through which he had passed, and by amusing the household after supper with marvellous saintly legends, and traveller's tales. He raised a little money for his inevitable travelling expenses by retailing holy trifles and curiosities, such as were sold wholesale at all the shrines frequented by pilgrims, and which were usually supposed to have some saintly efficacy attached to them. Sometimes the pilgrim would take a bolder flight, and carry with him some fragment of a relic—a joint of a bone, or a pinch of dust, or a nail-paring, or a couple of hairs of the saint, or a rag of his clothing; and the people gladly paid the pilgrim for thus bringing to their doors some of the advantages of the holy shrines which he had visited. Thus Chaucer's Pardoner—" That strait was comen from the Court of Rome "—

" In his mail‡ he had a pilwebere,§
Which as he saidé was oure Lady's veil ;

---

* King Horn, having taken the disguise of a palmer—" Horn took bourden and scrip " —went to the palace of Athulf and into the hall, and took his place among the beggars " in beggar's row," and sat on the ground.—*Thirteenth Century Romance of King Horn* (Early English Text Society). That beggars and such persons did usually sit on the ground in the hall and wait for a share of the food, we learn also from the " Vision of Piers Ploughman," xii. 198—

" Right as sum man gave me meat, and set me amid the floor,
I have meat more than enough, and not so much worship
As they that sit at side table, or with the sovereigns of the hall,
But sit as a beggar boardless by myself on the ground."

† In the romance of King Horn, the hero meets a palmer and asks his news—

" A palmere he there met
And fair him grette [greeted] :
Palmer, thou shalt me tell
All of thine spell."

‡ Wallet. § Pillow covering.

He said he had a gobbet of the sail
Thatte St. Peter had whan that he went
Upon the sea, till Jesu Christ him hent.*
He had a cross of laton full of stones;†
And in a glass he haddé piggés bones.‡
But with these relics whanné that he fond
A poure parson dwelling upon lond,
Upon a day he gat him more monie
Than that the parson gat in monthes tweie.
And thus with feined flattering and japes,
He made the parson and the people his apes."

In a subsequent chapter, on the Merchants of the Middle Ages, will be found some illustrations of mediæval shipping, which also illustrate the present subject. One is a representation of Sir John Mandeville and his companions in mantle, hat, and staff, just landed at a foreign town on their pilgrimage to the Holy Land. Another represents Richard Beauchamp, Earl of Warwick, in mantle, hat, and staff, embarking in his own ship on his departure for a similar pilgrimage. Another illustration in the subsequent chapter on Secular Clergy represents Earl Richard at Rome, being presented to the Pope.

But those who could not spare time or money to go to Jerusalem, or Rome, or Compostella, could spare both for a shorter expedition; and pilgrimages to English shrines appear to have been very common. By far the most popular of our English pilgrimages was to the shrine of St. Thomas-à-Becket, at Canterbury, and it was popular not only in England, but all over Europe. The one which stood next in popular estimation, was the pilgrimage to Our Lady of Walsingham. But nearly every cathedral and great monastery, and many a parish church besides, had its famous saint to whom the people resorted. There was St. Cuthbert at Durham, and St. William at York, and little St. William at Norwich, and St. Hugh at Lincoln, and St. Edward Confessor at Westminster, and St. Erkenwald in the cathedral of London, and St. Wulstan at Worcester, and St. Swithin at Winchester, and St. Edmund at Bury, and SS. Etheldreda

---

* Called or took.
† *i.e.* Latten (a kind of bronze) set with (mock) precious stones.
‡ Pretending them to be relics of some saint.

and Withburga at Ely, and many more, whose remains were esteemed holy relics, and whose shrines were frequented by the devout. Some came to pray at the tomb for the intercession of the saint in their behalf; or to seek the cure of disease by the touch of the relic; or to offer up thanks for deliverance believed to have been vouchsafed in time of peril through the saint's prayers; or to obtain the number of days' pardon—*i.e.* of remission of their time in purgatory—offered by Papal bulls to those who should pray at the tomb. Then there were famous roods, the Rood of Chester and of Bromholme; and statues of the Virgin, as Our Lady of Wilsden, and of Boxley, and of this, that, and the other place. There were scores of holy wells besides, under saintly invocations, of which St. Winifred's well with her chapel over it still remains an excellent example.*
Some of these were springs of medicinal water, and were doubtless of some efficacy in the cures for which they were noted; in others a saint had baptized his converts; others had simply afforded water to a saint in his neighbouring cell.†

Before any man ‡ went on pilgrimage, he first went to his church, and received the Church's blessing on his pious enterprise, and her prayers for his good success and safe return. The office of pilgrims (*officium peregrinorum*) may be found in the old service-books. We give a few notes of it from a Sarum missal, date 1554, in the British Museum. § The pilgrim is

---

* See "Archæological Journal," vol. iii. p. 149.
†·Mr. Taylor, in his edition of "Blomfield's Norfolk," enumerates no less than seventy places of pilgrimage in Norfolk alone.
‡ A man might not go without his wife's consent, nor a wife without her husband's:—

    " To preche them also thou might not wonde [fear, hesitate],
    Both to wyf and eke husbande,
    That nowther of hem no penance take,
    Ny non a vow to chastity make,
    Ny no pylgrimage take to do
    But if bothe assente thereto.
    *   *   *   *   *
    Save the vow to Jherusalem,
    That is lawful to ether of them."
                      Instructions for Parish Priests. (Early English Text Society.)

§ Marked 3,395 d. 4to. The footnote on a previous page (p. 158) leads us to conjecture

Office for Blessing Pilgrims. 163

previously to have confessed. At the opening of the service he lies prostrate before the altar, while the priest and choir sing over him certain appropriate psalms, viz. the 24th, 50th, and 90th. Then follow some versicles, and three collects, for safety, &c., in which the pilgrim is mentioned by name, "thy servant, N." Then he rises, and there follows the benediction of his scrip and staff; and the priest sprinkles the scrip with holy water, and places it on the neck of the pilgrim, saying, " In the name of, &c., take this scrip, the habit of your pilgrimage, that, corrected and saved, you may be worthy to reach the thresholds of the saints to which you desire to go, and, your journey done, may return to us in safety." Then the priest delivers the staff, saying, " Take this staff, the support of your journey, and of the labour of your pilgrimage, that you may be able to conquer all the bands of the enemy, and to come safely to the threshold of the saints to which you desire to go, and, your journey obediently performed, return to us with joy." If any one of the pilgrims present is going to Jerusalem, he is to bring a habit signed with the cross, and the priest blesses it :—". . . . we pray that Thou wilt vouchsafe to bless this cross, that the banner of the sacred cross, whose figure is signed upon him, may be to Thy servant an invincible strength against the evil temptations of the old enemy, a defence by the way, a protection in Thy house, and may be to us everywhere a guard, through our Lord, &c." Then he sprinkles the habit with holy water, and gives it to the pilgrim, saying, " Take this habit, signed with the cross of the Lord our Saviour, that by it you may come safely to his sepulchre, who, with the

Lydgate's Pilgrim.

---

that in ancient as in modern times the pilgrim may have received a certificate of his having been blessed as a pilgrim, as now we give certificates of baptism, marriage, and holy orders.

Father," &c. Then follows mass; and after mass, certain prayers over the pilgrims, prostrate at the altar; then, "let them communicate, and so depart in the name of the Lord." The service runs in the plural, as if there were usually a number of pilgrims to be dispatched together.

There was a certain costume appropriate to the pilgrim, which old writers speak of under the title of pilgrims' weeds; the illustrations of this paper will give examples of it. It consisted of a robe and hat, a staff and scrip. The robe called *sclavina* by Du Cange, and other writers, is said to have been always of wool, and sometimes of shaggy stuff, like that represented in the accompanying woodcut of the latter part of the fourteenth century, from the Harleian MS., 4,826. It seems intended to represent St. John Baptist's robe of camel's hair. Its colour does not appear in the illuminations, but old writers speak of it as grey. The hat seems to be commonly a round hat, of felt, and, apparently, does not differ from the hats which travellers not uncommonly wore over their hoods in those days.*

The pilgrim who was sent on pilgrimage as a penance seems usually to have been ordered to go barefoot, and probably many others voluntarily inflicted this hardship upon themselves in order to heighten the merit and efficacy of their good deed. They often also made a vow not to cut the hair or beard until the pilgrimage had been accomplished. But the special insignia of a pilgrim were the staff and scrip. In the religious service with which the pilgrims initiated their journey, we have seen that the staff and scrip are the only insignia mentioned, except in the case of one going to the Holy Land, who has a robe signed with the cross; the staff and the scrip were specially blessed by the priest, and the pilgrim formally invested with them by his hands.

The staff, or bourdon, was not of an invariable shape. On a fourteenth-century grave-stone at Haltwhistle, Northumberland, it is like a rather long walking-stick, with a natural knob at the top. In the cut from Erasmus's "Praise of Folly," which forms the frontispiece of Mr. Nichols's "Pilgrimages of Canterbury and Walsingham," it is a similar walking-stick;

---

* See woodcut on p. 90.

but, usually, it was a long staff, some five, six, or seven feet long, turned in the lathe, with a knob at the top, and another about a foot lower down. Sometimes a little below the lower knob there is a hook, or a staple, to which we occasionally find a water-bottle or a small bundle attached. The hook is seen on the staff of Lydgate's pilgrim (p. 163). Sir John Hawkins tells us * that the staff was sometimes hollowed out into a kind of flute, on which the pilgrim could play. The same kind of staff we find in illuminated MSS. in the hands of beggars and shepherds, as well as pilgrims.

The scrip was a small bag, slung at the side by a cord over the shoulder, to contain the pilgrim's food and his few necessaries.† Sometimes it was made of leather; but probably the material varied according to the taste and wealth of the pilgrim. We find it of different shape and size in different examples. In the monumental effigy of a pilgrim of rank at Ashby-de-la-Zouch, the scrip is rather long, widest at bottom, and is ornamented with three tassels at the bottom, something like the bag in which the Lord Chancellor carries the great seal, and it has scallop shells fixed upon its front. In the grave-stone of a knight at Haltwhistle, already alluded to, the knight's arms, sculptured upon the shield on one side of his grave cross, are a *fess* between three *garbs* (*i.e.* wheat-sheaves);

Pilgrim, from Erasmus's "Praise of Folly."

and a *garb* is represented upon his scrip, which is square and otherwise plain. The tomb of Abbot Chillenham, at Tewkesbury, has the pilgrim's staff and scrip sculptured upon it as an architectural ornament; the scrip is

---

* "History of Music."

† "Conscience then with Patience passed, Pilgrims as it were,
Then had Patience, as pilgrims have, in his poke vittailes."
Piers Ploughman's Vision, xiii. 215.

like the mediæval purse, with a scallop shell on the front of it, very like that on p. 163.* The pilgrim is sometimes represented with a bottle, often with a rosary, and sometimes with other conveniences for travelling or helps to devotion. There is a very good example in Hans Burgmaier's " Images de Saints, &c., of the Familly of the Emp. Maximilian I." fol. 112.

But though the conventional pilgrim is always represented with robe, and hat, and staff, and scrip, the actual pilgrim seems sometimes to have dispensed with some, if not with all, of these insignia. For example, Chaucer minutely describes the costume of the principal personages in his company of Canterbury Pilgrims, and he not only does not describe what would have been so marked and picturesque features in their appearance, but his description seems to preclude the pilgrim's robe and hat. His knight is described in the ordinary jupon,

"Of fustian he wered a jupon."

And the squire—

"Short was his gowne with sleves long and wide."

And the yeoman—

"Was clad in cote and hood of green."

And the serjeant of the law—

"Rode but homely in a medlee cote,
Girt with a seint † of silk with barres small."

The merchant was in motley—

"And on his hed a Flaundrish bever hat."

And so with all the rest, they are clearly described in the ordinary dress of their class, which the pilgrim's robe would have concealed. It seems very doubtful whether they even bore the especial insignia of staff and scrip. Perhaps when men and women went their pilgrimage on horseback, they did not go through the mere form of carrying a long walking-staff. The equestrian pilgrim, of whom we shall give a woodcut hereafter, though he is very correctly habited in robe and hat, with pilgrim signs on each, and his rosary round his neck, does not carry the bourdon. The only trace of pilgrim costume about Chaucer's Pilgrims, is in the Pardoner—

---

* Grose's " Gloucestershire," pl. lvii.   † Girdle.

"A vernicle hadde he sewed in his cappe "—
but that was a sign of a former pilgrimage to Rome; and it is enough to prove—if proof were needed—that Chaucer did not forget to clothe his personages in pilgrim weeds, but that they did not wear them.

But besides the ordinary insignia of pilgrimage, every pilgrimage had its special signs, which the pilgrim on his return wore conspicuously upon his hat or his scrip, or hanging round his neck, in token that he had accomplished that particular pilgrimage. The pilgrim who had made a long pilgrimage, paying his devotions at every shrine in his way, might come back as thickly decorated with signs as a modern soldier, who has been through a stirring campaign, with medals and clasps.

The pilgrim to the Holy Land had this distinction above all others, that he wore a special sign from the very hour that he took the vow upon him to make that most honourable pilgrimage. This sign was a cross, formed of two strips of coloured cloth sewn upon the shoulder of the robe; the English pilgrim wore the cross of white, the French of red, the Flemish of green. Some, in their fierce earnestness, had the sacred sign cut into their flesh; in the romance of "Sir Isumbras," we read—

"With a sharpe knyfe he share
A cross upon his shoulder bare."

Others had it branded upon them with a hot iron; one pilgrim in the "Mirac. de S. Thomæ" of Abbot Benedict gives the obvious reason, that though his clothes should be torn away, no one should be able to tear the cross from his breast. At the end of the *Officium peregrinorum*, which we have described, we find a rubric calling attention to the fact, that burning the cross in the flesh is forbidden by the canon law on pain of the greater excommunication; the prohibition is proof enough that at one time it was a not uncommon practice. But when the pilgrim reached the Holy Land, and had visited the usual round of the holy places, he became entitled to wear the palm in token of his accomplishment of that great pilgrimage; and from this badge he derived the name of Palmer. How the palm was borne does not quite certainly appear; some say that it was a branch of palm, which the returning pilgrim bore in his hand or affixed to the top of his staff;* but probably in the general case it was in the shape of sprigs of palm sewn crosswise upon the hat and scrip.

The Roman pilgrimage seems always to have ranked next in popular estimation to that of the Holy Land;† and with reason, for Rome was then the great centre of the religion and the civilization of Western Christendom. The plenary indulgence which Boniface VIII. published in 1300, to all who should make the Jubilee pilgrimage to Rome, no doubt had its effect in popularizing this pilgrimage *ad limina apostolorum*. Two hundred thousand pilgrims, it is said, visited Rome in one month during the first Jubilee; and succeeding popes shortened the interval between these great spiritual fairs, first to fifty, then to thirty-three, and lastly to twenty-five years. The pilgrim to Rome doubtless visited many shrines in that great Christian capital, and was entitled to wear as many signs; but the chief signs of the Roman pilgrimage were a badge with the effigies of St. Peter and St. Paul, the cross-keys, and the vernicle. Concerning the first, there is a grant from Innocent III. to the arch-priest and canons of St. Peter's at Rome,‡ which confirms to them (or to those to whom they shall concede it) the right to cast and to sell the lead or pewter signs, bearing the effigies of the Apostles Peter and Paul, with which those who have visited their threshold decorate themselves for the increase of their devotion and a testimony of their pilgrimage. Dr. Rock says§ "that a friend of his has one of these Roman pilgrim signs, which was dug up at Launde Abbey, Leicestershire. It is of copper, in the shape of a quatrefoil, one and three-quarter inches in diameter, and has the cross-keys on one side, the other side being plain. An equestrian pilgrim represented in Hans Burgmaier's "Der Weise Kœnige," seems to bear on his cloak and his hat the cross-keys. The vernicle was the kerchief of Veronica, with which,

---

* One of the two pilgrims in our first cut, p. 158, carries a palm branch in his hand; they represent the two disciples at Emmaus, who were returning from Jerusalem.

† The existence of several accounts of the stations of Rome in English prose and poetry as early as the thirteenth century (published by the Early English Text Society), indicates the popularity of this pilgrimage.

‡ Innocente III., Epist. 536, lib. i., t. c., p. 305, ed. Baluzio. (Dr. Rock's "Church of our Fathers.")

§ "Church of our Fathers," vol. iii. p. 438, note.

said a very popular legend, she wiped the brow of the Saviour, when he fainted under His cross in the Via Dolorosa, and which was found to have had miraculously transferred to it an imprint of the sacred countenance. Chaucer's Pardoner, as we have already seen—

> "Strait was comen from the Court of Rome,"

and, therefore,

> "A vernicle had he sewed upon his cap."

The sign of the Compostella pilgrimage was the scallop shell.* The legend which the old Spanish writers give in explanation of the badge is this:—When the body of the saint was being miraculously conveyed in a ship without sails or oars, from Joppa to Galicia, it passed the village of Bonzas, on the coast of Portugal, on the day that a marriage had been celebrated there. The bridegroom with his friends were amusing themselves on horseback on the sands, when his horse became unmanageable and plunged into the sea; whereupon the miraculous ship stopped in its voyage, and presently the bridegroom emerged, horse and man, close beside it. A conversation ensued between the knight and the saint's disciples on board, in which they apprised him that it was the saint who had saved him from a watery grave, and explained the Christian religion to him. He believed, and was baptized there and then. And immediately the ship resumed its voyage, and the knight came galloping back over the sea to rejoin his astonished friends. He told them all that had happened, and they too were converted, and the knight baptized his bride with his own hand. Now, when the knight emerged from the sea, both his dress and the trappings of his horse were covered with scallop shells; and, therefore, the Galicians took the scallop shell as the sign of St. James. The legend is found represented in churches dedicated to St. James, and in ancient illuminated MSS.† The scallop shell is not unfrequently found in armorial bearings. It is hardly probable that it would be given to a

---

* It is seen on the scrip of Lydgate's Pilgrim in the woodcut on p. 163. See a paper on the Pilgrim's Shell, by Mr. J. E. Tennant, in the *St. James's Magazine*, No. 10, for Jan., 1862.

† "Anales de Galicia," vol. i. p. 95. Southey's "Pilgrim to Compostella."

man merely because he had made the common pilgrimage to Compostella; perhaps it was earned by service under the banner of Santiago, against the Moors in the Spanish crusades. The Popes Alexander III., Gregory IX., and Clement V., granted a faculty to the Archbishops of Compostella, to excommunicate those who sell these shells to pilgrims anywhere except in the city of Santiago, and they assign this reason, because the shells are the badge of the Apostle Santiago.* The badge was not always an actual shell, but sometimes a jewel made in the shape of a scallop shell. In the "Journal of the Archæological Association," iii. 126, is a woodcut of a scallop shell of silver gilt, with a circular piece of jet set in the middle, on which is carved an equestrian figure of Santiago.

The chief sign of the Canterbury pilgrimage was an ampul (*ampulla*, a flask); we are told all about its origin and meaning by Abbot Benedict, who wrote a book on the miracles of St. Thomas.† The monks had carefully collected from the pavement the blood of the martyr which had been shed upon it, and preserved it as one of the precious relics. A sick lady who visited the shrine, begged for a drop of this blood as a medicine; it worked a miraculous cure, and the fame of the miracle spread far and wide, and future pilgrims were not satisfied unless they too might be permitted the same high privilege. A drop of it used to be mixed with a chalice full of water, that the colour and flavour might not offend the senses, and they were allowed to taste of it. It wrought, says the abbot, miraculous cures; and so, not only vast crowds came to take this strange and unheard-of medicine, but those who came were anxious to take some of it home for their sick friends and neighbours. At first they put it into wooden vessels, but these were split by the liquid; and many of the fragments of these vessels were hung up about the martyr's tomb in token of this wonder. At last it came into the head of a certain young man to cast little flasks—*ampullæ*—of lead and pewter. And then the miracle of the breaking ceased, and they knew that it was the Divine will that the Canterbury medicine should be carried in these ampullæ throughout the world,

---

* "Anales de Galicia," vol. i. p. 96, quoted by Southey, "Pilgrim to Compostella."
† Dr. Rock's "Church of our Fathers," iii. 424.

Pilgrim Signs. 171

and that these ampullæ should be recognised by all the world as the sign of this pilgrimage and these wonderful cures. At first the pilgrims had carried the wooden vases concealed under their clothes; but these ampullæ were carried suspended round the neck; and when the pilgrims reached home, says another authority,* they hung these ampullæ in their churches for sacred relics, that the glory of the blessed martyr might be known throughout the world. Some of these curious relics still exist. They are thin, flat on one side, and slightly rounded on the other, with two little

The Canterbury Ampulla.

ears or loops through which a cord might be passed to suspend them. The mouth might have been closed by solder, or even by folding over the edges of the metal. There is a little flask figured in Gardner's "History of Dunwich," pl. iii., which has a T upon the side of it, and which may very probably have been one of these ampullæ. But one of a much more elaborate and interesting type is here engraved, from an example preserved in the museum at York. The principal figure is a somewhat stern repre-

---

* "Vita S. Thomæ apud Willebald," folio Stephani, ed. Giles, i. 312.

sentation of the blessed archbishop; above is a rude representation of his shrine; and round the margin is the rhyming legend—" Optimus egrorum : Medicus fit Thoma bonorum " (" Thomas is the best physician for the pious sick"). On the reverse of the ampul is a design whose intention is not very clear; two monks or priests are apparently saying some service out of a book, and one of them is laying down a pastoral staff; perhaps it represents the shrine with its attendants. From the style of art, this design may be of the early part of the thirteenth century. But though this ampul is clearly designated by the monkish writers, whom we have quoted, as the special sign of the Canterbury pilgrimage, there was another sign which seems to have been peculiar to it, and that is a bell. Whether these bells were hand-bells, which the pilgrims carried in their hands, and rang from time to time, or whether they were little bells, like hawks' bells, fastened to their dress—as such bells sometimes were to a canon's cope—does not certainly appear. W. Thorpe, in the passage hereafter quoted at length from Fox, speaks of "the noise of their singing and the sound of their piping, and the jangling of their Canterbury bells," as a body of pilgrims passed through a town. One of the prettiest of our wild-flowers, the *Campanula rotundifolia*, which has clusters of blue, bell-like flowers, has obtained the common name of Canterbury Bells.* There were other religious trinkets also sold and used by pilgrims as mementoes of their visit to the famous shrine. The most common of them seems to have been the head of St. Thomas,† cast in various ornamental devices, in silver or pewter; sometimes it was adapted to hang to a rosary,‡ more usually, in the examples which remain to us, it was made into a brooch to be fastened upon the cap or hood, or dress. In Mr. C. R. Smith's "Collectanea Antiqua," vol. i. pl. 31, 32, 33, and vol. ii. pl. 16, 17, 18, there are representations of no less than fifty-one English and foreign

---

* The lily of the valley was another Canterbury flower. It is still plentiful in the gardens in the precincts of the cathedral.

† The veneration of the times was concentrated upon the blessed head which suffered the stroke of martyrdom; it was exhibited at the shrine and kissed by the pilgrims; there was an abbey in Derbyshire dedicated to the Beauchef (beautiful head), and still called Beauchief Abbey.

‡ The late T. Caldecot, Esq., of Dartford, possessed one of these.

pilgrims' signs, of which a considerable proportion are heads of St. Thomas. The whole collection is very curious and interesting.*

The ampul was not confined to St. Thomas of Canterbury. When his ampuls became so very popular, the guardians of the other famous shrines adopted it, and manufactured " waters," " aquæ reliquiarum," of their own. The relic of the saint, which they were so fortunate as to possess, was washed with or dipped in holy water, which was thereupon supposed to possess—diluted—the virtues of the relic itself. Thus there was a " Durham water," being the water in which the incorruptible body of St. Cuthbert had been washed at its last exposure; and Reginald of Durham, in his book on the admirable virtues of the blessed Cuthbert,† tells us how it used to be carried away in ampuls, and mentions a special example in which a little of this pleasant medicine poured into the mouth of a sick man, cured him on the spot. The same old writer tells us how the water held in a bowl that once belonged to Editha, queen and saint, in which a little bit of rag, which had once formed part of St. Cuthbert's garments, was soaked, acquired from these two relics so much virtue that it brought back health and strength to a dying clerk who drank it. In Gardner's " History of Dunwich " (pl. iii.) we find drawings of ampullæ like those of St. Thomas, one of which has upon its front a W surmounted by a crown, which it is conjectured may be the pilgrim sign of Our Lady of Walsingham, and contained, perhaps, water from the holy wells at Walsingham, hereinafter described. Another has an R surmounted by one of the symbols of the Blessed Virgin, a lily in a pot; the author hazards a conjecture that it may be the sign of St. Richard of Chichester. The pilgrim who brought away one of these flasks of medicine, or one of these blessed relics, we may suppose, did not always hang it up in church as an *ex voto*, but sometimes preserved it carefully in his house for use in time of sickness, and would often be applied to by a sick neighbour for the gift of a portion of the precious fluid out of his ampul, or for a touch of the trinket which had touched the saint. In the " Collectanea Antiqua," is a

---

* A very beautiful little pilgrim sign of lead found at Winchester is engraved in the " Journal of the British Archæological Association," No. 32, p. 363.

† Dr. Rock's " Church of our Fathers," vol. iii. p. 430.

facsimile of a piece of paper bearing a rude woodcut of the adoration of the Magi, and an inscription setting forth that " Ces billets ont touché aux troi testes de saints Rois a Cologne : ils sont pour les voyageurs contre les malheurs des chemins, maux de teste, mal caduque, fièures, sorcellerie, toute sorte de malefice, et morte soubite." It was found upon the person of one William Jackson, who having been sentenced for murder in June, 1748-9, was found dead in prison a few hours before the time of his execution. It was the charmed billet, doubtless, which preserved him from the more ignominious death.

We find a description of a pilgrim in full costume, and decorated with signs, in " Piers Ploughman's Vision." He was apparelled—

> " In pilgrym's wise.
> He bare a burdoun* y-bounde with a broad list,
> In a withwinde-wise y-wounden about ;
> A bollet† and a bagge he bare by his side,
> An hundred of ampulles ; on his hat seten
> Signes of Synay‡ and shells of Galice,§
> And many a crouche‖ on his cloke and keys of Rome,
> And the vernicle before, for men sholde knowe,
> And se bi his signes, whom he sought hadde.
> These folk prayed¶ hym first fro whence he came ?
> 'From Synay,' he seide, ' and from our Lordes Sepulcre :
> In Bethlem and in Babiloyne I have ben in bothe ;
> In Armonye** and Alesaundre, in many other places.

---

* Fosbroke has fallen into the error of calling this a burden bound to the pilgrim's back with a list : it is the bourdon, the pilgrim's staff, round which a list, a long narrow strip of cloth, was wound cross-wise. We do not elsewhere meet with this list round the staff, and it does not appear what was its use or meaning. We may call to mind the list wound cross-wise round a barber's pole, and imagine that this list was attached to the pilgrim's staff for use, or we may remember that a vexillum, or banner, is attached to a bishop's staff, and that a long, narrow riband is often affixed to the cross-headed staff which is placed in our Saviour's hand in mediæval representations of the Resurrection. The staff in our cut, p. 163, looks as if it might have such a list wound round it.

† Fosbrooke, and Wright, and Dr. Rock, all understand this to be a bowl. Was it a bottle to carry drink, shaped something like a gourd, such as we not unfrequently find hung on the hook of a shepherd's staff in pictures of the annunciation to the shepherds, and such as the pilgrim from Erasmus's " Praise of Folly," bears on his back ?

‡ Sinai.   § Galice—Compostella in Galicia.   ‖ Cross.

¶ Asked : people ask him first of all from whence he is come.

** Armenia.

> Ye may se by my signes, that sitten in my hat,
> That I have walked ful wide in weet and in drye,
> And sought good seintes for my soules helthe.'"

The little bit of satire, for the sake of which this model pilgrim is introduced, is too telling—especially after the wretched superstitions which we have been noticing—to be omitted here. "Knowest thou?" asks the Ploughman—

> "'Kondest thou aught a cor-saint* that men calle Truthe?
> Canst thou aught weten† us the way where that wight dwelleth?

"Nay," replies the much-travelled pilgrim—

> "'Nay, so me God helpe,
> I saw nevere palmere with pyke and with scrippe
> Ask after hym, ever til now in this place.'"

---

* Holy body, object of pilgrimage. † Tell us.

CHAPTER II.

OUR LADY OF WALSINGHAM AND ST. THOMAS OF CANTERBURY.

WE shall not wonder that these various pilgrimages were so popular as they were, when we learn that there were not only physical panaceas to be obtained, and spiritual pardons and immunities to be procured at the shrines of the saints, but that moreover the journey to them was often made a very pleasant holiday excursion.

Far be it from us to deny that there was many a pilgrim who undertook his pilgrimage in anything but a holiday spirit, and who made it anything but a gay excursion; many a man who sought, howbeit mistakenly, to atone for wrong done, by making himself an outcast upon earth, and submitting to the privations of mendicant pilgrimage; many a one who sought thus to escape out of reach of the stings of remorse; many a one who tore himself from home and the knowledge of friends, and went to foreign countries to hide his shame from the eyes of those who knew him. Certainly, here and there, might have been met a man or a woman, whose coarse sackcloth robe, girded to the naked skin, and unshod feet, were signs of real if mistaken penitence; and who carried grievous memories and a sad heart through every mile of his weary way. We give here, from Hans Burgmaier's "Images de Saints, &c., de la Famille de l'Empereur Maximilian I.," a very excellent illustration of a pilgrim of this class. But this was not the general character of the home pilgrimages of which we are especially speaking. In the great majority of cases they seem to have been little more than a pleasant religious holiday.* No doubt the general

---

* The Knight of La Tour Landry, in one of his stories, tells us : " There was a young lady that had her herte moche on the worlde. And there was a squier that loved her and

intention was devotional; very likely it was often in a moment of religious fervour that the vow was taken; the religious ceremony with which the journey was begun, must have had a solemnising effect; and doubtless when the pilgrim knelt at the shrine, an unquestioning faith in all the tales which he had heard of its sanctity and occasional miraculous power, and the imposing effect of the scene, would affect his mind with an unusual religious warmth and exaltation. But between the beginning and the end of the pilgrimage there was a long interval, which we say— not in a censorious spirit—was usually occupied by a very pleasant excursion. The same fine work which has supplied us with so excellent an illustration of an ascetic pilgrim, affords another equally valuable companion-picture of a pilgrim of the more usual class. He travels on foot, indeed, staff in hand, but he is comfortably shod and clad; and while the one girds his sackcloth shirt to his bare body with an iron chain, the other has his belt well furnished with little conveniences of travel. It is quite clear that the journey was not necessarily on foot, the voluntary pilgrims might ride if they preferred it.* Nor did they beg their bread as penitential pilgrims did; but put good store of

Pilgrim in Hair Shirt and Cloak.

---

she hym. And for because that she might have better leiser to speke with hym, she made her husbande to understande that she had vowed in diverse pilgrimages; and her husband, as he that thought none evelle and wolde not displese her, suffered and held hym content that she should go wherin her lust. . . . . Alle thei that gone on pilgrimage to a place for foul plesaunce more than devocion of the place that thei go to, and covereth thaire goinge with service of God, fowlethe and scornethe God and our Ladie, and the place that thei goo to."—*Book of La Tour Landry*, chap. xxxiv.

* "I was a poor pilgrim," says one ("History of the Troubadours," p. 300), "when I came to your court; and have lived honestly and respectably in it on the wages you have given me; restore to me my mule, my wallet, and my staff, and I will return in the same manner as I came."

money in their purse at starting, and ambled easily along the green roads, and lived well at the comfortable inns along their way. In many instances when the time of pilgrimage is mentioned, we find that it was the spring; Chaucer's pilgrims started—

> "When that April with his showerés sote
> The drouth of March had perced to the root;"

and Fosbroke "apprehends that Lent was the usual time for these pilgrimages."

It was the custom for the pilgrims to associate in companies; indeed, since they travelled the same roads, about the same time of year, and stopped at the same inns and hospitals, it was inevitable; and they seem to have taken pains to make the journey agreeable to one another. Chaucer's "hoste of the Tabard" says to his guests :—

> "Ye go to Canterbury : God you speed,
> The blisful martyr quité you your mede;
> And well I wot, as ye go by the way,
> Ye shapen you to talken and to play;
> For trewely comfort and worthe is none,
> To riden by the way dumb as a stone."

Even the poor penitential pilgrim who travelled barefoot did not travel, all the way at least, on the hard and rough highway. Special roads seem to have been made to the great shrines. Thus the "Pilgrim's Road" may still be traced across Kent, almost from London to Canterbury; and if the Londoner wishes for a pleasant and interesting home excursion, he may put a scrip on his back, and take a bourdon in his hand, and make a summer's pilgrimage on the track of Chaucer's pilgrims. The pilgrim's road to Walsingham is still known as the "Palmer's Way" and the "Walsingham Green Way." It may be traced along the principal part of its course for sixty miles in the diocese of Norwich. The common people used to call the Milky Way the Walsingham Way.

Dr. Rock tells us[*] that "besides its badge, each pilgrimage had also its gathering cry, which the pilgrims shouted out as, at the grey of morn, they

---

[*] "Church of our Fathers," vol. iii. p. 442.

slowly crept through the town or hamlet where they had slept that night." By calling aloud upon God for help, and begging the intercession of that saint to whose shrine they were wending, they bade all their fellow pilgrims to come forth upon their road and begin another day's march.*

After having said their prayers and told their beads, occasionally did they strive to shorten the weary length of the way by song and music. As often as a crowd of pilgrims started together from one place, they seem always to have hired a few singers and one or two musicians to go with them. Just before reaching any town, they drew themselves up into a line, and thus walked through its streets in procession, singing and ringing their little hand-bells, with a player on the bagpipes at their head. They ought in strictness, perhaps, to have been psalms which they sung, and the tales with which they were accustomed to lighten the way ought to have been saintly legends and godly discourses; but in truth they were of very varied character, according to the character of the individual pilgrims. The songs were often love-songs; and though Chaucer's poor parson of a town preached a sermon and was listened to, yet the romances of chivalry or the loose faiblieux which were current probably formed the majority of the real "Canterbury tales." In Foxe's "Acts and Monuments," we have a very graphic and amusing little sketch of a company of pilgrims passing through a town :—

W. Thorpe tells Archbishop Arundel, "When diverse men and women will go thus after their own willes, and finding out one pilgrimage, they will order with them before to have with them both men and women that can well synge wanton songs; and some other pilgrims will have with them bagge-pipes, so that every towne they come throwe, what with the noyse of their singing and with the sound of their pipyng, and with the jingling of their Canterbury belles, and with barking out of dogges after them, that they make more noise than if the kinge came there awaye with all his clarions, and many other minstrelles. And if these men and women be a moneth on their pilgrimage, many of them shall be an half year after

---

* Thus Pope Calixtus tells us ("Sermones Bib. Pat.," ed. Bignio, xv. 330) that the pilgrims to Santiago were accustomed before dawn, at the top of each town, to cry with a loud voice, "Deus Adjuva!" "Sancte Jacobe!" "God Help!" "Santiago!"

great janglers, tale-tellers, and liars." The archbishop defends the fashion, and gives us further information on the subject, saying "that pilgremys have with them both syngers and also pipers, that when one of them that goeth barefoote striketh his toe upon a stone, and hurteth him sore, and maketh him to blede, it is well done that he or his fellow begyn than a songe, or else take out of his bosom a bagge-pipe, for to drive away with such myrthe the hurte of his fellow; for with soche solace the travell and weriness of pylgremies is lightly and merily broughte forth."

Erasmus's colloquy entitled "Peregrinatio Religionis ergo," enables us to accompany the pilgrim to the shrine of Our Lady of Walsingham, and to join him in his devotions at the shrine. We shall throw together the most interesting portions of the narrative from Mr. J. G. Nichols's translation of it. "It is," he says, "the most celebrated place throughout all England,[*] nor could you easily find in that island the man who ventures to reckon on prosperity unless he yearly salute her with some small offering according to his ability." "The town of Walsingham," he says, "is maintained by scarcely anything else but the number of its visitors." The shrine of Our Lady was not within the priory church; but on the north side was the wooden chapel dedicated to "Our Lady," about twenty-three feet by thirteen, enclosed within a chapel of stone forty-eight feet by thirty, which Erasmus describes as unfinished. On the west of the church was another wooden building, in which were two holy wells also dedicated to the Virgin. Erasmus describes these "holy places." "Within the church, which I have called unfinished, is a small chapel made of wainscot, and admitting the devotees on each side by a narrow little door. The light is small, indeed scarcely any but from the wax lights. A most grateful fragrance meets the nostrils. When you look in, you would say it was the mansion of the saints, so much does it glitter on all sides with jewels, gold, and silver. In the inner chapel one canon attends to receive and take charge of the offerings," which the pilgrims placed upon the altar. "To the east of this is a chapel full of wonders. Thither I go. Another guide receives me. There we worshipped for a short time. Presently the

---

[*] Surely he should have excepted St. Thomas's shrine?

joint of a man's finger is exhibited to us, the largest of three; I kiss it; and then I ask whose relics were these? He says, St. Peter's. The Apostle? I ask. He said, Yes. Then observing the size of the joint, which might have been that of a giant, I remarked, Peter must have been a man of very large size. At this, one of my companions burst into a laugh; which I certainly took ill, for if he had been quiet the attendant would have shown us all the relics. However, we pacified him by offering a few pence. Before the chapel was a shed, which they say was suddenly, in the winter season, when everything was covered with snow, brought thither from a great distance. Under this shed are two wells full to the brink; they say the spring is sacred to the Holy Virgin. The water is wonderfully cold, and efficacious in curing the pains of the head and stomach. We next turned towards the heavenly milk of the Blessed Virgin" (kept apparently in another chapel); "that milk is kept on the high-altar; in the centre of which is Christ; at his right hand for honour's sake, his mother; for the milk personifies the mother. As soon as the canon in attendance saw us, he rose, put on his surplice, added the stole to his neck, prostrated himself with due ceremony, and worshipped; anon he stretched forth the thrice-holy milk to be kissed by us. On this, we also, on the lowest step of the altar, religiously fell prostrate; and having first called upon Christ, we addressed the Virgin with a little prayer like this, which I had prepared for the purpose. . . . .

" 'A very pious prayer; what reply did she make?'

"Each appeared to assent, if my eyes were not deceived. For the holy milk seemed to leap a little, and the Eucharist shone somewhat brighter. Meanwhile the ministering canon approached us, saying nothing, but holding out a little box, such as are presented by the toll collectors on the bridges in Germany. I gave a few pence, which he offered to the Virgin."

The visitor on this occasion being a distinguished person, and performing a trifling service for the canons, was presented by the sub-prior with a relic. "He then drew from a bag a fragment of wood, cut from a beam on which the Virgin Mother had been seen to rest. A wonderful fragrance at once proved it to be a thing extremely sacred. For my part, having received so distinguished a present, prostrate and with uncovered head, I kissed it three or four times with the highest veneration, and placed it in my purse. I would not exchange that fragment, small as it is, for all the gold in the Tagus. I will enclose it in gold, but so that it may shine through crystal."

He is also shown some relics not shown to ordinary visitors. "Several wax candles are lighted, and a small image is produced, neither excelling in material nor workmanship; but in virtue most efficacious. He then exhibited the golden and silver statues. 'This one,' says he, 'is entirely of gold; this is silver gilt; he added the weight of each, its value, and the name of the donor.* Then he drew forth from the altar itself, a world of

---

* In the *Guardian* newspaper of Sept. 5, 1860, a visitor to Rome gives a description of the exhibition of relics there, which forms an interesting parallel with the account in the text: "Shortly before Ash-Wednesday a public notice ('Invito Sagro') is issued by authority, setting forth that inasmuch as certain of the principal relics and 'sacra immagini' are to be exposed during the ensuing season of Lent, in certain churches specified, the confraternities of Rome are exhorted by the pope to resort in procession to those churches. . . . . The ceremony is soon described. The procession entered slowly at the west door, moved up towards the altar, and when the foremost were within a few yards of it, all knelt down for a few minutes on the pavement of the church to worship. At a signal given by one of the party, they rose, and slowly defiled off in the direction of the chapel wherein is preserved the column of the flagellation (?). By the way, no one of the other sex may ever enter that chapel, except on one day in the year—the very day of which I am speaking; and on *that* day men are as rigorously excluded. Well, all knelt again for a few minutes, then rose, and moved slowly towards the door, departing as they came, and making way for another procession to enter. It was altogether a most interesting and agreeable spectacle. Utterly alien to our English tastes and habits certainly; but the institution evidently suited the tastes of the people exactly, and I dare say may be conducive to piety, and recommend itself to their religious instincts. Coming from their several parishes, and returning, they chant psalms.

"It follows naturally to speak a little more particularly about the adoration of relics, for this is just another of those many definite religious acts which make up the sum of popular devotion, and supply the void occasioned by the entire discontinuance of the old breviary offices. In the 'Diario Romano' (a little book describing what is publicly transacted, of a religious character, during every day in the year), daily throughout Lent, and indeed on every occasion of unusual solemnity (of which, I think, there are eighty-five in all), you read 'Stazione' at such a church. This (whatever it may imply beside) denotes that relics are displayed for adoration in that church on the day indicated. The pavement is accordingly strewed with box, lights burn on the altar, and there is a constant influx of visitors to that church throughout the day. For example, at St. Prisca's, a little church on the Aventine, there was a 'Stazione,' 3rd April. In the Romish Missal you will perceive that on the Feria tertia Majoris hebdomadæ (this year April 3), there is

admirable things, the individual articles of which, if I were to proceed to describe, this day would not suffice for the relation. So that pilgrimage terminated most fortunately for me. I was abundantly gratified with sights; and I bring away this inestimable gift, a token bestowed by the Virgin herself.

"'Have you made no trial of the powers of your wood?'

"I have: in an inn, before the end of three days, I found a man afflicted

Statio ad S. Priscam. A very interesting church, by the way, it proved, being evidently built on a site of immense antiquity—traditionally said to be the house of Prisca. You descend by thirty-one steps into the subterranean edifice. At this little out-of-the-way church, there were strangers arriving all the time we were there. Thirty young Dominicans from S. Sabina, hard by, streamed down into the crypt, knelt for a time, and then repaired to perform a similar act of worship above, at the altar. The friend who conducted me to the spot, showed me, in the vineyard immediately opposite, some extraordinary remains of the wall of Servius Tullius. On our return we observed fresh parties straggling towards the church, bent on performing their 'visits.' It should, perhaps, be mentioned that prayers have been put forth by authority, to be used on such occasions.

"I must not pass by this subject of relics so slightly, for it evidently occupies a considerable place in the public devotions of a Roman Catholic. Thus the 'Invito Sagro,' already adverted to, specifies *which* relics will be displayed in each of the six churches enumerated—(*e.g.* the heads of SS. Peter and Paul, their chains, some wood of the cross, &c.)—granting seven years of indulgence for every visit, by whomsoever paid; and promising plenary indulgence to every person who, after confessing and communicating, shall thrice visit each of the aforesaid churches, and pray for awhile on behalf of holy church. There are besides, on nine chief festivals, as many great displays of relics at Rome, the particulars of which may be seen in the 'Année Liturgique,' pp. 189—206. I witnessed *one*, somewhat leisurely, at the Church of the Twelve Apostles, on the afternoon of the 1st of May. There was a congregation of about two or three hundred in church, while somebody in a lofty gallery displayed the relics, his companion proclaiming with a loud voice what each was: 'Questo e il braccio,' &c., &c., which such an one gave to this 'alma basilica,'—the formula being in every instance very sonorously intoned. There was part of the arm of S. Bartholomew and of S. James the Less; part of S. Andrew's leg, arm, and cross; part of one of S. Paul's fingers; one of the nails with which S. Peter was crucified; S. Philip's right foot; liquid blood of S. James; some of the remains of S. John the Evangelist, of the Baptist, of Joseph, and of the Blessed Virgin; together with part of the manger, cradle, cross, and tomb of our Lord, &c., &c. .... I have dwelt somewhat disproportionally on relics, but they play so conspicuous a part in the religious system of the country, that in enumerating the several substitutes which have been invented for the old breviary services, it would not be nearly enough to have discussed the subject in a few lines. A visit paid to a church where such objects are exposed, is a distinct as well as popular religious exercise; and it always seemed to me to be performed with great reverence and devotion."

in mind, for whom charms were then in preparation. This piece of wood was placed under his pillow, unknown to himself; he fell into a sleep equally deep and prolonged; in the morning he rose of whole mind."

Chaucer left his account of the Canterbury Pilgrimage incomplete; but another author, soon after Chaucer's death, wrote a supplement to his great work, which, however inferior in genius to the work of the great master, yet admirably serves our purpose of giving a graphic contemporary picture of the doings of a company of pilgrims to St. Thomas, when arrived at their destination. Erasmus, too, in the colloquy already so largely quoted, enables us to add some details to the picture. The pilgrims of Chaucer's continuator arrived in Canterbury at "mydmorowe." Erasmus tells us what they saw as they approached the city. "The church dedicated to St. Thomas, erects itself to heaven with such majesty, that even from a distance it strikes religious awe into the beholders. . . . . . There are two vast towers that seem to salute the visitor from afar, and make the surrounding country far and wide resound with the wonderful booming of their brazen bells." Being arrived, they took up their lodgings at the "Chequers." *

"They toke their In and loggit them at midmorowe I trowe
Atte Cheker of the hope, that many a man doth know."

And mine host of the "Tabard," in Southwark, their guide, having given the necessary orders for their dinner, they all proceeded to the cathedral to make their offerings at the shrine of St. Thomas. At the church door they were sprinkled with holy water as they entered. The knight and the better sort of the company went straight to their devotions; but some of the pilgrims of a less educated class, began to wander about the nave of the church, curiously admiring all the objects around them. The miller and his companions entered into a warm discussion concerning the arms in the painted glass windows. At length the host of the "Tabard" called them together and reproved them for their negligence, whereupon they hastened to make their offerings :—

---

* From Mr. Wright's "Archæological Album," p. 19.

> "Then passed they forth boystly gogling with their hedds
> Kneeled down to-fore the shrine, and hertily their beads
> They prayed to St. Thomas, in such wise as they couth;
> And sith the holy relikes each man with his mouth
> Kissed, as a goodly monk the names told and taught.
> And sith to other places of holyness they raught,
> And were in their devocioune tyl service were al done."

Erasmus gives a very detailed account of these "holy relikes," and of the "other places of holiness":—

> "On your entrance [by the south porch] the edifice at once displays itself in all its spaciousness and majesty. To that part any one is admitted. There are some books fixed to the pillars, and the monument of I know not whom. The iron screens stop further progress, but yet admit a view of the whole space, from the choir to the end of the church. To the choir you mount by many steps, under which is a passage leading to the north. At that spot is shown a wooden altar, dedicated to the Virgin, but mean, nor remarkable in any respect, unless as a monument of antiquity, putting to shame the extravagance of these times. There the pious old man is said to have breathed his last farewell to the Virgin when his death was at hand. On the altar is the point of the sword with which the head of the most excellent prelate was cleft, and his brain stirred, that he might be the more instantly despatched. The sacred rust of this iron, through love of the martyr, we religiously kissed. Leaving this spot, we descended to the crypt. It has its own priests. There was first exhibited the perforated skull of the martyr, the forehead is left bare to be kissed, while the other parts are covered with silver. At the same time is shown a slip of lead, engraved with his name *Thomas Acrensis*.[*] There also hang in the dark the hair shirts, the girdles and bandages with which that prelate subdued his flesh; striking horror with their very appearance, and reproaching us with our indulgence and our luxuries. From hence we returned into the choir. On the north side the aumbrics were unlocked. It is wonderful to tell what a quantity of bones was there brought out: skulls, jaw-bones, teeth, hands, fingers, entire arms; on all which we devoutly bestowed our kisses;

---

[*] This slip of lead had probably been put into his coffin. He is sometimes called Thomas of Acre.

and the exhibition seemed likely to last for ever, if my somewhat unmanageable companion in that pilgrimage had not interrupted the zeal of the showman.

"'Did he offend the priest?'

"When an arm was brought forward which had still the bloody flesh adhering, he drew back from kissing it, and even betrayed some weariness. The priest presently shut up his treasures. We next viewed the table of the altar, and its ornaments, and then the articles which are kept under the altar, all most sumptuous; you would say Midas and Crœsus were beggars if you saw that vast assemblage of gold and silver. After this we were led into the sacristy. What a display was there of silken vestments, what an array of golden candlesticks! . . . . . From this place we were conducted back to the upper floor, for behind the high-altar you ascend again as into a new church. There, in a little chapel, is shown the whole figure of the excellent man, gilt and adorned with many jewels. Then the head priest (prior) came forward. He opened to us the shrine in which what is left of the body of the holy man is said to rest. A wooden canopy covers the shrine, and when that is drawn up with ropes, inestimable treasures are opened to view. The least valuable part was gold; every part glistened, shone, and sparkled with rare and very large jewels, some of them exceeding the size of a goose's egg. There some monks stood around with much veneration; the cover being raised we all worshipped. The prior with a white rod pointed out each jewel, telling its name in French, its value, and the name of its donor, for the principal of them were offerings sent by sovereign princes. . . . . . From hence we returned to the crypt, where the Virgin Mother has her abode, but a somewhat dark one, being edged in by more than one screen.

"'What wassh e afraid of?'

"Nothing, I imagine, but thieves; for I have never seen anything more burdened with riches. When lamps were brought, we beheld a more than royal spectacle. . . . . . Lastly we were conducted back to the sacristy; there was brought out a box covered with black leather; it was laid upon the table and opened; immediately all knelt and worshipped.

"'What was in it?'

"Some torn fragments of linen, and most of them retaining marks of dirt. . . . . . After offering us a cup of wine, the prior courteously dismissed us."

When Chaucer's pilgrims had seen such of this magnificence as existed in their earlier time, noon approaching, they gathered together and went to their dinner. Before they left the church, however, they bought signs "as the manner was," to show to all men that they had performed this meritorious act.

> "There as manere and custom is, signes there they bought
> For men of contre' should know whom they had sought.
> Each man set his silver in such thing as they liked,
> And in the meen while the miller had y-piked
> His bosom full of signys of Canterbury broches.
> Others set their signys upon their hedes, and some upon their cap,
> And sith to dinner-ward they gan for to stapp."

The appearance of these shrines and their surroundings is brought before our eyes by the pictures in a beautiful volume of Lydgate's "History of St. Edmund" in the British Museum (Harl. 2,278). At f. 40 is a representation of the shrine of St. Edmund in the abbey church of St Edmund's Bury. At f. 9 a still better representation of it, showing the iron grille which enclosed it, a monk worshipping at it, and a clerk with a wand, probably the custodian whose duty it was to show the various jewels and relics—as the prior did to Erasmus at Canterbury. At f. 47 is another shrine, with some people about it who have come in the hope of receiving miraculous cures; still another at f. 100 v., with pilgrims praying round it. At f. 109 a shrine, with two monks in a stall beside it saying an office, a clerk and others present. At f. 10 v. a shrine with a group of monks. Other representations of shrines (all no doubt intended to represent the one shrine of St. Edmund, but differing in details) are to be found at f. 108 v., 117, &c. In the MS. Roman " D'Alexandre," of the latter half of the fourteenth century, in the Bodleian Library, at f. 2,660, is a very good representation of the shrine of St. Thomas the Apostle, with several people about it, and in front are two pilgrims in rough habits, a broad hat slung over the shoulder, and a staff.

We have hitherto spoken of male pilgrims; but it must be borne in

mind that women of all ranks were frequently to be found on pilgrimage;*
and all that has been said of the costume and habits of the one sex applies

Female Pilgrim. (Strutt, pl. 134.)

equally to the other. We give here a cut of a female pilgrim with scrip, staff, and hat, from Pl. 134 of Strutt's "Dresses and Habits of the People of England," who professes to take it from the Harleian MS. 621. We also give a picture of a pilgrim monk (Cotton. MS. Tiberius, A. 7.) who bears the staff and scrip, but is otherwise habited in the proper costume of his order.

When the pilgrim had returned safely home, it was but natural and proper that as he had been sent forth with the blessing and prayers of the church, he should present himself again in church to give thanks for the accomplishment of his pilgrimage and his safe return. We do not find in the service-books—as we might have expected—any special service for this occasion, but we find sufficient indications that it was the practice. Knighton tells us, for example,

Pilgrim Monk. of the famous Guy, Earl of Warwick, that on his return

---

* Of Chaucer's Wife of Bath we read:—
"Thrice had she been at Jerusalem,
And haddé passed many a strangé stream;
At Rome she haddé been, and at Boloyne,
In Galice, at St. James, and at Coloyne."

from his pilgrimage to the Holy Land, before he took any refreshment, he went to all the churches in the city to return thanks. Du Cange tells us that palmers were received on their return home with ecclesiastical processions; but perhaps this was only in the case of men of some social importance. We have the details of one such occasion on record:* William de Mandeville, Earl of Essex, assumed the cross, and after procuring suitable necessaries, took with him a retinue, and among them a chaplain to perform divine offices, for all of whom he kept a daily

From "Le Pélerinage de la Vie Humaine" (French National Library).

table. Before he set out he went to Gilbert, Bishop of London, for his license and benediction. He travelled by land as far as Rome, over France, Burgundy, and the Alps, leaving his horse at Mantua. He visited every holy place in Jerusalem and on his route; made his prayers and offerings at each; and so returned. Upon his arrival, he made presents of silk cloths to all the churches of his see, for copes or coverings of the altars. The monks of Walden met him in procession, in albes and copes, singing, "Blessed is he who cometh in the name of the Lord;" and the

---

* Dugdale's "Monasticon."

earl coming to the high-altar, and there prostrating himself, the prior gave him the benediction. After this he rose, and kneeling, offered some precious relics in an ivory box, which he had obtained in Jerusalem and elsewhere. This offering concluded, he rose, and stood before the altar; the prior and convent singing the *Te Deum.* Leaving the church he went to the chapter, to give and receive the kiss of peace from the prior and monks. A sumptuous entertainment followed for himself and his suite; and the succeeding days were passed in visits to relatives and friends, who congratulated him on his safe return.

Du Cange says that palmers used to present their scrips and staves to their parish churches. And Coryatt[*] says that he saw cockle and mussel shells, and beads, and other religious relics, hung up over the door of a little chapel in a nunnery, which, says Fosbroke, were offerings made by pilgrims on their return from Compostella.

The illuminated MS., Julius E. VI., illustrates, among other events of the life of Richard Beauchamp, Earl of Warwick, various scenes of his pilgrimage to Rome and to Jerusalem. In an illumination (subsequently engraved in the chapter on Merchants) he is seen embarking in his own ship; in another, he is presented to the Pope and cardinals at Rome [†] (subsequently engraved in the chapter on Secular Clergy); in another, he is worshipping at the Holy Sepulchre, where he hung up his shield in remembrance of his accomplished vow.

The additional MS. 24,189, is part of St. John Mandeville's history of his travels, and its illuminations in some respects illustrate the voyage of a pilgrim of rank.

Hans Burgmaier's "Images de Saints," &c.,—from which we take the figure on the next page,—affords us a very excellent contemporary illustration of a pilgrim of high rank, with his attendants, all in pilgrim costume, and wearing the signs which show us that their pilgrimage has been successfully accomplished.

---

[*] "Crudities," p. 18.
[†] In Lydgate's "Life of St. Edmund" (Harl. 2,278) is a picture of King Alkmund on his pilgrimage, at Rome, receiving the Pope's blessing, in which the treatment of the subject is very like that of the illumination in the text.

Those who had taken any of the greater pilgrimages would probably be regarded with a certain respect and reverence by their untravelled neighbours, and the agnomen of Palmer or Pilgrim, which would naturally be added to their Christian name—as William the Palmer, or John the Pilgrim—is doubtless the origin of two sufficiently common surnames. The tokens of pilgrimage sometimes even accompanied a man to his grave, and were sculptured on his monument. Shells have not unfrequently been

Pilgrim on Horseback.

found in stone coffins, and are taken with great probability to be relics of the pilgrimage, which the deceased had once taken to Compostella, and which as sacred things, and having a certain religious virtue, were strewed over him as he was carried upon his bier in the funeral procession, and were placed with him in his grave. For example, when the grave of Bishop Mayhew, who died in 1516, in Hereford Cathedral, was opened some years ago, there was found lying by his side, a common, rough, hazel wand, between four and five feet long, and about as thick as a man's finger; and with it a mussel and a few oyster-shells. Four other instances of such hazel rods, without accompanying shells, buried with ecclesiastics, had previously been observed in the same cathedral.* The tomb of Abbot Cheltenham, at Tewkesbury, has the spandrels ornamented with shields charged with scallop shells, and the pilgrim staff and scrip are sculptured on the bosses of the groining of the canopy over the tomb. There is a gravestone at Haltwhistle, Northumberland, to which we have already more than once had occasion to refer,† on which is the usual device of a cross sculptured in relief, and on one side of the shaft of the cross are laid a sword and shield, charged with the arms of Blenkinsop, a fess between three garbs, indicating, we presume, that the deceased was a knight; on the other side of the shaft of the cross are laid a palmer's staff, and a scrip, bearing also garbs, and indicating that the knight had been a pilgrim.

In the church of Ashby-de-la-Zouch, Leicestershire, there is, under a monumental arch in the wall of the north aisle, a recumbent effigy, a good deal defaced, of a man in pilgrim weeds. A tunic or gown reaches half-way down between the knee and ankle, and he has short pointed laced boots; a hat with its margin decorated with scallop-shells lies under his head, his scrip tasselled and charged with scallop-shells is at his right side, and his rosary on his left, and his staff is laid diagonally across the body. The costly style of the monument,‡ the lion at his feet, and above all a collar of SS. round his neck, prove that the person thus commemorated was a person of distinction.

In the churchyard of Llanfihangel-Aber-Cowen, Carmarthenshire, there are three graves,§ which are assigned by the local tradition to three holy

---

* The shells indicate a pilgrimage accomplished, but the rod may not have been intended to represent the pilgrim's bourdon. In the Harl. MS. 5,102, fol. 68, a MS. of the beginning of the thirteenth century, is a bishop holding a slender rod (not a pastoral staff), and at fol. 17 of the same MS. one is putting a similar rod into a bishop's coffin. The priors of small cathedrals bore a staff without crook, and had the privilege of being arrayed in pontificals for mass; choir-rulers often bore staves. Dr. Rock, in the "Church of our Fathers," vol. iii., pt. ii., p. 224, gives a cut from a late Flemish Book of Hours, in which a priest, sitting at confession, bears a long rod.

† It is engraved in Mr. Boutell's "Christian Monuments in England and Wales," p. 79.

‡ Engraved in Nichols's "Leicestershire," vol. iii., pl. ii., p. 623.

§ Engraved in the "Manual of Sepulchral Slabs and Crosses," by the Rev. E. L. Cutts, pl. lxxiii.

palmers, " who wandered thither in poverty and distress, and being about to perish for want, slew each other: the last survivor buried his fellows and then himself in one of the graves which they had prepared, and pulling the stone over him, left it, as it is, ill adjusted." Two of the headstones have very rude demi-effigies, with a cross patée sculptured upon them. In one of the graves were found, some years ago, the bones of a female or youth, and half-a-dozen scallop-shells. There are also, among the curious symbols which appear on mediæval coffin-stones, some which are very likely intended for pilgrim staves. There is one at Woodhorn, Northumberland, engraved in the "Manual of Sepulchral Slabs and Crosses," and another at Alnwick-le-Street, Yorkshire, is engraved in Gough's "Sepulchral Monuments," vol. i. It may be that these were men who had made a vow of perpetual pilgrimage, or who died in the midst of an unfinished pilgrimage, and therefore the pilgrim insignia were placed upon their monuments. If every man and woman who had made a pilgrimage had had its badges carved upon their tombs, we should surely have found many other tombs thus designated; but, indeed, we have the tombs of men who we know had accomplished pilgrimages to Jerusalem, but have no pilgrim insignia upon their tombs.

Other illustrations of pilgrim costume may be found scattered throughout the illuminated MSS. References to some of the best of them are here added. In the Royal, 1,696, at f. 163, is a good drawing of St. James as a pilgrim. In the Add. MS. 17,687, at f. 33, another of the pilgrim saints with scrip and staff; in the MS. Nero E 2, a half-length of the saint with a scallop-shell in his hat; in the MS. 18,143, of early sixteenth-century date, at f. 57 v., another. In Lydgate's "History of St. Edmund," already quoted for its pictures of shrines, there are also several good pictures of pilgrims. On f. 79 is a group of three pilgrims, who appear again in different parts of the history, twice on page 80, and again at 84 and 85. At f. 81 the three pilgrims have built themselves a hermitage and chapel, surrounded by a fence of wicker-work. In Henry VII.'s chapel, Westminster, the figure of a pilgrim is frequently introduced in the ornamental sculpture of the side chapels and on the reredos, in allusion, no doubt, to the pilgrims who figure in the legendary history of St. Edmund the Confessor.

Having followed the pilgrim to his very tomb, there we pause. We cannot but satirise the troops of mere religious holiday-makers, who rode a pleasant summer's holiday through the green roads of merry England, feasting at the inns, singing amorous songs, and telling loose stories by the way; going through a round of sight-seeing at the end of it; and drinking foul water in which a dead man's blood had been mingled, or a dead man's bones had been washed. But let us be allowed to indulge the hope that every act of real, honest, self-denial—however mistaken—in remorse for sin, for the sake of purity, or for the honour of religion, did benefit the honest, though mistaken devotee. Is *our* religion so perfect and so pure, and is *our* practice so exactly accordant with it, that we can afford to sit in severe judgment upon honest, self-denying error?

THE SECULAR CLERGY OF THE MIDDLE AGES.

CHAPTER I.

THE PAROCHIAL CLERGY.

THE present organisation of the Church of England dates from the Council of Hertford, A.D. 673. Before that time the Saxon people were the object of missionary operations, carried on by two independent bodies, the Italian mission, having its centre at Canterbury, and the Celtic mission, in Iona. The bishops who had been sent from one or other of these sources into the several kingdoms of the Heptarchy, gathered a body of clergy about them, with whom they lived in common at the cathedral town; thence they made missionary progresses through the towns and villages of the Saxon "bush;" returning always to the cathedral as their head-quarters and home. The national churches which sprang from these two sources were kept asunder by some differences of discipline and ceremonial rather than of doctrine. These differences were reconciled at the Council of Hertford, and all the churches there and then recognised Theodore, Archbishop of Canterbury, as the Metropolitan of all England.

To the same archbishop we owe the establishment of the parochial organisation of the Church of England, which has ever since continued.

He pointed out to the people the advantage of having the constant ministrations of a regular pastor, instead of the occasional visits of a missionary. He encouraged the thanes to provide a dwelling-house and a parcel of glebe for the clergyman's residence; and permitted that the tithe of each manor—which the thane had hitherto paid into the common church-fund of the bishop—should henceforth be paid to the resident pastor, for his own maintenance and the support of his local hospitalities and charities; and lastly, he permitted each thane to select the pastor for his own manor out of the general body of the clergy. Thus naturally grew the whole establishment of the Church of England; thus each kingdom of the Heptarchy became, in ecclesiastical language, a diocese, each manor a parish; and thus the patronage of the benefices of England became vested in the lords of the manors.

At the same time that a rector was thus gradually settled in every parish, with rights and duties which soon became defined, and sanctioned by law, the bishop continued to keep a body of clergy about him in the cathedral, whose position also gradually became defined and settled. The number of clergy in the cathedral establishment became settled, and they acquired the name of canons; they were organised into a collegiate body, with a dean and other officers. The estates of the bishops were distinguished from those of the body of canons. Each canon had his own house within the walled space about the cathedral, which was called the Close, and a share in the common property of the Chapter. Besides the canons, thus limited in number, there gradually arose a necessity for other clergymen to fulfil the various duties of a cathedral. These received stipends, and lodged where they could in the town; but in time these additional clergy also were organised into a corporation, and generally some benefactor was found to build them a quadrangle of little houses within, or hard by, the Close, and often to endow their corporation with lands and livings. The Vicars' Close at Wells is a very good and well-known example of these supplementary establishments. It is a long quadrangle, with little houses on each side, a hall at one end, and a library at the other, and a direct communication with the cathedral. There also arose in process of time many collegiate churches in the kingdom, which, resembled the cathedral establishments of secular canons in every respect, except that no bishop had his see within their church. Some of the churches of these colleges of secular canons were architecturally equal to the cathedrals. Southwell Minster, for example, is not even equalled by many of the cathedral churches. It would occupy too much space to enter into any details of the constitution of these establishments.

These canons may usually be recognised in pictures by their cos-

tume. The most characteristic features were the square cap and the furred amys. The amys was a fur cape worn over the shoulders, with a hood attached, and usually has a fringe of the tails of the fur or sometimes of little bells, and two long ends in front. In the accompanying very beautiful woodcut we have a semi-choir of secular canons, seated in their stalls in the cathedral, with the bishop in his stall at the west end. They are habited in surplices, ornamented with needlework, beneath which may be seen their robes, some pink, some blue in colour.* One in the sub-sellæ seems to have his furred amys thrown over the arm of his stall; his right-hand neighbour seems to have his hanging over his shoulder. He, and one in the upper stalls, have round skull caps (birettas); others have the hood on their heads, where it assumes a horned shape, which may be seen in other pictures of canons. The woodcut is part of a full-page illumination of the interior of a church, in the Book of Hours of Richard II., in the British Museum (Domit. xvii.).

These powerful ecclesiastical establishments continued to flourish throughout the Middle Ages; their histories must be sought in Dugdale's "Monasticon," or Britton's or Murray's "Cathedrals," or the monographs of the several cathedrals. In the registers of the cathedrals there exists also a vast amount of unpublished matter, which would supply all the little life-like details that historians usually pass by, but which we need to enable us really to enter into the cathedral life of the Middle Ages. The world is indebted to Mr. Raine for the publication of some such details from the registry of York, in the very interesting "York Fabric Rolls," which he edited for the Surtees Society.

To return to the Saxon rectors. By the end of the Saxon period of our history we find the whole kingdom divided into parishes, and in each a rector resident. Probably the rectors were often related to the lords of the manors, as is natural in the case of family livings; they were not a learned clergy; speaking generally they were a married clergy; in other respects, too, they did not affect the ascetic spirit of monasticism; they ate and drank like other people; farmed their own glebes; spent a good deal of their leisure in hawking and hunting, like their brothers, and cousins, and neighbours; but all their interests were in the people and things of their own parishes; they seem to have performed their clerical functions fairly well; and they were bountiful to the poor; in short, they seem to have had the virtues and failings of the country rectors of a hundred years ago.

After the Norman conquest several causes concurred to deprive a large

---

* It will be shown hereafter that secular priests ordinarily wore dresses of these gay colours, all the ecclesiastical canons to the contrary notwithstanding.

majority of the parishes of the advantage of the cure of well-born, well-endowed rectors, and to supply their places by ill-paid vicars and parochial chaplains. First among these causes we may mention the evil of impropriations, from which so many of our parishes are yet suffering, and of which this is a brief explanation. Just before the Norman conquest there was a great revival of the monastic principle; several new orders of monks had been founded; and the religious feeling of the age set in strongly in favour of these religious communities which then, at least, were learned, industrious, and self-denying. The Normans founded many new monasteries in England, and not only endowed them with lands and manors, but introduced the custom of endowing them also with the rectories of which they were patrons. They gave the benefice to the convent, and the convent, as a religious corporation, took upon itself the office of rector, and provided a vicar to perform the spiritual duties of the cure. The apportionment of the temporalities of the benefice usually was, that the convent took the great tithe, which formed the far larger portion of the benefice, and gave the vicar the small tithe, and (if it were not too large) the rectory-house and glebe for his maintenance. The position of a poor vicar, it is easy to see, was very different in dignity and emolument, and in prestige in the eyes of his parishioners, and the means of conferring temporal benefits upon them, from that of the old rectors his predecessors in the cure. By the time of the Reformation, about half of the livings of England and Wales had thus become impropriate to monasteries, cathedral chapters, corporations, guilds, &c.; and since the great tithe was not restored to the parishes at the dissolution of the religious houses, but granted to laymen together with the abbey-lands, about half the parishes of England are still suffering from this perversion of the ancient Saxon endowments.

Another cause of the change in the condition of the parochial clergy was the custom of papal provisors. The popes, in the thirteenth century, gradually assumed a power of nominating to vacant benefices. Gregory IX. and Innocent IV., who ruled the church in the middle of this century, are said to have presented Italian priests to all the best benefices in England. Many of these foreigners, having preferment in their own country, never came near their cures, but employed parish chaplains to fulfil their duties, and sometimes neglected to do even that. Edward III. resisted this invasion of the rights of the patrons of English livings, and in the time of Richard II. it was finally stopped by the famous statute of Præmunire (A.D. 1392).

The custom of allowing one man to hold several livings was another means of depriving parishes of a resident rector, and handing them over to the care of a curate. The extent to which this system of Pluralities was carried in the Middle Ages seems almost incredible; we even read of one man having from four to five hundred benefices.

Another less known abuse was the custom of presenting to benefices men who had taken only the minor clerical orders. A glance at the lists of incumbents of benefices in any good county history will reveal the fact that rectors of parishes were often only deacons, sub-deacons, or acolytes.* It is clear that in many of these cases—probably in the majority of them—the men had taken a minor order only to qualify themselves for holding the temporalities of a benefice, and never proceeded to the priesthood at all; they employed a chaplain to perform their spiritual functions for them, while they enjoyed the fruits of the benefice as if it were a lay fee, the minor order which they had taken imposing no restraint upon their living an entirely secular life.† It is clear that a considerable number of priests

---

* Here is a good example from Baker's "Northamptonshire:"—"Broughton Rectory: Richard Meyreul, sub-deacon, presented in 1243. Peter de Vieleston, deacon, presented in 1346-7. Though still only a deacon, he had previously been rector of Cottisbrook from 1342 to 1345."

Matthew Paris tells us that, in 1252, the beneficed clergy in the diocese of Lincoln were urgently persuaded and admonished by their bishop to allow themselves to be promoted to the grade of priesthood, but many of them refused.

The thirteenth Constitution of the second General Council of Lyons, held in 1274, ordered curates to reside and to take priests' orders within a year of their promotion; the lists above quoted show how inoperative was this attempt to remedy the practice against which it was directed.

† A writer in the *Christian Remembrancer* for July, 1856, says:—" During the fourteenth century it would seem that half the number of rectories throughout England were held by acolytes unable to administer the sacrament of the altar, to hear confessions, or even to baptise. Presented to a benefice often before of age to be ordained, the rector preferred to marry and to remain a layman, or at best a clerk in minor orders. . . . . In short, during the time to which we refer, rectories were looked upon and treated as lay fees."

were required to perform the duties of the numerous parishes whose rectors were absent or in minor orders, who seem to have been called parochial chaplains. The emolument and social position of these parochial chaplains were not such as to make the office a desirable one; and it would seem that the candidates for it were, to a great extent, drawn from the lower classes of the people. Chaucer tells us of his poor parson of a town, whose description we give below, that

"With him there was a *ploughman* was his brother."

In the Norwich corporation records of the time of Henry VIII. (1521 A.D.), there is a copy of the examination of "Sir William Green," in whose sketch of his own life, though he was only a pretended priest, we have a curious history of the way in which many a poor man's son did really attain the priesthood. He was the son of a labouring man, learned grammar at the village grammar school for two years, and then went to day labour with his father. Afterwards removing to Boston, he lived with his aunt, partly labouring for his living, and going to school as he had opportunity. Being evidently a clerkly lad, he was admitted to the minor orders, up to that of acolyte, at the hands of "Friar Graunt," who was a suffragan bishop in the diocese of Lincoln. After that he went to Cambridge, where, as at Boston, he partly earned a livelihood by his labour, and partly availed himself of the opportunities of learning which the university offered, getting his meat and drink of alms. At length, having an opportunity of going to Rome, with two monks of Whitby Abbey (perhaps in the capacity of attendant, one Edward Prentis being of the company, who was, perhaps, his fellow-servant to the two monks), he there endeavoured to obtain the order of the priesthood, which seems to have been conferred rather indiscriminately at Rome, and without a "title;" but in this he was unsuccessful. After his return to England he laboured for his living, first with his brother in Essex, then at Cambridge, then at Boston, then in London. At last he went to Cambridge again, and, by the influence of Mr. Coney, obtained of the Vice-Chancellor a licence under seal to collect subscriptions for one year towards an exhibition to complete his education in the schools, as was often done by poor scholars.* Had he obtained money enough, completed his education, and obtained ordination in due course, it would have completed the story in a regular way. But here he fell into bad hands, forged first a new poor scholar's licence, and then letters of orders, and then wandered about begging alms as an unfortunate, destitute priest; he may furnish us with a type of the idle and vagabond priests, of whom there were only too many in the country, and of whom Sir Thomas More says, " the order is rebuked by the priests' begging and lewd living, which either is fain to walk at rovers and live upon trentals (thirty days' masses), or worse, or to serve in a secular man's house."† The original of this sketch is given at length in the note below.‡

---

* See Chaucer's poor scholar, hereinafter quoted, who—

"busily gan for the soulis pray
Of them that gave him wherewith to scholaie."

† "Dialogue on Heresies," book iii. c. 12.

‡ "Norwich Corporation Records." Sessions Book of 12th Henry VII. Memorand.—That on Thursday, Holyrood Eve, in the xijth of King Henry the VIIJ., Sir William Grene, being accused of being a spy, was examined before the mayor's deputy and others, and gave the following account of himself :—" The same Sir William saieth that he was borne in Boston, in the countie of Lincoln, and about xviij yeres nowe paste or there about, he dwellyd with Stephen 'at Grene, his father at Wantlet, in the saide countie of Lincolne, and lerned gramer by the space of ij yeres; after that by v or vj yeres used labour with his said father, sometyme in husbandrie and other wiles with the longe sawe; and after that dwelling in Boston at one Genet a Grene, his aunte, used labour and other wiles goyng to scole by the space of ij years, and in that time receyved benet and accolet [the first tonsure and acolytate] in the freres Austens in Boston of one frere Graunt, then beyinge suffragan of the diocese of Lincoln ["Frere Graunt" was William Grant, titular Bishop of Pavada, in the province of Constantinople. He was Vicar of Redgewell, in Essex, and Suffragan of Ely, from 1516 to 1525.—*Stubbs's Registrum Sacrum Anglicanum*]; after that dwelling within Boston wt. one Mr. Williamson, merchaunt, half a yere, and after that dwellinge in Cambridge by the space of half a yere, used labour by the day beryng of ale and pekynge of saffron, and sometyme going to the colleges, and gate his mete and drynke of almes; and aft that the same Sir William, with ij monks of Whitby Abbey, and one Edward Prentis, went to Rome, to thentent for to have ben made p'st, to which order he could not be admitted; and after abiding in Larkington, in the countie of Essex, used labour for his levyng wt. one Thom. Grene his broder; and after that the same Sr. Will. cam to Cambridge, and ther teried iiij or v wekes, and gate his levynge of almes; and after, dwelling in Boston, agen laboured with dyvs persones by vij or viij wekes; and after that dwelling in London, in Holborn,

This custom of poor scholars gaining their livelihood and the means of prosecuting their studies by seeking alms was very common. It should be noticed here that the Church in the Middle Ages was the chief ladder by which men of the lower ranks were able to climb up—and vast numbers did climb up—into the upper ranks of society, to be clergymen, and monks, and abbots, and bishops, statesmen, and popes. Piers Ploughman, in a very illiberal strain, makes it a subject of reproach—

> " Now might each sowter * his son setten to schole,
> And each beggar's brat in the book learne,
> And worth to a writer and with a lorde dwelle,
> Or falsly to a frere the fiend for to serven.
> So of that beggar's brat a Bishop that worthen,
> Among the peers of the land prese to sythen ;
> And lordes sons lowly to the lorde's loute,
> Knyghtes crooketh hem to, and coucheth ful lowe ;
> And his sire a sowter y-soiled with grees,†
> His teeth with toyling of lether battered as a sawe."

with one Rickerby, a fustian dyer, about iij wekes, and after that the same William resorted to Cambridge, and ther met agen wt. the said Edward Prentise ; and at instance and labour of one Mr. Cony, of Cambridge, the same Will. Grene and Edward Prentise obteyned a licence for one year of Mr. Cappes, than being deputee to the Chancellor of the said univ'sitie, under his seal of office, wherby the same Will. and Edward gathered toguether in Cambridgeshire releaff toward their exhibicon to scole by the space of viij weks, and after that the said Edward departed from the company of the same William. And shortly after that, one Robert Draper, scoler, borne at Feltham, in the countee of Lincoln, accompanyed wt. the same Willm., and they forged and made a newe licence, and putte therin ther bothe names, and the same sealed wt. the seale of the other licence granted to the same Will. and Edward as is aforeseid, by which forged licence the same Will. and Robt. gathered in Cambridgeshire and other shires. At Coventre the same Will. and Robt. caused one Knolles, a tynker, dwelling in Coventre, to make for them a case of tynne mete for a seale of a title which the same Robt. Draper holdde of Makby Abbey. And after that the same Willm. and Robt. cam to Cambridge, and ther met wt. one Sr. John Manthorp, the which hadde ben lately before at Rome, and ther was made a prest ; and the same Robert Draper copied out the bulle of orders of deken, subdeken, and p'stehod for the same Willm.; and the same Willm. toke waxe, and leyed and p'st it to the prynte of the seale of the title that the said Robert had a Makby aforeseid, and led the same forged seale in the casse of tynne aforeseid, and with labels fastned ye same to his said forged bull. And sithen the same Willm. hath gathered in dyvers shires, as Northampton, Cambridge, Suffolk, and Norfolk, alway shewyng and feyning hymself that he hadde ben at Rome, and ther was made preste, by means whereof he hath receyved almes of dyvers and many persones."—*Norfolk Archæology*, vol. iv. p. 342.

* Cobbler. † Grease.

The Church was the great protector and friend of the lower classes of society, and that on the highest grounds. In this very matter of educating the children of the poor, and opening to such as were specially gifted a suitable career, we find so late as the date of the Reformation, Cranmer maintaining the rights of the poor on high grounds. For among the Royal Commissioners for reorganising the cathedral establishment at Canterbury "were more than one or two who would have none admitted to the Grammar School but sons or younger brothers of gentlemen. As for others, husbandmen's children, they were more used, they said, for the plough and to be artificers than to occupy the place of the learned sort. Whereto the Archbishop said that poor men's children are many times endowed with more singular gifts of nature, which are also the gifts of God, as eloquence, memory, apt pronunciation, sobriety, and such like; and also commonly more apt to study than is the gentleman's son, more delicately educated. Hereunto it was, on the other part, replied that it was for the ploughman's son to go to plough, and the artificer's son to apply to the trade of his parent's vocation; and the gentleman's children are used to have the knowledge of government and rule of the commonwealth. 'I grant,' replied the Archbishop, 'much of your meaning herein as needful in a commonwealth; but yet utterly to exclude the ploughman's son and the poor man's son from the benefit of learning, as though they were unworthy to have the gifts of the Holy Ghost bestowed upon them as well as upon others, was much as to say as that Almighty God should not be at liberty to bestow his great gifts of grace upon any person, but as we and other men shall appoint them to be employed according to our fancy, and not according to his most goodly will and pleasure, who giveth his gifts of learning and other perfections in all sciences unto all kinds and states of people indifferently."

Besides the rectors and vicars of parishes, there was another class of beneficed clergymen in the middle ages, who gradually became very numerous, viz., the chantry priests. By the end of the ante-Reformation period there was hardly a church in the kingdom which had not one or more chantries founded in it, and endowed for the perpetual maintenance of a chantry priest, to say mass daily for ever for the soul's health of the founder and his family. The churches of the large and wealthy towns had sometimes ten or twelve such chantries. The chantry chapel was sometimes built on to the parish church, and opening into it; sometimes it was only a corner of the church screened off from the rest of the area by open-work wooden screens. The chantry priest had sometimes a chantry-house to live in, and estates for his maintenance, sometimes he had only an annual income, charged on the estate of the founder. The chantries were suppressed, and their endowments confiscated, in the reign of Edward VI., but the chantry chapels still remain as part of our parish churches, and where the parclose screens have long since been removed, the traces of the chantry altar are still very frequently apparent to the eye of the ecclesiastical antiquary. Sometimes more than one priest was provided for by wealthy people. Richard III. commenced the foundation of a chantry of one hundred chaplains, to sing masses in the cathedral church of York; the chantry-house was begun, and six altars were erected in York Minster, when the king's death at Bosworth Field interrupted the completion of the magnificent design.*

We have next to add to our enumeration of the various classes of the mediæval clergy another class of chaplains, whose duties were very nearly akin to those of the chantry priests. These were the guild priests. It was the custom throughout the middle ages for men and women to associate themselves in religious guilds, partly for mutual assistance in temporal matters, but chiefly for mutual prayers for their welfare while living, and for their soul's health when dead. These guilds usually maintained a chaplain, whose duty it was to celebrate mass daily for the brethren and sisters of the guild. These guild priests must have been numerous, *e.g.*, we learn from Blomfield's "Norfolk," that there were at the Reformation ten guilds in Windham Church, Norfolk, seven at Hingham, seven at Swaffham, seventeen at Yarmouth, &c. Moreover, a guild, like a chantry, had sometimes more than one guild priest. Leland tells us the guild of St. John's, in St. Botolph's Church, Boston, had ten priests, "living in a fayre house at the west end of the parish church yard." In St. Mary's Church, Lichfield, was a guild which had five priests.†

---

* York Fabric Rolls, p. 87, note.   † "Church of our Fathers," ii. 441.

The rules of some of these religious guilds may be found in Stow's "Survey of London," *e.g.*, of St. Barbara's guild in the church of St. Katherine, next the Tower of London (in book ii. p. 7 of Hughes's edition.)

We find bequests to the guild priests, in common with other chaplains, in the ancient wills, *e.g.*, in 1541, Henry Waller, of Richmond, leaves "to every gyld prest of thys town, vi^d. y^t ar at my beryall."*

Dr. Rock says,† "Besides this, every guild priest had to go on Sundays and holy days, and help the priests in the parochial services of the church in which his guild kept their altar. All chantry priests were bidden by our old English canons to do the same." The brotherhood priest of the guild of the Holy Trinity, at St. Botolph's, in London, was required to be "meke and obedient unto the qu'er in alle divine servyces duryng hys time, as custome is in the citye amonge alle other p'sts." Sometimes a chantry priest was specially required by his foundation deed to help in the cure of souls in the parish, as in the case of a chantry founded in St. Mary's, Maldon, and Little Bentley, Essex;‡ sometimes the chantry chapel was built in a hamlet at a distance from the parish church, and was intended to serve as a chapel of ease, and the priest as an assistant curate, as at Foulness Island and Billericay, both in Essex.

But it is very doubtful whether the chantry priests generally considered themselves bound to take any share in the parochial work of the parish.§ In the absence of any cure of souls, the office of chantry or guild priest was easy, and often lucrative; and we find it a common subject of complaint, from the fourteenth to the sixteenth centuries, that it was preferred to a cure of souls; and that even parochial incumbents were apt to leave their parishes in the hands of a parochial chaplain, and seek for themselves a chantry or guild, or one of the temporary engagements to celebrate annals, of which there were so many provided by the wills of which we shall shortly have to speak. Thus Chaucer reckons, among the virtues of his poore parson, that—

---

* Richmond Wills.
† "Church of our Fathers," ii. 408, note.
‡ Newcourt's "Repertorium."
§ Johnson's "Canons," ii. 421. Ang. Cath. Lib. Edition.

> "He set not his benefice to hire,
> And let his shepe accomber in the mire,
> And runne to London to Saint Poule's,
> To seken him a chauntrie for soules,
> Or with a brotherhood to be with-held,
> But dwelt at home, and kepte well his fold."

So also Piers Ploughman—

> " Parsons and parisshe preistes, pleyned hem to the bisshope,
> That hire parishes weren povere sith the pestilence tyme,
> To have a licence and leve at London to dwelle
> And syngen ther for symonie, for silver is swete."

Besides the chantry priests and guild priests, there was a great crowd of priests who gained a livelihood by taking temporary engagements to say masses for the souls of the departed. Nearly every will of the period we are considering provides for the saying of masses for the soul of the testator. Sometimes it is only by ordering a fee to be paid to every priest who shall be present at the funeral, sometimes by ordering the executors to have a number of masses, varying from ten to ten thousand, said as speedily as may be; sometimes by directing that a priest shall be engaged to say mass for a certain period, varying from thirty days to forty or fifty years. These casual masses formed an irregular provision for a large number of priests, many of whom performed no other clerical function, and too often led a dissolute as well as an idle life. Archbishop Islip says in his " Constitutions :"[*]—" We are certainly informed, by common fame and experience, that modern priests, through covetousness and love of ease, not content with reasonable salaries, demand excessive pay for their labours, and receive it; and do so despise labour and study pleasure, that they wholly refuse, as parish priests, to serve in churches or chapels, or to attend the cure of souls, though fitting salaries are offered them, that they may live in a leisurely manner, by celebrating annals for the quick and dead ; and so parish churches and chapels remain unofficiated, destitute of parochial chaplains, and even proper curates, to the grievous danger of souls." Chaucer has introduced one of this class into the Canon's Yeoman's tale :—

---

[*] Johnson's " Canons," ii. 421.

> " In London was a priest, an annueller,*
> That therein dwelled hadde many a year,
> Which was so pleasant and so serviceable
> Unto the wife there as he was at table
> That she would suffer him no thing to pay
> For board ne clothing, went he never so gay,
> And spending silver had he right ynoit." †

Another numerous class of the clergy were the domestic chaplains. Every nobleman and gentleman had a private chapel in his own house, and an ecclesiastical establishment attached, proportionate to his own rank and wealth. In royal houses and those of the great nobles, this private establishment was not unrequently a collegiate establishment, with a dean and canons, clerks, and singing men and boys, who had their church and quadrangle within the precincts of the castle, and were maintained by ample endowments. The establishment of the royal chapel of St. George, in Windsor Castle, is, perhaps, the only remaining example. The household book of the Earl of Northumberland gives us very full details of his chapel establishment, and of their duties, and of the emoluments which they received in money and kind. They consisted of a dean, who was to be a D.D. or LL.D. or B.D., and ten other priests, and eleven gentlemen and six children, who composed the choir.‡ But country gentle-

---

* One who sang annual or yearly masses for the dead.
† Enough.
‡ Chapel of Earl of Northumberland, from the Household Book of Henry Algernon, fifth Earl of Northumberland, born 1477, and died 1527. ("Antiq. Repertory," iv. 242.):
  First, a preist, a doctour of divinity, a doctor of law, or a bachelor of divinitie, to be dean of my lord's chapell.
  It. A preist for to be surveyour of my lorde's landes.
  It. A preist for to be secretary to my lorde.
  It. A preist for to be amner to my lorde.
  It. A preist for to be sub-dean for ordering and keaping the queir in my lorde's chappell daily.
  It A preist for a riding chaplein for my lorde.
  It. A preist for a chaplein for my lorde's eldest son, to waite upon him daily.
  It. A preist for my lorde's clark of the closet.
  It. A preist for a maister of gramer in my lorde's hous.
  It. A preist for reading the Gospell in the chapel daily.
  It. A preist for singing of our Ladies' mass in the chapell daily.
The number of these persons as chapleins and preists in houshould are xi. [The

men of wealth often maintained a considerable chapel establishment.

The gentlemen and children of my lorde's chappell which be not appointed to attend at no time, but only in exercising of Godde's service in the chapell daily at matteins, Lady-mass, hyhe-mass, evensong, and compeynge :—
First, a bass.
It. A second bass.
Third bass.
A maister of the childer, or counter-tenor.
Second and third counter-tenor.
A standing tenour.
A second, third, and fourth standing tenour.
The number of theis persons, as gentlemen of my lorde's chapell, xi.

Children of my lorde's chappell :—
Three trebles and three second trebles.
In all six.

A table of what the Earl and Lady were accustomed to offer at mass on all holydays "if he keep chappell," of offering and annual lights paid for at Holy Blood of Haillis (Hales, in Gloucestershire), our Lady of Walsingham, St. Margaret in Lincolnshire, our Lady in the Whitefriars, Doncaster, of my lord's foundation :—
Presents at Xmas to Barne, Bishop of Beverley and York, when he comes, as he is accustomed, yearly.
Rewards to the children of his chapell when they do sing the responde called Exaudivi at the mattynstime for xi. in vespers upon Allhallow Day, 6s. 8d.
On St. Nicholas Eve, 6s. 8d.
To them of his lordshipe's chappell if they doe play the play of the Nativitie upon Xmas Day in the mornynge in my lorde's chapell before his lordship, xxs.
For singing "Gloria in Excelsis" at the mattens time upon Xmas Day in the mg.
To the Abbot of Miserewle (Misrule) on Xmas.
To the yeoman or groom of the vestry for bringing him the hallowed taper on Candlemas Day.
To his lordship's chaplains and other servts. that play the Play before his lordship on Shrofetewsday at night, xxs.
That play the Play of Resurrection upon Estur Daye in the mg. in my lorde's chapell before his lordship.
To the yeoman or groom of the vestry on Allhallows Day for syngynge for all Cristynne soles the saide nyhte to it be past mydnyght, 3s. 4d.

The Earl and Lady were brother and sister of St. Christopher Gilde of Yorke, and pd. 6s. 8d. each yearly, and when the Master of the Gild brought my lord and my lady for their lyverays a yard of narrow violette cloth and a yard of narrow rayed cloth, 13s. 4d. (*i.e.*, a yard of each to each).
And to Procter of St. Robert's of Knasbrughe, when my lord and lady were brother and sister, 6s. 8d. each.

At pp. 272-278, is an elaborate programme of the ordering of my lord's chapel for

Henry Machyn, in his diary,* tells us, in noticing the death of Sir Thomas Jarmyn, of Rushbrooke Hall, Suffolk, in 1552, that "he was the best housekeeper in the county of Suffolk, and kept a goodly chapel of singing men." Knights and gentlemen of less means, or less love of goodly singing men, were content with a single priest as chaplain.† Even wealthy yeomen and tradesmen had their domestic chaplain. Sir Thomas More says,‡ there was "such a rabel [of priests], that every mean man must have a priest in his house to wait upon his wife, which no man almost lacketh now." The chapels of the great lords were often sumptuous buildings, erected within the precincts, of which St. George's, Windsor, and the chapel within the Tower of London may supply examples. Smaller chapels erected within the house were still handsome and ecclesiastically-designed buildings, of which examples may be found in nearly every old castle and manor house which still exists ; *e.g.*, the chapel of Colchester Castle of the twelfth century, of Ormsbro Castle of late twelfth century, of Beverstone Castle of the fourteenth century, engraved in Parker's "Domestic Architecture," III. p. 177; that at Igtham Castle of the fifteenth century, engraved in the same work, III. p. 173; that at Haddon

the various services, from which it appears that there were organs, and several of the singing men played them in turn.

At p. 292 is an order about the washing of the linen for the chapel for a year. Surplices washed sixteen times a year against the great feasts—eighteen surplices for men, and six for children—and seven albs to be washed sixteen times a year, and "five aulter-cloths for covering of the alters" to be washed sixteen times a year.

Page 285 ordered that the vestry stuff shall have at every removal (from house to house) one cart for the carrying the nine antiphoners, the four grailles, the hangings of the three altars in the chapel, the surplices, the altar-cloths in my lord's closet and my ladie's, and the sort (suit) of vestments and single vestments and copes "·accopeed" daily, and all other my lord's chapell stuff to be sent afore my lord's chariot before his lordship remove.

[Cardinal Wolsey, after the Earl's death, intimated his wish to have the books of the Earl's chapel, which a note speaks of as fine service books.—P. 314.]

* Edited by Mr. Gough Nichols for the Camden Society.

† Richard Burré, a wealthy yeoman and " ffarmer of the parsonage of Sowntyng, called the Temple, which I holde of the howse of St. Jonys," in 19 Henry VIII. wills that Sir Robert Bechton, " my chaplen, syng ffor my soule by the span of ix. yers ;" and further requires an obit for his soul for eleven years in Sompting Church.—("Notes on Wills," by M. A. Lower, "Sussex Archæological Collections," iii. p. 112.)

‡ "Dialogue of Heresies," iii. c. 12.

Hall of the fifteenth century. In great houses, besides the general chapel, there was often a small oratory besides for the private use of the lord of the castle, in later times called a closet; sometimes another oratory for the lady, as in the case of the Earl of Northumberland.* In some of these domestic chapels we find a curious internal arrangement; the western part of the apartment is divided into two stories by a wooden floor. This is the case also with the chapel of the preceptory of Chobham, Northumberland, of the Coyston Almshouses at Leicester (Parker's "Dom. Arch"). It is the case in one of the chapels in Tewkesbury Abbey Church, and in the case of a priory church in Norway. In some cases it was probably to accommodate the tenants of different stories of the house. The frequency with which in later times the lord of the house had a private gallery in the chapel (a similar arrangement occasionally occurs in parish churches) leads us to conjecture that in these cases of two floors the upper floor was for the members of the family, and the lower for the servants of the house. These chapels were thoroughly furnished with vessels, books, robes, and every usual ornament, and every object and appliance necessary for the performance of the offices of the church, with a splendour proportioned to the means of the master of the house. From the Household Book of the Earl of Northumberland, we gather that the chapel had three altars, and that my lord and my lady had each a closet, *i.e.*, an oratory, in which there were other altars. The chapel was furnished with hangings, and had a pair of organs. There were four antiphoners and four grails—service books—which were so famous for their beauty, that, at the earl's death, Wolsey intimated his wish to have them. We find mention, too, of the suits of vestments and single vestments, and copes and surplices, and altar-cloths for the five altars. All these things were under the care of the yeoman of the vestry, and were carried about with the earl at his removals from one to another of his houses. Minute catalogues and descriptions of the furniture of these domestic chapels may also be found in the inventories attached to ancient wills.†

---

* See note on previous page, "the altar-cloths in my lord's closet and my ladie's."
† Of the inventories to be found in wills, we will give only two, of the chapels of

We shall give hereafter a picture of one of these domestic chaplains, viz., of Sir Roger, chaplain of the chapel of the Earl of Warwick at Flamstead. There is a picture of another chaplain of the Earl of Warwick in the MS. Life of R. Beauchamp, Earl of Warwick (Julius E. IV.), where the earl and his chaplain are represented sitting together at dinner.

Besides the clergy who were occupied in these various kinds of spiritual work, there were also a great number of priests engaged in secular occupations. Bishops were statesmen, generals, and ambassadors, employing suffragan bishops* in the work of their dioceses. Priests were engaged in many ways in the king's service, and in that of noblemen and others. Piers Ploughman says:—

> " Somme serven the kyng, and his silver tellen,
> In cheker and in chauncelrie, chalangen his dettes,
> Of wardes and of wardemotes, weyves and theyves.
> And some serven as servantz, lordes and ladies,
> And in stede of stywardes, sitten and demen."

The domestic chaplains were usually employed more or less in secular duties. Thus such services are regularly allotted to the eleven priests in the chapel of the Earls of Northumberland; one was surveyor of my lord's lands, and another my lord's secretary. Mr. Christopher Pickering, in his will

---

country gentlemen. Rudulph Adirlay, Esq. of Colwick (" Testamenta Eboracensia," p. 30), Nottinghamshire, A.D. 1429, leaves to Alan de Cranwill, his chaplain, a little missal and another book, and to Elizabeth his wife " the chalice, vestment, with two candelabra of laton, and the little missal; with all other ornaments belonging to my chapel." In the inventories of the will of John Smith, Esq., of Blackmore, Essex, A.D. 1543, occur : " In the chappell chamber—Item a long setle yoyned. In the chappell— Item one aulter of yoyner's worke. Item a table with two leaves of the passion gilt. Item a long setle of waynscott. Item a bell hanging over the chapel. Chappell stuff: Copes and vestments thre. Aulter fronts foure. Corporall case one ; and dyvers peces of silk necessary for cusshyons v. Thomas Smith (to have) as moche as wyll serve his chappell, the resydue to be solde by myn executours." The plate and candlesticks of the chapel are not specially mentioned ; they are probably included among the plate which is otherwise disposed of, and " the xiiiij latyn candlestyckes of dyvers sorts," elsewhere mentioned.—*Essex Archæological Society's Transactions*, vol. iii. p. 60.

* See the Rev. W. Stubbs's learned and laborious " Registrum Sacrum Anglicanum," which gives lists of the suffragan (as well as the diocesan) bishops of the Church of England.

(A.D. 1542), leaves to " my sarvands John Dobson and Frances, xx^s. a-pece, besydes ther wages ; allso I gyve unto Sir James Edwarde my sarvand," &c. ; and one of the witnesses to the will is " Sir James Edwarde, preste," who was probably Mr. Pickering's chaplain.* Sir Thomas More says, every man has a priest to wait upon his wife ; and in truth the chaplain seems to have often performed the duties of a superior gentleman usher. Nicholas Blackburn, a wealthy citizen of York, and twice Lord Mayor, leaves (A.D. 1431-2) a special bequest to his wife " to find her a gentlewoman, and a priest, and a servant."† Lady Elizabeth Hay leaves bequests in this order, to her son, her chaplain, her servant, and her maid.‡

---

* " Richmondshire Wills," p. 34.   † " Test. Ebor.," 220.
‡ Ibid., p. 39.

CHAPTER II.

CLERKS IN MINOR ORDERS.

IT is necessary, to a complete sketch of the subject of the secular clergy, to notice, however briefly, the minor orders, which have so long been abolished in the reformed Church of England, that we have forgotten their very names. There were seven orders through which the clerk had to go, from the lowest to the highest step in the hierarchy. The Pontifical of Archbishop Ecgbert gives us the form of ordination for each order; and the ordination ceremonies and exhortations show us very fully what were the duties of the various orders, and by what costume and symbols of office we may recognise them. But these particulars are brought together more concisely in a document of much later date, viz., in the account of the degradation from the priesthood of Sir William Sawtre, the first of the Lollards who died for heresy, in the year 1400 A.D., and a transcript of it will suffice for our present purpose. The archbishop, assisted by several bishops, sitting on the bishop's throne in St. Paul's—Sir William Sawtre standing before him in priestly robes—proceeded to the degradation as follows:—" In the name, &c., we, Thomas, &c., degrade and depose you from the order of priests, and in token thereof we take from you the paten and the chalice, and deprive you of all power of celebrating mass; we also strip you of the chasuble, take from you the sacerdotal vestment, and deprive you altogether of the dignity of the priesthood. Thee also, the said William, dressed in the habit of a deacon, and having the book of the gospels in thy hands, do we degrade and depose from the order of deacons, as a condemned and relapsed heretic; and in token hereof we take from thee the book of the gospels, and the stole, and deprive thee of the power of reading the gospels. We degrade thee from the order of subdeacons, and in token thereof take from thee the albe and maniple. We degrade thee from the order of an acolyte, taking from thee in token thereof this small pitcher and taper staff. We degrade thee from the order of an exorcist, and take from thee in token thereof the book of exorcisms. We degrade thee from the order of reader, and take from thee in token thereof the book of divine lessons. Thee also, the said William Sawtre, vested in a surplice as an ostiary,* do we degrade from that order, taking from thee the surplice and the keys of the church. Furthermore, as a sign of actual degradation, we have caused the crown and clerical tonsure to be shaved off in our presence, and to be entirely obliterated like a layman; we have also caused a woollen cap to be put upon thy head, as a secular layman."

The word *clericus*—clerk—was one of very wide and rather vague significance, and included not only the various grades of clerks in orders, of whom we have spoken, but also all men who followed any kind of occupation which involved the use of reading and writing; finally, every man who could read might claim the "benefit of clergy," *i.e.*, the legal immunities of a clerk. The word is still used with the same comprehensiveness and vagueness of meaning. Clerk in Orders is still the legal description of a clergyman; and men whose occupation is to use the pen are still called clerks, as lawyers' clerks, merchants' clerks, &c. Clerks were often employed in secular occupations; for example, Alan Middleton, who was

---

* In a pontifical of the middle of the fifteenth century, in the British Museum, (Egerton, 1067) at f. 19, is an illumination at the beginning of the service for ordering an ostiary, in which the act is represented. The bishop, habited in a green chasuble and white mitre, is delivering the keys to the clerk, who is habited in a surplice over a black cassock, and is tonsured. At f. 35 of the same MS. is a pretty little picture, showing the ordination of priests; and at f. 44 v., of the consecration of bishops. Other episcopal acts are illustrated in the same MS.: confirmation at f. 12; dedication of a church, f. 100; consecration of an altar, f. 120; benediction of a cemetery, f. 149 v.; consecration of chalice and paten, f. 163; reconciling penitents, f. 182 and f. 186 v.; the "feet-washing," f. 186.

employed by the convent of St. Alban's to collect their rents, and who is represented on page 63 ante in the picture from their "Catalogus Benefactorum" (Nero D. vii., British Museum), is tonsured, and therefore was a clerk. Chaucer gives us a charming picture of a poor clerk of Oxford, who seems to have been a candidate for holy orders, and is therefore germane to our subject:—

> "A clerke there was of Oxenforde also,
> That unto logike hadde long ygo,
> As lene was his horse as is a rake,
> And he was not right fat, I undertake,
> But looked holwe and thereto soberly.
> Ful thredbare was his overest courtepy,*
> For he hadde getten him yet no benefice,
> Ne was nought worldly to have an office.†
> For him was lever han at his beddes hed
> A twenty bokes, clothed in black or red,
> Of Aristotle and his philosophie,
> Than robes riche, or fidel or sautrie.
> But all be that he was a philosophre,
> Yet hadde he but little gold in cofre,
> But all that he might of his frendes hente,‡
> On bokes and on lerning he it spente;
> And besely gan for the soules praye
> Of hem that yave him wherewith to scholaie,§
> Of studie toke he moste cure and hede.
> Not a word spake he more than was nede,
> And that was said in forme and reverence,
> And short and quike, and ful of high sentence.
> Souning in moral vertue was his speche,
> And gladly wolde he lerne and gladly teche."

In the Miller's Tale Chaucer gives us a sketch of another poor scholar of Oxford. He lodged with a carpenter, and

> "A chambre had he in that hostelerie,
> Alone withouten any compaynie,
> Ful fetisly 'ydight with herbés sweet."

His books great and small, and his astrological apparatus

---

* Outer short cloak.
† Was not sufficiently a man of the world to be fit for a secular occupation.
‡ Obtain. § To pursue his studies.

"On shelvés couched at his beddé's head,
His press ycovered with a falding red,
And all about there lay a gay sautrie
On which he made on nightés melodie
So swetély that all the chamber rung,
And *Angelus ad Virginem* he sung."

We give a typical illustration of the class from one of the characters in a Dance of Death at the end of a Book of the Hours of the Blessed Virgin Mary, in the British Museum. It is described beneath as " Un Clerc." *

One of this class was employed by every parish to perform certain duties on behalf of the parishioners, and to assist the clergyman in certain functions of his office. The Parish Clerk has survived the revolution which swept away the other minor ecclesiastical officials of the middle ages, and still has his legal status in the parish church. Probably many of our readers will be surprised to hear that the office is an ancient one, and will take interest in a few original extracts which throw light on the subject.

A Clerk.

In the wills he frequently has a legacy left, together with the clergy— *e.g.*, " Item I leave to my parish vicar iij$^{s.}$ iiij$^{d.}$ Item I leave to my parish clerk xij$^{d.}$ Item I leave to every chaplain present at my obsequies and mass iiij$^{d.}$" (Will of John Brompton, of Beverley, merchant, 1443.)† Elizabeth del Hay, in 1434, leaves to "every priest ministering at my obsequies vi$^{d.}$; to every parish clerk iiij$^{d.}$; to minor clerks to each one ij$^{d.}$"‡ Hawisia Aske, of York, in 1450-1 A.D., leaves to the " parish chaplain of St. Michael iij$^{s.}$ iiij$^{d.}$; to every chaplain of the said church xx$^{d.}$; to

---

* For another good illustration of a clerk of time of Richard II. see the illumination of that king's coronation in the frontispiece of the MS. Royal, 14, E iv., where he seems to be in attendance on one of the bishops. He is habited in blue cassock, red liripipe, black urse, with penner and inkhorn.

† " Test. Ebor.," vol. ii. p. 98.   ‡ Ibid., vol. ii. p. 38.

the parish clerk of the said church xx^d; to the sub-clerk of the same church x^d."* John Clerk, formerly chaplain of the chapel of the Blessed Mary Magdalen, near York, in 1449, leaves to "the parish clerk of St. Olave, in the suburbs of York, xij^d; to each of the two chaplains of the said church being present at my funeral and mass iiij^d; to the parish clerk of the said church iiij^d; to the sub-clerk of the said church ij^d; among the little boys of the said church wearing surplices iiij^d, to be distributed equally."† These extracts serve to indicate the clerical staff of the several churches mentioned.

From other sources we learn what his duties were. In 1540 the parish of Milend, near Colchester, was presented to the archdeacon by the rector, because in the said church there was "nother clerke nor sexten to go withe him in tyme of visitacion [of the sick], nor to helpe him say masses, nor to rynge to servyce."‡ And in 1543 the Vicar of Kelveden, Essex, complains that there is not "caryed holy water,§ nor ryngyng to evensonge accordyng as the clerke shuld do, with other dutees to him belongyng." ‖ In the York presentations we find a similar complaint at Wyghton in 1472; they present that the parish clerk does not perform his services as he ought, because when he ought to go with the vicar to visit the sick, the clerk absents himself, and sends a boy with the vicar.¶ The clerk might be a married man, for in 1416 Thomas Curtas, parish clerk of the parish of St. Thomas the Martyr, is presented, because with his wife he has hindered, and still hinders, the parish clerk of St. Mary Bishophill, York [in which parish he seems to have lived] from entering his house on the Lord's days with holy water, as is the custom of the city. Also it is complained that the said Thomas and his wife refuse to come to hear divine service at their parish church, and withdraw their oblat ions. In the Royal MS., 10, E iv., is a series of illustrations of a mediæval tale, which

---

* "Test. Ebor.," vol. ii. p. 143. † Ibid., vol. ii. p. 149.
‡ Archdeacon Hale's "Precedents in Criminal Causes," p. 113.
§ From the duty of carrying holy water, mentioned here and in other extracts, the clerk derived the name of *aqua bajulus*, by which he is often called, *e.g.*, in many of the places in Archdeacon Hale's " Precedents in Criminal Causes."
‖ Ibi l., p. 122.   ¶ York Fabric Rolls, p. 257.   ** Ibid., p. 248.

turns on the adventures of a parish clerk, as he goes through the parish aspersing the people with holy water. Two of the pictures will suffice to show the costume and the holy water-pot and aspersoir, and to indicate

The Parish Clerk sprinkling the Cook.

how he went into all the rooms of the house—now into the kitchen sprinkling the cook, now into the hall sprinkling the lord and lady who are at breakfast. In the woodcut on p. 241, will be seen how he precedes an

The Parish Clerk sprinkling the Knight and Lady.

ecclesiastical procession, sprinkling the people on each side as he goes. The subsequent description (p. 221) of the parish clerk Absolon, by Chaucer, indicates that sometimes—perhaps on some special festivals—the clerk went about censing the people instead of sprinkling them.

To continue the notes of a parish clerk's duties, gathered from the churchwardens' presentations: at Wyghton, in 1510, they find "a faut with our parish clerk yt he hath not done his dewtee to ye kirk, yt is to say, ryngyng of ye morne bell and ye evyn bell; and also another fawt [which may explain the former one], he fyndes yt pour mene pays hym not his wages."* At Cawood, in 1510 A.D., we find it the duty of the parish clerk "to keepe ye clok and ryng corfer [curfew] at dew tymes appointed by ye parrish, and also to ryng ye day bell." † He had his desk in church near the clergyman, perhaps on the opposite side of the chancel, as we gather from a presentation from St. Maurice, York, in 1416, that the desks in the choir on both sides, especially where the parish chaplain and parish clerk are accustomed to sit, need repair.‡ A story in Matthew Paris§ tells us what his office was worth: "It happened that an agent of the pope met a petty clerk of a village carrying water in a little vessel, with a sprinkler and some bits of bread given him for having sprinkled some holy water, and to him the deceitful Roman thus addressed himself: 'How much does the profit yielded to you by this church amount to in a year?' To which the clerk, ignorant of the Roman's cunning, replied, 'To twenty shillings I think;' whereupon the agent demanded the per-centage the pope had just demanded on all ecclesiastical benefices. And to pay that small sum this poor man was compelled to hold schools for many days, and by selling his books in the precincts, to drag on a half-starved life." The parish clerks of London formed a guild, which used to exhibit miracle plays at its annual feast, on the green, in the parish of St. James, Clerkenwell. The parish clerks always took an important part in the conduct of the miracle plays; and it was natural that when they united their forces in such an exhibition on behalf of their guild the result should be an exhibition of unusual excellence. Stow tells us that in 1391 the guild performed before the king and queen and whole court three days successively, and that in 1409 they produced a play of the creation of the world, whose representation occupied

---

* York Fabric Rolls, p. 265. † Ibid., p. 266.
‡ Ibid., p. 248. § Bohn's Edition, ii. 388.

eight successive days. The Passion-play, still exhibited every ten years at Ober-Ammergau, has made all the world acquainted with the kind of exhibition in which our forefathers delighted. These miracle-plays still survive also in Spain, and probably in other Roman Catholic countries.

Chaucer has not failed to give us, in his wonderful gallery of contemporary characters (in the Miller's Tale), a portrait of the parish clerk:—

> "Now was ther of that churche a parish clerk,
> The which that was ycleped Absolon.
> Crulle was his here,* and as the gold it shon,
> And strouted as a fanne large and brode;
> Ful streight and even lay his jolly shode.
> His rode† was red, his eyen grey as goos,
> With Poules windowes carven on his shoos,
> In hosen red he went ful fetisly,‡
> Yclad he was ful smal and proprely,
> All in a kirtle of a light waget,§
> Ful faire and thicke ben the pointes set.
> An' therupon he had a gay surplise,
> As white as is the blossome upon the rise.‖
> A mery child he was, so God me save,
> Wel coud he leten blod, and clippe, and shave,
> And make a chartre of lond and a quitance;
> In twenty manere could he trip and dance,
> (After the scole of Oxenforde tho)
> And playen songes on a smal ribible,¶
> Therto he song, sometime a loud quinible,¶
> And as wel could he play on a giterne.
> In all the toun n'as brewhouse ne taverne
> That he ne visited with his solas,
> Ther as that any galliard tapstere was.
>   This Absolon, that joly was and gay,
> Goth with a censor on the holy day,
> Censing the wives of the parish faste,**
> And many a lovely loke he on hem caste.
>   *   *   *   *
> Sometime to shew his lightnesse and maistrie,
> He plaieth Herode on a skaffold hie."

---

* Hair.   † Complexion.   ‡ Neatly.
§ *Watchet*, a kind of cloth.   ‖ Small twigs or trees.   ¶ Musical instruments.
** As the parish clerk of St. Mary, York, used to go to the people's houses with holy water on Sundays.

CHAPTER III.

THE PARISH PRIEST.

WE shall obtain further help to a comprehension of the character, and position, and popular estimation of the mediæval seculars—the parish priests—if we compare them first with the regulars—the monks and friars—and then with their modern representatives the parochial clergy. One great point of difference between the regulars and the seculars was that the monks and friars affected asceticism, and the parish priests did not. The monks and friars had taken the three vows of absolute poverty, voluntary celibacy, and implicit obedience to the superior of the convent. The parish priests, on the contrary, had their benefices and their private property; they long resisted the obligations of celibacy, which popes and councils tried to lay upon them; they were themselves spiritual rulers in their own parishes, subject only to the constitutional rule of the bishop. The monks professed to shut themselves up from the world, and to mortify their bodily appetites in order the better, as they considered, to work out their own salvation. The friars professed to be the schools of the prophets, to have the spirit of Nazariteship, to be followers of Elijah and John Baptist, to wear sackcloth, and live hardly, and go about as preachers of repentance. The secular clergy had no desire and felt no need to shut themselves up from the world like monks; they did not feel called upon, with the friars, to imitate John Baptist, "neither eating nor drinking," seeing that a greater than he came " eating and drinking" and living the common life of men. They rather looked upon Christian priests and clerks as occupying the place of the priests and Levites of the ancient church, set apart to minister in holy things like them, but not condemned to poverty or asceticism any more than they were. The difference told unfavourably for the parish clergy in the popular estimation; for the unreasoning crowd is always impressed by the dramatic exhibition of austerity of life and the profession of extraordinary sanctity, and undervalues the virtue which is only seen in the godly regulation of a life of ordinary every-day occupations. The lord monks were the aristocratic order of the clergy. Their convents were wealthy and powerful, their minsters and houses were the glory of the land, their officials ranked with the nobles, and the greatness of the whole house reflected dignity upon each of its monks.

The friars were the popular order of the clergy. The Four Orders were great organizations of itinerant preachers; powerful through their learning and eloquence, their organization, and the Papal support; cultivating the favour of the people by which they lived by popular eloquence and demagogic arts.

Between these two great classes stood the secular clergy, upon whom the practical pastoral work of the country fell. A numerous body, but disorganized; diocesan bishops acting as statesmen, and devolving their ecclesiastical duties on suffragans; rectors refusing to take priests' orders, and living like laymen; the majority of the parishes practically served by parochial chaplains; every gentleman having his own chaplain dependent on his own pleasure; hundreds of priests engaged in secular occupations.

Between the secular priests and the friars, as we have seen, pp. 46 *et seq.*, there was a direct rivalry and a great deal of bitter feeling. The friars accused the parish priests of neglect of duty and ignorance in spiritual things and worldliness of life, and came into their parishes whenever they pleased, preaching and visiting from house to house, hearing confessions and prescribing penances, and carrying away the offerings of the people. The parish priests looked upon the friars as intruders in their parishes, and accused them of setting their people against them and undermining their spiritual influence; of corrupting discipline, by receiving the confessions of those who were ashamed to confess to their pastor who knew them, and enjoining light penances in order to encourage people to come to them; and lastly, of using all the arts of low popularity-seeking in order to extract gifts and offerings from their people.

We have already given one contemporary illustration of this from Chaucer, at p. 46 *ante*. We add one or two extracts from Piers Ploughman's Vision. In one place of his elaborate allegory he introduces Wrath, saying :—

> "I am Wrath, quod he, I was sum tyme a frere,
> And the convent's gardyner for to graff impes*
> On limitoures and listers lesyngs I imped
> Till they bere leaves of low speech lordes to please
> And sithen thier blossomed abrode in bower to hear shriftes.
> And now is fallen therof a fruite, that folk have well liever
> Shewen her shriftes to hem than shryve hem to ther parsones.
> And now, parsons have perceyved that freres part with hem,
> These possessioners preache and deprave freres,
> And freres find hem in default, as folk beareth witness."—v. 143.

And again on the same grievance of the friars gaining the confidence of the people away from their parish priests—

> "And well is this y-holde : in parisches of Engelonde,
> For persones and parish prestes : that shulde the peple shryve,
> Ben curatoures called : to know and to hele.
> Alle that ben her parishens : penaunce to enjoine,
> And shulden be ashamed in her shrifte : an shame maketh hem wende,
> And fleen to the freres : as fals folke to Westmynstere,
> That borwith and bereth it thider."†

When we compare the mediæval seculars with the modern clergy, we find that the modern clergy form a much more homogeneous body. In the mediæval seculars the bishop was often one who had been a monk or friar ; the cathedral clergy in many dioceses were regulars. Then, besides the parsons and parochial chaplains, who answer to our incumbents and curates, there were the chantry and gild priests, and priests who "lived at rovers on trentals;" the great number of domestic chaplains must have considerably affected the relations of the parochial clergy to the gentry. Of the inferior ecclesiastical people, deacons, sub-deacons, acolytes, readers, exorcists, and ostiaries it is probable that in an ordinary parish there

---

* Grafted lies.
† As debtors flee to sanctuary at Westminster, and live on what they have borrowed, and set their creditors at defiance.

would be only a parish clerk and a boy-acolyte; in larger churches an ostiary besides, answering to our verger, and in cathedrals a larger staff of minor officials; but it is doubtful whether there was any real working staff of sub-deacons, readers, exorcists, any more than we in these days have a working order of deacons; men passed through those orders on their way upwards to the priesthood, but made no stay in them.

But a still greater difference between the mediæval secular clergy and the modern parochial clergy is in their relative position with respect to society generally. The homogeneous body of "the bishops and clergy" are the only representatives of a clergy in the eyes of modern English society; the relative position of the secular clergy in the eyes of the mediæval world was less exclusive and far inferior. The seculars were only one order of the clergy, sharing the title with monks and friars, and they were commonly held as inferior to the one in wealth and learning, and to the other in holiness and zeal.

Another difference between the mediæval seculars and the modern clergy is in the superior independence of the latter. The poor parochial chaplain was largely dependent for his means of living on the fees and offerings of his parishioners. The domestic chaplain was only an upper servant. Even the country incumbent, in those feudal days when the lord of the manor was a petty sovereign, was very much under the influence of the local magnate.

In some primitive little villages, where the lord of the manor continues to be the sovereign of his village, it is still the fashion for the clergyman not to begin service till the squire comes. The Book of the Knight of La Tour Landry gives two stories which serve to show that the deference of the clergyman to the squire was sometimes carried to very excessive lengths in the old days of which we are writing. " I have herde of a knight and of a lady that in her youthe delited hem to rise late. And so they used longe, tille many tymes that thei lost her masse, and made other of her parisshe to lese it, for the knight was lorde and patron of the chirche, and therfor the priest durst not disobeye hym. And so it happed that on a Sunday the knight sent unto the chirche that thei shulde abide hym. And whane he come, it was passed none, wherfor thir might not that day have no masse, for every man saide it was passed tyme of the day, and therfor thei durst not singe. And so that Sunday the knight, the lady, and alle the parisshe was without masse, of the whiche the pepelle were sori, but thir must needs suffre." And on a night there came a vision to the parson, and the same night the knight and lady dreamed a dream. And the parson came to the knight's house, and he told him his vision, and the priest his, of which they greatly marvelled, for their dreams were like. " And the priest said unto the knight, 'There is hereby in a forest an holy ermyte that canne telle us what this avision menithe.' And than thei yede to hym, and tolde it hym fro point to point, and as it was. And the wise holi man, the which was of blessed lyff, expounded and declared her avision."

The other story is of "a ladi that dwelled faste by the chirche, that toke every day so long time to make her redy that it made every Sunday the person of the chirche and the parisshenes to abide after her. And she happed to abide so longe on a Sunday that it was fer dayes, and every man said to other, 'This day we trow shall not this lady be kemed and arraied.'"

The condition of the parochial clergy being such as we have sketched, it might seem as if the people stood but a poor chance of being Christianly and virtuously brought up. But when we come to inquire into that part of the question the results are unexpectedly satisfactory. The priests in charge of parishes seem, on the whole, to have done their duty better than we should have anticipated; and the people generally had a knowledge of the great truths of religion, greater probably than is now generally possessed—it was taught to them by the eye in sculptures, paintings, stained glass, miracle plays; these religious truths were probably more constantly in their minds and on their lips than is the case now—they occur much more frequently in popular literature; and though the people were rude and coarse and violent and sensual enough, yet it is probable that religion was a greater power among them generally than it is now; there was probably more crime, but less vice; above all, an elevated sanctity in individuals was probably more common in those times than in these.

One interesting evidence of the actual mode of pastoral ministrations in those days is the handbooks, which were common enough, teaching the parish priest his duties. The Early English Text Society has lately done us a service by publishing one of these manuals of "Instructions for Parish Priests," which will enable us to give some notes on the subject. "Great numbers," says the editor, "of independent works of this nature were produced in the Middle Ages. There is probably not a language or dialect in Europe that has not now, or had not once, several treatises of this nature among its early literature. The growth of languages, the Reformation, and the alteration in clerical education consequent on that great revolution, have caused a great part of them to perish or become forgotten. A relic of this sort fished up from the forgotten past is very useful to us as a help towards understanding the sort of life our fathers lived. To many it will seem strange that these directions, written without the least thought of hostile criticism, when there was no danger in plain speaking, and no inducements to hide or soften down, should be so free from superstition. We have scarcely any of the nonsense which some people still think made up the greater part of the religion of the Middle Ages, but instead thereof good sound morality, such as it would be pleasant to hear preached at the present day."

The book in question is by John Myrk, a canon regular of St. Austin, of Lilleshall, in Shropshire; the beautiful ruins of his monastery may still be seen in the grounds of the Duke of Sutherland's shooting-box at Lilleshall. He tells us that he translated it from a Latin book called "Pars Oculi." It is worthy of note that a former prior of Lilleshall, Johannes Miræus, had written a work on the same subject, called "Manuale Sacerdotis," to which John Myrk's bears much resemblance, both in subject and treatment. The editor's sketch of the argument of the "Instructions to Parish Priests" will help us to give a sufficient idea of its contents for our present purpose.

The author begins by telling the parish priest what sort of man he himself should be. Not ignorant, because

"Whenne the blynde ledeth the blynde
Into the dyche they fallen both."

He must himself be an example to his people :—

> " What thee nedeth hem to teche
> And whyche thou muste thy self be.
> For lytel is worth thy prechynge
> If thou be of evyle lyvynge."

He must be chaste, eschew lies and oaths, drunkenness, gluttony, pride, sloth, and envy. Must keep from taverns, trading, wrestling, and shooting, and the like manly sports; from hunting, hawking, and dancing. Must not wear cutted clothes or pyked shoes, or dagger, but wear becoming clothes, and shave his crown and beard. Must be given to hospitality, both to poor and rich, read his psalter, and remember doomsday; return good for evil, eschew jesting and ribaldry, despise the world, and follow after virtue.

The priest must not be content with knowing his own duties. He must be prepared to teach those under his charge all that Christian men and women should do and believe. We are told that when any one has done a sin he must not continue long with it on his conscience, but go straight to the priest and confess it, lest he should forget before the great shriving time at Eastertide. Pregnant women, especially, are to go to their shrift, and receive the Holy Communion at once. Our instructor is very strict on the duties of midwives—women they were really in those days, and properly licensed to their office by the ecclesiastical authorities. They are on no account to permit children to die unbaptized. If there be no priest at hand, they are to administer that sacrament themselves if they see danger of death. They must be especially careful to use the right form of words, such as our Lord taught; but it does not matter whether they say them in Latin or English, or whether the Latin be good or bad, so that the intention be to use the proper words. The water, and the vessel that contained it, are not to be again employed in domestic use, but to be burned or carried to the church and cast into the font. If no one else be at hand, the parents themselves may baptize their children. All infants are to be christened at Easter and Whitsuntide in the newly-blessed fonts, if there have not been necessity to administer the Sacrament before. Godparents are to be careful to teach their godchildren the *Pater Noster*, *Ave Maria*, and *Credo;* and are not to be sponsors to their godchildren at their Confirmation, for they have already contracted a spiritual relationship. Before weddings banns are to be asked on three holidays, and all persons who contract irregular marriages, and the priests, clerks, and others that help thereat, are cursed for the same. The real presence of the body and blood of our Saviour in the Sacrament of the Altar is to be fully held; but the people are to bear in mind that the wine and water given them after they have received Communion is not a part of the Sacrament. It is an important thing to behave reverently in church, for the church is God's house, not a place for idle prattle. When people go there they are not to jest, or loll against the pillars and walls, but kneel down on the floor and pray to their Lord for mercy and grace. When the Gospel is read they are to stand up, and sign themselves with the cross; and when they hear the Sanctus bell ring, they are to kneel and worship their Maker in the Blessed Sacrament. All men are to show reverence when they see the priest carrying the Host to the sick. He is to teach them the "Our Father," and "Hail, Mary," and "I believe," of which metrical versions are given, with a short exposition of the Creed.

The author gives some very interesting instructions about churchyards, which show that they were sometimes treated with shameful irreverence. It was not for want of good instructions that our ancestors, in the days of the Plantagenets, played at rustic games, and that the gentry held their manorial courts, over the sleeping-places of the dead.

Of witchcraft we hear surprisingly little. Myrk's words are such that one might almost think he had some sceptical doubts on the subject. Not so with usury: the taking interest for money, or lending anything to get profit thereby, is, we are shown, "a synne full grevus."

After these and several more general instructions of a similar character, the author gives a very good commentary on the Creed, the Sacraments, the Commandments, and the deadly sins. The little tract ends with a few words of instruction to priests as to the "manner of saying mass, and of giving Holy Communion to the sick." On several subjects the author gives very detailed instructions and advice as to the best way of dealing with people, and his counsels are so right and sensible, that they might well be read now, not out of mere curiosity, but for profit. Here is his conclusion, as a specimen of the English and versification :—

" Hyt ys I-made hem* to schonne
That have no bokes of here† owne,
And other that beth of mene lore
That wolde fayn conne ‡ more,
And those that here-in learnest most,
Thonke yerne the Holy Gost,
That geveth wyt to eche mon
To do the gode that he con,
And by hys travayle and hys dede
Geveth hym heven to hys mede;
The mede and the joye of heven lyht
God us graunte for hys myht. Amen."

That these instructions were not thrown away upon the mediæval parish priests we may infer from Chaucer's beautiful description of the poor parson of a town, who was one of his immortal band of Canterbury Pilgrims, which we here give as a fitting conclusion of this first part of our subject:—

" A good man there was of religioun,
That was a poure persone of a toun;
But riche he was of holy thought and werk.
He was also a lerned man, a clerk,
That Criste's gospel trewely wolde preche,
His parishens devoutly wolde he teche.
Benigne he was and wonder diligent,
And in adversite ful patient;
And such he was yproved often sithes.
Full loth were he to cursen for his tithes,
But rather wolde he given out of doubte
Unto his poure parishens about,
Of his offering and eke of his substance.
He could in litel thing have suffisance.
Wide was his parish, and houses fer asunder,
But he ne left nought for no rain ne thunder,
In sikenesse and in mischief to visite
The farthest in his parish much and lite,§
Upon his fete, and in his hand a staff.
This noble ensample to his sheep he gaf ‖
That first he wrought, and afterward he taught.
Out of the gospel he the wordes caught,
And this figure he added yet thereto,
That if gold rusté what should iren do ?

---

* Them. † Their. ‡ Know.
§ Great and little. ‖ Gave.

> For if a priest be foul, on whom we trust,
> No wonder is a léwéd man to rust;
> Well ought a preest ensample for to give,
> By his clenenesse how his shepe shulde live.
> He sette not his benefice to hire,
> And lefte his sheep accumbered in the mire,
> And ran unto London, unto Seint Poules,
> To seeken him a chanterie for souls,
> Or with a brotherhede to be withold,
> But dwelt at home and kepté well his fold.
> He was a shepherd and no mercenare;
> And though he holy were and vertuous,
> He was to sinful men not despitous, *
> Ne of his speché dangerous ne digne,†
> But in his teaching discrete and benigne.
> To drawen folk to heaven with fairénesse,
> By good ensample was his businesse.
> But it were any persone obstinat,
> What so he were of highe or low estate,
> Him wolde he snibben‡ sharply for the nones,
> A better preest I trow that nowhere none is.
> He waited after no pomp ne reverence,
> Ne maked him no spiced§ conscience,
> But Christés lore, and his apostles twelve,
> He taught, but first he followed it himself."

Thus, monk, and friar, and hermit, and recluse, and rector, and chantry priest, played their several parts in mediæval society, until the Reformation came and swept away the religious orders and their houses, the chantry priests and their superstitions, and the colleges of seculars, with all their good and evil, and left only the parish churches and the parish priests remaining, stripped of half their tithe, and insufficient in number, in learning, and in social *status* to fulfil the office of the ministry of God among the people. Since then, for three centuries the people have multiplied, and the insufficiency of the ministry has been proportionately aggravated. It has been left to our day to complete the work of the Reformation by multiplying bishops and priests, and creating an order of deacons, re-distributing the ancient revenues and supplying what more is needed, and by effecting a general reorganization of the ecclesiastical establishment to adapt it to the actual spiritual needs of the people.

---

* Angry.   † Difficult nor proud.   ‡ Smite, rebuke.   § Scrupulous.

CHAPTER IV.

CLERICAL COSTUME.

WE proceed to give some notes on the costume of the secular clergy; first the official costume which they wore when performing the public functions of their order, and next the ordinary costume in which they walked about their parishes and took part in the daily affairs of the mediæval society of which they formed so large and important a part. The first branch of this subject is one of considerable magnitude; it can hardly be altogether omitted in such a series of papers as this, but our limited space requires that we should deal with it as briefly as may be.

Representations of the pope occur not infrequently in ancient paintings. His costume is that of an archbishop, only that instead of the usual mitre he wears a conical tiara. In later times a cross with three crossbars has been used by artists as a symbol of the pope, with two crossbars of a patriarch, and with one crossbar of an archbishop; but Dr. Rock assures us that the pope never had a pastoral staff of this shape, but of one crossbar only; that patriarchs of the Eastern Church used the cross of two bars, but never those of the Western Church; and that the example of Thomas-à-Becket with a cross of two bars, in Queen Mary's Psalter (Royal, 2 B. vii.) is a unique example (and possibly an error of the artist's). A representation of Pope Leo III. from a contemporary picture is engraved in the "Annales Archæologique," vol. viii. p. 257; another very complete and clear representation of the pontifical costume of the time of Innocent III. is engraved by Dr. Rock (" Church of our Fathers," p. 467) from a fresco painting at Subiaco, near Rome. Another representation, of late thirteenth-century date, is given in the famous MS. called the "Psalter of Queen Mary," in the British Museum (Royal, 2 B. vii.); there the pope is in nothing more than ordinary episcopal costume—alb, tunic, chasuble, without the pall—and holds his cross-staff of only one bar in his right hand, and his canonical tiara has one crown round the base. Beside him stands a bishop in the same costume, except that he wears

Pope, Cardinal, and Bishop.

the mitre and holds a crook. A good fourteenth-century representation of a pope and cardinals is in the MS. August. V. f. 459. We give a woodcut of the fifteenth century, from a MS. life of Richard Beauchamp, Earl of Warwick, in the British Museum (Julius E. iv. f. 207); the subject is the presentation of the pilgrim earl to the pope, and it enables us to bring into one view the costumes of pope, cardinal, and bishop. A later picture of considerable artistic merit may be found in Hans Burgmair's "Der Weise König," where the pope, officiating at a royal marriage, is habited in a chasuble, and has the three crowns on his tiara.

The cardinalate is not an ecclesiastical "order." Originally the name was applied to the priests of the chief churches of Rome, who formed the chapter of the Bishop of Rome. In later times they were the princes of the papal sovereignty, and the dignity was conferred not only upon the highest order of the hierarchy, but upon priests, deacons,* and even upon men who had only taken minor orders to qualify themselves for holding office in the papal kingdom. The red hat, which became their distinctive symbol, is said to have been given them first by Innocent VI. at the Council of Lyons in 1245; and De Curbio says they first wore it in 1246, at the interview between the pope and Louis IX. of France. A representation of it may be seen in the MS. Royal, 16 G. vi., which is engraved in the "Pictorial History of England," vol. i. 869. Another very clear and good representation of the costume of a cardinal is in the plate in Hans Burgmair's "Der Weise König," already mentioned; a group of them is on the right side of the drawing, each with a fur-lined hood on his head, and his hat over the hood. It is not the hat which is peculiar to cardinals, but the colour of it, and the number of its tassels. Other ecclesiastics wore the hat of the same shape, but only a cardinal wears it of scarlet. Moreover, a priest wore only one tassel to each string, a bishop three, a cardinal seven. It was not the hat only which was scarlet. Wolsey, we read, was in the habit of dressing entirely in scarlet for his ordinary costume. In the Decretals of Pope Gregory, Royal, 10 E. iv. f. 3 v., are representations of cardinals in red gown and hood and hat. On the following page they are represented, in *pontificalibus*.

The archbishop wore the habit of a bishop, his differences being in the crosier and pall.† His crozier had a cross head instead of a curved head

---

* Cardinal Otho, the Papal legate in England in the time of Henry III., was a deacon (Matthew Paris, Sub. Ann. 1237); Cardinal Pandulph, in King John's time, was a sub-deacon (R. Wendover, Sub. Ann. 1212).

† There is a very fine drawing of an archbishop in *pontificalibus* of the latter part of the thirteenth century in the MS. Royal, 2 A. f. 219 v.

like the bishop's. Over the chasuble he wore the pall, which was a flat circular band, or collar, placed loosely round the shoulders, with long ends hanging down behind and before, made of lambs' wool, and marked with a number of crosses. Dr. Rock has engraved[*] two remarkably interesting early representations of archbishops of Ravenna, in which a very early form of the pontifical garments is given, viz., the sandals, alb, stole, tunic, chasuble, pall, and tonsure. They are not represented with either mitre or staff. Other representations of archbishops may be found of the eleventh century in the Bayeux tapestry, and of the thirteenth in the Royal MS., 2 B. vii. In the Froissart MS., Harl. 4,380, at f. 170, is a fifteenth-century representation of the Archbishop of Canterbury in ordinary dress—a lavender-coloured gown and red liripipe.

The bishop wore the same habit as the priest, with the addition of sandals, gloves, a ring, the pastoral staff with a curved head, and the mitre. The chasuble was only worn when celebrating the Holy Communion; on any other ceremonial occasion the cope was worn, *e.g.*, when in choir, as in the woodcut on p. 197: or when preaching, as in a picture in the Harl. MS. 1319, engraved in the "Pictorial History of England," vol. i. 806; or when attending parliament. In illuminated MSS. bishops are very commonly represented dressed in alb and cope only, and this seems to have been their most usual habit. If the bishop were a monk or friar he wore the cope over the robe proper to his order. We might multiply indefinitely references to representations of bishops and other ecclesiastics in the illuminated MS. We will content ourselves with one reference to a beautifully drawn figure in the psalter of the close of the 14th century (Harl. 2,897, f. 380). In the early fourteenth-century MS. (Royal, 14 E. iii. at ff. 16 and 25), we find two representations of a bishop in what we may suppose was his ordinary unofficial costume; he wears a blue-grey robe and hood with empty falling sleeves, through which appear the blue sleeves of his under robe; it is the ordinary civil and clerical costume of the period, but he is marked out as a bishop by a white mitre. In the Pontifical of the middle of the fifteenth century, already referred to (Eger-

---

[*] "Church of our Fathers," i. 319.

ton, 1067) at f. 186 in the representation of the ceremony of the feet-washing, the bishop in a long black sleeveless robe* over a white alb, and a biretta.

The earliest form of the mitre was that of a simple cap, like a skull-cap, of which there is a representation, giving in many respects a clear and elaborate picture of the episcopal robes, in a woodcut of St. Dunstan in the MS. Cotton, Claudius A. iii.† In this early shape it has already the infulæ—two narrow bands hanging down behind. In the twelfth century it is in the form of a large cap, with a depression in the middle, which produces two blunt horns at the sides. There is a good representation of this in the MS. Cotton, Nero C. iv. f. 34, which has been engraved by Strutt, Shaw, and Dr. Rock.

In the Harl. MS. 5,102, f. 17, is a picture of the entombment of an archbishop, in which is well shown the transition shape of the mitre from the twelfth century, already described, to the cleft and pointed shape which was used in the thirteenth and fourteenth centuries. The depression is here deepened into a partial cleft, and the mitre is put on so that the horns come before and behind, instead of at the sides, but the horns are still blunt and rounded. The archbishop's gloves in this picture are white, like the mitre, and in shape are like mittens, *i.e.*, not divided into fingers.

The shape in the thirteenth and fourteenth century presented a stiff low triangle in front and behind, with a gap between them. It is well shown in a MS. of the close of the twelfth century, Harl. 2,800, f. 6, and, in a shape a little further developed, in the pictures in the Royal MS., 2 B. vii., already noticed. In the fifteenth century the mitre began to be made taller, and with curved sides, as seen in the beautiful woodcut of a bishop and his canons in choir given in our last chapter, p. 197. The latest example in the English Church is in the brass of Archbishop Harsnett, in Chigwell Church, in which also occur the latest examples of the alb, stole, dalmatic, and cope.

The pastoral staff also varied in shape at different times. The earliest

---

* In a Spansh Book of Hours (Add. 1819—3), at f. 86 v., is a representation of an ecclesiastic in a similar robe of dark purple with a hood, he wears a cardinal's hat and holds a papal tiara in his hand.

† Engraved by Dr. Rock, ii. 97.

examples of it are in the representations of St. Mark and St. Luke,* in the " Gospels of MacDurnan," in the Lambeth Library, a work of the middle of the ninth century. St. Luke's staff is short, St. Mark's longer than himself; in both cases the staff terminates with a plain, slightly reflexed curve of about three-fourths of a circle. Some actual examples of the metal heads of these Celtic pastoral staves remain ; one is engraved in the " Archæologia Scotica," vol. ii., another is in the British Museum ; that of the abbots of Clonmacnoise, and that of the ancient bishops of Waterford, are in the possession of the Duke of Devonshire. They were all brought together in 1863 in the Loan Exhibition at South Kensington. One of the earliest English representations of the staff is in the picture of the consecration of a church, in a MS. of the ninth century, in the Rouen Library, engraved in the " Archæologia," vol. xxv. p. 17, in the " Pictorial History of England," and by Dr. Rock, ii. p. 24. Here the staff is about the length of an ordinary walking-stick, and is terminated by a round knob.

Odo, Bishop of Bayeux, is represented on his great seal with a short staff, with a tau-cross or crutch head. An actually existing staff of this shape, which belonged to Gerard, Bishop of Limoges, who died in 1022, is engraved in the " Annales Archæologique," vol. x. p. 176. The staves represented in illuminations of the twelfth and thirteenth centuries have usually a plain spiral curve of rather more than a circle;† in later times they were ornamented with foliage, and sometimes with statuettes, and were enamelled and jewelled. Numerous representations and actual examples exist; some may be seen in the South Kensington Museum. From early in the fourteenth century downward, a napkin of linen or silk is often found attached by one corner to the head of the staff, whose origin and meaning seem to be undetermined.

The official costume of the remaining orders, together with the symbols significant of their several offices, are well brought out in the degradation of W. Sawtre, already given at p. 214.

Some of the vestments there mentioned may need a few words of explana-

---

* Engraved in the *Archæological Journal*, vii. 17 and 19.

† A plain straight staff is sometimes seen in illuminations being put into a bishop's grave ; such staves have been actually found in the coffins of bishops.

tion. The alb was a kind of long coat with close fitting sleeves made of white* linen, and usually, at least during the celebration of divine service, ornamented with four to six square pieces of cloth of gold, or other rich stuff, or of goldsmith's work, which were placed on the skirt before and behind, on the wrist of each sleeve, and on the back and breast. The dalmatic of the deacon was a kind of tunic, reaching generally a little below the knees, and slit some way up the sides, and with short, broad sleeves; it was usually ornamented with a broad hem, which passed round the side slits. The sub-deacon's tunicle was like the dalmatic, but rather shorter, and less ornamented. The cope was a kind of cloak, usually of rich material, fastened across the chest by a large brooch; it was worn by priests in choir and in processions, and on other occasions of state and ceremony. The chasuble was the Eucharistic vestment; originally it was a circle of rich cloth with a slit in the middle, through which the head was passed, and then it fell in ample folds all round the figure. Gradually it was made oval in shape, continually decreasing in width, so as to leave less of the garment to encumber the arms. In its modern shape it consists of two stiff rectangular pieces of cloth, one piece falling before, the other behind, and fastened together at the shoulders of the wearer. The ancient inventories of cathedrals, abbeys, and churches show us that the cope and chasuble were made in every colour, of every rich material, and sometimes embroidered and jewelled. Indeed, all the official robes of the clergy were of the costliest material and most beautiful workmanship which could be obtained. England was celebrated for its skill in the arts employed in their production; and an anecdote of the time of Henry III. shows us that the English ecclesiastical vestments excited admiration and cupidity even at Rome. Their richness had nothing to do with personal pride or luxury on the part of the priests. They were not the property of the clergy, but were generally presented to the churches, to which they belonged in perpetuity; and they were made thus costly on the principle of honouring the divine worship. As men gave their costliest material and

---

* The alb was often of coloured materials. We find coloured albs in the mediæval inventories. In Louandre's "Arts Somptuaires," vol. i. xi. siecle, is a picture of the canons of St. Martin of Tours in blue albs. Their costume is altogether worth notice.

noblest Art for the erection of the place in which it was offered, so also for the appliances used in its ministration, and the robes of the ministrants.

In full sacerdotal habit the priests wore the apparelled alb, and stole, and over that the dalmatic, and either the cope or the chasuble over all, with the amys thrown back like a hood over the cope or chasuble. Representations of priests *in pontificalibus* abound in illuminated MSS., and in their monumental effigies, to such an extent that we need hardly quote any particular examples. Representations of the inferior orders are comparatively rare. Examples of deacons may be found engraved in Dr. Rock's "Church of our Fathers," i. 376, 378, 379, 443, and 444. Two others of early fourteenth-century date may be found in the Add. MS. 10,294, f. 72, one wearing a dalmatic of cloth of gold, the other of scarlet, over the alb. Two others of the latter part of the fourteenth century are seen in King Richard II.'s Book of Hours (Dom. A. xvii. f. 176), one in blue dalmatic embroidered with gold, the other red embroidered with gold. A monumental effigy of a deacon under a mural arch at Avon Dassett, Warwickshire, was referred to by Mr. M. H. Bloxam, in a recent lecture at the Architectural Museum, South Kensington. The effigy, which is of the thirteenth century, is in alb, stole, and dalmatic. We are indebted to Mr. Bloxam for a note of another mutilated effigy of a deacon of the fourteenth century among the ruins of Furness Abbey; he is habited in the alb only, with a girdle round the middle, whose tasselled knobs hang down in front. The stole is passed across the body from the left shoulder, and is fastened together at the right hip.

Dr. Rock, vol. i. p. 384, engraves a very good representation of a ninth-century sub-deacon in his tunicle, holding a pitcher in one hand and an empty chalice in the other; and in vol. ii. p. 89, an acolyte, in what seems to be a surplice, with a scarlet hood—part of his ordinary costume —over it, the date of the drawing being *cir.* 1395 A.D. We have already noted the costume of an ostiary at p. 215. In the illuminations we frequently find an inferior minister attending upon a priest when engaged in his office, but in many cases it is difficult to determine whether he is deacon, sub-deacon, or acolyte, *e.g.*—in the early fourteenth-century MS., Add. 10,294, at f. 72, is a priest officiating at a funeral, attended by a minister, who is habited in a pink under robe—his ordinary dress—and over it a short white garment with wide loose sleeves, which may be either a deacon's dalmatic, or a sub-deacon's tunic, or an acolyte's surplice. In the Add. MS. 10,293, at f. 154, is a representation of a priest celebrating mass in a hermitage, with a minister kneeling behind him, habited in a white alb only, holding a lighted taper. Again, in the MS. Royal, 14 E. iii. f. 86, is a picture of a prior dressed like some of the canons in

Coronation Procession of Charles V. of France.

our woodcut from Richard II.'s Book of Hours, in a blue under robe, white surplice, and red stole crossed over the breast, and his furred hood on his head; he is baptizing a heathen king, and an attendant minister, who is dressed in the ordinary secular habit of the time, stands beside, holding the chrismatory. In the same history of Richard Earl of Warwick which we have already quoted, there is at f. 213 v., a boy in a short surplice with a censer. In the early fourteenth-century MS., Royal, 14 E. iii. at f. 84 v., is a picture of a bishop anointing a king; an attendant minister, who carries a holy water vessel and aspersoir, is dressed in a surplice over a pink tunic. The surplice is found in almost as many and as different shapes in the Middle Ages as now; sometimes with narrow sleeves and tight up to the neck; sometimes with shorter and wider sleeves and falling low at the neck; sometimes longer and sometimes shorter in the skirt; never, however, so long as altogether to hide the cassock beneath. In addition to the references already given, it may be sufficient to name as further authorities for ecclesiastical costumes generally:—for Saxon times, the Benedictional of St. Ethelwold, engraved in the Archæologia; for the thirteenth century, Queen Mary's Psalter, Royal, 2 B. vii.; for the fourteenth, Royal, 20, c. vii.; for the fifteenth century, Lydgate's "Life of St. Edmund;" for the sixteenth century, Hans Burgmaier's "Der Weise König," and the various works on sepulchral monuments and monumental brasses.

The accompanying woodcut from Col. Johnes's Froissart, vol. i. p. 635, representing the coronation procession of Charles V. of France, will help us to exhibit some of the orders of the clergy with their proper costume and symbols. First goes the aquabajalus, in alb, sprinkling holy water; then a cross-bearer in cassock and surplice; then two priests, in cassock, surplice, and cope; then follows a canon in his cap (biretta), with his furred amys over his arm.*

But the clergy wore these robes only when actually engaged in some official act. What was their ordinary costume is generally little known, and it is a part of the subject in which we are especially interested in these papers. From the earliest times of the English Church downwards it was considered by the rulers of the Church that clergymen ought to be distinguished from laymen not only by the tonsure, but also by their dress. We do not find that any uniform habit was prescribed to them, such as distinguished the regular orders of monks and friars from the laity, and from one another; but we gather from the canons of synods, and the injunctions of bishops, that the clergy were expected to wear their clothes

---

* For another ecclesiastical procession which shows very clearly the costume of the various orders of clergy, see Achille Jubinal's "Anciennes Tapisseries," plate ii.

not too gay in colour, and not too fashionably cut; that they were to abstain from wearing ornaments or carrying arms; and that their horse furniture was to be in the same severe style. We also gather from the frequent repetition of canons on the subject, and the growing earnestness of their tone, that these injunctions were very generally disregarded. We need not take the reader through the whole series of authorities which may be found in the various collections of councils; a single quotation from the injunctions of John (Stratford) Archbishop of Canterbury, A.D. 1342, will suffice to give us a comprehensive sketch of the general contents of the whole series.

"The external costume often shows the internal character and condition of persons; and though the behaviour of clerks ought to be an example and pattern of the laity, yet the abuse of clerks, which has gained ground more than usually in these days in tonsures, in garments, in horse trappings, and other things, has now generated an abominable scandal among the people, while persons holding ecclesiastical dignities, rectories, honourable prebends, and benefices with cure of souls, even when ordained to holy orders, scorn to wear the crown (which is the token of the heavenly kingdom and of perfection), and, using the distinction of hair extended almost to the shoulders like effeminate persons, walk about clothed in a military rather than a clerical outer habit, viz., short, or notably scant, and with excessively wide sleeves, which do not cover the elbows, but hang down, lined, or, as they say, turned up with fur or silk, and hoods with tippets of wonderful length, and with long beards; and rashly dare, contrary to the canonical sanctions, to use rings indifferently on their fingers; and to be girt with zones, studded with precious stones of wonderful size, with purses engraved with various figures, enamelled and gilt, and attached to them (*i.e.* to the girdle), with knives, hanging after the fashion of swords, also with buskins red and even checked, green shoes and peaked and cut* in many ways, with cruppers (*croperiis*) to their saddles, and horns hanging to their necks, capes and cloaks furred openly at the edges to such an extent, that little or no distinction appears of clerks from laymen, whereby

---

* *Incisis*, cut and slashed so as to show the lining.

they render themselves, through their demerits, unworthy of the privilege of their order and profession.

"We therefore, wishing henceforward to prevent such errors, &c., command and ordain, that whoever obtain ecclesiastical benefices in our province, especially if ordained to holy orders, wear clerical garments and tonsure suitable to their status; but if any clerks of our province go publicly in an outer garment short, or notably scant, or in one with long or excessively wide sleeves, not touching the elbow round about, but hanging, with untonsured hair and long beard, or publicly wear their rings on their fingers, &c., if, on admonition, they do not reform within six months, they shall be suspended, and shall only be absolved by their diocesan, and then only on condition that they pay one-fifth of a year's income to the poor of the place through the diocesan," &c., &c.

The authorities tried to get these canons observed. Grostête sent back a curate who came to him for ordination " dressed in rings and scarlet like a courtier." * Some of the vicars of York Cathedral † were presented in 1362 A.D. for being in the habit of going through the city in short tunics, ornamentally trimmed, with knives and baselards ‡ hanging at their girdles. But the evidence before us seems to prove that it was not only the acolyte-rectors, and worldly-minded clerics, who indulged in such fashions, but that the secular clergy generally resisted these endeavours to impose upon them anything approaching to a regular habit like those worn by the monks and friars, and persisted in refusing to wear sad colours, or to cut their coats differently from other people, or to abstain from wearing a gold ring or an ornamented girdle. In the drawings of the secular clergy in the illuminated MSS., we constantly find them in the ordinary civil costume. Even in representations of the different orders and ranks of the secular clergy drawn by friendly hands, and intended to represent them *comme il faut*, we find them dressed in violation of the canons.

* Monumenta Franciscana, lxxxix. Master of the Rolls' publications.
† York Fabric Rolls, p. 243.
‡ This word, which will frequently occur, means a kind of ornamental dagger, which was worn hanging at the girdle in front by civilians, and knights when out of armour. The instructions to parish priests, already quoted, says—
    In honeste clothes thow muste gon
    Baselard ny bawdryke were thou non.

We have already had occasion to notice a bishop in a blue-grey gown and hood, over a blue under-robe; and a prior performing a royal baptism, and canons performing service under the presidency of their bishop, with the blue and red robes of every-day life under their ritual surplices. The MSS. furnish us with an abundance of other examples, *e.g.*—In the early fourteenth-century MS., Add. 10,293, at f. 131 v., is a picture showing "how the priests read before the barony the letter which the false queen sent to Arthur." One of the persons thus described as priests has a blue gown and hood and black shoes, the other a claret-coloured gown and hood and red shoes.

But our best examples are those in the book (Cott. Nero D. vii.) before quoted, in which the grateful monks of St. Alban's have recorded the names and good deeds of those who had presented gifts or done services to the convent. In many cases the scribe has given us a portrait of the benefactor in the margin of the record; and these portraits supply us with an authentic gallery of typical portraits of the various orders of society of the time at which they were executed. From these we have taken the three examples we here present to the reader. On f. 100 v. is a portrait of one Lawrence, a clerk, who is dressed in a brown robe; another clerk, William by name, is in a scarlet robe and hood; on f. 93 v., Leofric, a deacon, is in a blue robe and hood. The accompanying woodcut, from folio 105, is Dns. Ricardus de Threton, sacerdos,—Sir Richard de Threton, priest,—who was executor of Sir Robert de Thorp, knight, formerly chancellor of the king, and who gave twenty marks to the convent. Our woodcut gives only the outlines of the full-length portrait. In the original the robe and hood are of full bright blue, lined with white; the under sleeves,

Dns. Ricardus de Threton, Sacerdos.

which appear at the wrists, are of the same colour; and the shoes are red. At f. 106 v. is Dns. Bartholomeus de Wendone, rector of the church of Thakreston, and the character of the face leads us to think that it may have been intended for a portrait. His robe and hood and sleeves are scarlet, with black shoes. Another rector, Dns. Johannes Rodland (at f. 105), rector of the church of Todyngton, has a green robe and scarlet hood. Still another rector, of the church of Little Waltham, is represented half-length in pink gown and purple hood. On f. 108 v. is the full-length portrait which is here represented. It is of Dns. Rogerus, chaplain

Dns. Barth. de Wendone, Rector.   *Dns. Rogerus, Capellanus.*

of the chapel of the Earl of Warwick, at Flamsted. Over a scarlet gown, of the same fashion as those in the preceding pictures, is a pink cloak lined with blue; the hood is scarlet, of the same suit as the gown; the buttons at the shoulder of the cloak are white, the shoes red. It will be seen also that all three of these clergymen wear the moustache and beard.

Dominus Robertus de Walsham, precentor of Sarum (f. 100 v.), is in his choir habit, a white surplice, and over it a fur amys fastened at the throat with a brooch. Dns. Robertus de Hereforde, Dean of Sarum

(f. 101), has a lilac robe and hood fastened by a gold brooch. There is another dean, Magister Johnnes Appleby, Dean of St. Paul's, at f. 105, whose costume is not very distinctly drawn. It may be necessary to assure some of our readers, that the colours here described were not given at the caprice of a limner wishing to make his page look gay. The portraits were perhaps imaginary, but the personages are habited in the costume proper to their rank and order. The series of Benedictine abbots and

John Ball, Priest.

monks in the same book are in black robes; other monks introduced are in the proper habit of their order; a king in his royal robes; a knight sometimes in armour, sometimes in the civil costume of his rank, with a sword by his side, and a chaplet round his flowing hair; a lady in the fashionable dress of the time; a burgher in his proper habit, with his hair cut short. And so the clergy are represented in the dress which they usually wore; and, for our purpose, the pictures are more valuable than if they were actual portraits of individual peculiarities of costume, because we are the more sure that they give us the usual and recognised costume of the several characters. Indeed, it is a rule, which has very rare exceptions, that the mediæval illuminators represented contemporary subjects with scrupulous accuracy. We give another representation from the picture of John Ball, the priest who was concerned in Wat Tyler's rebellion, taken from a MS. of Froissart's Chronicle, in the Bibliothèque Impériale at Paris. The whole picture is interesting; the background is a church, in whose churchyard are three tall crosses. Ball is preaching from the pulpit of his saddle to the crowd of insurgents who occupy the left side of the picture. In the Froissart MS. Harl. 4,380, at f. 20, is a picture of *un vaillant homme et clerque nommé Maistre Johan Warennes*, preaching against Pope Boniface; he is in a pulpit panelled in green and gold, with a pall hung over the front, and the people sit on benches before him; he is habited in a blue robe and hood lined with white.

The author of Piers Ploughman, carping at the clergy in the latter half of the fourteenth century, says it would be better

"If many a priest bare for their baselards and their brooches,
A pair of beads in their hand, and a book under their arm.
Sire* John and Sire Geffrey hath a girdle of silver,
A baselard and a knife, with botons overgilt."

---

* The honorary title of Sir was given to priests down to a late period. A law of Canute declared a priest to rank with the second order of thanes—*i.e.*, with the landed gentry. "By the laws, armorial, civil, and of arms, a priest in his place in civil conversation is always before any esquire, as being a knight's fellow by his holy orders, and the third of the three Sirs which only were in request of old (no baron, viscount, earl, nor marquis being then in use), to wit, Sir King, Sir Knight, and Sir Priest. . . . . . . But afterwards Sir in English was restrained to these four,—Sir Knight, Sir Priest, and Sir Graduate, and, in common speech, Sir Esquire; so always, since distinction of titles were, Sir Priest was ever the second."—A Decacordon of Quodlibetical Questions concerning Religion and State, quoted in Knight's Shakespeare, Vol. I. of Comedies, note to Sc. 1, Act i. of "Merry Wives of Windsor." In Shakespeare's characters we have *Sir Hugh Evans* and *Sir Oliver Martext*, and, at a later period still, "Sir John" was the popular name for a priest. Piers Ploughman (Vision XI. 304) calls them "God's knights,"

And also in the Psalter says David to overskippers,
*Psallite Deo nostro, psallite; quoniam rex terre
Deus Israel; psallite sapienter.*
The Bishop shall be blamed before God, as I leve [believe]
That crowneth such goddes knightes that conneth nought *sapienter*
Synge ne psalmes rede ne segge a masse of the day.
Ac never neyther is blameless the bisshop ne the chapleyne,
For her either is endited; and that of *ignorancia
Non excusat episcopos, nec idiotes prestes.*

A little later, he speaks of proud priests habited in patlocks,—a short jacket worn by laymen,—with peaked shoes and large knives or daggers. And in the poems of John Audelay, in the fifteenth century, a parish priest is described in

"His girdle harnesched with silver, his baselard hangs by."

In the wills of the clergy they themselves describe their "togas" of gay colours, trimmed with various furs, and their ornamented girdles and purses, and make no secret of the objectionable knives and baselards. In the Bury St. Edmunds Wills, Adam de Stanton, a chaplain, A.D. 1370, bequeaths one girdle, with purse and knife, valued at 5s.—a rather large sum of money in those days. In the York wills, John Wynd-hill, Rector of Arnecliffe, A.D. 1431, bequeaths a pair of amber beads, such as Piers Ploughman says a priest ought "to bear in his hand, and a book under his arm;" and, curiously enough, in the next sentence he leaves "an English book of Piers Ploughman;" but he does not seem to have been much influenced by the popular poet's invectives, for he goes on to bequeath two green gowns and one of murrey and one of sanguine colour, besides two of black, all trimmed with various furs; also, one girdle of sanguine silk, ornamented with silver, and gilded, and another zone of green and white, ornamented with silver and gilded ; and he also leaves behind him— *proh pudor*—his best silver girdle, and a baselard with ivory and silver handle. John Gilby, Rector of Knesale, 1434-5, leaves a red toga, furred with byce, a black zone of silk with gilt bars, and a zone ornamented with silver. J. Bagule, Rector of All Saints, York, A.D. 1438, leaves a little baselard, with a zone harnessed with silver, to Sir T. Astell, a chaplain. W. Duffield, a chantry priest at York, A.D. 1443, leaves a black zone silvered, a purse called a "gypsire," and a white purse of "Burdeux." W. Siverd, chaplain, leaves to H. Hobshot a hawk-bag ; and to W. Day, parochial chaplain of Calton, a pair of hawk-bag rings ; and to J. Sarle, chaplain, "my ruby zone, silvered, and my toga, furred with 'bevers ;'" and to the wife of J. Bridlington, "a ruby purse of satin." R. Rolleston, provost of the church of Beverley, A.D. 1450, leaves a "toga lunata" with a red hood, a toga and hood of violet, a long toga and hood of black, trimmed with martrons, and a toga and hood of violet. J. Clyft, chaplain,

A.D. 1455, leaves a zone of silk, ornamented with silver. J. Tidman, chaplain, A.D. 1458, a toga of violet and one of meld. C. Lassels, chaplain, A.D. 1461, a green toga and a white zone, silvered. T. Horneby, rector of Stokesley, A.D. 1464, a red toga and hood; and, among the Richmondshire Wills, we find that of Sir Henry Halled, Lady-priest of the parish of Kirby-in-Kendal, in 1542 A.D. (four years before the suppression of the chantries), who leaves a short gown and a long gown, whose colour is not specified, but was probably black, which seems by this time to have been the most usual clerical wear.

The accompanying woodcut will admirably illustrate the ornamented girdle, purse, and knife, of which we have been reading. It is from a MS. of Chaucer's poem of the Romaunt of the Rose (Harl. 4,425, f. 143), and represents a priest confessing a lady in a church. The characters in the scene are, like the poem, allegorical; the priest is Genius, and the lady is Dame Nature; but it is not the less an accurate picture of a confessional scene of the latter part of the fourteenth century. The priest is habited in a robe of purple, with a black cap and a black liripipe attached to it, brought over the shoulder to the front, and falling over the arm. The tab, peeping from beneath the cap above the ear, is red;

A Priest Confessing a Lady.

the girdle, purse, and knife, are, in the original illumination, very clearly represented. In another picture of the same person, at f. 106, the black girdle is represented as ornamented with little circles of gold.

Many of these clergymen had one black toga with hood *en suite*—not for constant use in divine service, for, as we have already seen, they are generally represented in the illuminations with coloured "togas" under their surplices,—but perhaps, for wear on mourning occasions. Thus, in the presentations of York Cathedral, A.D. 1519, "We thynke it were convenient that whene we fetche a corse to the churche, that we shulde be in our blak abbettes [habits] mornyngly, w^t our hodes of the same of our hedes, as is used in many other places." *

At the time of the Reformation, when the English clergy abandoned the mediæval official robes, they also desisted from wearing the tonsure, which had for many centuries been the distinguishing mark of a cleric, and they seem generally to have adopted the academical dress, for the model both of their official and their ordinary dress. The Puritan clergy adopted a costume which differed little, if at all, from that of the laity of the same school. But it is curious that this question of clerical dress continued to be one of complaint on one side, and resistance on the other, down to the end of our ecclesiastical legislation. The 74th canon of 1603 is as rhetorical in form, and as querulous in tone, and as minute in its description of the way in which ecclesiastical persons should, and the way in which they should not, dress, as is the Injunction of 1342, which we have already quoted. "The true, ancient, and flourishing churches of Christ, being ever desirous that their prelacy and clergy might be had as well in outward reverence, as otherwise regarded for the worthiness of their ministry, did think it fit, by a prescript form of decent and comely apparel, to have them known to the people, and thereby to receive the honour and estimation due to the special messengers and ministers of Almighty God : we, therefore, following their grave judgment and the ancient custom of the Church of England, and hoping that in time new fangleness of apparel in some factious persons will die of itself, do constitute and appoint, that the archbishops and bishops shall not intermit to use the accustomed apparel of their degree. Likewise, all deans, masters of colleges, archdeacons, and prebendaries, in cathedrals and collegiate churches (being priests or deacons), doctors in divinity, law, and physic, bachelors in divinity, masters of arts, and bachelors of law, having any ecclesiastical living, shall wear gowns with standing collars, and sleeves straight at the hands, or wide sleeves, as is used in the universities, with hoods or tippets of silk or sarcenet, and square caps; and that all

---

* York Fabric Rolls, p. 268.

Canonical Costume. 251

other ministers admitted, or to be admitted, into that function, shall also usually wear the like apparel as is aforesaid, except tippets only. We do further in like manner ordain, that all the said ecclesiastical persons above mentioned shall usually wear on their journeys cloaks with sleeves, commonly called Priests' Cloaks, without guards, welts, long buttons, or cuts. And no ecclesiastical person shall wear any coif, or wrought nightcap, but only plain night caps of black silk, satin, or velvet. In all which particulars concerning the apparel here prescribed, our meaning is not to attribute any holiness or special worthiness to the said garments, but for decency, gravity, and order, as is before specified. In private houses and in their studies the said persons ecclesiastical may use any comely and scholarlike apparel, provided that it be not cut or pinkt; and that in public they go not in their doublet and hose without coats or cassocks; and that they wear not any light-coloured stockings. Likewise, poor beneficed men and curates (not being able to provide themselves long gowns) may go in short gowns of the fashion aforesaid."

The portraits prefixed to the folio works of the great divines of the sixteenth and seventeenth centuries have made us familiar with the fact, that at the time of the Reformation the clergy wore the beard and moustache. They continued to wear the cassock and gown as their ordinary out-door costume until as late as the time of George II.; but in the fashion of doublet and hose, hats, shoes, and hair, they followed the custom of other gentlemen. Mr. Fairholt, in his "Costume in England," p. 327, gives us a woodcut from a print of 1680 A.D., which admirably illustrates the ordinary out-door dress of a clergyman of the time of William and Mary.

CHAPTER V.

PARSONAGE HOUSES.

WHEN, in our endeavour to realise the life of these secular clergymen of the Middle Ages, we come to inquire, What sort of houses did they live in? how were these furnished? what sort of life did their occupants lead? what kind of men were they? it is curious how little seems to be generally known on the subject, compared with what we know about the houses and life and character of the regular orders. Instead of gathering together what others have said, we find ourselves engaged in an original investigation of a new and obscure subject. The case of the cathedral and collegiate clergy, and that of the isolated parochial clergy, form two distinct branches of the subject. The limited space at our disposal will not permit us to do justice to both; the latter branch of the subject is less known, and perhaps the more generally interesting, and we shall therefore devote the bulk of our space to it. We will only premise a few words on the former branch.

The bishop of a cathedral of secular canons had his house near his cathedral, in which he maintained a household equal in numbers and expense to that of the secular barons among whom he took rank; the chief difference being, that the spiritual lord's family consisted rather of chaplains and clerks than of squires and men-at-arms. The bishop's palace at Wells is a very interesting example in an unusually perfect condition. Britton gives an engraving of it as it appeared before the reign of Edward VI. The bishop besides had other residences on his manors, some of which were castles like those of the other nobility. Farnham, the present residence of the see of Winchester, is a noble example, which still serves its original purpose. Of the cathedral closes many still remain sufficiently unchanged to enable us to understand their original condition. Take Lincoln for example. On the north side of the church, in the angle between the nave and transept, was the cloister, with the polygonal chapter-house on the east side. The lofty wall which enclosed the precincts yet remains, with its main entrance in the middle of the west wall, opposite the great doors of the cathedral. This gate, called the Exchequer Gate, has chambers over it, devoted probably to the official business of the diocese. There are two other smaller gates at the north-east and south-east corners of the close, and there is a postern on the south side. The bishop's palace, whose beautiful and interesting ruins and charming grounds still remain, occupied the slope of the southern hill outside the close. The vicar's court is in the corner of the close near the gateway to the palace grounds. A fourteenth-century house, which was the official residence of the chaplain of one of the endowed chantries, still remains on the south side of the close, nearly opposite the choir door. On the east side of the close the fifteenth-century houses of several of the canons still remain, and are interesting examples of the domestic architecture of the time. It is not difficult from these data to picture to ourselves the original condition of this noble establishment when the cathedral, with its cloister and chapter-house, stood isolated in the middle of the green sward, and the houses of the canons and chaplains formed a great irregular quadrangle round it, and the close walls shut them all in from the outer world, and the halls and towers of the bishop's palace were still perfect amidst its hanging gardens enclosed within their own walls, the quadrangle of houses which had been built for the cathedral vicars occupying a corner cut out of the bishop's grounds beside his gateway. And we can repeople the restored close. Let it be on the morning of one of the great festivals; let the great bells be ringing out their summons to high mass; and we shall see the dignified canons in amice and cap crossing the green singly on their way from their houses to their stalls in the choir; the vicars conversing in a little group as they come across from their court; the surpliced chorister boys under the charge of their schoolmaster; a band of minstrels with flutes, and hautboys, and viols, and harps, and organs, coming in from the city, to use their instruments in the rood-loft to aid the voices of the choir; scattered clerks and country clergy, and townspeople, are all converging to the great south door; and last of all the lord bishop, in cope and mitre, emerges from his gateway, preceded by his cross-bearer, attended by noble or royal guests, and followed by a suite of officials and clerks; while over all the great bells ring out their joyous peal to summon the people to the solemn worship of God in the mother church of the vast diocese.

But we must turn to our researches into the humbler life of the country rectors and vicars. And first, what sort of houses did they live in? We have not been able to find one of the parsonage houses of an earlier date than the Reformation still remaining in a condition sufficiently unaltered to enable us to understand what they originally were. There is an ancient rectory house of the fourteenth century at West Deane, Sussex,* of which we give a ground-plan and north-east view on the following page; but the rectory belonged to the prior and convent of Benedictine Monks of Wilmington, and this house was probably their grange, or cell, and may have been inhabited by two of their monks, or by their tenant, and not by the parish priest. Again, there is a very picturesque rectory house, of the fifteenth century, at Little Chesterton, near Cambridge,† but this again is believed to have been a grange, or cell, of a monastic house.

In the absence of actual examples, we are driven to glean what information we can from other sources. There remain to us a good many of the deeds of the thirteenth and fourteenth centuries, by which, on the impropriation of the benefices, provision was made for the permanent endowment of vicarages in them. In the majority of cases the old rectory house was assigned as the future vicarage house, and no detailed description of it was necessary; but in the deed by which the rectories of Sawbridgeworth, in Herts, and Kelvedon, in Essex, were appropriated to the convent of Westminster, we are so fortunate as to find descriptions of the fourteenth-century parsonage houses, one of which is so detailed as to enable any one who is acquainted with the domestic architecture of the

---

* Described and engraved in the Sussex Archæological Collections, vii. f. 13.
† Described and engraved in Mr. Parker's "Domestic Architecture."

time to form a very definite picture of the whole building. In the case of Sawbridgeworth, the old rectory house was assigned as the vicarage house, and is thus described—" All the messuage which is called the priest's

Rectory House, West Deane, Sussex.

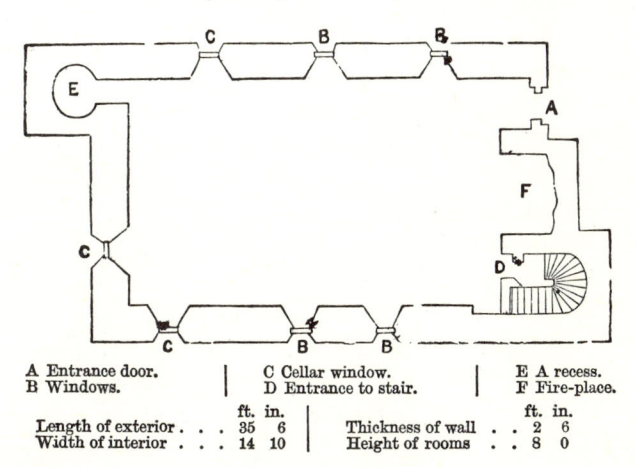

A Entrance door. C Cellar window. E A recess.
B Windows. D Entrance to stair. F Fire-place.

	ft.	in.		ft.	in.
Length of exterior	35	6	Thickness of wall	2	6
Width of interior	14	10	Height of rooms	8	0

messuage, with the houses thereon built, that is to say, one hall with two chambers, with a buttery, cellar, kitchen, stable, and other fitting and decent houses, with all the garden as it is enclosed with walls to the said messuage belonging." The description of the parsonage house at Kelvedon is much more definite and intelligible. For this the deed tells us the convent assigned—" One hall situate in the manor of the said abbot and convent near the said church, with a chamber and soler at one end of the hall and with a buttery and cellar at the other. Also one other house in three parts, that is to say, for a kitchen with a convenient chamber in the end of the said house for guests, and a bakehouse. Also one other house in two parts, next the gate at the entrance of the manor, for a stable and cowhouse. He (the vicar) shall also have a convenient grange, to be built within a year at the expense of the prior and convent. He shall also have the curtilage with the garden adjoining to the hall on the north side, as it is enclosed with hedges and ditches." The date of the deed is 1356 A.D., and it speaks of these houses as already existing. Now the common arrangement of a small house at that date, and for near a century before and after, was this, " a hall in the centre, with a soler at one end and offices at the other."* A description which exactly agrees with the account of the Kelvedon house, and enables us to say with great probability that in the Sawbridgeworth " priest's messuage " also, the two chambers were at one end of the hall, and the buttery, cellar, and kitchen at the other, the stable and other fitting and decent houses being detached from and not forming any portion of the dwelling house.

Confining ourselves, however, to the Kelvedon house, a little study will enable us to reconstruct it conjecturally with a very high probability of being minutely accurate in our conjectures. First of all, a house of this character in the county of Essex would, beyond question, be a timber house. To make our description clearer we have given a rough diagram of our conjectural arrangement. Its principal feature was, of course, the " one hall " (A). We know at once what the hall of a timber house of this period of architecture would be. It would be a rather spacious and lofty apartment, with an open timber roof; the principal door of the house would open into the "screens" (D), at the lower end of the hall, and the back door of the house would be at the other end of the screens. At the

---

* Parker's "Domestic Architecture," ii. p. 87.

upper end of the hall would be the raised dais (B), at which the master of the house sat with his family. The fireplace would either be an open hearth in the middle of the hall, like that which still exists in the fourteenth-century hall at Penshurst Place, Kent, or it would be an open fireplace, under a projecting chimney, at the further side of the hall, such as is frequently seen in MS. illuminations of the small houses of the period. There was next " a chamber and soler at one end of the hall." The soler of a mediæval house was the chief apartment after the hall, it answered to the " great chamber " of the sixteenth century, and to the parlour or drawing-room of more modern times. It was usually adjacent to the upper end

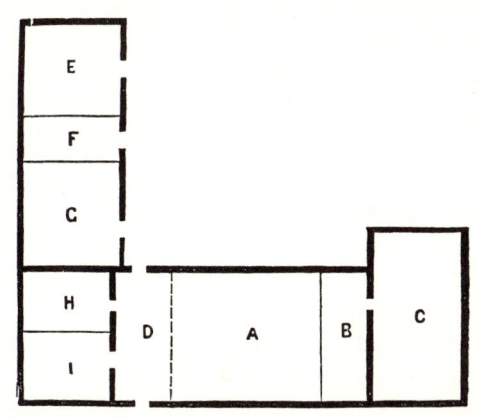

Conjectural Plan of Rectory-House at Kelvedon, Essex.

of the hall, and built on transversely to it, with a window at each end. It was usually raised on an undercroft, which was used as a storeroom or cellar, so that it was reached by a stair from the upper end of the hall. Sometimes, instead of a mere undercroft, there was a chamber under the soler, which was the case here, so that we have added these features to our plan (c). Next there was "a buttery and cellar at the other" end of the hall. In the buttery in those days were kept wine and beer, table linen, cups, pots, &c. : and in the cellar the stores of eatables which, it must be remembered, were not bought in weekly from the village shop, or the next market town, but were partly the produce of the glebe and tithe, and partly were laid in yearly or half-yearly at some neighbouring fair. The buttery and cellar—they who are familiar with old houses, or with our colleges, will remember—are always at the lower end of the hall, and open upon the screens, with two whole or half doors side by side; we may therefore add them thus upon our plan (H, I).

The deed adds, " Also one other house in three parts." In those days the rooms of a house were not massed compactly together under one roof, but were built in separate buildings more or less detached, and each building was called a house; " One other house in three parts, that is to say, a kitchen with a convenient chamber at one end of the said house for guests, and a bakehouse." "The kitchen," says Mr. Parker, in his " Domestic Architecture," "was frequently a detached building, often connected with the hall by a passage or alley leading from the screens;" and it was often of greater relative size and importance than modern usage would lead us to suppose; the kitchens of old monasteries, mansion houses, and colleges often have almost the size and architectural character of a second hall. In the case before us it was a section of the " other house," and probably occupied its whole height, with an open timber roof (G). In the disposition of the bakehouse and convenient chamber for guests which were also in this other house, we meet with our first difficulty; the " chamber " might possibly be over the bakehouse, which took the usual form of an undercroft beneath the guest chamber; but the definition that the house was divided "in three parts" suggests that it was divided from top to bottom into three distinct sections. Inclining to the latter opinion, we have so disposed these apartments in our plan (F, E).

The elevation of the house may be conjectured with as much probability as its plan. Standing in front of it we should have the side of the hall towards us, with the arched door at its lower end, and perhaps two windows in the side with carved wood tracery* in their heads. To the right would be the gable end of the chamber with soler over it; the soler would probably have a rather large arched and traceried window in the end, the chamber a smaller and perhaps square-headed light. On the left would be

---

* There are numerous curious examples of fifteenth-century timber window-tracery in the Essex churches.

the building, perhaps a lean-to, containing the buttery and cellar, with only a small square-headed light in front. The accompanying wood-cut of a fourteenth-century house, from the Add. MSS. 10,292, will help to illustrate our conjectural elevation of Kelvedon Rectory. It has the hall with its great door and arched traceried window, and at the one end a chamber

A Fourteenth Century House.

and soler over it. It only wants the offices at the other end to make the resemblance complete.*

---

* The deed of settlement of the vicarage of Bulmer, in the year 1425, gives us the description of a parsonage house of similar character. It consisted of one hall with two chambers annexed, the bakehouse, kitchen, and larder-house, one chamber for the vicar's servant, a stable, and a hay-soller (*Soler*, loft), with a competent garden. Ingrave rectory house was a similar house; it is described, in a terrier of 1610, as "a house containing a hall, a parlour, a buttery, two lofts, and a study, also a kitchen, a milk-house, and a house for poultry, a barn, a stable and a hay-house."—*Newcourt*, ii. p. 281.

Ingatestone rectory, in the terrier of 1610, was "a dwelling-house with a hall, a parlour, and a chamber within it; a study newly built by the then parson; a chamber over the parlour, and another within that with a closet; without the dwelling-house a kitchen and two little rooms adjoining to it, and a chamber over them; two little butteries over against the hall, and next them a chamber, and one other chamber over the same; without the kitchen there is a dove-house, and another house built by the then parson; a barn and a stable very ruinous."—*Newcourt*, ii. 348. Here, too, we seem to have an old house with hall in the middle, parlour and chamber at one end and two butteries at the other, in the midst of successive additions.

There is also a description of the rectory house of West Haningfield, Essex, in Newcourt, ii. 309, and of North Bemfleet, ii. 46.

Of later date probably and greater size, resembling a moated manor house, was the rectory of Great Bromley, Essex, which is thus described in the terrier of 1610 A.D.: "A large parsonage house compass'd with a Mote, a Gate-house, with a large chamber, and a substantial bridge of timber adjoining to it, a little yard, an orchard, and a little garden, all within the Mote, which, together with the Circuit of the House, contains about half an Acre of Ground; and without the Mote there is a Yard, in which there is another Gate-house and a stable, and a hay house adjoining; also a barn of 25 yards long and 9 yards wide, and about 79 Acres and a-half of glebe-land."* The outbuildings were perhaps arranged as a courtyard outside the moat to which the gate-house formed an entrance, so that the visitor would pass through this outer gate, through the court of offices, over the bridge, and through the second gate-house into the base court of the house. This is the arrangement at Ightham Mote, Kent.

The parish chaplains seem to have had houses of residence provided for them. The parish of St. Michael-le-Belfry, York, complained in its visitation presentment, in the year 1409, that there was no house assigned for the parish chaplain or for the parish clerk. That they were small houses we gather from the fact that in some of the settlements of vicarages it is required that a competent house shall be built for the vicar where the parish chaplain has been used to live; *e.g.* at Great Bentley, Essex, it was ordered in 1323, that the vicars "shall have one competent dwelling-house with a sufficient curtilage, where the parish chaplain did use to abide, to be prepared at the cost of the said prior and convent." † And at the settlement of the vicarage of St. Peter's, Colchester, A.D. 1319, it was required that "the convent of St. Botolph's, the impropriators, should prepare a competent house for the vicar in the ground of the churchyard where a house was built for the parish chaplain of the said church." At Radwinter, Essex, we find by the terrier of 1610 A.D., that there were two mansions belonging to the benefice, "on the south side of the church, towards the west end, one called the great vicarage, and in ancient time the Domus Capellanorum, and the other the less vicarage," which latter "formerly

---

* Newcourt's "Repertorum," ii. 97.   † Newcourt, ii. 49.

served for the ease of the Parson, and, as appears by evidence, first given to the end that if any of the parish were sick, the party might be sure to find the Parson or his curate near the church ready to go and visit him." At the south-west corner of the churchyard of Doddinghurst, Essex, there still exists a little house of fifteenth-century date, which may have been such a curate's house.

From a comparison of these parsonages with the usual plan and arrangement of the houses of laymen of the fourteenth century, may be made the important deduction that the houses of the parochial clergy had no ecclesiastical peculiarities of arrangement; they were not little monasteries or great recluse houses, they were like the houses of the laity; and this agrees with the conclusions to which we have arrived already by other roads, that the secular clergy lived in very much the same style as laymen of a similar degree of wealth and social standing. The poor clerk lived in a single chamber of a citizen's house; the town priest had a house like those of the citizens; the country rector or vicar a house like the manor houses of the smaller gentry.

As to the furniture of the parsonage, the wills of the clergy supply us with ample authorities. We will select one of about the date of the Kelvedon parsonage house which we have been studying, to help us to conjecturally furnish the house which we have conjecturally built. Here is an inventory of the goods of Adam de Stanton, a chaplain, date 1370 A.D., taken from Mr. Tymms's collection of Bury wills. "Imprimis, in money vj$^s.$ viij$^d.$ and i seal of silver worth ijs." The money will seem a fair sum to have in hand when we consider the greater value of money then and especially the comparative scarcity of actual coin. The seal was probably his official seal as chaplain of an endowed chantry; we have extant examples of such seals of the beneficed clergy. "Item, iij brass pots and i posnet worth xj$^s.$ vj$^d.$ Item, in plate, xxij$^d.$ Item, a round pot with a laver, j$^s.$ vj$^{d.}$," probably an ewer and basin for washing the hands, like those still used in Germany, &c. "Item, in iron instruments, vj^s viiij$^d.$ and vj$^{d.}$," perhaps fire-dogs and poker, spit, and pothook. "Item, in pewter vessels, iiij$^s.$ ij$^{d.}$," probably plates, dishes, and spoons. "Item, of wooden utensils," which, from comparison with other inventories of about the same period, we suppose may be boards and trestles for tables, and benches, and a chair, and perhaps may include trenchers and bowls. "Item, i portiforum, x$^{s.}$" a book of church service so called, which must have been a handsome one to be worth ten shillings, perhaps it was illuminated. "Item, j book de Lege and j Par Statutorum, and j Book of Romances.* Item, j girdle with purse and knife, v$^{s.}$" on which we have already commented in our last chapter. "Item, j pair of knives for the table, xij$^{d.}$ Item, j saddle with bridle and spurs, iij$^{s.}$ Item, of linen and woollen garments, xxviij$^{s.}$ and xij$^{d.}$ Item, of chests and caskets, vj$^{s.}$ ij$^{d.}$" Chests and caskets then served for cupboards and drawers.†

If we compare these clerical inventories with those of contemporary laymen of the same degree, we shall find that a country parson's house was furnished like a small manor house, and that his domestic economy was very like that of the gentry of a like income. Matthew Paris tells us an anecdote of a certain handsome clerk, the rector of a rich church, who surpassed all the knights living around him in giving repeated entertainments and acts of hospitality.‡ But usually it was a rude kind of life which the country squire or parson led, very like that which was led by the substantial farmers of a few generations ago, when it was the fashion for the unmarried farm labourers to live in the farm-house, and for the farmer and his household all to sit down to meals together. These were their hours:—

"Rise at five, dine at nine,
Sup at five, and bed at nine,
Will make a man live to ninety-and-nine."

The master of the house sat in the sole arm-chair, in the middle of the

---

* George Darell, A.D. 1432, leaves one book of statutes, containing the statutes of Kings Edward III., Richard II., and Henry IV.; one book of law, called "Natura Brevium;" one Portus, and one Par Statutorum Veterum.—*Testamenta Eboracensia*, ii. p. 27.

† There are other inventories of the goods of clerics, which will help to throw light upon their domestic economy at different periods, *e.g.*, of the vicar of Waghen, A.D. 1462, in the York Wills, ii. 261, and of a chantry priest, A.D. 1542, in the Sussex Archæological Collections, iii. p. 115.

‡ Bohn's Edition, vol. ii. p. 278.

high table on the dais, with his family on either side of him; and his men sat at the movable tables of boards and trestles, with a bench on each side, which we find mentioned in the inventories: or the master sat at the same table with his men, only he sat above the salt and they below; he drank his ale out of a silver cup while they drank it out of horn; he ate white bread while they ate brown, and he a capon out of his curtilage while they had pork or mutton ham; he retired to his great chamber when he desired privacy, which was not often perhaps; and he slept in a tester bed in the great chamber, while they slept on truckle beds in the hall.

One item in the description of the Kelvedon parsonage requires special consideration, and opens up a rather important question as to the domestic economy of the parochial clergy over and above what we have hitherto gleaned. "The convenient chamber for guests" there mentioned was not a best bedroom for any friend who might pay him a visit. It was a provision for the efficient exercise of the hospitality to which the beneficed parochial clergy were bound. It is a subject which perhaps needs a little explanation. In England there were no inns where travellers could obtain food and lodging until the middle of the fourteenth century; and for long after that period they could only be found in the largest and most important towns; and it was held to be a part of the duty of the clergy to "entertain strangers," and be "given to hospitality." It was a charity not very likely to be abused; for, thanks to bad roads, unbridged fords, no inns, wild moors, and vast forests haunted by lawless men, very few travelled, except for serious business; and it was a real act of Christian charity to afford to such travellers the food and shelter which they needed, and would have been hard put to it to have obtained otherwise. The monasteries, we all know, exercised this hospitality on so large a scale, that in order to avoid the interruption a constant succession of guests would have made in the seclusion and regularity of conventual life, they provided special buildings for it, called the hospitium or guest house, a kind of inn within the walls, and they appointed one of the monks, under the name of the hospitaller or guest master, to represent the convent in entertaining the guests. Hermitages also, we have seen, were frequently built along the high roads, especially near bridges and fords, for the purpose of aiding travellers.

Along the road which led towards some famous place of pilgrimage hospitals, which were always religious foundations, were founded especially for the entertainment of poor pilgrims. And the parochial clergy were expected to exercise a similar hospitality. Thus in the replies of the rectors of Berkshire to the papal legate, in 1240 A.D., they say that " their churches were endowed and enriched by their patrons with lands and revenues for the especial purpose that the rectors of them should receive guests, rich as well as poor, and show hospitality to laity as well as clergy, according to their means, as the custom of the place required." * Again, in 1246, the clergy, on a similar occasion, stated that " a custom has hitherto prevailed, and been observed in England, that the rectors of parochial churches have always been remarkable for hospitality, and have made a practice of supplying food to their parishioners who were in want, ... and if a portion of their benefices be taken away from them, they will be under the necessity of refusing their hospitality, and abandoning their accustomed offices of piety. And if these be withdrawn, they will incur the hatred of those subject to them [their parishioners], and will lose the favour of passers-by [travellers] and their neighbours." † Again, in 1253 A.D., Bishop Grostête, in his remonstrance to the Pope, says of the foreigners who were intruded into English benefices, that they " could not even take up their residence, to administer to the wants of the poor, and to receive travellers." ‡

There is an interesting passage illustrative of the subject quoted in Parker's " Domestic Architecture," i. p. 123. Æneus Sylvius, afterwards Pope Pius II., describing his journey from Scotland into England, in the year 1448, says that he entered a large village in a wild and barbarous part of the country, about sunset, and " alighted at a rustic's house, and supped there with the priest of the place and the host." The special mention of the priest in the first place almost leads us to conjecture that the foreign ecclesiastic had first gone to the priest of the place for the usual hospitality, and had been taken on by him to the manor house—for

---

* Matthew Paris, vol. i. p. 285 (Bohn's edition).
† Ibid., vol. ii. p. 193.
‡ Ibid., vol iii. p. 48.

the "rustic" seems to have been a squire—as better able to afford him a suitable hospitality. Sundry pottages, and fowls, and geese, were placed on the table, but there was neither bread nor wine. He had, however, brought with him a few loaves and a roundel of wine, which he had received at a certain monastery. Either a stranger was a great novelty, or the Italian ecclesiastic had something remarkable in his appearance, for he says all " the people of the place ran to the house to stare at him."

Kelvedon being on one of the great high roads of the country, its parson would often be called upon to exercise his duty of hospitality, hence the provision of a special guest chamber in the parsonage house. And so in our picture of the domestic economy and ordinary life of a mediæval country parson we must furnish his guest chamber, and add a little to the contents of buttery and cellar, to provide for his duty of hospitality; and we must picture him not always sitting in solitary dignity at his high table on the dais, but often playing the courteous host to knight and lady, merchant, minstrel, or pilgrim; and after dinner giving the broken meat to the poor, who in the days when there was no poor law were the regular dependants on his bounty.

THE MINSTRELS OF THE MIDDLE AGES.

CHAPTER I.

IT would carry us too far a-field to attempt to give a sketch of the early music of the principal nations of antiquity, such as might be deduced from the monuments of Egypt and Nineveh and Greece. We may, however, briefly glance at the most ancient minstrelsy of the Israelites; partly for the sake of the peculiar interest of the subject itself, partly because the early history of music is nearly the same in all nations, and this earliest history will illustrate and receive illustration from a comparison with the history of music in mediæval England.

Musical instruments, we are told by the highest of all authorities, were invented in the eighth generation of the world—that is in the third generation before the flood—by Tubal, " the Father of all such as handle the harp and organ, both stringed and wind instruments." The ancient Israelites used musical instruments on the same occasions as the mediæval Europeans—in battle; in their feasts and dances; in processions, whether of religious or civil ceremony; and in the solemnising of divine worship. The trumpet and the horn were then, as always, the instruments of warlike music—" If ye go to war then shall ye blow an alarm with the silver trumpets."* The trumpet regulated the march of the hosts of Israel through the wilderness. When Joshua compassed Jericho, the seven

---

* Numb. x. 9.

priests blew trumpets of rams' horns. Gideon and his three hundred discomfited the host of the Midianites with the sound of their trumpets.

The Tabret was the common accompaniment of the troops of female dancers, whether the occasion were religious or festive. Miriam the prophetess took a timbrel in her hand, and all the women went out after her with timbrels and with dances, singing a solemn chorus to the triumphant song of Moses and of the Children of Israel over the destruction of Pharaoh in the Red Sea,—

> " Sing ye to the Lord, for he hath triumphed gloriously;
> The horse and his rider hath he thrown into the sea."*

Jephthah's daughter went to meet her victorious father with timbrels and dances :—

> " The daughter of the warrior Gileadite,
> From Mizpeh's tower'd gate with welcome light,
> With timbrel and with song."

And so, when King Saul returned from the slaughter of the Philistines, after the shepherd David had killed their giant champion in the valley of Elah, the women came out of all the cities to meet the returning warriors " singing and dancing to meet King Saul, with tabrets, with joy, and with instruments of music;" and the women answered one another in dramatic chorus—

> " Saul hath slain his thousands,
> And David his ten thousands."†

Laban says that he would have sent away Jacob and his wives and children, " with mirth and with songs, with tabret and with harp." And Jeremiah prophesying that times of ease and prosperity shall come again for Israel, says: " O Virgin of Israel, thou shalt again be adorned with thy tabrets, and shalt go forth in the dances of them that make merry." ‡

In their feasts these and many other instruments were used. Isaiah tells us § that they had " the harp, and the viol, the tabret, and pipe, and wine in their feasts;" and Amos tells us of the luxurious people who lie upon beds of ivory, and " chant to the sound of the viol, and invent to

---

* Exod. xv. 21.   † 1 Sam. xviii. 7.   ‡ Jer. xxxi. 4.   § Is. v. 12.

themselves instruments of music like David," and drink wine in bowls, and anoint themselves with the costliest perfumes.

Instruments of music were used in the colleges of Prophets, which Samuel established in the land, to accompany and inspire the delivery of their prophetical utterances. As Saul, newly anointed, went up the hill of God towards the city, he met a company of prophets coming down, with a psaltery, and a tabret, and a pipe, and a harp before them, prophesying; and the spirit of the Lord came upon Saul when he heard, and he also prophesied.* When Elisha was requested by Jehoram to prophesy the fate of the battle with the Moabites, he said : " Bring me a minstrel ; and when the minstrel played, the hand of the Lord came upon him, and he prophesied."

When David brought up the ark from Gibeah, he and all the house of Israel played before the Lord on all manner of instruments made of firwood, even on harps, psalteries, timbrels, cornets, and cymbals.† And in the song which he himself composed to be sung on that occasion,‡ he thus describes the musical part of the procession :—

> " It is well seen how thou goest,
> How thou, my God and King, goest to the sanctuary;
> The singers go before, the minstrels follow after,
> In the midst are the damsels playing with the timbrels."

The instruments appointed for the regular daily service of the Temple " by David, and Gad the king's seer, and Nathan the prophet, for so was the commandment of the Lord by his prophets," were cymbals, psalteries, and harps, which David made for the purpose, and which were played by four thousand Levites.

Besides the instruments already mentioned,—the harp, tabret, timbrel, psaltery, trumpet, cornet, cymbal, pipe, and viol,—they had also the lyre, bag-pipes, and bells; and probably they carried back with them from Babylon further additions, from the instruments of " all peoples, nations, and languages " with which they would become familiarised in that capital of the world. But from the time of Tubal down to the time when the

---

* 1 Sam. x. 5.   † 2 Sam. vi. 5.   ‡ Psalm lxviii.

royal minstrel of Israel sang those glorious songs which are still the daily solace of thousands of mankind, and further down to the time when the captive Israelites hanged their unstrung harps upon the willows of Babylon, and could not sing the songs of Zion in a strange land, the harp continued still the fitting accompaniment of the voice in all poetical utterance of a dignified and solemn character :—the recitation of the poetical portions of historical and prophetical Scripture, for instance, would be sustained by it, and the songs of the psalmists of Zion were accompanied by its strains. And thus this sketch of the history of the earliest music closes, with the minstrel harp still in the foreground; while in the distance we hear the sound of the fanfare of cornet, flute, harp, sackbut, psaltery, dulcimer, and all kinds of music, which were concerted on great occasions; such as that on which they resounded over the plain of Dura, to bow that bending crowd of heads, as the ripe corn bends before the wind, to the great Image of Gold :—an idolatry, alas! which the peoples, nations, and languages still perform almost as fervently as of old.

The northern Bard, or Scald, was the father of the minstrels of mediæval Europe. Our own early traditions afford some picturesque anecdotes, proving the high estimation in which the character was held by the Saxons and their kindred Danes; and showing that they were accustomed to wander about to court, and camp, and hall; and were hospitably received, even though the Bard were of a race against which his hosts were at that very time encamped in hostile array. We will only remind the reader of the Royal Alfred's assumption of the character of a minstrel, and his visit in that disguise to the Danish camp (A.D. 878); and of the similar visit, ten years after, of Anlaff the Danish king to the camp of Saxon Athelstane. But the earliest anecdote of the kind we shall have hereafter to refer to, and may therefore here detail at length. It is told us by Geoffrey of Monmouth, that Colgrin, the son of Ella, who succeeded Hengist in the leadership of the invading Saxons, was shut up in York, and closely besieged by King Arthur and his Britons. Baldulf, the brother of Colgrin, wanted to gain access to him, to apprise him of a reinforcement which was coming from Germany. In order to accomplish this design, he assumed the character of a minstrel. He shaved his head and beard; and dressing himself in the habit of that profession, took his harp in his hand. In this disguise he walked up and down the trenches without suspicion, playing all the while upon his instrument as a harper. By little and little he approached the walls of the city; and, making himself known to the sentinels, was in the night drawn up by a rope.

The harper continued throughout the Middle Ages to be the most dignified of the minstrel craft, the reciter, and often the composer, of heroic legend and historical tale, of wild romance and amorous song. Frequently, and perhaps especially in the case of the higher class of harpers, he travelled alone, as in the cases which we have already seen of Baldulf, and Alfred, and Anlaff. But he also often associated himself with a band of minstrels, who filled up the intervals of his recitations and songs with their music, much as vocal and instrumental pieces are alternated in our modern concerts. With a band of minstrels there was also very usually associated a mime, who amused the audience with his feats of agility and leger-de-main. The association appears at first sight somewhat undignified—the heroic harper and the tumbler—but the incongruity was not peculiar to the Middle Ages; the author of the "Iliad" wrote the "Battle of the Frogs,"—the Greeks were not satisfied without a satiric drama after their grand heroic tragedy; and in these days we have a farce or a pantomime after Shakspeare. We are not all Heraclituses, to see only the tragic side of life, or Democrituses, to laugh at everything; the majority of men have faculties to appreciate both classes of emotion; and it would seem, from universal experience, that, as the Russian finds a physical delight in leaping from a vapour-bath into the frozen Neva, so there is some mental delight in the sudden alternate excitation of the opposite emotions of tragedy and farce. If we had time to philosophise, we might find the source of the delight deeply seated in our nature :—alternate tears and laughter—it is an epitome of human life!

In the accompanying woodcut from a Late Saxon MS. in the British Museum (Cott. Tiberius C. vi.) we have a curious evidence of the way in which custom blinded men to any incongruity there may be in the association of the harper and the juggler, for here we have David singing his Psalms and accompanying himself on the harp, the dove reminding us that he sang and harped under the influence of inspiration. He is accompanied by performers who must be Levites; and yet the Saxon illuminator was so used to see a mime form one of a minstrel band, that he

Saxon Band of Minstrels.

has introduced one playing the common feat of tossing three knives and three balls.

The Saxons were a musical people. We learn from Bede's anecdote of the poet Cædmon, that it was usual at their feasts to pass the harp round from hand to hand, and every man was supposed to be able to sing in his turn, and accompany himself on the instrument. They had a considerable number of musical instruments. In a MS. in the British Museum, Tiberius C. vi., folios 16 v., 17 v., 18, are a few leaves of a formal treatise on the subject, which give us very carefully drawn pictures of different instruments, with their names and descriptions. There are also illustrations of them in the Add. 11,695, folios 86, 86 v., 164, 170 v., 229, and in Cleopatra E. viii. Among them are the Psaltery of various shapes, the Sambuca or sackbut, the single and double Chorus, &c. Other instruments we find in Saxon MSS. are the lyre, viol, flute, cymbals, organ, &c. A set of hand-bells (carillons) which the player struck with two hammers, was a favourite instrument. We often find different instruments played

Saxon Organ.

together. At folio 93 v. of the MS. Claudius B iv. there is a group of twelve female harpists playing together; one has a small instrument, probably a kind of lyre, the rest have great harps of the same pattern. They probably represent Miriam and the women of Israel joining in the triumphal song of Moses over the destruction of the Egyptians in the Red Sea.

The organ, already introduced into divine service, became, under the hands of St. Dunstan, a large and important instrument. William of·

Malmesbury says that Dunstan gave many to churches which had pipes of brass and were inflated with bellows. In a MS. psalter in Trinity College, Cambridge, is a picture of one of considerable size, which has no less than four bellows played by four men. It is represented in the accompanying wood-cut.

The Northmen who invaded and gave their name to Normandy, took their minstrels with them; and the learned assert that it was from them that the troubadours of Provence learned their art, which ripened in their sunny clime into *la joyeuse science*, and thence was carried into Italy, France, and Spain. It is quite certain that minstrelsy was in high repute among the Normans at the period of the Conquest. Every one will remember how Taillefer, the minstrel-knight, commenced the great battle of Hastings. Advancing in front of the Norman host, he animated himself and them to a chivalric daring by chanting the heroic tale of Charlemagne and his Paladins, at the same time showing feats of skill in tossing his sword into the air; and then rushed into the Saxon ranks, like a divinely-mad hero of old, giving in his own self-sacrifice an augury of victory to his people.

From the period of the Conquest, authorities on the subject of which we are treating, though still not so numerous as could be desired, become too numerous to be all included within the limits to which our space restricts us. The reader may refer to Wharton's "History of English Poetry," to Bishop Percy's introductory essay to the "Reliques of Early English Poetry," and to the introductory essay to Ellis's "Early English Metrical Romances," for the principal published authorities. For a series of learned essays on mediæval musical instruments he may consult M. Didron's "Annales Archæologiques," vol. iii. pp. 76, 142, 260; vol. iv. pp. 25, 94; vol. vi. p. 315; vol. vii. pp. 92, 157, 244, 325; vol. viii. p. 242; vol. ix. pp. 289, 329.* We propose only from these and other published and unpublished materials to give a popular sketch of the subject.

Throughout this period minstrelsy was in high estimation with all

---

* Also a paper read before the London and Middlesex Architectural Society in June, 1871.

classes of society. The king himself, like his Saxon* predecessors, had a king's minstrel, or king of the minstrels, who probably from the first was at the head of a band of royal minstrels.†

This fashion of the royal court, doubtless, like all its other fashions, obtained also in the courts of the great nobility (several instances will be observed in the sequel), and in their measure in the households of the lesser nobility. Every gentleman of estate had probably his one, two, or more minstrels as a regular part of his household. It is not difficult to discover their duties. In the representations of dinners, which occur plentifully in the mediæval MSS., we constantly find musicians introduced; sometimes we see them preceding the servants, who are bearing the dishes to table—a custom of classic usage, and which still lingers to this day at Queen's College, Oxford, in the song with which the choristers usher in the boar's head on Christmas-day, and at our modern public dinners,

---

* The king's minstrel of the last Saxon king is mentioned in Domesday Book as holding lands in Gloucestershire.

† In the reign of Henry I., Rayer was the King's Minstrel. Temp. Henry II., it was Galfrid, or Jeffrey. Temp. Richard I., Blondel, of romantic memory. Temp. Henry III., Master Ricard. It was the Harper of Prince Edward (afterwards King Edward I.) who brained the assassin who attempted the Prince's life, when his noble wife Eleanor risked hers to extract the poison from the wound. In Edward I.'s reign we have mention of a King Robert, who may be the impetuous minstrel of the Prince. Temp. Edward II., there occur two: a grant of houses was made to William de Morley, the King's Minstrel, which had been held by his predecessor, John de Boteler. At St. Bride's, Glamorganshire, is the insculpt effigy of a knightly figure, of the date of Edward I., with an inscription to John le Boteler; but there is nothing to identify him with the king of the minstrels. Temp. Richard II., John Camuz was the king of his minstrels. When Henry V. went to France, he took his fifteen minstrels, and Walter Haliday, their Marshal, with him. After this time the chief of the royal minstrels seems to have been styled *Marshal* instead of King; and in the next reign but one we find a *Sergeant* of the Minstrels. Temp. Henry VI., Walter Haliday was still Marshal of the Minstrels; and this king issued a commission for *impressing* boys to supply vacancies in their number. King Edward IV. granted to the said long-lived Walter Haliday, Marshal, and to seven others, a charter for the restoration of a Fraternity or Gild, to be governed by a marshal and two wardens, to regulate the minstrels throughout the realm (except those of Chester). The minstrels of the royal chapel establishment of this king were thirteen in number; some trumpets, some shalms, some small pipes, and others singers. The charter of Edward IV. was renewed by Henry VIII. in 1520, to John Gilman, his then marshal, on whose death Hugh Wodehouse was promoted to the office.

276   *The Minstrels of the Middle Ages.*

when the band strikes up " Oh the Roast Beef of Old England," as that national dish is brought to table.

We give here an illustration of such a scene from a very fine MS. of the early part of the fourteenth century, in the British Museum (marked Royal 2 B vii., f. 184 v. and 185). A very fine representation of a similar scene occurs at the foot of the large Flemish Brass of Robert Braunche and his two wives in St. Margaret's Church, Lynn; the scene is intended as a delineation of a feast given by the corporation of Lynn to King Edward III. Servants from both sides of the picture are bringing in that famous dish of chivalry, the peacock with his tail displayed; and two bands of minstrels are ushering

A Royal Dinner.

in the banquet with their strains: the date of the brass is about 1364 A.D. In the fourteenth-century romance of " Richard Cœur de Lion," we read of some knights who have arrived in presence of the romance king whom they are in quest of; dinner is immediately prepared for them; "trestles," says Ellis in his abstract of it, " were immediately set; a table covered with a silken cloth was laid; a rich repast, ushered in by the sound of trumpets and shalms, was served up."*

Having introduced the feast, the minstrels continued to play during its progress. We find numerous representations of dinners in the illuminations, in which one or two minstrels are standing beside the table, playing their instruments during the progress of the meal. In a MS. volume of romances

* Ellis's " Earl English Metrical Romances " (Bohn's edition), p. 287.

Domestic Minstrels.

of the early part of the fourteenth century in the British Museum (Royal 14 E iii.), the title-page of the romance of the "Quête du St. Graal" (at folio 89 of the MS.) is adorned with an illumination of a royal banquet; a squire on his knee (as in the illustration given on opposite page) is carving, and a minstrel stands beside the table playing the violin; he is dressed in a parti-coloured tunic of red and blue, and wears his hat. In the Royal MS. 2 B vii., at folio 168, is a similar representation of a dinner, in which a minstrel stands playing the violin; he is habited in a red tunic, and is

Royal Dinner of the time of Edward IV.

bareheaded. At folio 203 of the same MS. (Royal 2 B vii.), is another representation of a dinner, in which two minstrels are introduced; one (wearing his hood) is playing a cittern, the other (bareheaded) is playing a violin: and these references might be multiplied.

We reproduce here, in further illustration of the subject, engravings of a royal dinner of about the time of our Edward IV., "taken from an illumination of the romance of the Compte d'Artois, in the possession of

M. Barrois, a distinguished and well-known collector in Paris."* The other is an exceedingly interesting representation of a grand imperial ban-

Imperial Banquet.

quet, from one of the plates of Hans Burgmair, in the volume dedicated to the exploits of the Emperor Maximilian, contemporary with our

---

* From Mr. T. Wright's "Domestic Manners of the English."

Henry VIII. It represents the entrance of a masque, one of those strange entertainments, of which our ancestors, in the time of Henry and Elizabeth, were so fond, and of which Mr. C. Kean some years ago gave the play-going world of London so accurate a representation in his *mise en scene* of Henry VIII. at the Princess's Theatre. The band of minstrels who have been performing during the banquet, are seen in the left corner of the picture.

So in "The Squier's Tale" of Chaucer, where Cambuscan is "holding his feste so solempne and so riche."

"It so befel, that after the thridde cours,
While that this king sat thus in his nobley,*
Harking his ministralles her† thinges play,
Beforne him at his bord deliciously," &c.

The custom of having instrumental music as an accompaniment of dinner

Harper.

is still retained by her Majesty and by some of the greater nobility, by military messes, and at great public dinners. But the musical accompaniment of a mediæval dinner was not confined to instrumental performances. We frequently find a harper introduced, who is doubtless reciting some romance or history, or singing chansons of a lighter character. He is often represented as sitting upon the floor, as in the accompanying illustration, from the Royal MS., 2 B vii., folio 71 b. Another similar representation

---

* Among his nobles. † Their.

occurs at folio 203 b of the same MS. In the following very charming picture, from a MS. volume of romances of early fourteenth century date in the British Museum (Additional MS., 10,292, folio 200), the harper is sitting upon the table.

Gower, in his "Confessio Amantis," gives us a description of a scene of the kind. Appolinus is dining in the hall of King Pentapolin, with the king and queen and their fair daughter, and all his "lordes in estate.' Appolinus was reminded by the scene of the royal estate from which he is

Royal Harper.

fallen, and sorrowed and took no meat; therefore the king bade his daughter take her harp and do all that she can to enliven that "sorry man."

>"And she to dou her fader's hest,
> Her harpe fette, and in the feste
> Upon a chaire which thei fette,
> Her selve next to this man she sette."

Appolinus in turn takes the harp, and proves himself a wonderful proficient, and

>"When he hath harped all his fille,
> The kingis hest to fulfille,
> A waie goth dishe, a waie goth cup,
> Doun goth the borde, the cloth was up,
> Thei risen and gone out of the halle."

In the sequel, the interesting stranger was made tutor to the princess, and among other teachings,

> "He taught hir till she was certeyne
> Of harpe, citole, and of riote,
> With many a tewne and many a note,
> Upon musike, upon measure,
> And of her harpe the temprure,
> He taught her eke, as he well couth."

Another occasion on which their services would be required would be for the dance. Thus we read in the sequel of "The Squire's Tale," how the king and his "nobley," when dinner was ended, rose from table, and, preceded by the minstrels, went to the great chamber for the dance :—

> "Wan that this Tartar king, this Cambuscán,
> Rose from his bord ther as he sat ful hie;
> Beforne him goth the loudé minstralcie,
> Til he come to his chambre of parements,*
> Theras they sounden divers instruments,
> That it is like an Heaven for to here.
> Now dauncen lusty Venus children dere," &c.

In the tale of Dido and Æneas, in the legend of "Good Women," he calls it especially the dancing chamber :—

Mediæval Dance.

> "To dauncing chambers full of paraments,
> Of riché bedés † and of pavements,
> This Eneas is ledde after the meat."

---

* Great chamber, answering to our modern drawing-room.   † Couches.

But the dance was not always in the great chamber. Very commonly it took place in the hall. The tables were only movable boards laid upon trestles, and at the signal from the master of the house, " A hall ! a hall !" they were quickly put aside ; while the minstrels tuned their instruments anew, and the merry folly at once commenced. In the illustration, of early fourteenth-century date, which we give on the preceding page, from folio 174 of the Royal MS., 2 B vii., the scene of the dance is not indicated ; the minstrels themselves appear to be joining in the saltitation which they inspire.

In the next illustration, reproduced from Mr. Wright's " Domestic

A Dance in the Gallery.

Manners of the English," we have a curious picture of a dance, possibly in the gallery, which occupied the whole length of the roof of most fifteenth-century houses; it is from M. Barrois's MS. of the " Compte D'Artois," of fifteenth-century date. In all these instances the minstrels are on the floor with the dancers, but in the latter part of the Middle Ages they were probably—especially on festal occasions—placed in the music gallery over the screens, or entrance-passage, of the hall.

Marriage processions were, beyond doubt, attended by minstrels. **An illustration of a band consisting of tabor, bagpipes, regal, and violin, head-**

ing a marriage procession, may be seen in the Roman d'Alexandre (Bodleian Library) at folio 173; and at folios 173 and 174 the wedding feast is enlivened by a more numerous band of harp, gittern, violin, regal, tabor, bagpipes, hand-bells, cymbals, and kettle-drums—which are carried on a boy's back.*

---

* For other illustrations of musical instruments see a good representation of Venus playing a rote, with a plectrum in the right hand, pressing the strings with the left, in the Sloane MS. 3,985, f. 44 v. Also a band, consisting of violin, organistrum (like the modern hurdy-gurdy), harp, and dulcimer, in the Harl. MS. 1,527; it represents the feast on the return of the prodigal son. In the Arundel MS. 83, f. 155, is David with a band of instruments of early fourteenth-century date, and other instruments at f. 630. In the early fourteenth-century MS. 28,162, at f. 6 v., David is tuning his harp with a key; at f. 10 v. is Dives faring sumptuously, with carver and cup-bearer, and musicians with lute and pipe.

CHAPTER II.

SACRED MUSIC.

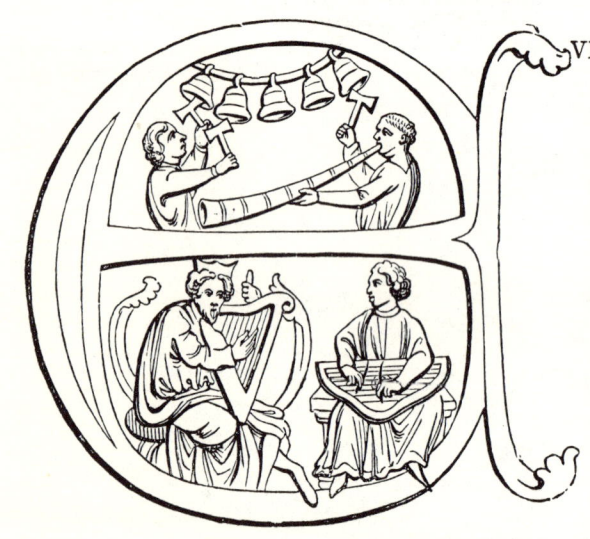

EVERY nobleman and gentleman in the Middle Ages, we have seen, had one or more minstrels as part of his household, and among their other duties they were required to assist at the celebration of divine worship. Allusions occur perpetually in the old romances, showing that it was the universal custom to hear mass before dinner, and even-song before supper, *e.g.*: " And so they went home and unarmed them, and so to even-song and supper. . . . And on the morrow they heard mass, and after went to dinner, and to their counsel, and made many arguments what were best to do."* "The Young Children's Book," a kind of mediæval "Chesterfield's Letters to his Son," pub-

---

* Mallory's "History of Prince Arthur," vol. i. p. 44.

lished by the Early English Text Society, from a MS. of about 1500 A.D., in the Bodleian Library, bids its pupils—

> "Aryse be tyme oute of thi bedde,
> And blysse* thi brest and thi forhede,
> Then wasche thi handes and thi face,
> Keme thi hede and ask God grace
> The to helpe in all thi workes;
> Thou schalt spede better what so thou carpes.
> Then go to the chyrche and here a massé,
> There aske mersy for thi trespasse.
> When thou hast done go breke thy faste
> With mete and drynk a gode repast."

In great houses the service was performed by the chaplain in the chapel of the hall or castle, and it seems probable that the lord's minstrels assisted in the musical part of the service.

The organ doubtless continued to be, as we have seen it in Saxon times, the most usual church instrument. Thus the King of Hungary in "The Squire of Low Degree," tells his daughter:—

> "Then shal ye go to your even song,
> With tenours and trebles among;
>   *   *   *   *
> Your quere nor organ song shal want
> With countre note and dyscant;
> The other half on organs playing,
> With young children ful fayn synging."

And in inventories of church furniture in the Middle Ages we find organs enumerated:† Not only the organ, but all instruments in common use, were probably also used in the celebration of divine worship. We meet with repeated instances in which David singing the psalms is accompanied by a band of musicians, as in the Saxon illumination on p. 272, and again in the initial letter of this chapter, which is taken from a psalter

---

* Viz., by making the sign of the cross upon them.

† Edward VI.'s commissioners return a pair of organs in the church of St. Peter Mancroft, Norwich, which they value at 40s., and in the church of St. Peter, Parmentergate, in the same city, a pair of organs which they value at £10 (which would be equal to about £70 or £80 in these days), and soon after we find that 8d. were "paied to a carpenter for makyng of a plaunche (a platform of planks) to sette the organs on."

of early thirteenth-century date in the British Museum (Harl. 5,102). The men of those days were in some respects much more real and practical, less sentimental and transcendental, than we in religious matters. We must have everything relating to divine worship of different form and fashion from ordinary domestic appliances, and think it irreverent to use things of ordinary domestic fashion for religious uses, or to have domestic things in the shapes of what we call religious art. They had only one art, the best they knew, for all purposes; and they were content to apply the best of that to the service of God. Thus to their minds it would not appear at all unseemly that the minstrels who had accompanied the divine service in chapel should walk straight out of chapel into the hall, and tune their instruments anew to play symphonies, or accompany chansons during dinner, or enliven the dance in the great chamber in the evening—no more unseemly than that their master and his family should dine and dance as well as pray. The chapel royal establishment of Edward IV. consisted of trumpets, shalms, and pipes, as well as voices; and we may be quite sure that the custom of the royal chapel was imitated by noblemen and gentlemen of estate. A good fifteenth-century picture of the interior of a church, showing the organ in a gallery, is engraved in the "Annales Archæologiques," vol. xii., p. 349. A very good representation of an organ of the latter part of the sixteenth century (1582) is in the fine MS. Plut. 3,469, folio 27.* An organ of about this date is still preserved in that most interesting old Manor House, Igtham Mote, in Kent. They were sometimes placed at the side of the chancel, sometimes in the rood-loft, which occupied the same relative position in the choir which the music gallery did in the hall.

In the MSS. we not unfrequently find the ordinary musical instruments placed in the hands of the angels; *e.g.*, in the early fourteenth-century MS. Royal 2 B. vii., in a representation of the creation, with the morning stars singing together, and all the sons of God shouting for joy, an angelic choir are making melody on the trumpet, violin, cittern, shalm (or psaltery), and harp. There is another choir of angels at p. 168 of the same MS., two

---

* Another, with kettle-drums and trumpets, in the MS. Add. 27,675, f. 13.

citterns and two shalms, a violin and trumpet. Similar representations occur very significantly in churches. On the arch of the Porta Della Gloria of Saragossa Cathedral, of the eleventh century, from which there is a cast at the entrance to the South Kensington Museum, are a set of angel minstrels with musical instruments. In the bosses of the ceiling of Tewkesbury Abbey Church we find angels playing the cittern (with a plectrum), the harp (with its cover seen enveloping the lower half of the instrument)*

The Morning Stars singing together.

and the cymbals. A set of angel musicians is sculptured on the rood loft of York Minster. In the triforum of the nave of Exeter Cathedral is a projecting gallery for the minstrels, with sculptures of them on the front playing instruments.† In the choir of Lincoln Cathedral, some of the noble series of angels which fill the spandrels of its arcades, and which have given to it the name of the Angel Choir, are playing instruments, viz., the trumpet, double pipe, pipe and tabret, dulcimer, viol and harp. They represent the heavenly choir attuning their praises in harmony with the human choir below: "Therefore with angels and archangels, and with all the company of heaven, we laud and magnify thy glorious name." There is a band of musicians sculptured on the grand portal of the Cathedral at Rheims; a sculptured capital from the church of St. Georges

---

* A harp with its case about the lower part is in the Add. MS. 18,854, f. 91.
† There are casts of these in the Mediæval Court of the Crystal Palace.

de Bocherville, now in the Museum at Rouen, represents eleven crowned figures playing different instruments.* On the chasse of St. Ursula at Bruges are angels playing instruments beautifully painted by Hemling.† We cannot resist the temptation to introduce here another charming little drawing of an angelic minstrel, playing a psaltery, from the Royal MS. 14 E iii.; others occur at folio 1 of the same MS. The band of village musicians with flute, violin, clarinet, and bass-viol, whom most of us have seen occupying the singing-gallery of some country church, are the representatives of the band of minstrels who occupied the rood-lofts in mediæval times.

Clerical censors of manners during the Middle Ages frequently denounce the dissoluteness of minstrels, and the minstrels take their revenge by lampooning the vices of the clergy. Like all sweeping censures of whole classes of men, the accusations on both sides must be received cautiously. However, it is certain that the minstrels were patronised by the clergy. We shall presently find a record of the minstrels of the Bishop of Winchester in the fourteenth century; and the Ordinance of Edward II., quoted at p. 296, tells us that minstrels flocked to the houses of prelates as well as of nobles and gentlemen. In the thirteenth century, that fine sample of an English bishop, Grostête of Lincoln, was a great patron of minstrel science: he himself composed an allegorical romance, the Chasteau d'Amour. Robert de Brunne, in his English paraphrase of Grostête's Manuel de Peches (begun in 1303), gives us a charming anecdote of the Bishop's love of minstrelsy.

An Angel Minstrel.

> "Y shall yow telle as y have herde,
> Of the bysshope seynt Robérde,
> Hys to-name ys Grostet.
> Of Lynkolne, so seyth the gest

---

* "Annales Archæologiques," vol. vi. p. 315. † Ibid., vol. ix. p. 329.

> He loved moche to here the harpe,
> For mannys witte hyt makyth sharpe.
> Next hys chaumber, besyde his stody,
> Hys harpers chaumbre was fast therby.
> Many tymes be nyght and dayys,
> He had solace of notes and layys.
> One askede hym onys resun why
> He hadde delyte in mynstralsy?
> He answered hym on thys manere
> Why he helde the harper so dere.
> The vertu of the harpe, thurghe skylle and ryght,
> Wyl destroy the fendes myght;
> And to the croys by gode skylle
> Ys the harpe lykened weyle.
> Tharfor gode men, ye shul lere
> Whan ye any gleman here,
> To wurschep Gode al youre powére,
> As Dauyde seyth yn the sautére."

We know that the abbots lived in many respects as other great people did; they exercised hospitality to guests of gentle birth in their own halls, treated them to the diversions of hunting and hawking over their manors and in their forests, and did not scruple themselves to partake in those amusements; possibly they may have retained minstrels wherewith to solace their guests and themselves. It is quite certain at least that the wandering minstrels were welcome guests at the religious houses; and Warton records many instances of the rewards given to them on those occasions. We may record two or three examples.

The monasteries had great annual feasts, on the ecclesiastical festivas, and often also in commemoration of some saint or founder; there was a grand service in church, and a grand dinner afterwards in the refectory. The convent of St. Swithin, in Winchester, used thus to keep the anniversary of Alwyne the Bishop; and in the year A.D. 1374 we find that six minstrels, accompanied by four harpers, performed their minstrelsies at dinner, in the hall of the convent, and during supper sang the same gest in the great arched chamber of the prior, on which occasion the chamber was adorned, according to custom on great occasions, with the prior's great dorsal (a hanging for the wall behind the table), having on it a picture of the three kings of Cologne. These minstrels and harpers belonged partly to the Royal household in Winchester Castle, partly to the Bishop of Winchester. Similarly at the priory of Bicester, in Oxfordshire, in the year A.D. 1432, the treasurer of the monastery gave four shillings to six minstrels from Buckingham, for singing in the refectory, on the Feast of the Epiphany, a legend of the Seven Sleepers. In A.D. 1430 the brethren of the Holie Crosse at Abingdon celebrated their annual feast; twelve priests were hired for the occasion to help to sing the dirge with becoming solemnity, for which they received four pence each; and twelve minstrels, some of whom came from the neighbouring town of Maidenhead, were rewarded with two shillings and four pence each, besides their share of the feast and food for their horses. At Mantoke Priory, near Coventry, there was a yearly obit; and in the year A.D. 1441, we find that eight priests were hired from Coventry to assist in the service, and the six minstrels of their neighbour, Lord Clinton, of Mantoke Castle, were engaged to sing, harp, and play, in the hall of the monastery, at the grand refection allowed to the monks on the occasion of that anniversary. The minstrels amused the monks and their guests during dinner, and then dined themselves in the painted chamber (*camera picta*) of the monastery with the sub-prior, on which occasion the chamberlain furnished eight massy tapers of wax to light their table.

These are instances of minstrels formally invited by abbots and convents to take part in certain great festivities; but there are proofs that the wandering minstrel, who, like all other classes of society, would find hospitality in the guest-house of the monastery, was also welcomed for his minstrel skill, and rewarded for it with guerdon of money, besides his food and lodging. Warton gives instances of entries in monastic accounts for disbursements on such occasions; and there is an anecdote quoted by Percy of some dissolute monks who one evening admitted two poor priests whom they took to be minstrels, and ill-treated and turned them out again when they were disappointed of their anticipated gratification.

On the next page is a curious illumination from the Royal MS. 2 B vii., representing a friar and a nun themselves making minstrelsy.

At tournaments the scene was enlivened by the strains of minstrels, and horses and men inspirited to the charge by the loud fanfare of their

Nun and Friar with Musical Instruments.

instruments. Thus in "The Knight's Tale," at the tournament of Palamon and Arcite, as the king and his company rode to the lists :—

> "Up gon the trumpets and the melodie,
> And to the listés ride the companie."

And again :—

> "Then were the gates shut, and cried was loude
> Now do your devoir youngé knightés proud.
> The heralds left their pricking up and down,
> Now ringen trumpets loud and clarioun.
> There is no more to say, but East and West
> In go the spearés sadly in the rest;
> In goeth the sharpé spur into the side;
> There see men who can just and who can ride.
> Men shiveren shaftés upon shieldés thick,
> He feeleth thro the hearte-spoon the prick."

In actual war only the trumpet and horn and tabor seem to have been used. In "The Romance of Merlin" we read of

> "Trumpés beting, tambours classing"

in the midst of a battle; and again, in Chaucer's "Knight's Tale"—

> "Pipes, trumpets, nakeres,* and clariouns
> That in the battle blowen bloody sounds;"

---

* Kettle-drums.

and again, on another occasion—

> " The trumping and the tabouring,
> Did together the knights fling."

There are several instances in the Royal MS., 2 B vii., in which trumpeters are sounding their instruments in the rear of a company of charging chevaliers.

Again, when a country knight and his neighbour wished to keep their spears in practice against the next tournament, or when a couple of errant knights happened to meet at a manor-house, the lists were rudely staked out in the base-court of the castle, or in the meadow under the castle-walls; and, while the ladies looked on and waved their scarfs from the windows or the battlements, and the vassals flocked round the ropes, the minstrels gave animation to the scene. In the illustration on p. 414 from the title-page of the Royal MS., 14 E iii., a fine volume of romances of early fourteenth-century date, we are made spectators of a scene of the kind; the herald is arranging the preliminaries between the two knights who are about to joust, while a band of minstrels inspire them with their strains.

Not only at these stated periods, but at all times, the minstrels were liable to be called upon to enliven the tedium of their lord or lady with music and song; the King of Hungary (in " The Squire of Low Degree "), trying to comfort his daughter for the loss of her lowly lover by the promise of all kinds of pleasures, says that in the morning—

> " Ye shall have harpe, sautry, and songe,
> And other myrthes you among."

And again a little further on, after dinner—

> " When you come home your menie amonge,
> Ye shall have revell, daunces, and songe;
> Lytle children, great and smale,
> Shall syng as doth the nightingale."

And yet again, when she is gone to bed—

> " And yf ye no rest can take,
> All night mynstrels for you shall wake."

Doubtless many of the long winter evenings, when the whole household was assembled round the blazing wood fire in the middle of the hall, would be passed in listening to those interminable tales of chivalry which my lord's chief harper would chant to his harp, while his fellows would play a symphony between the "fyttes." Of other occasions on which the minstrels would have appropriate services to render, an entry in the Household Book of the Percy family in A.D. 1512 gives us an indication: There were three of them at their castle in the north, a tabret, a lute, and a rebec; and we find that they had a new-year's gift, "xx*s*. for playing at my lordes chamber doure on new yeares day in the mornynge; and for playinng at my lordes sone and heire's chamber doure, the lord Percy, ii*s*.; and for playing at the chamber dours of my lord's yonger sonnes, my yonge masters, after viii. the piece for every of them."

But besides the official minstrels of kings, nobles, and gentlemen, bishops, and abbots, and corporate towns, there were a great number of "minstrels unattached," and of various grades of society, who roamed abroad singly or in company, from town to town, from court to camp, from castle to monastery, flocking in great numbers to tournaments and festivals and fairs, and welcomed everywhere.

The summer-time was especially the season for the wanderings of these children of song,[*] as it was of the knight-errant[†] and of the pilgrim[‡] also. No wonder that the works of the minstrels abound as they do with charming outbursts of song on the return of the spring and summer, and the delights which they bring. All winter long the minstrel had lain in some town, chafing at its miry and unsavoury streets, and its churlish, money-getting citizens; or in some hospitable castle or manor-house, perhaps, listening to the wind roaring through the broad forests, and howling among the

---

[*] In the accomt of the minstrel at Kenilworth, subsequently given, he is described as "a squiere minstrel of Middlesex, that travelled the country this summer time."

[†] "Miri it is in somer's tide
Swainés gin on justing ride."

[‡] "Whanne that April with his shourés sote," &c.
"Than longen folk to gon on pilgrimages."

turrets overhead, until he pined for freedom and green fields; his host, perchance, grown tired of his ditties, and his only occupation to con new ones; this, from the "Percy Reliques," sounds like a verse composed at such a time :—

> "In time of winter alange* it is!
> The foules lesen† her bliss!
> The leves fallen off the tree;
> Rain alangeth ‡ the countree."

No wonder they welcomed the return of the bright, warm days, when they could resume their gay, adventurous, open-air life, in the fresh, flowery meadows, and the wide, green forest glades; roaming to town and village, castle and monastery, feast and tournament; alone, or in company with a band of brother minstrels; meeting by the way with gay knights adventurous, or pilgrims not less gay—if they were like those of Chaucer's company; welcomed everywhere by priest and abbot, lord and loon. These are the sort of strains which they carolled as they rested under the white hawthorn, and carelessly tinkled an accompaniment on their harps :—

> "Merry is th' enté of May;
> The fowles maketh merry play;
> The time is hot, and long the day.
> The joyful nightingale singeth,
> In the grene mede flowers springeth.
>   *   *   *
> "Merry it is in somer's tide;
> Fowles sing in forest wide;
> Swaines gin on justing ride,
> Maidens liffen hem in pride."

The minstrels were often men of position and wealth. Rayer, or Raherus, the first of the king's minstrels whom we meet with after the Conquest, founded the Priory and Hospital of St. Bartholomew, in Smithfield, London, in the third year of Henry I., A.D. 1102, and became the first prior of his own foundation. He was not the only minstrel who turned religious. Foulquet de Marseille, first a merchant, then a minstrel of note—some of his songs have descended to these days—at length turned monk, and was made abbot of Tournet, and at length Archbishop of

---

* Tedious, irksome. † Lose their. ‡ Renders tedious.

Toulouse, and is known in history as the persecutor of the Albigenses: he died in 1231 A.D. It seems to have been no unusual thing for men of family to take up the wandering, adventurous life of the minstrel, much as others of the same class took up the part of knight adventurous; they frequently travelled on horseback, with a servant to carry their harp; flocking to courts and tournaments, where the graceful and accomplished singer of chivalrous deeds was perhaps more caressed than the large-limbed warrior who achieved them; and obtained large rewards, instead of huge blows, for his guerdon.

There are some curious anecdotes showing the kind of people who became minstrels, their wandering habits, their facility of access to all companies and places, and the uses which were sometimes made of their privileges. All our readers will remember how Blondel de Nesle, the minstrel of Richard Cœur de Lion, wandered over Europe in search of his master. There is a less known instance of a similar kind and of the same period. Ela, the heiress of D'Evereux, Earl of Salisbury, had been carried abroad and secreted by her French relations in Normandy. To discover the place of her concealment, a knight of the Talbot family spent two years in exploring that province; at first under the disguise of a pilgrim; then, having found where she was confined, in order to gain admittance, he assumed the dress and character of a harper; and being a jocose person, exceedingly skilled in the Gests of the ancients, he was gladly received into the family. He succeeded in carrying off the lady, whom he restored to her liege lord the king, who bestowed her in marriage, not upon the adventurous knight-minstrel, as ought to have been the ending of so pretty a novelet, but upon his own natural brother, William Longespée, to whom she brought her earldom of Salisbury in dower.

Many similar instances, not less valuable evidences of the manners of the times because they are fiction, might be selected from the romances of the Middle Ages; proving that it was not unusual for men of birth and station[*] to assume, for a longer or shorter time, the character and life of the wandering minstrel.

---

[*] Fontenelle ("Histoire du Théâtre," quoted by Percy) tells us that in France, men, who by the division of the family property had only the half or the fourth part of an old

But besides these gentle minstrels, there were a multitude of others of the lower classes of society, professors of the joyous science; descending through all grades of musical skill, and of respectability of character. We find regulations from time to time intended to check their irregularities. In 1315 King Edward II. issued an ordinance addressed to sheriffs, &c., as follows: "Forasmuch as .... many idle persons under colour of mynstrelsie, and going in messages[*] and other faigned busines, have been and yet be receaved in other men's houses to meate and drynke, and be not therwith contented yf they be not largely considered with gyftes of the Lordes of the Houses, &c. ..... We wyllyng to restrayne such outrageous enterprises and idlenes, &c., have ordeyned .... that to the houses of Prelates, Earls, and Barons, none resort to meate and drynke unless he be a mynstrell, and of these mynstrels that there come none except it be three or four mynstrels of honour at most in one day unless he be desired of the Lorde of the House. And to the houses of meaner men, that none come unlesse he be desired; and that such as shall come so holde themselves contented with meate and drynke, and with such curtesie as the Master of the House wyl shewe unto them of his owne good wyll, without their askyng of any thyng. And yf any one do against this ordinaunce at the first tyme he to lose his minstrelsie, and at the second tyme to forsweare his craft, and never to be received for a minstrell in any house." This curious ordinance gives additional proof of several facts which we have before noted, viz., that minstrels were well received everywhere, and had even become exacting in their expectations; that they used to wander about in bands; and the penalties seem to indicate that the minstrels were already incorporated in a guild. The first positive evidence of such a

---

seignorial castle, sometimes went rhyming about the world, and returned to acquire the remainder of their ancestral castle.

[*] In the MS. illuminations of the thirteenth and fourteenth centuries, the messenger is denoted by peculiarities of equipment. He generally bears a spear, and has a very small, round target (or, perhaps, a badge of his lord's arms) at his girdle—*e.g.*, in the MS. Add. 11,639 of the close of the thirteenth century, folio 203 v. In the fifteenth century we see messengers carrying letters openly, fastened in the cleft of a split wand, in the MS. of about the same date, Harl. 1,527, folio 1,080, and in the fourteenth century MS. Add. 10,293, folio 45; **and in Hans Burgmaier's Der Weise Könige.**

Organization of Minstrels.

guild is in the charter (already alluded to) of 9th King Edward IV, A.D. 1469, in which he grants to Walter Haliday, *Marshall*, and seven others, his own minstrels, a charter by which he restores a Fraternity or perpetual Guild (such as he understands the brothers and sisters of the Fraternity of Minstrels had in times past), to be governed by a marshall, appointed for life, and by two wardens, to be chosen annually, who are empowered to admit brothers and sisters into the guild, and are authorised to examine the pretensions of all such as affect to exercise the minstrel profession; and to regulate, govern, and punish them throughout the realm—those of Chester excepted. It seems probable that the King's Minstrel, or the King of the Minstrels, had long previously possessed an authority of this kind over all the members of the profession, and that the organization very much resembled that of the heralds. The two are mentioned together in the Statute of Arms for Tournaments, passed in the reign of Edward I., A.D. 1295. "E qe nul Roy de Harraunz ne Menestrals* portent privez armez:" that no King of the Heralds or of the Minstrels shall carry secret weapons. That the minstrels attended all tournaments we have already mentioned. The heralds and minstrels are often coupled in the same sentence; thus Froissart tells us that at a Christmas entertainment given by the Earl of Foix, there were many minstrels, as well his own as strangers, "and the Earl gave to Heraulds and Minstrelles the sum of fyve hundred frankes; and gave to the Duke of Tourayne's mynstreles gowns of cloth of gold furred with ermine, valued at 200 frankes."†

---

* It is right to state that one MS. of this statute gives Mareschans instead of Menestrals; but the reading in the text is that preferred by the Record Commission, who have published the whole of the interesting document.

† In the romance of Richard Cœur de Lion we read that, after the capture of Acre, he distributed among the "heralds, disours, tabourers, and trompours," who accompanied him, the greater part of the money, jewels, horses, and fine robes which had fallen to his share. We have many accounts of the lavish generosity with which chivalrous lords propitiated the favourable report of the heralds and minstrels, whose good report was fame.

CHAPTER III.

GUILDS OF MINSTRELS.

IT is not unlikely that the principal minstrel of every great noble exercised some kind of authority over all minstrels within his lord's jurisdiction. There are several famous instances of something of this kind on record. The earliest is that of the authority granted by Ranulph, Earl of Chester, to the Duttons over all minstrels of his jurisdiction; for the romantic origin of the grant the curious reader may see the Introductory Essay to Percy's "Reliques," or the original authorities in Dugdale's "Monasticon," and D. Powel's "History of Cambria."

The Beverley Minstrels.

The ceremonies attending the exercise of this authority are thus described by Dugdale, as handed down to his time:—viz., "That at Midsummer fair there, all the minstrels of that countrey resorting to Chester, do attend the heir of Dutton from his lodging to St. John's Church (he being then accompanied by many gentlemen of the countrey), one of the minstrels walking before him in a surcoat of his arms, depicted on taffeta; the rest of his fellows proceeding two and two, and playing on their several sorts of musical instruments. And after divine service ended, gave the like attendance on him back to his lodging; where a court being kept by his (Mr. Dutton's) steward, and all the minstrels formally called, certain orders and laws are usually made for the better government of that society, with penalties on those that transgress." This court, we have seen, was exempted from the jurisdiction of the King of the Minstrels by Edward IV., as it was also from the operation of all Acts of Parliament on the subject down to so late a period as the seventeenth year of George II., the last of them. In the fourth year of King Richard II., John* of Gaunt created a court of minstrels at Tutbury, in Staffordshire, similar to that at Chester; in the charter (which is quoted in Dr. Plott's "History of Staffordshire," p. 436) he gives them a King of the Minstrels and four officers, with a legal authority over the men of their craft in the five adjoining counties of Stafford, Derby, Notts, Leicester, and Warwick. The form of election, as it existed at a comparatively late period, is fully detailed by Dr. Plott.

Another of these guilds was the ancient company or fraternity of minstrels in Beverley, of which an account is given in Poulson's "Beverlac" (p. 302). When the fraternity originated we do not know; but they were of some consideration and wealth in the reign of Henry VI., when the Church of St. Mary's, Beverley, was built; for they gave a pillar to it, on the capital of which a band of minstrels are sculptured, of whom we here re-produce a drawing from Carter's "Ancient Painting and Sculpture," to which we shall have presently to ask the reader's further attention. The oldest existing document of the fraternity is a copy of laws of the time of Philip and Mary. They are similar to those by which all trade guilds were governed: their officers were an alderman and two stewards or sears

---

* May we infer from the exemption of the jurisdiction of the Duttons, and not of that of the court of Tutbury and the guild of Beverley, that the jurisdiction of the King of the Minstrels over the whole realm was established after the former, and before the latter? The French minstrels were incorporated by charter, and had a king in the year 1330, forty-seven years before Tutbury. In the ordonnance of Edward II., 1315, there is no allusion to such a general jurisdiction.

(*i.e.* seers, searchers); the only items in their laws which throw much additional light upon our subject are the one already partly quoted, that they should not take " any new brother except he be mynstrell to some man of honour or worship (proving that men of honour and worship still had minstrels), or waite * of some towne corporate or other ancient town, or else of such honestye and conyng as shall be thought laudable and pleasant to the hearers there." And again, " no myler, shepherd, or of

Goatherds playing Musical Instruments.

other occupation, or husbandman, or husbandman servant, playing upon pype or other instrument, shall sue any wedding, or other thing that pertaineth to the said science, except in his own parish." We may here

---

* One of the minstrels of King Edward the Fourth's household (there were thirteen others) was called the *wayte;* it was his duty to "pipe watch." In the romance of "Richard Cœur de Lion," when Richard, with his fleet, has come silently in the night under the walls of Jaffa, which was besieged on the land side by the Saracen army :—

"They looked up to the castel,
They heard no pipe, ne flagel,[1]
They drew em nigh to land,
If they mighten understand,
And they could ne nought espie,
Ne by no voice of minstralcie,
That quick man in the castle were."

And so they continued in uncertainty until the spring of the day, then

"A wait there came, in a kernel,[2]
And piped a nott in a flagel."

And when he recognised King Richard's galleys,

"Then a merrier note he blew,
And piped, ' Seigneurs or sus! or sus!
King Richard is comen to us!'"

[1] Flageolet.   [2] Battlement.

digress for a moment to say that the shepherds, throughout the Middle Ages, seem to have been as musical as the swains of Theocritus or Virgil; in the MS. illuminations we constantly find them represented playing upon instruments; we give a couple of goatherds from the MS. Royal 2 B vii. folio 83, of early fourteenth-century date.

Besides the pipe and horn, the bagpipe was also a rustic instrument. There is a shepherd playing upon one in folio 112 of the same MS.; and again, in the early fourteenth-century MS. Royal 2 B vi., on the reverse of folio 8, is a group of shepherds, one of whom plays a small pipe, and another the bagpipes. Chaucer (3rd Book of the "House of Fame") mentions—

"Pipes made of greené corne,
As have these little herd gromes,
That keepen beastés in the bromes."

Shepherd with Bagpipes.

It is curious to find that even at so late a period as the time of Queen Mary, the shepherds still officiated at weddings and other merrymakings in their villages, so as to excite the jealousy of the professors of the joyous science.

Rustic Merry-making.

The accompanying wood-cut, from a MS. in the French National Library, may represent such a rustic merry-making

One might, perhaps, have been disposed to think that the good minstrels of Beverley were only endeavouring to revive usages which had fallen into desuetude; but we find that in the time of Elizabeth the profession of minstrelsy was sufficiently universal to call for the inquiry, in the Injunctions of 1559, "Whether any minstrells, or any other persons, do use to sing any songs or ditties that be vile or unclean."

Ben Jonson gives us numerous allusions to them: *e.g.*, in the "Tale of a Tub," old Turve talks of "old Father Rosin, the chief minstrel here—chief minstrel, too, of Highgate; she has hired him, and all his two boys, for a day and a half." They were to be dressed in bays, rosemary, and ribands, to precede the bridal party across the fields to church and back, and to play at dinner. And so in "Epicœne," act iii. sc. 1:—

"Well, there be guests to meat now; how shall we do for music?" [for Morose's wedding.]

Clerimont.—The smell of the venison going thro' the street will invite one noise of fiddlers or other.

Dauphine.—I would it would call the trumpeters hither!

Clerimont.—Faith, there is hope: they have intelligence of all feasts. There's a good correspondence betwixt them and the London cooks: 'tis twenty to one but we have them."

And Dryden, so late as the time of William III., speaks of them—

> "These fellows
> Were once the minstrels of a country show,
> Followed the prizes through each paltry town,
> By trumpet cheeks and bloated faces known."

There were also female minstrels throughout the Middle Ages; but, as might be anticipated from their irregular wandering life, they bore an indifferent reputation. The romance of "Richard Cœur de Lion" says that it was a female minstrel, and, still worse, an Englishwoman, who recognised and betrayed the knight-errant king and his companions, on their return from the Holy Land, to his enemy, the "King of Almain." The passage is worth quoting, as it illustrates several of the traits of minstrel habits which we have already recorded. After Richard and his companions had dined on a goose, which they cooked for themselves at a tavern—

> "When they had drunken well afin,
> A minstralle com therin,·
> And said 'Gentlemen, wittily,
> Will ye have any minstrelsey ?'
> Richard bade that she should go.
> That turned him to mickle woe!
> The minstralle took in mind,[*]
> And saith, 'Ye are men unkind;
> And if I may, ye shall for-think [†]
> Ye gave neither meat nor drink.
> For gentlemen should bede [‡]
> To minstrels that abouten yede [§]
> Of their meat, wine, and ale;
> For los [||] rises of minstrale.'
> She was English, and well true
> By speech, and sight, and hide, and hue."

Stow tells that in 1316, while Edward II. was solemnizing his Feast of Pentecost in his hall at Westminster, sitting royally at table, with his peers about him, there entered a woman adorned like a minstrel, sitting on a great horse, trapped as minstrels then used, who rode round about the tables showing her pastime. The reader will remember the use which Sir E. B. Lytton has made of a troop of tymbesteres in "The Last of the Barons," bringing them in at the epochs of his tale with all the dramatic effect of the Greek chorus: the description which he gives of their habits is too sadly truthful. The daughter of Herodias dancing before Herod is scornfully represented by the mediæval artists as a female minstrel performing the tumbling tricks which were part of their craft. We give a representation of a female minstrel playing the tambourine from the MS. Royal, 2 B vii. folio 182.

Female Minstrel.

A question of considerable interest to artists, no less than to antiquaries, is whether the minstrels were or not distinguished

---

[*] Was offended.   ‡ Repent.   ‡ Give.   § Travel. || Praise

by any peculiar costume or habit. Bishop Percy* and his followers say that they were, and the assertion is grounded on the following evidences: Baldulph, the Saxon, in the anecdote already related, when assuming the disguise of a minstrel, is described as shaving his head and beard, and dressing himself in the habit of that profession. Alfred and Aulaff were known at once to be minstrels. The two poor priests who were turned out of the monastery by the dissolute monks were at first mistaken for minstrels. The woman who entered Westminster Hall at King Edward the Second's Pentecost feast was adorned like a minstrel, sitting on a great horse, trapped as minstrels then used.

The Knight of La Tour-Landry (chap. xvii.) tells a story which shows that the costume of minstrels was often conspicuous for richness and fashion: "As y have herde telle, Sir Piere de Luge was atte the feste where as were gret foyson of lordes, ladies, knightes, and squieres, and gentilwomen, and so there came in a yonge squier before hem that was sette atte dyner and salued the companie, and he was clothed in a cote-hardy † upon the guyse of Almayne, and in this wise he come further before the lordes and ladies, and made hem goodly reverence. And so the said Sir Piere called this yonge squier with his voys before alle the statis, and saide unto hym and axed hym, where was his fedylle or hys ribible, or suche an instrument as longethe unto a mynstralle. 'Syr,' saide the squier, 'I canne not medille me of such thinge, it is not my craft nor science.' 'Sir,' saide the knight, 'I canne not trowe that ye saye, for ye be counterfait in youre araye and lyke unto a mynstralle; for I have knowe herebefore alle youre aunsetours, and the knightes and squiers of youre kin, which were alle worthie men; but I sawe never none of hem that were [wore] counterfait, nor that clothed hem in such array.' And thanne the yonge squier answered the knight and saide, 'Sir, by as moche as it mislykithe you it shalle be amended,' and cleped a pursevant and gave him the cote-hardy. And he abled hym selff in an other gowne, and come agen into the halle, and thanne the anncyen knight saide openly, 'This yonge squier shalle have

---

* Introduction to his "Reliques of Early English Poetry."

† The close-fitting outer garment worn in the fourteenth century, shown in the engravings on p. 350.

worshipe for he hath trowed and do bi the counsaile of the elder withoute ani contraryenge.'"

In the time of Henry VII. we read of nine ells of *tawny* cloth for three minstrels; and in the "History of Jack of Newbury," of "a noise [*i.e.* band] of musicians in *townie* coats, who, putting off their caps, asked if they would have music." And lastly, there is a description of the person who personated "an ancient mynstrell" in one of the pageants which were played before Queen Elizabeth at her famous visit to Kenilworth, which is curious enough to be quoted. "A person, very meet seemed he for the purpose, of a forty-five years old, apparalled partly as he would himself. His cap off; his head seemly rounded tonsterwise;* fair kembed, that with a sponge daintily dipped in a little capon's grease was finely smoothen, to make it shine like a mallard's wing. His beard smugly shaven; and yet his shirt after the new trick, with ruffs fair starched, sleeked and glistering like a paire of new shoes, marshalled in good order with a setting stick and strut, that every ruff stood up like a wafer. A side (*i.e.* long) gown of Kendal Green, after the freshness of the year now, gathered at the neck with a narrow gorget, fastened afore with white clasp and keeper close up to the chin; but easily, for heat to undo when he list. Seemly begirt in a red caddis girdle: from that a pair of capped Sheffield knives hanging a' two sides. Out of his bosom drawn forth a lappel of his napkin (*i.e.* handkerchief) edged with a blue lace, and marked with a true love, a heart, and a D. for Damian, for he was but a batchelor yet. His gown had side (*i.e.* long) sleeves down to midleg, slit from the shoulder to the hand, and lined with white cotton. His doublet sleeves of black worsted: upon them a pair of paynets (perhaps points) of tawny chamlet laced along the wrist with blue threaden points, a weall towards the hand of fustian-a-napes. A pair of red neather socks. A pair of pumps on his feet, with a cross cut at the toes for corns: not new, indeed, yet cleanly blackt with soot, and shining as a shoeing horn. About his neck a red ribband suitable to his girdle. His harp in good grace dependant before him. His wrest tyed to a green lace, and hanging by; under the gorget

---

* Which Percy supposes to mean "tonsure-wise," like priests and monks.

of his gown a fair flaggon chain (pewter for) silver, as a squire-minstrel *
of Middlesex that travelled the country this summer season, unto fairs and
worshipful men's houses. From this chain hung a scutcheon, with metal
and colour resplendant upon his breast, of the ancient arms of Islington,"
to which place he is represented as belonging.

From these authorities Percy would deduce that the minstrels were
tonsured and apparelled very much after the same fashion as priests. The

A Band of Minstrels.

pictorial authorities do not bear out any such conclusion. There are
abundant authorities for the belief that the dress of the minstrels was
remarkable for a very unclerical sumptuousness; but in looking through
the numerous ancient representations of minstrels we find no trace of the
tonsure, and no peculiarity of dress; they are represented in the ordinary
costume of their time; in colours blue, red, grey, particoloured, like other
civilians; with hoods, or hats, or without either; frequently the different
members of the same band of minstrels present all these differences of

---

* Percy supposes from this expression that there were inferior orders, as yeomen-
minstrels. May we not also infer that there were superior orders, as knight-minstrels,
over whom was the king-minstrel? for we are told "he was but a batchelor (whose
chivalric signification has no reference to matrimony) yet." We are disposed to believe
that this was a real minstrel. Langham tells us that he was dressed "partly as he would
himself:" probably, the only things which were not according to his wont, were that my
Lord of Leicester may have given him a new coat; that he had a little more capon's
grease than usual in his hair; and that he was set to sing " a solemn song, warranted for
story, out of King Arthur's Acts," instead of more modern minstrel ware.

costume, as in the instance here given, from the title-page of the fourteenth century MS. Add., 10,293; proving that the minstrels did not affect any uniformity of costume whatever.

The household minstrels probably wore their master's badge* (liveries were not usual until a late period); others the badge of their guild. Thus in the Morte Arthur, Sir Dinadan makes a reproachful lay against King Arthur, and teaches it an harper, that hight Elyot, and sends him to sing it before King Mark and his nobles at a great feast. The king asked, "Thou harper, how durst thou be so bold to sing this song before me?" "Sir," said Elyot, "wit you well I am a minstrell, and I must doe as I am commanded of these lords that *I bear the armes of;*" and in proof of the privileged character of the minstrel we find the outraged king replying, "Thou saiest well, I charge thee that thou hie thee fast out of my sight." So the squire-minstrel of Middlesex, who belonged to Islington, had a

Cymbals and Trumpets.

chain round his neck, with a scutcheon upon it, upon which were blazoned the arms of Islington. And in the effigies of the Beverley minstrels, which we have given on page 298, we find that their costume is the ordinary costume of the period, and is not alike in all; but that each of them has a chain round his neck, to which is suspended what is probably a scutcheon, like that of the Islington minstrel. In short, a

---

* Heralds in the fourteenth century bore the arms of their lord on a small scutcheon fastened at the side of their girdle.

careful examination of a number of illustrations in illuminated MSS. of various dates, from Saxon downwards, leaves the impression that minstrels

Regals and Double Pipe (Royal 2 B vii).

wore the ordinary costume of their period, more or less rich in material, or fashionable in cut, according to their means and taste ; and that the only

Regals or Organ (Royal, 14 E iii).

distinctive mark of their profession was the instrument which each bore, or, as in the case of the Kenilworth minstrel, the tuning wrest hung by a riband to his girdle; and in the case of a household minstrel the badge of the lord whom he served.

The forms of the most usual musical instruments of various periods may be gathered from the illustrations which have already been given. The most common are the harp, fiddle, cittern or lute, hand-organ, the shalm or psaltery, the pipe and tabor, pipes of various sizes played like clarionets, but called flutes, the double pipe, hand-bells, trumpets and horns, bagpipes, tambourine, tabret, drum, and cymbals. Of the greater number of these we have already incidentally given illustrations; we add, on the last page, other illustrations, from the Royal MS., 2 B vii., and Royal MS. 14 E iii. In the fourteenth century new instruments were invented. Guillaume de Marhault in his poem of "Le Temps Pastour," gives us an idea of the multitude of instruments which composed a grand concert of the fifteenth century; he says *—

> "Là je vis tout en un cerne
> Viole, rubebe, guiterne,
> L'enmorache, le micamon,
> Citole et Psalterion,
> Harpes, tabours, trompes, nacaires,
> Orgues, cornes plus de dix paires,
> Cornemuse, flajos et chevrettes
> Douceines, simbales, clochettes,
> Tymbre, la flauste lorehaigne,
> Et le grand cornet d'Allemayne,
> Flacos de sans, fistule, pipe,
> Muse d'Aussay, trompe petite,
> Buisine, eles, monochorde,
> Ou il n' y a qu'une corde ;
> Et muse de blet tout ensemble.
> Et certainment il me semble
> Qu' oncques mais tèle mélodie
> Ne feust oncques vene ne oye ;
> Car chascun d'eux, selon l'accort
> De son instrument sans descort,
> Vitole, guiterne, citole,
> Harpe, trompe, corne, flajole,
> Pipe, souffle, muse, naquaire,
> Taboure et qu eunque ou put faire

---

* "Annales Archæologiques," vii. p. 323.

> De dois, de peune et à l'archet,
> Ois et vis en ce porchet."

In conclusion we give a group of musical instruments from one of the illustrations of "Der Weise König," a work of the close of the fifteenth century.

Musical Instruments of the 15th Century.

THE KNIGHTS OF THE MIDDLE AGES.

CHAPTER I.

SAXON ARMS AND ARMOUR.

WE proceed, in this division of our work, to select out of the inexhaustible series of pictures of mediæval life and manners contained in illuminated MSS., a gallery of subjects which will illustrate the armour and costume, the military life and chivalric adventures, of the Knights of the Middle Ages; and to append to the pictures such explanations as they may seem to need, and such discursive remarks as the subjects may suggest.

For the military costume of the Anglo-Saxon period we have the authority of the descriptions in their literature, illustrated by drawings in their illuminated MSS.; and if these leave anything wanting in definiteness, the minutest details of form and ornamentation may often be recovered from the rusted and broken relics of armour and weapons which have been recovered from their graves, and are now preserved in our museums.

Saxon freemen seem to have universally borne arms. Tacitus tells us of their German ancestors, that swords were rare among them, and the majority did not use lances, but that spears, with a narrow, sharp and short head, were the common and universal weapon, used either in distant or close fight; and that even the cavalry were satisfied with a shield and one of these spears.

The law in later times seems to have required freemen to bear arms for the common defence; the laws of Gula, which are said to have been originally established by Hacon the Good in the middle of the eighth century, required every man who possessed six marks besides his clothes to furnish himself with a red shield and a spear, an axe or a sword; he who was worth twelve marks was to have a steel cap also; and he who was worth eighteen marks a byrnie, or shirt of mail, in addition. Accordingly, in the exploration of Saxon graves we find in those of men "spears and javelins are extremely numerous," says Mr. C. Roach Smith, "and of a variety of shapes and sizes." . . . . . "So constantly do we find them in the Saxon graves, that it would appear no man above the condition of a serf was buried without one. Some are of large size, but the majority come under the term of javelin or dart." The rusty spear-head lies beside the skull, and the iron boss of the shield on his breast; the long, broad, heavy, rusted sword is comparatively seldom found beside the skeleton; sometimes, but rarely, the iron frame of a skull-cap or helmet is found about the head.

Saxon Soldiers.

An examination of the pictures in the Saxon illuminated MSS. confirms the conclusion that the shield and spear were the common weapons. Their bearers are generally in the usual civil costume, and not infrequently are bare-headed. The spear-shaft is almost always spoken of as being of ash-wood; indeed, the word *æsc* (ash) is used by metonymy for a spear; and the common poetic name for a soldier is *æsc-berend*, or *æsc-born*, a spear-bearer; just as, in later times, we speak of him as a swordsman.

We learn from the poets that the shield—"the broad war disk"—was made of linden-wood, as in Beowulf:—

"He could not then refrain,
but grasped his shield
the yellow linden,
drew his ancient sword."

From the actual remains of shields, we find that the central boss was of iron, of conical shape, and that a handle was fixed across its concavity by which it was held in the hand.

The helmet is of various shapes; the commonest are the three repre-

Saxon Horse Soldiers.

sented in our first four wood-cuts. The most common is the conical shape seen in the large wood-cut on p. 316.

The Phrygian-shaped helmet, seen in the single figure on p. 314 is also a very common form; and the curious crested helmet worn by all the warriors in our first two wood-cuts of Saxon soldiers is also common. In some cases the conical helmet was of iron, but perhaps more frequently it was of leather, strengthened with a frame of iron.

In the group of four foot soldiers in our first wood-cut, it will be observed that the men wear tunics, hose, and shoes; the multiplicity of folds and fluttering ends in the drapery is a characteristic of Saxon art, but the spirit and elegance of the heads is very unusual and very admirable.

Our first three illustrations are taken from a beautiful little MS. of Prudentius in the Cottonian Library, known under the press mark, Cleopatra C. IV. The illuminations in this MS. are very clearly and skilfully drawn with the pen; indeed, many of them are designed with so much spirit and skill and grace, as to make them not only of antiquarian interest, but also of high artistic merit. The subjects are chiefly illustrations of Scripture history or of allegorical fable; but, thanks to the custom which prevailed throughout the Middle Ages of representing all such subjects in contemporary costume, and according to contemporary manners and customs, the Jewish patriarchs and their servants afford us perfectly correct representations of Saxon thanes and their *cheorls;* Goliath, a perfect picture of a Saxon warrior, armed *cap-à-pied*; and Pharaoh and his nobles of a Saxon Basileus and his witan. Thus, our second wood-cut is an illustration of the incident of Lot and his family being carried away captives by the Canaanitish kings after their successful raid against the cities of the plain; but it puts before our eyes a group of the armed retainers of a Saxon king on a military expedition. It will be seen that they wear the ordinary Saxon civil costume, a tunic and cloak; that they are all armed with the spear, all wear crested helmets; and the last of the group carries a round shield suspended at his back. The variety of attitude, the spirit and life of the figures, and the skill and gracefulness of the drawing, are admirable.

Another very valuable series of illustrations of Saxon military costume will be found in a MS. of Ælfric's Paraphrase of the Pentateuch and Joshua, in the British Museum (Cleopatra B. IV.); at folio 25, for example, we have a representation of Abraham pursuing the five kings in order to rescue Lot: in the version of the Saxon artist the patriarch and his Arab servants are translated into a Saxon thane and his house carles, who are represented marching in a long array which takes up two bands of drawing across the vellum page.

Saxon Soldier, in Leather Armour.

The Anglo-Saxon poets let us know that chieftains and warriors wore a body defence, which they call a byrnie or a battle-sark. In the illuminations we find this sometimes of leather, as in the wood-cut here given from the Prudentius which has already supplied us with two illustrations. It is very usually Vandyked at the edges, as here represented. But the epithets, "iron byrnie," and "ringed byrnie," and "twisted battle-sark," show that the hauberk was often made of iron mail. In some of the illuminations it is represented as if detached rings of iron were sewn flat upon it: this may be really a representation of a kind of jazerant work, such as was frequently used in later times, or it may be only an unskilful way of representing the ordinary linked mail.

A document of the early part of the eighth century, given in Mr. Thorpe's Anglo-Saxon Laws, seems to indicate that at that period the mail hauberk was usually worn only by the higher ranks. In distinguishing between the eorl and the cheorl it says, if the latter thrive so well that he have a helmet and byrnie and sword ornamented with gold, yet if he have not five hydes of land, he is only a cheorl. By the time of the end of the Saxon era, however, it would seem that the men-at-arms were usually furnished with a coat of fence, for the warriors in the battle of Hastings are nearly all so represented in the Bayeux tapestry.

In Ælfric's Paraphrase, already mentioned (Cleopatra B. IV.), at folio 64, there is a representation of a king clothed in such a mail shirt, armed with sword and shield, attended by an armour-bearer, who carries a second shield but no offensive weapon, his business being to ward off the blows aimed at his lord. We should have given a wood-cut of this interesting group, but that it has already been engraved in the "Pictorial History of England" (vol. i.) and in Hewitt's "Ancient Armour" (vol. i. p. 60). This king with his shield-bearer does not occur in an illustration of Goliath and the man bearing a shield who went before him, nor of Saul and his armour-bearer, where it would be suggested by the text; but is one of the three kings engaged in battle against the cities of the plain; it seems therefore to indicate a Saxon usage. Another of the kings in the same picture has no hauberk, but only the same costume as the warrior in the wood-cut on the next page.

In the Additional MS. 11,695, in the British Museum, a work of the eleventh century, there are several representations of warriors thus fully armed, very rude and coarse in drawing, but valuable for the clearness with which they represent the military equipment of the time. At folio 194 there is a large figure of a warrior in a mail shirt, a conical helmet, strengthened with iron ribs converging to the apex, the front rib extending downwards, into what is called a nasal, *i.e.*, a piece of iron extending downwards over the nose, so as to protect the face from a sword-cut across the upper part of it. At folio 233 of the same MS. is a group of six warriors, two on horseback and four on foot. We find them all with

No. 4.

hauberk, iron helmets, round shields, and various kinds of leg defences; they have spears, swords, and one of the horsemen bears a banner of characteristic shape, *i.e.*, it is a right-angled triangle, with the shortest side applied to the spear-shaft, so that the right angle is at the bottom.

A few extracts from the poem of Beowulf, a curious Saxon fragment, which the best scholars concur in assigning to the end of the eighth century, will help still further to bring these ancient warriors before our mind's eye.

Here is a scene in King Hrothgar's hall:

> "After evening came
> and Hrothgar had departed
> to his court,
> guarded the mansion
> countless warriors,
> as they oft ere had done,
> they bared the bench-floor
> it was overspread
> with beds and bolsters.
> they set at their heads
> their disks of war,
> their shield-wood bright;
> there on the bench was
> over the noble,
> easy to be seen,
> his high martial helm,
> his ringed byrnie
> and war-wood stout."

Beowulf's funeral pole is said to be—

> "with helmets, war brands,
> and bright byrnies behung."

And in this oldest of Scandinavian romances we have the natural reflections—

> "the hard helm shall
> adorned with gold
> from the fated fall;
> mortally wounded sleep
> those who war to rage
> by trumpet should announce;
> in like manner the war shirt
> which in battle stood
> over the crash of shields
> the bite of swords
> shall moulder after the warrior;
> the byrnie's ring may not

>   after the martial leader
>   go far on the side of heroes;
>   there is no joy of harp
>   no glee-wood's mirth,
>   no good hawk
>   swings through the hall,
>   nor the swift steed
>   tramps the city place.
>   Baleful death
>   has many living kinds
>   sent forth."

Reflections which Coleridge summed up in the brief lines—

>   " Their swords are rust,
>   Their bones are dust,
>   Their souls are with the saints, we trust."

The wood-cut on page 316 is taken from a collection of various Saxon pictures in the British Museum, bound together in the volume marked Tiberius C. VI., at folio 9. Our wood-cut is a reduced copy. In the original the warrior is seven or eight inches high, and there is, therefore, ample room for the delineation of every part of his costume. From the embroidery of the tunic, and the ornamentation of the shield and helmet, we conclude that we have before us a person of consideration, and he is represented as in the act of combat; but we see his armour and arms are only those to which we have already affirmed that the usual equipment was limited. The helmet seems to be strengthened with an iron rim and converging ribs, and is furnished with a short nasal.

The figure is without the usual cloak, and therefore the better shows the fashion of the tunic. The banding of the legs was not for defence, it is common in civil costume. The quasi-banding of the forearm is also sometimes found in civil costume; it seems not to be an actual banding, still less a spiral armlet, but merely a fashion of wearing the tunic sleeve. We see how the sword is, rather inartificially, slung by a belt over the shoulder; how the shield is held by the iron handle across its hollow spiked umbo; and how the barbed javelin is cast.

On the preceding page of this MS. is a similar figure, but without the sword.

Saxon Weapons.

There were some other weapons frequently used by the Saxons which we have not yet had occasion to mention. The most important of these is the axe. It is not often represented in illuminations, and is very rarely found in graves, but it certainly was extensively in use in the latter part of the Anglo-Saxon period, and was perhaps introduced by the Danes. The house carles of Canute, we are expressly told, were armed with axes, halberds, and swords, ornamented with gold. In the ship which Godwin presented to Hardicanute, William of Malmesbury tells us the soldiers wore two bracelets of gold on each arm, each bracelet weighing sixteen ounces; they had gilt helmets; in the right hand they carried a spear of iron, and in the left a Danish axe, and they wore swords hilted with gold. The axe was also in common use by the Saxons at the battle of Hastings. There are pictorial examples of the single axe in the Cottonian MS., Cleopatra C. VIII.; of the double axe—the bipennis—in the Harleian MS., 603; and of various forms of the weapon, including the pole-axe, in the Bayeux tapestry.

The knife or dagger was also a Saxon weapon. There is a picture in the Anglo-Saxon MS. in the Paris Library, called the Duke de Berri's Psalter, in which a combatant is armed with what appears to be a large double-edged knife and a shield, and actual examples of it occur in Saxon graves. The *seax*, which is popularly believed to have been a dagger and a characteristic Saxon weapon, seems to have been a short single-edged slightly curved weapon, and is rarely found in England. It is mentioned in Beowulf:—he—

> "drew his deadly seax,
> bitter and battle sharp,
> that he on his byrnie bore."

The sword was usually about three feet long, two-edged and heavy in the blade. Sometimes, especially in earlier examples, it is without a guard. Its hilt was sometimes of the ivory of the walrus, occasionally of gold, the blade was sometimes inlaid with gold ornaments and runic verses. Thus in Beowulf—

> "So was on the surface
> of the bright gold

> with runic letters
> rightly marked,
> set and said, for whom that sword,
> costliest of irons,
> was first made,
> with twisted hilt and
> serpent shaped."

The Saxons indulged in many romantic fancies about their swords. Some swordsmiths chanted magical verses as they welded them, and tempered them with mystical ingredients. Beowulf's sword was a—

> "tempered falchion
> that had before been one
> of the old treasures;
> its edge was iron
> tainted with poisonous things
> hardened with warrior blood;
> never had it deceived any man
> of those who brandished it with hands."

Favourite swords had names given them, and were handed down from father to son, or passed from champion to champion, and became famous. Thus, again, in Beowulf, we read—

> "He could not then refrain,
> but grasped his shield,
> the yellow linden,
> drew his ancient sword
> that among men was
> a relic of Eanmund,
> Ohthere's son,
> of whom in conflict was,
> when a friendless exile,
> Weohstan the slayer
> with falchions edges,
> and from his kinsmen bore away
> the brown-hued helm,
> the ringed byrnie,
> the old Eotenish* sword
> which him Onela had given."

There is a fine and very perfect example of a Saxon sword in the

---

* "Eoten," a giant; "Eotenish," made by or descended from the giants.

British Museum, which was found in the bed of the river Witham, at Lincoln. The sheath was usually of wood, covered with leather, and tipped, and sometimes otherwise ornamented with metal.

The spear was used javelin-wise, and the warrior going into battle sometimes carried several of them. They are long-bladed, often barbed, as represented in the woodcut on p. 316, and very generally have one or two little cross-bars below the head, as in cuts on pp. 313 and 314. The Saxon artillery, besides the javelin, was the bow and arrows. The bow is usually a small one, of the old classical shape, not the long bow for which the English yeomen afterwards became so famous, and which seems to have been introduced by the Normans.

In the latest period of the Saxon monarchy, the armour and weapons were almost identical with those used on the Continent. We have abundant illustrations of them in the Bayeux tapestry. In that invaluable historical monument, the minutest differences between the Saxon and Norman knights and men-at-arms seem to be carefully observed, even to the national fashions of cutting the hair; and we are therefore justified in assuming that there were no material differences in the military equipment, since we find none indicated, except that the Normans used the long bow and the Saxons did not. We have abstained from taking any illustrations from the tapestry, because the whole series has been several times engraved, and is well known, or, at least, is easily accessible, to those who are interested in the subject. We have preferred to take an illustration from a MS. in the British Museum, marked Harleian 2,895, from folio 82 v. The warrior, who is no less a person than Goliath of Gath, has a hooded hauberk, with sleeves down to the elbow, over a green tunic. The legs are tinted blue in the drawing, but seem to be unarmed, except for the green boots, which reach half way to the knee. He wears an iron helmet with a nasal, and the hood appears to be fastened to the nasal, so as to protect the lower part of the face. The large shield is red, with a yellow border, and is hung from the neck by a chain. The belt round his waist is red. The well-armed giant leans upon his spear, looking down contemptuously on David, whom it has not been thought necessary to include in our copy of the picture. The group forms a very appropriate filling-in of the great initial letter B of the Psalm *Benedictus Dns. Ds. Ms. qui docet manus meas ad prælium et digitos meos ad bellum* (Blessed be the Lord my God, who teacheth my hands to war and my fingers to fight). In the same MS., at folio 70, there are two men armed with helmet and sword, and at folio 81 v. a group of armed men on horseback, in sword, shield, and spurs.

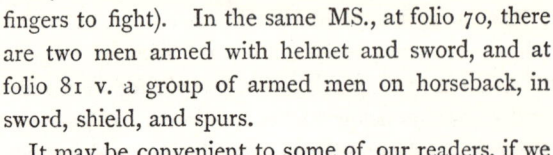

It may be convenient to some of our readers, if we indicate here where a few other examples of Saxon military costume may be found which we have noted down, but have not had occasion to refer to in the above remarks.

In the MS. of Prudentius (Cleopatra C. VIII.), from which we have taken our first three woodcuts, are many other pictures well worth study. On the same page (folio 1 v.) as that which contains our wood-cut p. 312, there is another very similar group on the lower part of the page; on folio 2 is still another group, in which some of the faces are most charming in drawing and expression. At folio 15 v. there is a spirited combat of two footmen, armed with sword and round shield, and clad in short leather coats of fence, vandyked at the edges. At folio 24 v. is an allegorical female figure in a short leather tunic, with shading on it which seems to indicate that the hair of the leather has been left on, and is worn outside, which we know from other sources was one of the fashions of the time. In the MS. of Ælfric's Paraphrase (Claud. B. iv.) already quoted, there are, besides the battle scene at folio 24 v., in which occurs the king and his armour-bearer, at folio 25 two long lines of Saxon horsemen marching across the page, behind Abraham, who wears a crested Phrygian helm. On the reverse of folio 25 there is another group, and also on folios 62 and 64. On folio 52 is another troop, of Esau's horsemen, marching across the page in ranks of four abreast, all bareheaded and armed with spears. At folio 96 v. is another example of a warrior, with a shield-bearer. The pictures in the latter part of this MS. are not nearly so clearly delineated as in the former part, owing to their having been tinted with colour; the colour, however, enables us still more completely to fill in to the mind's eye the distinct forms which we have gathered from the former part of the book. The large troops of soldiers are valuable, as showing us the style of equipment which was common in the Saxon militia.

There is another MS. of Prudentius in the British Museum of about the same date, and of the same school of art, though not quite so finely executed, which is well worth the study of the artist in search of authorities for Saxon military (and other) costume, and full of interest for the amateur of art and archæology. Its press mark is Cottonian, Titus D. xvi. On the reverse of folio 2 is a group of three armed horsemen, representing the confederate kings of Canaan carrying off Lot, while Abraham, at the head of another group of armed men, is pursuing them. On folio 3 is another group of armed horsemen. After these Scripture histories come some allegorical subjects, conceived and drawn with great spirit. At folio 6 v., "*Pudicitia pugnat contra Libidinem,*" Pudicitia being a woman armed with hauberk, helmet, spear, and shield. On the opposite page Pudicitia—in a very spirited attitude—is driving her spear through the throat of Libido. On folio 26 v., "*Discordia vulnerat occulte Concordium.*" Concord is represented as a woman armed with a loose-sleeved hauberk, helmet, and sword. Discord is lifting up the skirt of Concord's hauberk, and thrusting a sword into her side. In the Harleian MS. 2,803, is a Vulgate Bible, of date about 1170 A.D.; there are no pictures, only the initial letters of the various books are illuminated. But while the illuminator was engaged upon the initial of the Second Book of Kings, his eye seems to have been caught by the story of Saul's death in the last chapter of the First Book, which happens to come close by in the parallel column of the great folio page:—*Arripuit itaqu, gladium et erruit sup. eum* (Therefore Saul took a sword, and fell upon it); and he has sketched in the scene with pen-and-ink on the margin of the page, thus affording us another authority for the armour of a Saxon king when actually engaged in battle. He wears a hauberk, with an ornamented border, has his crown on his head, and spurs on his heels; has placed his sword-hilt on the ground, and fallen upon it.

In the Additional MS. 11,695, on folio 102 v., are four armed men on horseback, habited in hauberks without hoods. Two of them have the sleeves extending to the wrist, two have loose sleeves to the elbow only, showing that the two fashions were worn contemporaneously. They all have mail hose; one of them is armed with a bow, the rest with the sword. There are four men in similar armour on folio 136 v. of the same MS. Also at folio 143, armed with spear, sword, and round ornamented shield. At folio 222 v. are soldiers manning a gate-tower.

When the soldiers so very generally wore the ordinary citizen costume, it becomes necessary, in order to give a complete picture of the military costume, to say a few words on the dress which the soldier wore in common with the citizen. The tunic and mantle composed the national costume of the Saxons. The tunic reached about to the knee: sometimes it was slit up a little way at the sides, and it often had a rich ornamented border round the hem, extending round the side slits, making the garment almost exactly resemble the ecclesiastical tunic or Dalmatic. It had also very generally a narrower ornamental border round the opening for the neck. The tunic was sometimes girded round the waist.

The Saxons were famous for their skill in embroidery, and also in metal-work; and there are sufficient proofs that the tunic was often richly embroidered. There are indications of it in the wood-cut on p. 316; and in the relics of costume found in the Saxon graves are often buckles of elegant workmanship, which fastened the belt with which the tunic was girt.

The mantle was in the form of a short cloak, and was usually fastened at the shoulder, as in the wood-cuts on pp. 312, 313, 314, so as to leave the right arm unencumbered by its folds. The brooch with which this cloak was fastened formed a very conspicuous item of costume. They were of large size, some of them of bronze gilt, others of gold, beautifully ornamented with enamels; and there is this interesting fact about them, they seem to corroborate the old story, that the Saxon invaders were of three different tribes—the Jutes, Angles, and Saxons—who subdued and inhabited different portions of Britain. For in Kent and the Isle of Wight, the settlements of the Jutes, brooches are found of circular form, often of gold and enamelled. In the counties of Yorkshire, Derby, Leicester, Nottingham, Northampton, and in the eastern counties, a large gilt bronze brooch of peculiar form is very commonly found, and seems to denote a peculiar fashion of the Angles, who inhabited East Anglia, Mercia, and Northumbria. Still another variety of fashion, shaped like a saucer, has been discovered in the counties of Gloucester, Oxford, and Buckingham, on the border between the Mercians and West Saxons. It is curious to find these peculiar fashions thus confirming the ancient and obscure tradition about the original Saxon settlements. The artist will bear in mind that the Saxons seem generally to have settled in the open country, not in the towns, and to have built timber halls and cottages after their own custom, and to have avoided the sites of the Romano-British villas, whose blackened ruins must have thickly dotted at least the southern and south-eastern parts of the island. They appear to have built no fortresses, if we except a few erected at a late period, to check the incursions of the Danes. But they had the old Roman towns left, in many cases with their walls and gates tolerably entire. In the Saxon MS. Psalter, Harleian 603, are several illuminations in which walled towns and gates are represented. But we do not gather that they were very skilful either in the attack or defence of fortified places. Indeed, their weapons and armour were of a very primitive kind, and their warfare seems to have been conducted after a very unscientific fashion. Little chance had their rude Saxon hardihood against the military genius of William the Norman and the disciplined valour of his bands of mercenaries.

CHAPTER II.

ARMS AND ARMOUR, FROM THE NORMAN CONQUEST DOWNWARDS.

THE Conquest and subsequent confiscations put the land of England so entirely into the hands of William the Conqueror, that he was able to introduce the feudal system into England in a more simple and symmetrical shape than that in which it obtained in any other country of Europe. The system was a very intelligible one. The king was supposed to be the lord of all the land of the kingdom. He retained large estates in his own hands, and from these estates chiefly he derived his personal followers and his royal revenues. The rest of the land he let in large lordships to his principal nobles, on condition that they should maintain for the defence of the kingdom a certain number of men armed after a stipulated fashion, and should besides aid him on certain occasions with money payments, with which we have at present no concern.

These chief tenants of the crown followed the example of the sovereign. Each retained a portion of the land in his own hands, and sub-let the rest in estates of larger or smaller size, on condition that each noble or knight who held of him should supply a proportion of the armed force he was required to furnish to the royal standard, and contribute a proportion of the money payments for which he was liable to be called upon. Each knight let the farms on his manor to his copyholders, on condition that they provided themselves with the requisite arms, and assembled under his banner when called upon for military suit and service; and they rendered certain personal services, and made certain payments in money or in kind besides, in lieu of rent. Each manor, therefore, furnished its troop of soldiers; the small farmers, perhaps, and the knight's personal retainers fighting on foot, clad in leather jerkins, and armed with pike or bow; two or three of his greater copyholders in skull caps and coats of fence; his younger brothers or grown-up sons acting as men-at-arms and esquires, on horseback, in armour almost or quite as complete as his own; while the knight himself, on his war horse, armed from top to toe—*cap-à-pied*—with shield on arm and lance in hand, with its knight's pennon fluttering from the point, was the captain of the little troop. The troops thus furnished by his several manors made up the force which the feudal lord was bound to furnish the king, and the united divisions made up the army of the kingdom.

Besides this feudal army bound to render suit and service at the call of its sovereign, the laws of the kingdom also required all men of fit age—between sixteen and sixty—to keep themselves furnished with arms, and made them liable to be called out *en masse* in great emergencies. This was the *Posse Comitatus*, the force of the county, and was under the command of the sheriff. We learn some particulars on the subject from an assize of arms of Henry II., made in 1181, which required all his subjects being free men to be ready in defence of the realm. Whosoever holds one knight's fee, shall have a hauberk, helmet, shield and lance, and every knight as many such equipments as he has knight's fees in his domain. Every free layman having ten marks in chattels shall have a habergeon, iron cap, and lance. All burgesses and the whole community of freemen shall have each a coat of fence (padded and quilted, a *wambeys*), iron cap, and lance. Any one having more arms than those required by the statute, was to sell or otherwise dispose of them, so that they might be utilised for the king's service, and no one was to carry arms out of the kingdom.

There were two great points of difference between the feudal system as introduced into England and as established on the Continent. William made all landowners owe fealty to himself, and not only the tenants *in capite*. And next, though he gave his chief nobles immense possessions, these possessions were scattered about in different parts of the kingdom. The great provinces which had once been separate kingdoms of the Saxon heptarchy, still retained, down to the time of the Confessor, much of their old political feeling. Kentish men, for example, looked on one another as brothers, but Essex men, or East Anglians, or Mercians, or Northumbrians, were foreigners to them. If the Conqueror had committed the blunder of giving his great nobles all their possessions together, Rufus might have found the earls of Mercia or Northumbria semi-independent, as the kings of France found their great vassals of Burgundy, and Champagne, and Normandy, and Bretagne. But, by the actual arrangement, every county was divided; one powerful noble had a lordship here, and another had half-a-dozen manors there, and some religious community had one or two manors between. The result was, that though a combination of great barons was powerful enough to coerce John or Henry III., or a single baron like Warwick was powerful enough, when the nobility were divided into two factions, to turn the scale to one side or the other, no one was ever able to set the power of the crown at defiance, or to establish a semi-independence; the crown was always powerful enough to enforce a sufficiently arbitrary authority over them all. The consequence was that there was little of the clannish spirit among Englishmen. They rallied round their feudal superior, but the sentiment of loyalty was warmly and directly towards the crown.

We must not, however, pursue the general subject further than we have done, in order to obtain some apprehension of the position in the body politic occupied by the class of persons with whom we are specially concerned. Of their social position we may perhaps briefly arrive at a correct estimate, if we call to mind that nearly all our rural parishes are divided into several manors, which date from the Middle Ages, some more, some less remotely; for as population increased and land increased in value, there was a tendency to the subdivision of old manors and the creation of new ones out of them. Each of these manors, in the times to which our researches are directed, maintained a family of gentle birth and knightly rank. The head of the family was usually a knight, and his sons were eligible for, and some of them aspirants to, the same rank in chivalry. So that the great body of the knightly order consisted of the country gentlemen—the country *squires* we call them now, then they were the country *knights*—whose wealth and social importance gave them a claim to the rank; and to these we must add such of their younger brothers and grown-up sons as had ambitiously sought for and happily achieved the chivalric distinction by deeds of arms. The rest of the brothers and sons who had not entered the service of the Church as priest or canon, monk or friar, or into trade, continued in the lower chivalric and social rank of squires.

When we come to look for authorities for the costume and manners of the knights of the Middle Ages, we find a great scarcity of them for the period between the Norman Conquest and the beginning of the Edwardian era. The literary authorities are not many; there are as yet few of the illuminated MSS., from which we derive such abundant material in the fourteenth and fifteenth centuries;* the sepulchral monuments are not numerous; the valuable series of monumental brasses has not begun; the Bayeux tapestry, which affords abundant material for the special time to which it relates, we have abstained from drawing upon; and there are few subjects in any other class of pictorial art to help us out.

The figure of Goliath, which we gave in our last chapter (p. 322), will serve very well for a general representation of a knight of the twelfth century. In truth, from the Norman Conquest down to the introduction of plate armour at the close of the thirteenth century, there was wonderfully little alteration in the knightly armour and costume. It would seem that the body armour consisted of garments of the ordinary fashion, either quilted in their substance to deaden the force of a blow, or covered with *mailles* (rings) on the exterior, to resist the edge of sword or point of lance. The ingenuity of the armourer showed itself in various ways of quilting, and various methods of applying the external defence of metal. Of the quilted armours we know very little. In the illuminations is often seen armour covered over with lines arranged in a lozenge pattern, which perhaps represents garments stuffed and sewn in this commonest of all patterns of quilting; but it has been suggested that it may represent lozenged-shaped scales, of horn or metal, fastened upon the face of the garments. In the wood-cut

* The Harl. MS. 603, of the close of the eleventh century, contains a number of military subjects rudely drawn, but conveying suggestions which the artist will be able to interpret and profit by. In the Add. MS. 28,107, of date A.D. 1096, at f. 25 v., is a Goliath; and at f. 1,630 v., a group of soldiers.

here given from the MS. Caligula A. vii., we have one of the clearest and best extant illustrations of this quilted armour.

In the mail armour there seem to have been different ways of applying the *mailles*. Sometimes it is represented as if the rings were sewn by one edge only, and at such a distance that each overlapped the other in the same row, but the rows do not overlap one another. Sometimes they look as if each row of rings had been sewn upon a strip of linen or leather and then the strips applied to the garment. Sometimes the rings were interlinked, as in a common steel purse, so that the garment was entirely of steel rings. Very frequently we find a surcoat or chausses represented, as if rings or little discs of metal were sewn flat all over the garment. It is possible that this is only an artistic way of indicating that the garment was covered with rings, after one of the methods above described; but it is also possible that a light armour was composed of rings thus sparely sewn upon a linen or leather garment. It is possible also that little round plates of metal or horn were used in this way for defence, for we have next to mention that *scale* armour is sometimes, though rarely, found; it consisted of small scales, usually rectangular, and probably usually of horn, though sometimes of metal, attached to a linen or leather garment.

Quilted Armour.

The shield and helmet varied somewhat in shape at various times. The shield in the Bayeux tapestry was kite-shaped, concave, and tolerably large, like that of Goliath on p. 322. The tendency of its fashion was continually to grow shorter in proportion to its width, and flatter. The round Saxon target continued in use throughout the Middle Ages, more especially for foot-soldiers.

The helmet, at the beginning of the period, was like the old Saxon conical helmet, with a nasal; and this continued in occasional use far into the fourteenth century. About the end of the twelfth century, the cylindrical helmet of iron enclosing the whole head, with horizontal slits for vision, came into fashion. Richard I. is represented in one on his second great seal. A still later fashion is seen in the next woodcut, p. 334. William Longespée, A.D. 1227, has a flat-topped helmet.

The only two inventions of the time seem to be, first, the surcoat, which began to be worn over the hauberk about the end of the twelfth century. The seal of King John is the first of the series of great seals in which we see it introduced. It seems to have been of linen or silk.

The other great invention of this period was that of armorial bearings, properly so called. Devices painted upon the shield were common in classical times. They are found ordinarily on the shields in the Bayeux tapestry, and were habitually used by the Norman knights. In the Bayeux tapestry they seem to be fanciful or merely decorative; later they were symbolical or significant. But it was only towards the close of the twelfth century that each knight assumed a fixed device, which was exclusively appropriated to him, by which he was known, and which became hereditary in his family.

The offensive weapons used by the knights were most commonly the sword and spear. The axe and mace are found, but rarely. The artillery consisted of the crossbow, which was the most formidable missile in use, and the long bow, which, however, was not yet the great arm of the English yeomanry which it became at a later period; but these were hardly the weapons of knights and gentlemen, though men-at-arms were frequently armed with the crossbow, and archers were occasionally mounted. The sling was sometimes used, as were other very rude weapons, by the half-armed crowd who were often included in the ranks of mediæval armies.

We have said that there is a great scarcity of pictorial representations of the military costume of the thirteenth century, and of the few which exist the majority are so vague in their definition of details, that they add nothing to our knowledge of costume, and have so little of dramatic character, as to throw no light on manners and customs. Among the best are some knightly figures in the Harleian Roll, folio 6, which contains a life of St. Guthlac of about the end of the twelfth century. The figures are armed in short-sleeved and hooded hauberk; flat-topped iron helmet, some with, some without, the nasal; heater-shaped shield and spear; the legs undefended, except by boots like those of the Goliath on p. 322.

The Harleian MS. 4,751, a MS. of the beginning of the thirteenth century, shows at folio 8 a group of soldiers attacking a fortification; it contains hints enough to make one earnestly desire that the subject had been more fully and artistically worked out. The fortification is represented by a timber projection carried on brackets from the face of the wall. Its garrison is represented by a single knight, whose demi-figure only is seen; he is represented in a short-sleeved hauberk, with a surcoat over it having a cross on the breast. He wears a flat-topped cylindrical helmet, and is armed with a crossbow. The assailants would seem to be a rabble of half-armed men; one is bareheaded, and armed only with a sling; others have round hats, whether of felt or iron does not appear; one is armed in a hooded hauberk and carries an axe, and a cylindrical helmet also appears amidst the crowd.

In the Harleian MS. 5,102, of the beginning of the thirteenth century, at folio 32, there is a representation of the martyrdom of St. Thomas of Canterbury, which gives us the effigies of the three murderers in knightly costume. They all wear long-sleeved hauberks, which have the peculiarity of being slightly slit up the sides, and the tunic flows from beneath them. Fitzurse (known by the bear on his shield) has leg defences fastened behind, like those in our next woodcut, p. 334, and a circular iron helmet. One of the others wears a flat-topped helmet, and the third has the hood of mail fastened on the cheek, like that in the same woodcut. The drawing is inartistic, and the picture of little value for our present purposes.

The Harleian MS. 3,244 contains several MSS. bound together. The second of these works is a Penitential, which has a knightly figure on horseback for its frontispiece. It has an allegorical meaning, and is rather curious. The inscription over the figure is *Milicia est vita hominis super terram.* (The life of man upon the earth is a warfare.) The knightly figure represents the Christian man in the spiritual panoply of this warfare;

and the various items of armour and arms have inscriptions affixed to tell us what they are. Thus over the helmet is *Spes futuri gaudii* (For a helmet the hope of salvation); his sword is inscribed, *Verbum di;* his spear, *Persevancia;* its pennon, *Regni cælesti desiderium*, &c. &c. The shield is charged with the well-known triangular device, with the enunciation of the doctrine of the Trinity, *Pater est Deus*, &c., *Pater non est Filius*, &c. The knight is clad in hauberk, with a rather long flowing surcoat; a helmet, in general shape like that in the next woodcut, but not so ornamental; he has chausses of mail; shield, sword, and spear with pennon, and prick spurs; but there is not sufficient definiteness in the details, or character in the drawing, to make it worth while to reproduce it. But there is one MS. picture which fully atones for the absence of others by its very great merit. It occurs in a small quarto of the last quarter of the thirteenth century, which contains the Psalter and Ecclesiastical Hymns. Towards the end of the book are several remarkably fine full-page drawings, done in outline with a pen, and partially tinted with colour; large, distinct, and done with great spirit and artistic skill. The first on the verso of folio 218 is a king; on the opposite page is the knight, who is here given on a reduced scale; on the opposite side of the page is St. Christopher, and on the next page an archbishop.

The figure of the knight before us shows very clearly the various details of a suit of thirteenth-century armour. In the hauberk will be noticed the mode in which the hood is fastened at the side of the head, and the way in which the sleeves are continued into gauntlets, whose palms are left free from rings, so as to give a firmer grasp. The thighs, it will be seen, are protected by haut-de-chausses, which are mailed only in the exposed parts, and not on the seat. The legs have chausses of a different kind of armour. In the MS. drawings we often find various parts of the armour thus represented in different ways, and, as we have already said, we are sometimes tempted to think the unskilful artist has only used different modes of representing the same kind of mail. But here the drawing is so careful, and skilful, and self-evidently accurate, that we cannot doubt that the defence of the legs is really of a different kind of armour from the mail of the hauberk and haut-de-chausses. The surcoat is of graceful fashion, and embroidered with crosses, which appear also on the pennon, and one of them is used as an ornamental genouillière on the shoulder. The helmet is elaborately and very elegantly ornamented. The attitude of the figure is spirited and dignified, and the drawing unusually good. Altogether we do not know a finer representation of a knight of this century.

Knight of the latter part of the Thirteenth Century.

A few, but very valuable, authorities are to be found in the sculptural monumental effigies of this period. The best of them will be found in Stothard's "Monumental Effigies," and his work not only brings these examples together, and makes them easily accessible to the student, but it has this great advantage, that Stothard well understood his subject, and gives every detail with the most minute accuracy, and also elucidates obscure points of detail. Those in the Temple Church, that of William

Longespée in Salisbury Cathedral, and that of Aymer de Valence in Westminster Abbey, are the most important of the series. Perhaps, after all, the only important light they add to that already obtained from the MSS. is, they help us to understand the fabrication of the mail-armour, by giving it in fac-simile relief. There are also a few foreign MSS., easily accessible, in the library of the British Museum, which the artist student will do well to consult; but he must remember that some of the peculiarities of costume which he will find there are foreign fashions, and are not to be introduced in English subjects. For example, the MS. Cotton, Nero, c. iv., is a French MS. of about 1125 A.D., which contains some rather good drawings of military subjects. The Additional MS. 14,789, of German execution, written in 1128 A.D., contains military subjects; among them is a figure of Goliath, in which the Philistine has a hauberk of chain mail, and chausses of jazerant work, like the knight in the last woodcut. The Royal MS. 20 D. i., is a French MS., very full of valuable military drawings, executed probably at the close of the thirteenth century, belonging, however, in the style of its Art and costume, rather to the early part of the next period than to that under consideration. The MS. Addit. 17,687, contains fine and valuable German drawings, full of military authorities, of about the same period as the French MS. last mentioned.

Knight and Men-at-Arms of the end of the Thirteenth Century.

The accompanying wood-cut represents various peculiarities of the armour in use towards the close of the thirteenth century. It is taken from the Sloane MS. 346, which is a metrical Bible. In the original drawing a female figure is kneeling before the warrior, and there is an inscription over the picture, *Abygail placet iram regis David* (Abigail appeases the anger of King David). So that this group of a thirteenth-century knight and his men-at-arms is intended by the mediæval artist to represent David and his followers on the march to revenge the churlishness of Nabal. The reader will notice the round plates at the elbows and knees, which are the first *visible* introduction of plate armour—breast-plates, worn under the hauberk, had been occasionally used from Saxon times. He will observe, too, the leather gauntlets which David wears, and the curious defences for the shoulders called *ailettes*: also that the shield is hung round the neck by its strap (*guige*), and the sword-belt round the hips, while the surcoat is girded round the waist by a silken

Knight of the end of the Thirteenth Century.

cord. The group is also valuable for giving us at a glance three different fashions of helmet. David has a conical bascinet, with a movable visor. The man immediately behind him wears an iron hat, with a wide rim and a raised crest, which is not at all unusual at this period. The other two men wear the globular helmet, the most common head-defence of the time.

The next cut is a spirited little sketch of a mounted knight, from the same MS. The horse, it may be admitted, is very like those which children draw nowadays, but it has more life in it than most of the drawings of that day; and the way in which the knight sits his horse is much more artistic. The picture shows the equipment of the knight very clearly, and it is specially valuable as an early example of horse trappings, and as an authority for the shape of the saddle, with its high pommel and croupe. The inscrption over the picture is, *Tharbis defendit urbem Sabea ab impugnanti Moysi;* and over the head of this cavalier is his name *Moyses*—Moses, as a knight of the end of the thirteenth century!

CHAPTER III.

ARMOUR OF THE FOURTEENTH CENTURY.

IN arriving at the fourteenth century, we have reached the very heart of our subject. For this century was the period of the great national wars with France and Scotland; it was the time when the mercenaries raised in the Italian wars first learnt, and then taught the world, the trade of soldier and trained their captains in the art of war; it was the period when the romantic exploits and picturesque trappings of chivalry were in their greatest vogue; the period when Gothic art was at its highest point of excellence. It was a period, too, of which we have ample knowledge from public records and serious histories, from romance writers in poetry and prose, from Chaucer and Froissart, from MS. illuminations and monumental effigies. Our difficulty amid such a profusion of material is to select that which will be most serviceable to our special purpose.

Let us begin with some detailed account of the different kinds and fashions of armour and equipment. In the preceding period, it has been seen, the most approved knightly armour was of mail. The characteristic feature of the armour of the fourteenth century is the intermixture of mail and plate. We see it first in small supplementary defences of plate introduced to protect the elbow and knee-joints. Probably it was found that the rather heavy and unpliable sleeve and hose of mail pressed inconveniently upon these joints; therefore the armourer adopted the expedient which proved to be the "thin end of the wedge" which gradually brought plate armour into fashion. He cut the mail hose in two; the lower part, which was then like a modern stocking, protected the leg, and the upper part protected the thigh, each being independently fastened below and above the knee, leaving the knee unprotected. Then he hollowed a piece of plate iron so as to form a cap for the knee, called technically a *genouillière*, within which the joint could work freely without chafing or pressure; perhaps it was padded or stuffed so as to deaden the effect of a blow; and it was fashioned so as effectually to cover all the part left undefended by the mail. The sleeve of the hauberk was cut in the same

Men-at-Arms, Fourteenth Century.

way, and the elbow was defended by a cap of plate-iron called a *coudière*. Early examples of these two pieces of plate armour will be seen in the later illustrations of our last chapter, for they were introduced a little before the end of the thirteenth century. The two pieces of plate were introduced simultaneously, and they appear together in the woodcut of David and his men in our last chapter; but we often find the genouillière used while the arm is still defended only by the sleeve of the hauberk, as in the first woodcut in the present chapter, and again in the cut on p. 348. It is easy to see that the pressure of the chausses of mail upon the knee in riding would be constant and considerable, and a much more serious inconvenience than the pressure upon the elbow in the usual attitude of the arm.

Next, round plates of metal, called *placates* or *roundels*, were applied to shield the armpits from a thrust; and sometimes they were used also at the elbow to protect the inner side of the joint where, for the convenience of motion, it was destitute of armour. An example of a roundel at the shoulder will be seen in one of the men-at-arms in the woodcut on p. 339. Another curious fashion which very generally prevailed at this time—that is, at the close of the thirteenth and beginning of the fourteenth century—was the *ailette*. It was a thin, oblong plate of metal, which was attached behind the shoulder. It would to some extent deaden the force of a blow directed at the neck, but it would afford so inartificial and ineffective a defence, that it is difficult to believe it was intended for anything more than an ornament. It is worn by the foremost knight in the cut on p. 335.

Perhaps the next great improvement was to protect the foot by a shoe made of plates of iron overlapping, like the shell of a lobster, the sole being still of leather. Then plates of iron, made to fit the limb, were applied to the shin and the upper part of the forearm, and sometimes a small plate is applied to the upper part of the arm in the place most exposed to a blow. Then the shin and forearm defences were enlarged so as to enclose the limb completely, opening at the side with a hinge, and closing with straps or rivets. Then the thigh and the upper arm were similarly enclosed in plate.

It is a little difficult to trace exactly the changes which took place in the body defences, because all through this period it was the fashion to wear a surcoat of some kind, which usually conceals all that was worn beneath it. It is however probable that at an early period of the introduction of plate a breastplate was introduced, which was worn over the hauberk, and perhaps fastened to it. Then, it would seem, a back plate was added also, worn over the hauberk. Next, the breast and back plate were made to enclose the whole of the upper part of the body, while only a skirt of mail remained; *i.e.* a garment of the same shape as the hauberk was worn, unprotected with mail, where the breast and back plate would come upon it, but still having its skirt covered with rings. In an illumination in the MS., is a picture of a knight putting off his jupon, in which the " pair of plates," as Chaucer calls them in a quotation hereafter given, is seen, tinted blue (steel colour), with a skirt of mail. At this time the helmet had a fringe of mail, called the *camail*, attached to its lower margin, which fell over the body armour, and defended the neck. It is clearly seen in the hindermost knight of the group in the woodcut on p. 339, and in the effigy of John of Eltham, on p. 342.

It is not difficult to see the superiority of defence which plate afforded over mail. The edge of sword or axe would bite upon the mail; if the rings were unbroken, still the blow would be likely to bruise; and in romances it is common enough to hear of huge cantles of mail being hewn out by their blows, and the doughty champions being spent with loss of blood. But many a blow would glance off quite harmless from the curved and polished, and well-tempered surface of plate; so that it would probably require not only a more dexterous blow to make the edge of the weapon bite at all on the plate, but also a harder blow to cut into it so as to wound. In " Prince Arthur" we read of Sir Tristram and Sir Governale—" they avoided their horses, and put their shields before them, and they strake together with bright swords like men that were of might, and either wounded other wondrous sore, so that the blood ran upon the grass, and of their harness they had hewed off many pieces." And again, in a combat between Sir Tristram and Sir Elias, after a course in which " either smote other so hard that both horses and knights went to the earth," " they both lightly rose up and dressed their shields on their shoulders, with naked swords in their hands, and they dashed together like as there had been a flaming fire about them. Thus they traced and traversed, and hewed on helms and hauberks, and cut away many pieces and cantles of their shields, and either wounded other passingly sore, so that the hot blood fell fresh upon the earth."

We have said that a surcoat of some kind was worn throughout this period, bu tit differed in shape at different times, and had different names applied to it. In the early part of the time of which we are now speaking, *i.e.* when the innovation of plate armour was beginning, the loose and flowing surcoat of the thirteenth century was still used, and is very clearly seen in the nearest of the group of knights in woodcut on p. 339. It was usually of linen or silk, sleeveless, reached halfway between the knee and ankle, was left unstiffened to fall in loose folds, except that it was girt by a silk cord round the waist, and its skirts flutter behind as the wearer gallops on through the air. The change of taste was in the direction of shortening the skirts of the surcoat, and making it scantier about the body, and stiffening it so as to make it fit the person without folds; at last it was tightly fitted to the breast and back plate, and showed their outline; and it was not uncommonly covered with embroidery, often of the armorial bearings of the wearer. The former garment is properly called a surcoat, and the latter a jupon; the one is characteristic of the greater part of the thirteenth century, the latter of the greater part of the fourteenth. But the fashion did not change suddenly from the one to the other; there was a transitional phase called the *cyclas*, which may be briefly described. The cyclas opened up the sides instead of in front, and it had this curious peculiarity, that the front skirt was cut much shorter than the hind skirt—behind it reached to the knees, but in front not very much below the hips. The fashion has this advantage for antiquarians, that the shortness of the front skirt allows us to see a whole series of military garments beneath, which are hidden by the long surcoat and even by the shorter jupon. A suit of armour of this period is represented in the Roman d'Alexandre (Bodleian Library), at folio 143 v., and elsewhere in the MS. The remainder of the few examples of the cyclas which remain, and which, so far as our observation extends, are all in sepulchral monuments, range

John of Eltham.

between the years 1325 and 1335, the shortening of the cyclas enables us to see. We have chosen for our illustration the sepulchral effigy in Westminster Abbey of John of Eltham, the second son of King Edward II., who died in 1334. Here we see first and lowest the hacqueton; then the hauberk of chain mail, slightly pointed in front, which was one of the fashions of the time, as we see it also in the monumental brasses of Sir John de Creke, at Westley-Waterless, Cambridgeshire, and of Sir J. D'Aubernoun, the younger, at Stoke D'Abernon, Surrey; over the hauberk we see the ornamented gambeson; and over all the cyclas. It is a question whether knights generally wore this whole series of defences, but the monumental effigies are usually so accurate in their representations of actual costume, that we must conclude that at least on occasions of state solemnity they were all worn. In the illustration it will be seen that the cyclas is confined, not by a silk cord, but by a narrow belt, while the sword-belt of the thirteenth century is still worn in addition. The jupon is seen in the two knights tilting, in the woodcut on p. 348. In the knight on the left will be seen how it fits tightly, and takes the globular shape of the breastplate. It will be noticed that on this knight the skirt of the jupon is scalloped, on the other it is plain. The jupon was not girded with a silk cord or a narrow belt; it was made to fit tight without any such fastening. The sword-belt worn with it differs in two important respects from that worn previously. It does not fall diagonally across the person, but horizontally over the hips; and it is not merely a leather belt ornamented, but the leather foundation is completely concealed by plates of metal in high relief, chased, gilt, and filled with enamels, forming a gorgeous decoration. The general form will be seen in the woodcut on p. 350, but its elaboration and splendour are better understood on an examination of some of the sculptured effigies, in which the forms of the metal plates are preserved in facsimile, with traces of their gilding and colour still remaining.

It would be easy, from the series of sculptured effigies in relief and monumental brasses, to give a complete chronological view of these various changes which were continually progressing throughout the fourteenth century. But this has already been done in the very accessible works by

Stothard, the Messrs. Waller, Mr. Boutell, and Mr. Haines, especially devoted to monumental effigies and brasses. It will be more in accordance with the plan we have laid down for ourselves, if we take from the less known illuminations of MSS. some subjects which will perhaps be less clear and fine in detail, but will have more life and character than the formal monumental effigies.

We must, however, pause to mention some other kinds of armour which were sometimes used in place of armour of steel. And first we may mention leather. Leather was always more or less used as a cheap kind of defence, from the Saxon leather tunic with the hair left on it, down to the buff jerkin of the time of the Commonwealth, and even to the thick leather gauntlets and jack boots of the present Life Guardsman. But at the time of which we are speaking pieces of armour of the same shape as those we have been describing were sometimes made, for the sake of lightness, of *cuir bouilli* instead of metal. Cuir bouilli was, as its name implies, leather which was treated with hot water, in such a way as to make it assume a required shape; and often it was also impressed, while soft, with ornamental devices. It is easy to see that in this way armour might be made possessing great comparative lightness, and yet a certain degree of strength, and capable, by stamping, colouring, and gilding, of a high degree of ornamentation. It was a kind of armour very suitable for occasions of mere ceremonial, and it was adopted in actual combat for parts of the body less exposed to injury; for instance, it seems to be especially used for the defence of the lower half of the legs. We shall find presently, in the description of Chaucer's Sire Thopas, the knight adventurous, that "his jambeux were of cuirbouly." In external form and appearance it would be so exactly like metal armour that it may be represented in some of the ornamental effigies and MSS. drawings, where it has the appearance of, and is usually assumed to be, metal armour. Another form of armour, of which we often meet with examples in drawings and effigies, is one in which the piece of armour appears to be studded, at more or less distant regular intervals, with small round plates. There are two suggestions as to the kind of armour intended. One is, that the armour thus represented was a garment of cloth, silk, velvet, or other textile material, lined with plates of metal, which are fastened to the garment with metal rivets, and that the heads of these rivets, gilt and ornamented, were allowed to be seen powdering the coloured face of the garment by way of ornament. Another suggestion is that the garment was merely one of the padded and quilted armours which we shall have next to describe, in which, as an additional precaution, metal studs were introduced, much as an oak door is studded with iron bolts. An example of it will be seen in the armour of the forearms of King Meliadus in the woodcut on p. 350. Chaucer seems to speak of this kind of defence, in his description of Lycurgus at the great tournament in the "Knight's Tale," under the name of coat armour:—

>"Instede of cote-armure on his harnais,
>With nayles yelwe and bryght as any gold,
>He had a bere's skin cole-blake for old."

Next we come to the rather large and important series of quilted defences. We find the names of the *gambeson*, *hacqueton*, and *pourpoint*, and sometimes the *jacke*. It is a little difficult to distinguish one from the other in the descriptions; and in fact they appear to have greatly resembled one another, and the names seem often to have been used interchangeably. The gambeson was a sleeved tunic of stout coarse linen, stuffed with flax and other common material, and sewn longitudinally. The hacqueton was a similar garment, only made of buckram, and stuffed with cotton; stiff from its material, but not so thick and clumsy as the gambeson. The pourpoint was very like the hacqueton, only that it was made of finer material, faced with silk, and stitched in ornamental patterns. The gambeson and hacqueton were worn under the armour, partly to relieve its pressure upon the body, partly to afford an additional defence. Sometimes they were worn, especially by the common soldiers, without any other armour. The pourpoint was worn over the hauberk, but sometimes it was worn alone, the hauberk being omitted for the sake of lightness. The jacke, or jacque, was a tunic of stuffed leather, and was usually worn by the common soldiers without other armour, but sometimes as light armour by knights.

In the first wood-cut on the next page, from the Romance of King

Meliadus, we have a figure which appears to be habited in one of these quilted armours, perhaps the hacqueton. There is another figure in the same group, in a similar dress, with this difference—in the first the skirt seems to fall loose and light, in the second the skirt seems to be stuffed and quilted like the body of the garment. At folio 214 of the same Romance is a squire, attendant upon a knight-errant, who is habited in a similar

Squire in Hacqueton.   *Sir Robert Shurland.*

hacqueton to that we have represented; the squires throughout the MS. are usually quite unarmed. In the monumental effigy of Sir Robert Shurland, who was made a knight-banneret in 1300, we seem to have a curious and probably unique effigy of a knight in the gameson. We give a woodcut of it, reduced from Stothard's engraving. The smaller figure of the man placed at the feet of the effigy is in the same costume, and affords us an additional example. Stothard conjectures that the garment in the effigy of John of Eltham (1334, A.D.), whose vandyked border appears beneath his hauberk, is the buckram of the hacqueton left unstuffed, and ornamentally scalloped round the border. In the MS. of King Meliadus, at f. 21, and again on the other side of the leaf, is a knight, whose red jupon, slit up at the sides, is thrown open by his attitude, so that we see the skirt of mail beneath, which is silvered to represent metal; and beneath that is a scalloped border of an under habit, which is left white, and, if Stothard's conjecture be correct, is another example of the hacqueton under the hauberk. But the best representation which we have met with of the quilted armours is in the MS. of the Romance of the Rose (Harleian, 4,425), at folio 133, where, in a battle scene, one knight is conspicuous among the blue steel and red and green jupons of the other knights by a white body armour quilted in small squares, with which he wears a steel bascinet and ringed camail. He is engraved on p. 389.

And now to turn to a description of some of the MS. illuminations which illustrate this chapter. That on p. 339 is a charming little subject from a famous MS. (Royal 2 B. VII.) of the beginning of the Edwardian period, which will illustrate half-a-dozen objects besides the mere suit of knightly armour. First of all there is the suit of armour on the knight in the foreground, the hooded hauberk and chausses of mail and genouillières, the chapeau de fer, or war helm, and the surcoat, and the shield. But we get also a variety of helmets, different kinds of weapons, falchion and axe, as well as sword and spear, and the pennon attached to the spear; and, in addition, the complete horse trappings, with the ornamental crest which was used to set off the arching neck and tossing head. Moreover, we learn that this variety of arms and armour was to be found in a single troop of men-at-arms; and we see the irregular but picturesque effect which such a group presented to the eyes of the monkish illuminator as it pranced beneath the gateway into the outer court of the abbey, to seek the hospitality which the hospitaller would hasten to offer on behalf of the convent.

This mixture of armour and weapons is brought before us by Chaucer in his description of Palamon's party in the great tournament in the "Knight's Tale:"—

> "And right so ferden they with Palamon,
> With him ther wenten knights many one,
> Som wol ben armed in an habergeon,
> And in a brestplate and in a gipon;
> And some wol have a pair of plates large;
> And some wol have a Pruce shield or a targe;
> And some wol ben armed on his legge's wele,
> And have an axe, and some a mace of stele,
> Ther was no newe guise that it was old,
> Armed they weren, as I have you told,
> Everich after his opinion."

The illustration here given and that on p. 350 are from a MS. which we cannot quote for the first time without calling special attention to it. It is a MS. of one of the numerous romances of the King Arthur cycle, the Romance

Jousting.

of the King Meliadus, who was one of the Companions of the Round Table. The book is profusely illustrated with pictures which are invaluable to the student of military costume and chivalric customs. They are by different hands, and not all of the same date, the earlier series being probably about 1350, the later perhaps as late as near the end of the century. In both these dates the MS. gives page after page of large-sized pictures drawn with great spirit, and illustrating every variety of incident which could take place in single combat and in tournament, with many scenes of civil and domestic life besides. Especially there is page after page in which, along the lower portion of the pages, across the whole width of the book, there are pictures of tournaments. There is a gallery of spectators along the top, and in some of these—especially in those at folio 151 v. and 152, which are sketched in with pen and ink, and left uncoloured —there are more of character and artistic drawing than the artists of the time are usually believed to have possessed. Beneath this gallery is a confused mêlée of knights in the very thickest throng and most energetic action of a tournament. The wood-cut on p. 348 represents one out of many incidents of a single combat. It does not do justice to the drawing, and looks tame for want of the colouring of the original; but it will serve to show the armour and equipment of the time. The victor knight is habited in a hauberk of banded mail, with gauntlets of plate, and the legs are cased entirely in plate. The body armour is covered by a jupon; the tilting helmet has a knight's chapeau and drapery carrying the lion crest. The armour in the illumination is silvered to represent metal. The knight's jupon is red, and the trappings of his helmet red, with a golden lion; his shield bears gules, a lion rampant argent; the conquered knight's jupon is blue, his shield argent, two bandlets gules. We see here the way in which the shield was carried, and the long slender spear couched, in the charge.

The next wood-cut hardly does credit to the charming original. It represents the royal knight-errant himself sitting by a fountain, talking with his squire. The suit of armour is beautiful, and the face of the knight has much character, but very different from the modern conventional type of a mediæval knight-errant. His armour deserves particular examination. He wears a hauberk of banded mail; whether he wears a breastplate, or pair of plates, we are unable to see for the jupon, but we can see the hauberk which protects the throat above the jupon, and the skirt of it where the attitude of the wearer throws the skirt of the jupon open at the side. It will be seen that the sleeves of the hauberk are not continued, as in most examples, over the hands, or even down to the wrist; but the forearm is defended by studded armour, and the hands by gauntlets which are proably of plate. The leg defences are admirably exhibited; the hose of banded mail, the knee cap, and shin pieces of plate, and the boots of over-lapping plates. The helmet also, with its royal crown and curious double crest, is worth notice. In the original drawing the whole suit of armour is brilliantly executed. The armour is all silvered to represent steel, the jupon is green, the military belt gold, the helmet silvered, with its drapery

A Knight-Errant.

blue powdered with gold fleurs-de-lis, and its crown, and the fleur-de-lis which terminate its crest, gold. The whole dress and armour of a knight of the latter half of the fourteenth century are described for us by Chaucer in a few stanzas of his Rime of Sire Thopas :—

"He didde* next his white lere
Of cloth of lake fine and clere
A breche and eke a sherte ;

---

* *Didde*—did on next his white skin.

> And next his shert an haketon,
> And over that an habergeon,
>   For percing of his herte.
>
> And over that a fine hauberk,
> Was all ye wrought of Jewes werk,
>   Full strong it was of plate ;
> And over that his coat armoure,
> As white as is the lily floure,
>   In which he could debate.*
>
> His jambeux were of cuirbouly,†
> His swerde's sheth of ivory,
>   His helm of latoun‡ bright,
> His sadel was of rewel bone,
> His bridle as the sonne shone,
>   Or as the mone-light.§
>
> His sheld was all of gold so red,
> And therein was a bore's hed,
>   A charboncle beside ;
> And then he swore on ale and bred,
> How that the geaunt shuld be ded,
>   Betide what so betide.
>
> His spere was of fine cypres,
> That bodeth warre and nothing pees,
>   The hed ful sharpe yground.
> His stede was all of dapper gray,
> It goth an amble in the way,
>   Ful softely in londe."

There is so much of character in his squire's face in the same picture, and that character so different from our conventional idea of a squire, that we are tempted to give a sketch of it on p. 352, as he leans over the horse's back talking to his master. This MS. affords us a whole gallery of squires attendant upon their knights. At folio 66 v. is one carrying his master's spear and

---

* *Debate*—contend.
† *Cuirbouly*—stamped leather.
‡ *Latoun*—brass.
§ Compare Tennyson's description of Sir Lancelot, in the " Lady of Shalot."
> " His gemmy bridle glittered free,
>   Like to some branch of stars we see ;
>   Hung in the golden galaxy,
>   As he rode down to Camelot."

shield, who has a round cap with a long feather, like that in the woodcut. In several other instances the squire rides bareheaded, but has his hood hanging behind on his shoulders ready for a cold day or a shower of rain. In another place the knight is attended by two squires, one bearing his master's tilting helmet on his shoulder, the other carrying his spear and shield. In all cases the squires are unarmed, and mature men of rather heavy type, different from the gay and gallant youths whom we are apt to picture to ourselves as the squires of the days of chivalry attendant on

The Knight-Errant's Squire.

noble knights adventurous. In other cases we see the squires looking on very phlegmatically while their masters are in the height of a single combat; perhaps a knight adventurous was not a hero to his squire. But again we see the squire starting into activity to catch his master's steed, from which he has been unhorsed by an antagonist of greater strength or skill, or good fortune. We see him also in the lists at a tournament, handing his master a new spear when he has splintered his own on an opponent's shield; or helping him to his feet when he has been overthrown, horse and man, under the hoofs of prancing horses.

CHAPTER IV.

THE DAYS OF CHIVALRY.

WE have no inclination to deny that life is more safe and easy in these days than it was in the Middle Ages, but it certainly is less picturesque, and adventurous, and joyous. This country then presented the features of interest which those among us who have wealth and leisure now travel to foreign lands to find. There were vast tracts of primeval forest, and wild unenclosed moors and commons, and marshes and meres. The towns were surrounded by walls and towers, and the narrow streets of picturesque, gabled, timber houses were divided by wide spaces of garden and grove, above which rose numerous steeples of churches full of artistic wealth. The villages consisted of a group of cottages scattered round a wide green, with a village cross in the middle, and a maypole beside it. And there were stately monasteries in the rich valleys; and castles crowned the hills; and moated manor-houses lay buried in their woods; and hermitages stood by the dangerous fords. The high roads were little more than green lanes with a narrow beaten track in the middle, poached into deep mud in winter; and the by-roads were bridle-paths winding from village to village; and the costumes of the people were picturesque in fashion, bright in colour, and characteristic. The gentleman pranced along in silks and velvets, in plumed hat, and enamelled belt, and gold-hilted sword and spurs, with a troop of armed servants behind him; the abbot, in the robe of his order, with a couple of chaplains, all on ambling palfreys; the friar paced along in serge frock and sandals; the minstrel, in gay coat, sang snatches of lays as he wandered along from hall to castle, with a lad at his back carrying his harp or gittern; the traders went from fair to fair, taking their goods on strings of pack horses; a pilgrim, passed now and then, with staff and scrip and cloak; and, now and then, a knight-errant in full armour rode by on his war-horse, with a squire carrying his helm and spear. It was a wild land, and the people were rude, and the times lawless; but every mile furnished pictures for the artist, and every day offered the chance of adventures. The reader must picture to himself the aspect of the country and the manners of the times, before he can appreciate the spirit of knight-errantry, to which it is necessary that we should devote one of these chapters on the Knights of the Middle Ages.

The knight-errant was usually some young knight who had been lately dubbed, and who, full of courage and tired of the monotony of his father's manor-house, set out in search of adventures. We could envy him as, on some bright spring morning, he rode across the sounding drawbridge, followed by a squire in the person of some young forester as full of animal spirits and reckless courage as himself; or, perhaps, by some steady old warrior practised in the last French war, whom his father had chosen to take care of him. We sigh for our own lost youth as we think of him, with all the world before him—the mediæval world, with all its possibilities of wild adventure and romantic fortune; with caitiff knights to overthrow at spear-point, and distressed damsels to succour; and princesses to win as the prize of some great tournament; and rank and fame to gain by prowess and daring, under the eye of kings, in some great stricken field.

The old romances enable us to follow such an errant knight through all his travels and adventures; and the illuminations leave hardly a point in the history unillustrated by their quaint but naïve and charming pictures. Tennyson has taken some of the episodes out of these old romances, and filled up the artless but suggestive stories with the rich detail and artistic finish which adapt them to our modern taste, and has made them the favourite subjects of modern poetry. But he has left a hundred others behind; stories as beautiful, with words and sentences here and there full of poetry, destined to supply material for future poems and new subjects for our painters.

It is our business to quote from these romances some of the scenes which will illustrate our subject, and to introduce some of the illuminations that will present them to the eye. In selecting the literary sketches, we shall use almost exclusively the translation which Sir Thomas Mallory made, and Caxton printed, of the cycle of Prince Arthur romances, because it comprises a sufficient number for our purpose, and because the language, while perfectly intelligible and in the best and most vigorous English, has enough of antique style to give the charm which would be wanting if we

A Squire.

were to translate the older romances into modern phraseology. In the same way we shall content ourselves with selecting pictorial illustrations chiefly from MSS. of the fourteenth century, the date at which many of these romances were brought into the form in which they have descended to us.

A knight was known to be a knight-errant by his riding through the peaceful country in full armour, with a single squire at his back, as surely as a man is now recognised as a fox-hunter who is seen riding easily along the strip of green sward by the roadside in a pink coat and velvet cap. " Fair knight," says Sir Tristram, to one whom he had found sitting by a fountain, "ye seem for to be a knight-errant by your arms and your harness, therefore dress ye to just with one of us :" for this was of course inevitable when knights-errant met; the whole passage is worth transcribing :—" Sir Tristram and Sir Kay rode within the forest a mile or more. And at the last Sir Tristram saw before him a likely knight and a well-made man, all armed, sitting by a clear fountain, and a mighty horse near unto him tied to a great oak, and a man [his squire] riding by him, leading an horse that was laden with spears. Then Sir Tristram rode near him, and said, 'Fair knight, why sit ye so drooping, for ye seem to be an errant knight by your arms and harness, and therefore dress ye to just with one of us or with both.' Therewith that knight made no words, but took his shield and buckled it about his neck, and lightly he took his horse and leaped upon him, and then he took a great spear of his squire, and departed his way a furlong."

And so we read in another place :—" Sir Dinadan spake on high and said, 'Sir Knight, make thee ready to just with me, for it is the custom of all arrant knights one for to just with another.' 'Sir,' said Sir Epinogris, 'is that the rule of your arrant knights, for to make a knight to just whether he will or not?' 'As for that, make thee ready, for here is for me.' And therewith they spurred their horses, and met together so hard that Sir Epinogris smote down Sir Dinadan "—and so taught him the truth of the adage " that it is wise to let sleeping dogs lie."

But they did not merely take the chance of meeting one another as they journeyed. A knight in quest of adventures would sometimes station himself at a ford or bridge, and mount guard all day long, and let no knight-errant pass until he had jousted with him. Thus we read "then they rode forth all together, King Mark, Sir Lamorake, and Sir Dinadan, till that they came unto a bridge, and at the end of that bridge stood a fair tower. Then saw they a knight on horseback, well armed, brandishing a spear, crying and proffering himself to just." And again, "When King Mark and Sir Dinadan had ridden about four miles, they came unto a bridge, whereas hoved a knight on horseback, and ready to just. 'So,' said Sir Dinadan unto King Mark, 'yonder hoveth a knight that will just, for there shall none pass this bridge but he must just with that knight.'"

And again: "They rode through the forest, and at the last they were ware of two pavilions by a priory with two shields, and the one shield was renewed with white and the other shield was red. 'Thou shalt not pass this way,' said the dwarf, 'but first thou must just with yonder knights that abide in yonder pavilions that thou seest.' Then was Sir Tor ware where two pavilions were, and great spears stood out, and two shields hung on two trees by the pavilions." In the same way a knight would take up his abode for a few days at a wayside cross where four ways met, in order to meet adventures from east, west, north, and south. Notice of adventures was sometimes affixed upon such a cross, as we read in "Prince Arthur": "And so Sir Galahad and he rode forth all that week ere they found any adventure. And then upon a Sunday, in the morning, as they were departed from an abbey, they came unto a cross which departed two ways. And on that cross were letters written which said thus: *Now ye knights-errant that goeth forth for to seek adventures, see here two ways,*" &c.

Wherever they went, they made diligent inquiry for adventures. Thus "Sir Launcelot departed, and by adventure he came into a forest. And in the midst of a highway he met with a damsel riding on a white palfrey, and either saluted other: 'Fair damsel,' said Sir Launcelot, 'know ye in this country any adventures?' 'Sir Knight,' said the damsel, 'here are adventures near at hand, an thou durst prove them.' 'Why should I not prove adventures,' said Sir Launcelot, 'as for that cause came I hither?'" And on another occasion, we read, Sir Launcelot passed out of the (King Arthur's) court to seek adventures, and Sir Ector made him ready to meet Sir Launcelot, and as he had ridden long in a great forest, he met with a man that was like a forester.—These frequent notices of "riding long through a great forest," are noticeable as evidences of the condition of the country in those days.—"Fair fellow," said Sir Ector, "knowest thou in this country any adventures which be here nigh at hand?" "Sir," said the forester, "this country know I well, and here within this mile is a strong manor and well ditched"—not well walled; it was the fashion of the Middle Ages to choose low sites for their manor-houses, and to surround them with moats—such moats are still common round old manor-houses in Essex—" and by that manor on the left hand is a fair ford for horses to drink, and over that ford there groweth a fair tree, and thereon hangeth many fair shields that belonged some time unto good knights; and at the bole of the tree hangeth a bason of copper and laten; and strike upon that bason with the end of the spear thrice, and soon after

Preliminaries of Combat in Green Court of Castle.

thou shalt hear good tidings, and else hast thou the fairest grace that many a year any knight had that passed through this forest."

Every castle offered hope, not only of hospitality, but also of a trial of arms; for in every castle there would be likely to be knights and squires glad of the opportunity of running a course with bated spears with a new and skilful antagonist. Here is a picture from an old MS. which represents the preliminaries of such a combat on the green between the castle walls and the moat. In many castles there was a special tilting-ground. Thus we read, "Sir Percivale passed the water, and when he came unto the castle gate, he said to the porter, 'Go thou unto the good knight within the castle, and tell him that here is came an errant knight to just with him.' 'Sir,' said the porter, 'ride ye within the castle, and there shall ye find a common place for justing, that lords and ladies may behold you.'" At Carisbrook Castle, in the Isle of Wight, the tilting-ground remains to this day; a plot of level green sward, with raised turfed banks round it, that at the same time served as the enclosure of the lists, and a vantage-ground from which the spectators might see the sport. At Gawsworth, also, the ancient tilting-ground still remains. But in most castles of any size, the outer court afforded room enough for a course, and at the worst there was the green meadow outside the castle walls. In some castles they had special customs; just as in old-fashioned country-houses one used to be told it was "the custom of the house" to do this and that; so it was "the custom of the castle" for every knight to break three lances, for instance, or exchange three strokes of sword with the lord — a quondam errant knight be sure, thus creating adventures for himself at home when marriage and cares of property forbade him to roam in search of them. Thus, in the Romance:—" Sir Tristram and Sir Dinadan rode forth their way till they came to some shepherds and herdsmen, and there they asked if they knew any lodging or harbour thereabout." " Forsooth, fair lords," said the herdsmen, "nigh hereby is a good lodging in a castle, but such a custom there is that there shall no knight be lodged but if he first just with two knights, and if ye be beaten, and have the worse, ye shall not be lodged there, and if ye beat them, ye shall be well lodged." The Knights of the Round Table easily vanquished the two knights of the castle, and were hospitably received; but while they were at table came Sir Palomides, and Sir Gaheris, " requiring to have the custom of the castle." "And now," said Sir Tristram, "must we defend the custom of the castle, inasmuch as we have the better of the lord of the castle."

Here is the kind of invitation they were sure to receive from gentlemen living peaceably on their estates, but sympathising with the high spirit and love of adventure which sent young knights a wandering through their woods and meadows, and under their castle walls:—Sir Tristram and Sir Gareth " were ware of a knight that came riding against [towards] them unarmed, and nothing about him but a sword; and when this knight came nigh them he saluted them, and they him again. 'Fair knights,' said that knight, 'I pray you, inasmuch as ye are knights errant, that ye will come and see my castle, and take such as ye find there, I pray you heartily.' And so they rode with him to his castle, and there they were brought to the hall that was well appareled, and so they were unarmed and set at a board."

We have already heard in these brief extracts of knights lodging at castles and abbeys: we often find them received at manor-houses. Here is one of the most graphic pictures:—"Then Sir Launcelot mounted upon his horse and rode into many strange and wild countries, and through many waters and valleys, and evil was he lodged. And at the last, by fortune, it happened him against a night to come to a poor courtilage, and therein he found an old gentleman, which lodged him with a good will, and there he and his horse were well cheered. And when time was, his host brought him to a fair garret over a gate to his bed. There Sir Launcelot unarmed him, and set his harness by him, and went to bed, and anon he fell in sleep. So, soon after, there came one on horseback, and knocked at the gate in great haste. And when Sir Launcelot heard this, he arose up and looked out at the window, and saw by the moonlight three knights that came riding after that one man, and all three lashed upon him at once with their swords, and that one knight turned on them knightly again, and defended himself." And Sir Launcelot, like an errant knight, "took his harness and went out at the window by a sheet," and made them yield, and commanded them at Whit Sunday to go to King Arthur's court, and there yield them unto Queen Guenever's grace and mercy; for so errant knights gave to their lady-loves the evidences of their prowess, and did them honour, by sending them a constant succession of vanquished knights, and putting them "unto her grace and mercy."

Very often the good knight in the midst of forest or wild found a night's shelter in a friendly hermitage, for hermitages, indeed, were established partly to afford shelter to belated travellers. Here is an example. Sir Tor asks the dwarf who is his guide, "'Know ye any lodging?' 'I know none,' said the dwarf; 'but here beside is an hermitage, and there ye must take such lodging as ye find.' And within a while they came to the hermitage and took lodging, and there was grass and oats and bread for their horses. Soon it was spread, and full hard was their supper; but there they rested them all the night till on the morrow, and heard a mass devoutly, and took their leave of the hermit, and Sir Tor prayed the hermit to pray for him, and he said he would, and betook him to God; and so he mounted on horseback, and rode towards Camelot."

But sometimes not even a friendly hermitage came in sight at the hour of twilight, when the forest glades darkened, and the horse track across the moor could no longer be seen, and the knight had to betake himself to a soldier's bivouac. It is an incident often met with in the Romances. Here is a more poetical description than usual:—"And anon these knights made them ready, and rode over holts and hills, through forests and woods, till they came to a fair meadow full of fair flowers and grass, and there they rested them and their horses all that night." Again, "Sir Launcelot rode into a forest, and there he met with a gentlewoman riding upon a white palfrey, and she asked him, 'Sir Knight, whither ride ye?' 'Certainly, damsel,' said Sir Launcelot, 'I wot not whither I ride, but as fortune leadeth me.' . . . . . Then Sir Launcelot asked her where he might be harboured that night. 'Ye shall none find this day nor night, but tomorrow ye shall find good harbour.' And then he commended her unto God. Then he rode till he came to a cross, and took that for his host as for that night. And he put his horse to pasture, and took off his helm and shield, and made his prayers to the cross, that he might never again fall into deadly sin, and so he laid him down to sleep, and anon as he slept it befel him that he had a vision," with which we will not trouble the reader; but we commend the incident to any young artist in want of a subject for a picture: the wayside cross where the four roads meet in the forest, the gnarled tree-trunks with their foliage touched with autumn tints, and the green bracken withering into brown and yellow and red, under the level rays of the sun which fling alternate bars of light and shade across the scene; and the noble war-horse peacefully grazing on the short sweet forest grass, and the peerless knight in glorious gilded arms, with his helmet at his feet, and his great spear leaned against a tree-trunk, kneeling before the cross, with his grave noble face, and his golden hair gleaming in the sun-light, "making his prayers that he might never again fall into deadly sin."

In the old monumental brasses in which pictures of the knightly costume are preserved to us with such wonderful accuracy and freshness, it is very common to find the knight represented as lying with his tilting helm under his head by way of pillow. One would take it for a mere artistic arrangement for raising the head of the recumbent figure, and for introducing this important portion of his costume, but that the Romances tell us that knights did actually make use of their helm for a pillow; a hard pillow, no doubt—but we have all heard of the veteran who kicked from under his

Knights, Damsel, and Squire.

son's head the snowball which he had rolled together for a pillow at his bivouac in the winter snow, indignant at his degenerate effeminacy. Thus we read of Sir Tristram and Sir Palomides, "They mounted upon their horses, and rode together into the forest, and there they found a fair well with clear water burbelling. 'Fair Sir,' said Sir Tristram, 'to drink of that water have I a lust.' And then they alighted from their horses, and then were they ware by them where stood a great horse tied to a tree, and ever he neighed, and then were they ware of a fair knight armed under a tree, lacking no piece of harness, save his helm lay under his head. Said Sir Tristram, 'Yonder lieth a fair knight, what is best to do?' 'Awake him,' said Sir Palomides. So Sir Tristram waked him with the end of his spear."

They had better have let him be, for the knight, thus roused, got him to horse and overthrew them both. Again, we read how "Sir Launcelot bad his brother, Sir Lionel, to make him ready, for we two, said he, will seek adventures. So they mounted upon their horses, armed at all points, and rode into a deep forest, and after they came into a great plain, and then the weather was hot about noon, and Sir Launcelot had great lust to sleep. Then Sir Lionel espied a great apple-tree that stood by a hedge, and said, 'Brother, yonder is a fair shadow; there may we rest us, and our horses.' 'It is well said, fair brother,' said Sir Launcelot, 'for all the seven year I was not so sleepy as I am now.' And so they alighted there, and tied their horses unto sundry trees, and so Sir Launcelot laid him down under an apple-tree, and laid his helm under his head. And Sir Lionel waked while he slept."

The knight did not, however, always trust to chance for shelter, and risk a night in the open air. Sometimes we find he took the field in this mimic warfare with a baggage train, and had his tent pitched for the night wherever night overtook him, or camped for a few days wherever a pleasant glade, or a fine prospect, or an agreeable neighbour, tempted him to prolong his stay. And he would picket his horse hard by, and thrust his spear into the ground beside the tent door, and hang his shield upon it. Thus we read:—"Now turn we unto Sir Launcelot, that had long been riding in a great forest, and at last came into a low country, full of fair rivers and meadows, and afore him he saw a long bridge, and three pavilions stood thereon of silk and sendal of divers hue, and without the pavilions hung three white shields on truncheons of spears, and great long spears stood upright by the pavilions, and at every pavilion's door stood three fresh squires, and so Sir Launcelot passed by them, and spake not a word." We may say here that it was not unusual for people in fine weather to pitch a tent in the courtyard or garden of the castle, and live there instead of indoors, or to go a-field and pitch a little camp in some pleasant place, and spend the time in justing and feasting, and mirth and minstrelsy. We read in one of the Romances how "the king and queen—King Arthur and Queen Guenever, to wit—made their pavilions and their tents to be pitched in the forest, beside a river, and there was daily hunting, for there were ever twenty knights ready for to just with all them that came in at that time." And here, in the woodcut below, is a picture of the scene.

Usually, perhaps, there was not much danger in these adventures of a knight-errant. There was a fair prospect of bruises, and a risk of broken bones if he got an awkward fall, but not more risk perhaps than in the modern hunting-field. Even if the combat went further than the usual three courses with bated spears, if they did draw swords and continue the combat on foot, there was usually no more real danger than in a duel of German students. But sometimes cause of anger would accidentally

King, &c., in Pavilion before Castle.

rise between two errant knights, or the combat begun in courtesy would fire their hot blood, and they would resolve "worshipfully to win worship, or die knightly on the field," and a serious encounter would take place. There were even some knights of evil disposition enough to take delight in making every combat a serious one; and some of the adventures in which we take most interest relate how these bloodthirsty bullies, attacking in ignorance some Knight of the Round Table, got a well-deserved blood-letting for their pains.

We must give one example of a combat—rather a long one, but it combines many different points of interest. "So as they (Merlin and King

Arthur) went thus talking, they came to a fountain, and a rich pavilion by it. Then was King Arthur aware where a knight sat all armed in a chair. 'Sir Knight,' said King Arthur, 'for what cause abidest thou here, that there may no knight ride this way, but if he do just with thee; leave that custom.' 'This custom,' said the knight, 'have I used, and will use maugre who saith nay, and who is grieved with my custom, let him amend it that will.' 'I will amend it,' saith King Arthur. 'And I shall defend it,' saith the knight. Anon he took his horse, and dressed his shield, and took a spear; and they met so hard either on other's shield, that they shivered their spears. Therewith King Arthur drew his sword. 'Nay, not so,' saith the knight, 'it is fairer that we twain run more together with

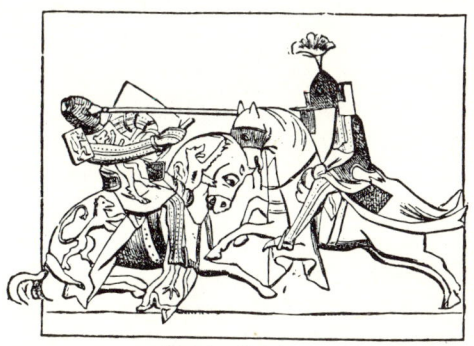

Knights Justing.

sharp spears.' 'I will well,' said King Arthur, 'an I had any more spears.' 'I have spears enough,' said the knight. So there came a squire, and brought two good spears, and King Arthur took one, and he another; so they spurred their horses, and came together with all their might, that either break their spears in their hands. Then King Arthur set hand to his sword. 'Nay,' said the knight, 'ye shall do better; ye are a passing good juster as ever I met withal; for the love of the high order of knighthood let us just it once again.' 'I assent me,' said King Arthur. Anon there were brought two good spears, and each knight got a spear, and therewith they ran together, that King Arthur's spear broke to shivers. But the knight hit him so hard in the middle of the shield, that horse and man fell to the earth, wherewith King Arthur was sore angered, and drew out his sword, and said, 'I will assay thee, Sir Knight, on foot, for I have lost the honour on horseback.' 'I will be on horseback,' said the knight. Then was King Arthur wrath, and dressed his shield towards him with his sword drawn. When the knight saw that, he alighted for him, for he thought it was no worship to have a knight at such advantage, he to be on horseback, and the other on foot, and so alighted, and dressed himself to King Arthur. Then there began a strong battle with many great strokes, and so hewed with their swords that the cantels flew on the field, and much blood they bled both, so that all the place where they fought was all bloody; and thus they fought long and rested them, and then they went to battle again, and so hurtled together like two wild boars, that either of them fell to the earth. So at the last they smote together, that both their swords met even together. But the sword of the knight smote King Arthur's sword in two pieces, wherefore he was heavy. Then said the knight to the king, 'Thou art in my danger, whether me list to slay thee or save thee; and but thou yield thee as overcome and recreant, thou shalt die.' 'As for death,' said King Arthur, 'welcome be it when it cometh, but as to yield me to thee as recreant, I had liever die than be so shamed.' And therewithal the king leapt upon Pelinore, and took him by the middle, and threw him down, and rased off his helmet. When the knight felt that he was a dread, for he was a passing big man of might; and anon he brought King Arthur under him, and rased off his helmet, and would have smitten off his head. Therewithal came Merlin, and said, 'Knight, hold thy hand.'"

Happy for the wounded knight if there were a religious house at hand, for there he was sure to find kind hospitality and such surgical skill as the times afforded. King Bagdemagus had this good fortune when he had been wounded by Sir Galahad. "I am sore wounded," said he, "and full hardly shall I escape from the death. Then the squire fet [fetched] his horse, and brought him with great pain to an abbey. Then was he taken down softly and unarmed, and laid in a bed, and his wound was looked into, for he lay there long and escaped hard with his life." So Sir Tristram, in his combat with Sir Marhaus, was so sorely wounded, "that unneath he might recover, and lay at a nunnery half a year." Such adventures sometimes, no doubt, ended fatally, as in the case of the unfortunate Sir Marhaus, and there was a summary conclusion to his adventures; and there was nothing left but to take him home and bury him in his parish church, and hang his sword and helmet over his tomb. Many a knight would be satisfied with the series of adventures which finished by laying him on a sick bed for six months, with only an ancient nun for his nurse; and as soon as he was well enough he would get himself conveyed home on a horse litter, a sadder and a wiser man. The modern romances have good mediæval authority, too, for making marriage a natural conclusion of their three volumes of adventures; we have no less authority for it than that of Sir Launcelot:—" Now, damsel," said he, at the conclusion of an adventure, " will ye any more service of me?" " Nay, sir," said she at this time, " but God preserve you, wherever ye go or ride, for the courtliest knight thou art, and meekest to all ladies and gentlewomen that now liveth. But, Sir Knight, one thing me thinketh that ye lack, ye that are a knight wifeless, that ye will not love some maiden or gentlewoman, for I could never hear say that ye loved any of no manner degree, wherefore many in this country of high estate and low make great sorrow." " Fair damsel," said Sir Launcelot, " to be a wedded man I think never to be, for if I were, then should I be bound to tarry with my wife, and leave arms and tournaments, battles and adventures."

We have only space left for a few examples of the quaint and poetical phrases that, as we have said, frequently occur in these Romances, some of which Tennyson has culled, and set like uncut mediæval gems in his circlet of " Idyls of the King." In the account of the great battle between King Arthur and his knights against the eleven kings " and their chivalry," we read " they were so courageous, that many knights shook and trembled for eagerness," and " they fought together, that the

---

* In the MS. Royal, 1,699, is a picture in which are represented a sword and hunting-horn hung over a tomb. The helmet, sword, and shield of Edward the Black Prince still hang over his tomb in Canterbury Cathedral; Henry IV.'s saddle and helmet over his tomb in Westminster Abbey; and in hundreds of parish churches helmets, swords, gauntlets, spurs, &c., still hang over the tombs of mediæval knights.

sound rang by the water and the wood," and "there was slain that morrow-tide ten thousand of good men's bodies." The second of these expressions is a favourite one; we meet with it again: "when King Ban came into the battle, he came in so fiercely, that the stroke resounded again from the water and the wood." Again we read, King Arthur "commanded his trumpets to blow the bloody sounds in such wise that the earth trembled and dindled." He was "a mighty man of men;" and "all men of worship said it was merry to be under such a chieftain, that would put his person in adventure as other poor knights did."

CHAPTER V.

KNIGHTS-ERRANT.

IN the British Museum are two volumes containing a rather large number of illuminated pictures which have been cut out of MSS., chiefly of the early fourteenth century, by some collector who did not understand how much more valuable they would have been, even as pictures, if left each by itself in the appropriate setting of its black letter page, than when pasted half-a-dozen together in a scrap-book. That they are severed from the letterpress which they were intended to illustrate is of the less importance, because they seem all to be illustrations of scenes in romances, and it is not difficult to one who is well versed in those early writings either to identify the subjects or to invent histories for them. Each isolated picture affords a subject in which an expert, turning the book over and explaining it to an amateur, would find material for a little lecture on mediæval art and architecture, costume, and manners.

In presenting to the reader the subjects which illustrate this chapter, we find ourselves placed by circumstances in the position of being obliged to treat them like those scrap-book pictures of which we have spoken, viz., as isolated pictures, illustrating generally our subject of the Knights of the Middle Ages, needing each its independent explanation.

The first subject represents a scene from some romance, in which the good knight, attended by his squire, is guided by a damsel on some adventure. As in the scene which we find in Caxton's " Prince Arthur " : " And the good knight, Sir Galahad, rode so long, till that he came that night to the castle of Carberecke; and it befel him that he was benighted in an hermitage. And when they were at rest there came a gentlewoman knocking at the door, and called Sir Galahad, and so the hermit came to the door to ask what she would. Then she called the hermit, Sir Ulfric, 'I am a gentlewoman that would speak with the knight that is with you.' Then the good man awaked Sir Galahad, and bade him rise and speak 'with a gentlewoman which seemeth hath great need of you.' Then Sir Galahad went to her, and asked what she would. 'Sir Galahad,' said she, 'I will that you arm you and mount upon your horse and follow me, for I will show you within these three days the highest adventure that ever knight saw. Anon, Sir Galahad armed him, and took his horse and com-

Lady, Knight, and Squire.

mended him to God, and bade the gentlewoman go, and he would follow her there as she liked. So the damsel rode as fast as her palfrey might gallop till that she came to the sea."

Here then we see the lady ambling through the forest, and she rides as ladies rode in the middle ages, and as they still ride, like female centaurs, in the Sandwich Islands. She turns easily in her saddle, though going at a good pace, to carry on an animated conversation with the knight. He, it will be seen, is in hauberk and hood of banded mail, with the curious ornaments called *ailettes*—little wings—at his shoulders. He seems to have *genouillières*—knee-pieces of plate; but it is doubtful whether he has also plate armour about the leg, or whether the artist has omitted the lines which would indicate that the legs were, as is more probably the case, also protected by banded mail. He wears the prick spur; and his body-armour is protected from sun and rain by the surcoat. Behind him prances his squire. The reader will not fail to notice the character which the artist has thrown into his attitude and the expression of his features. It will be seen that he is not armed, but wears the ordinary civil costume, with a hood and hat; he carries his master's spear, and the shield is suspended at his back by its guige or strap; its hollow shape and the rampant lion emblazoned on it will not be overlooked.

Romance writers are sometimes accused of forgetting that their heroes are human, and need to eat and drink and sleep. But this is hardly true of the old romancers, who, in relating knightly adventures, did not draw

Knight at Supper.

upon their imagination, but described the things which were continually happening about them; and the illuminators in illustrating the romances drew from the life—the life of their own day—and this it is which makes their pictures so naive and truthful in spite of their artistic defects, and so valuable as historical authorities. In the engraving above is a subject which would hardly have occurred to modern romancer or illustrator. The crowd of tents tells us that the scene is cast in the " tented field," either of real war or of the mimic war of some great tournament. The combat of the day is over. · The modern romancer would have dropped the curtain for the day, to be drawn up again next morning when the trumpets of the heralds called the combatants once more to the field. Our mediæval illuminator has given us a charming episode in the story. He has followed the good knight to his pavilion pitched in the meadow hard by. The knight has doffed his armour, and taken his bath, and put on his robes of peace, and heard vespers, and gone to supper. The lighted candles show that it is getting dusk. It is only by an artistic license that the curtains of the tent are drawn aside to display the whole interior; in reality they were close drawn; these curtains are striped of alternate breadths of gay colours—gold and red and green and blue. Any one who has seen how picturesque a common bell tent, pitched on the lawn, looks from the outside, when one has been tempted by a fine summer evening to stay out late and "have candles," will be able to perceive how picturesque the striped curtains of this pavilion would be, how eminently picturesque the group of such pavilions here indicated, with the foliage of trees overhead and the grey walls and towers of a mediæval town in the background, with the stars coming out one by one among the turrets and spires sharply defined against the fading sky.

The knight, like a good chevalier and humane master, has first seen his war-horse groomed and fed. And what a sure evidence that the picture is from the life is this introduction of the noble animal sharing the shelter of the tent of his master, who waits for supper to be served. The furniture of the table is worth looking at—the ample white table-cloth, though the table is, doubtless, only a board on trestles; and the two candlesticks of massive and elegant shape, show that the candlesticks now called altar-candlesticks are only of the ordinary domestic mediæval type, obsolete now in domestic use, but still retained, like so many other ancient fashions, in ecclesiastical use. There, too, are the wine flagon and cup, and the salt between them; the knife is at the knight's right hand. We almost expect to see the squire of the last picture enter from behind, bearing aloft in both hands a fat capon on an ample pewter platter.

The little subject which is next engraved will enable us to introduce from the Romance of Prince Arthur a description of an adventure and a graphic account of the different turns and incidents of a single combat, told in language which is rich in picturesque obsolete words. "And so they rode forth a great while till they came to the borders of that country, and there they found a full fair village, with a strong bridge like a fortress.* And when Sir Launcelot and they were at the bridge, there start forth before them many gentlemen and yeomen, which said, 'Fair lord, ye may not pass over this bridge and this fortress but one of you at once, therefore choose which of you shall enter within this bridge first.' Then Sir Launcelot proffered himself first to enter within this bridge. 'Sir,' said

Defending the Bridge.

Sir La Cote Male Taile, 'I beseech you let me enter first within this fortress, and if I speed well I will send for you, and if it happen that I be slain there it goeth; and if so be that I am taken prisoner then may ye come and rescue me.' 'I am loath,' said Sir Launcelot, 'to let you take this passage.' 'Sir,' said he, 'I pray you let me put my body in this adventure.' 'Now go your way,' said Sir Launcelot, 'and God be your speed.' So he entered, and anon there met with him two brethren, the one hight Sir Pleine de Force and that other hight Sir Pleine de Amours; and anon they met with Sir La Cote Male Taile, and first Sir La Cote Male Taile smote down Sir Pleine de Force, and soon after he smote down Sir

---

* Probably a bridge with a tower to defend the approach to it.

Pleine de Amours; and then they dressed themselves to their shields and swords, and so they bade Sir La Cote Male Taile alight, and so he did, and there was dashing and foining with swords. And so they began full hard to assay Sir La Cote Tale Maile, and many great wounds they gave him upon his head and upon his breast and upon his shoulders. And as he might ever among he gave sad strokes again. And then the two brethren traced and traversed for to be on both hands of Sir La Cote Male Taile. But by fine force and knightly prowess he got them afore him. And so then when he felt himself so wounded he doubled his strokes, and gave them so many wounds that he felled them to the earth, and would have slain them had they not yielded them. And right so Sir La Cote Male Taile took the best horse that there was of them two, and so rode forth his way to that other fortress and bridge, and there he met with the third brother, whose name was Sir Plenorius, a full noble knight, and there they justed together, and either smote other down, horse and man, to the earth. And then they two avoided their horses and dressed their shields and drew their swords and gave many sad strokes, and one while the one knight was afore on the bridge and another while the other. And thus they fought two hours and more and never rested. Then Sir La Cote Male Taile sunk down upon the earth, for what for wounds and what for blood he might not stand. Then the other knight had pity of him, and said, 'Fair young knight, dismay you not, for if ye had been fresh when ye met with me, as I was, I know well I should not have endured so long as ye have done, and therefore for your noble deeds and valiantness I shall show you great kindness and gentleness in all that ever I may.' And forthwith the noble knight, Sir Plenorius, took him up in his arms and led him into his tower. And then he commended him the more and made him for to search him and for to stop his bleeding wounds. 'Sir,' said Sir La Cote Male Taile, 'withdraw you from me, and hie you to yonder bridge again, for there will meet you another manner knight than ever I was.' Then Sir Plenorius gat his horse and came with a great spear in his hand galloping as the hurl wind had borne him towards Sir Launcelot, and then they began to feutre* their spears, and came together like

---

* Couch.

thunder, and smote either other so mightily that their horses fell down under them; and then they avoided their horses and drew out their swords, and like two bulls they lashed together with great strokes and foins; but ever Sir Launcelot recovered ground upon him, and Sir Plenorius traced to have from about him, and Sir Launcelot would not suffer that, but bore him backer and backer, till he came nigh the gate tower, and then said Sir Launcelot, ' I know thee well for a good knight, but wot thou well thy life and death is in my hands, and therefore yield thou to me and thy prisoners.' The other answered not a word, but struck mightily upon Sir Launcelot's helm that fire sprang out of his eyes; then Sir Launcelot doubled his strokes so thick and smote at him so mightily that he made him to kneel upon his knees, and therewith Sir Launcelot lept upon him, and pulled him down grovelling; then Sir Plenorius yielded him and his tower and all his prisoners at his will, and Sir Launcelot received him and took his troth." We must tell briefly the chivalrous sequel. Sir Launcelot offered to Sir La Cote Male Taile all the possessions of the conquered knight, but he refused to receive them, and begged Sir Launcelot to let Sir Plenorius retain his livelihood on condition he would be King Arthur's knight,—"' Full well,' said Sir Launcelot; 'so that he will come to the court of King Arthur and become his man and his three brethren. And as for you, Sir Plenorius, I will undertake, at the next feast, so there be a place void, that ye shall be Knight of the Round Table.' Then Sir Launcelot and Sir La Cote Male Taile rested them there, and then they had merry cheer and good rest and many good games, and there were many fair ladies." In the woodcut we see Sir La Cote Male Taile, who has just overthrown Sir Pleine de Force at the foot of the bridge, and the gentlemen and yeomen are looking on out of the windows and over the battlements of the gate tower.

The illuminators are never tired of representing battles and sieges; and the general impression which we gather from them is that a mediæval combat must have presented to the lookers-on a confused *melée* of rushing horses and armoured men in violent action, with a forest of weapons overhead—great swords, and falchions, and axes, and spears, with pennons fluttering aloft here and there in the breeze of the combat.

We almost fancy we can see the dust caused by the prancing horses, and hear the clash of weapons and the hoarse war-cries, and sometimes can almost hear the shriek which bursts from the maddened horse, or the groan of the man who is wounded and helpless under the trampling hoofs. The woodcut introduced represents such a scene in a very spirited way. But it is noticeable among a hundred similar scenes for one incident, which is very unusual, and which gives us a glimpse of another aspect of mediæval war. It will be seen that the combat is taking place outside a castle or fortified town; and that, on a sudden, in the con-

A Sally across the Drawbridge.

fusion of the combat, a side gate has been opened, and the bridge lowered, and a solid column of men-at-arms, on foot, is marching in military array across the bridge, in order to turn the flank of the assailant chivalry. We do not happen to know a representation of this early age of anything so thoroughly soldierly in its aspect as this sally. The incident itself indicates something more like regular war than the usual confused mingling of knights so well represented on the left side of the picture. The fact of men-at-arms, armed *cap-a-pied*, acting on foot, is not very usual at this period; their unmistakable military order, as they march two and two with shields held in the same attitude and spears sloped at the same angle, speaks of accurate drill. The armorial bearings on the shield of one of the foremost rank perhaps point out the officer in command.

It seems to be commonly assumed that the soldiers of the Middle Ages had little, if anything, like our modern drill and tactics; that the men were simply put into the field in masses, according to some rude initial plan of the general, but that after the first charge the battle broke up into a series of chance-medley combats, in which the leaders took a personal share; and that the only further piece of generalship consisted in bringing up a body of reserve to strengthen a corps which was giving ground, or to throw an overwhelming force upon some corps of the enemy which seemed to waver.

It is true that we find very little information about the mediæval drill or tactics, but it is very possible that there was more of both than is commonly supposed. Any man whose duty it was to marshal and handle a body of troops would very soon, even if left to his own wit, invent enough of drill to enable him to move his men about from place to place, and to put them into the different formations necessary to enable them effectively to act on the offensive or defensive under different circumstances. A leader whose duty it was to command several bodies of troops would invent the elements of tactics, enough to enable him to combine them in a general plan of battle, and to take advantage of the different turns of the fight. Experience would rapidly ripen the knowledge of military men, and of experience they had only too much. It is true that the armies of mediæval England consisted chiefly of levies of men who were not professional soldiers, and the officers and commanders were marked out for leadership by their territorial possessions, not by their military skill. But the men were not unaccustomed to their weapons, and were occasionally mustered for feudal display; and the country gentlemen who officered them were trained to military exercises as a regular part of their education, and, we may assume, to so much of military skill as was necessary to fulfil their part as knights. Then there were mercenary captains, who by continuous devotion to war acquired great knowledge and experience in all military affairs; and the men who had to do with them, either as friends or foes, learnt from them. We need only glance down the line of our kings to find abundance of great captains among them—William the Conqueror, and Stephen, and Richard I., and Edward I. and III., and Henry IV. and V., and Edward IV., and Richard III. And military skill equal to the direction of armies was no less common among the. nobility; and ability to take command of his own contingent was expected of every one who held his lands on condition of being always ready and able to follow his lord's banner to the field.

In the Saxon days the strength of the army seems to have consisted of footmen, and their formation was generally in close and deep ranks, who, joining their shoulders together, formed an impenetrable defence; wielding long heavy swords and battle-axes, they made a terrible assault. Some insight into the tactics of the age is given by William of Malmesbury's assertion that at Hastings the Normans made a feigned flight, which drew the Saxons from their close array, and then turning upon them, took them at advantage; and repeated this manœuvre more than once at the word of command.

The strength of the Norman armies, on the other hand, consisted of knights and mounted men-at-arms. The military engines were placed in front, and commenced the engagement with their missiles; the archers and slingers were placed on the wings. The crowd of half-armed footmen usually formed the first line; the mounted troops were drawn up behind them in three lines, whose successive charges formed the main attack of the engagement. Occasionally, however, dismounted men-at-arms seem to have been used by some skilful generals with great effect. In several of the battles of Stephen's reign, this unusual mode appears to have been followed, under the influence of the foreign mercenary captains in the king's pay.

Generals took pains to secure any possible advantage from the nature of the ground, and it follows that the plan of the battle must have turned sometimes on the defence or seizure of some commanding point which formed the key of the position. Ambuscades were a favourite device of which we not unfrequently read, and night surprises were equally common.

We read also occasionally of stratagems, especially in the capture of fortresses, which savour rather of romance than of the stern realities of war. In short, perhaps the warfare of that day was not so very inferior in military skill to that of our own times as some suppose. In our last war the charge at Balaklava was as chivalrous a deed as ever was done in the Middle Ages, and Inkerman a fight of heroes; but neither of them displayed more military science than was displayed by the Norman chivalry who charged at Hastings, or the Saxon billmen whose sturdy courage all but won the fatal day.

CHAPTER VI.

MILITARY ENGINES.

TO attempt to represent the knights in their manor-houses and castles would be to enter upon an essay on the domestic and military architecture of the Middle Ages, which would be beyond the plan of these sketches of the mediæval chivalry. The student may find information on the subject in Mr. Parker's "Domestic Architecture," in Grose's "Military Antiquities," in Viollet le Duc's "Architecture du Moyen Age," and scattered over the publications of the various antiquarian and architectural societies. We must, however, say a few words as to the way in which the knight defended his castle when attacked in it, and how he attacked his neighbour's castle or his enemy's town, in private feud or public war.

It seems to be a common impression that the most formidable aspect of mediæval war was a charge of knights with vizor down and lance in rest; and that these gallant cavaliers only pranced their horses round and round the outer margin of the moat of a mediæval castle, or if they did dismount and try to take the fortress by assault, would rage in vain against its thick walls and barred portcullis; as in the accompanying woodcut from a MS. romance of the early part of the 14th century (Add. 10,292, f. v., date A.D. 1316), where the king on his curveting charger couches his lance against the castle wall, and has only his shield to oppose to the great stone which is about to be hurled down upon his head. The impression is, no doubt, due to the fact that many people have read romances, ancient and modern, which concern themselves with the personal adventures of their heroes, but have not read mediæval history, which tells—even more than enough—of battles and sieges. They have only had the knight put before them—as in the early pages of these chapters—in the pomp and pageantry of chivalry. They have not seen him as the captain and soldier, directing and wielding the engines of war.

Suppose the king and his chivalry in the following woodcut to be only summoning the castle; and suppose them, on receiving a refusal to surrender, to resolve upon an assault. They retire a few hundred yards and dismount, and put their horses under the care of a guard. Presently they return supported by a strong body of archers, who ply the mail-clad de-

Summoning the Castle.

fenders with such a hail of arrows that they are driven to seek shelter behind the battlements. Seizing that moment, a party of camp followers run forward with a couple of planks, which they throw over the moat to make a temporary bridge. They are across in an instant, and place scaling-ladders against the walls. The knights, following close at their heels, mount rapidly, each man carrying his shield over his head, so that the bare ladder is converted into a covered stair, from whose shield-roof arrows glint and stones roll off innocuous. It is easy to see that a body of the enemy might thus, in a few minutes, effect a lodgment on the castle-wall, and open a way for the whole party of assailants into the interior.

But the assailed may succeed in throwing down the ladders; or in beating the enemy off them by hurling down great stones ready stored against such an emergency, or heaving the coping-stones off the battlements; or they may succeed in preventing the assailants from effecting a lodgment on the wall by a hand to hand encounter; and thus the assault may be foiled and beaten off. Still our mediæval captain has other resources; he will next order up his " gyns," *i.e.* engines of war.

The name applies chiefly to machines constructed for the purpose of hurling heavy missiles. The ancient nations of antiquity possessed such machines, and the knowledge of them descended to mediæval times. There

The Assault.

seems, however, to be this great difference between the classical and the mediæval engines, that the former were constructed on the principle of the bow, the latter on the principle of the sling. The classical *ballista* was, in fact, a huge cross-bow, made in a complicated way and worked by machinery. The mediæval *trebuchet* was a sling wielded by a gigantic arm of wood. In mediæval Latin the ancient name of the ballista is sometimes found, but in the mediæval pictures the principle of the engines illustrated is always that which we have described. We meet also in mediæval writings with the names of the *mangona* and *mangonella* and the *catapult*, but they were either different names for the same engine, or names for different species of the same genus. The woodcut here introduced from the MS. Add. 10,294, f. 81 v., gives a representation of a trebuchet. A still earlier representation—viz., of the thirteenth century—of machines of the same kind is to be found in the Arabic MS. quoted in a treatise, "Du feu Grégois," by MM. Favé and Reinaud, and leads to the supposition that the sling principle in these machines may have been introduced from the East. There are other representations of a little later date than that in the text (viz., about A.D. 1330) in the Royal MS. 16 G. VI., which are engraved in Shaw's " Dresses and Decorations." We also possess a contemporary description of the machine in the work of Gilles Colonne (who died A.D. 1316), written for Philip the Fair of France.* " Of *perriers*," he says, " there are four kinds, and in all these machines there is a beam which is raised and lowered by means of a counterpoise, a sling being attached to the end of the beam to discharge the stone. Sometimes the counterpoise is not sufficient, and then they attach ropes to it to move the beam." This appears to be the case in our illustration. The rope seems to be passed through a ring in the platform of the engine, so that the force applied to the rope acts to the greater advantage in aid of the weight of the beam. " The counterpoise may either be fixed or movable, or both at once. In the fixed counterpoise a box is fastened to the end of the beam, and filled with stones or sand, or any heavy body." One would not, perhaps, expect such a machine to possess any precision of action, but according to our author the case was far otherwise. " These machines," he continues, " anciently called *trabutium*, cast their missiles with the utmost exactness, because the weight acts in a uniform manner. Their aim is so sure, that one may, so to say, hit a needle. If the gyn carries too far, it must be drawn back or loaded with a heavier stone ; if the contrary, then it must be advanced or a smaller stone supplied ; for without attention to the weight of the stone, one cannot hope to reach the given mark." " Others of these machines have a movable counterpoise attached to the beam, turning upon an axis. This variety the Romans called *biffa*. The third kind, which is called *tripantum*, has two weights, one fixed to the beam and the other movable round it. By this means it throws with

---

* Hewitt's " Ancient Armour," i. p. 349.

more exactness than the *biffa*, and to a greater distance than the trebuchet. The fourth sort, in lieu of weights fixed to the beam, has a number of ropes, and is discharged by means of men pulling simultaneously at the cords. This last kind does not cast such large stones as the others, but it has the advantage that it may be more rapidly loaded and discharged than they. In using the perriers by night it is necessary to attach a lighted body to the projectile. By this means one may discover the force of the machine, and regulate the weight of the stone accordingly." * This, then, is the engine which our captain, repulsed in his attempt to take the place by a *coup de main*, has ordered up, adjusting it, no doubt, like a good captain, with his own eye and hand, until he has got it, "so to say, to hit a neeedle," on the weak points of the place. It was usual in great sieges to have several of them, so that a whole battery might be set to work to overmaster the defence.

We must bear in mind that similar engines were, it is probable, usually mounted on the towers of the castle. We should judge from the roundness of the stones which the defenders in both the preceding woodcuts are throwing down by hand upon the enemy immediately beneath, that they are the stones provided for the military engines. We find that, as in modern times cannon is set to silence the cannon of the enemy, so that a battle becomes, for a time at least, an artillery duel, so engine was set to silence engine. In the account which Guillaume des Ormes gives of his defence of the French town of Carcasonne in 1240 A.D., he says: "They set up a mangonel before our barbican, when we lost no time in opposing to it from within an excellent Turkish petrary, which played upon the mangonel and those about it, so that when they essayed to cast upon us, and saw the beam of our petrary in motion, they fled, utterly abandoning their mangonel."

There was also an engine called an *arbalast*, or *spurgardon*, or *espringale*, which was a huge cross-bow mounted on wheels, so as to be movable like a field-piece; it threw great pointed bolts with such force as to pass successively through several men.

If the engines of the besiegers were silenced, or failed to produce any

---

* The album of Villars de Hônnecourt, of the thirteenth century, contains directions for constructing the trebuchet.

decisive impression on the place, the captain of the assailants might try the effect of the ram. We seldom, indeed, hear of its use in the Middle Ages, but one instance, at least, is recorded by Richard of Devizes, who says that Richard I., at the siege of Messina, forced in the gates of the city by the application of the battering-ram, and so won his way into the place, and captured it. The walls of mediæval fortifications were so immensely thick, that a ram would be little likely to break them. The gates, too, of a castle or fortified gate-tower were very strong. If the reader will look at the picture of a siege of a castle, given on page 373, he will see a representation of a castle-gate, which will help him to understand its defences. First he will see that the drawbridge is raised, so that the assailant has to bridge the moat before he can bring his battering-ram to bear. Suppose the yawning gulf bridged with planks or filled in with fascines, and the ram brought into position, under fire from the loops of the projecting towers of the gate as well as from the neighbouring battlements, then the bridge itself forms an outer door which must first be battered down. Behind it will be found the real outer-door, made as strong as oak timber and iron bolts can make it. That down, there is next the grated portcullis seen in two previous woodcuts, against which the ram would rattle with a great clang of iron; but the grating, with its wide spaces, and having plenty of "play" in its stone groove, would baffle the blows by the absence of a solid resistance, and withstand them by the tenacity of wrought-iron. Even if the bars were bent and torn till they afforded a passage, the assailants would find themselves in the narrow space within the gate-tower confronted by another door, and exposed to missiles poured upon them from above. It is, perhaps, no wonder that we hear little of the use of the ram in mediæval times; though it might be useful occasionally to drive in some ill-defended postern.

The use of the regular mine for effecting a breach in the wall of a fortified place was well known, and often brought to bear. The miners began their work at some distance, and drove a shaft underground towards the part of the fortifications which seemed most assailable; they excavated beneath the foundations of the wall, supporting the substructure with wooden props until they had finished their work. Then they set fire to the props, and retired to see the unsupported weight of the wall bringing it down in a heap of ruins. The operation of mining was usually effected under the protection of a temporary pent-house, called a *cat* or *sow*. William of Malmesbury describes the machine as used in the siege of Jerusalem, at the end of the eleventh century. " It is constructed," he says, " of slight timbers, the roof covered with boards and wicker-work, and the sides protected with undressed hides, to protect those who are within, who proceed to undermine the foundations of the walls." Our next woodcut gives a very clear illustration of one of these machines, which has been moved on its wheels up to the outer wall of a castle, and beneath its protection a party of men-at-arms are energetically plying their miner's tools, to pick away the foundation, and so allow a portion of the wall to settle down and leave an entrance. The methods in which this mode of attack was met were various. We all remember the Border heroine, who, when her castle was thus attacked, declared she would make the sow farrow, viz., by casting down a huge fragment of stone upon it. That this was one way of defence is shown in the woodcut, where one of the defenders, with energetic action, is casting down a huge stone upon the sow.

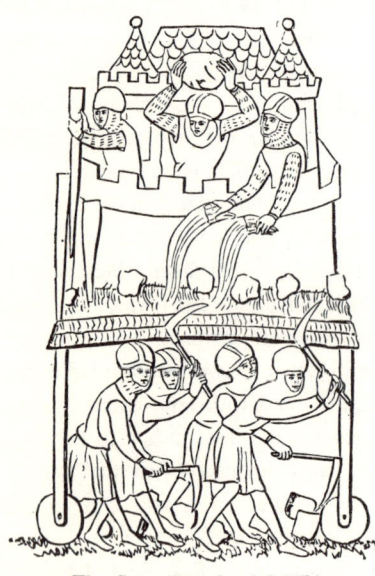

The Cat. (Royal, 16 G VI.)

That the roof was made strong enough to resist such a natural means of offence is shown by the stones which are represented as lodged all along it. Another more subtle counteraction, shown in the woodcut, was to pour boiling water or boiling oil upon it, that it might fall through the interstices of the roof, and make the interior untenable. No doubt means were taken to make the roof liquid-tight, for the illustration represents another mode of counter-action (of which we have met with no other suggestion), by driving sharp-pointed piles into the roof, so as to make holes and cracks through which the boiling liquid might find an entrance. If these means of counteracting the work of the cat seemed likely to be unavailing, it still remained to throw up an inner line of wall, which, when the breach was made, should extend from one side to the other of the unbroken wall, and so complete the circumvallation. This, we have evidence, was sometimes done with timber and planks, and a sort of scaffolding was erected on the inner side, which maintained the communication along the top of the walls, and enabled the soldiers to man the top of this wooden wall and offer a new resistance to the besiegers as they poured into the breach. The mine was also, in ancient as in modern times, met by a counter-mine.

Another usual machine for facilitating the siege of fortified places was a movable tower. Such an engine was commonly prepared beforehand, and taken to pieces and transported with the army as a normal part of the siege-train. When arrived at the scene of operations, it was put together at a distance, and then pushed forward on wheels, until it confronted the walls of the place against which it was to operate. It was intended to put the besiegers on a level and equality with the besieged. From the roof the assailants could command the battlements and the interior of the place, and by their archers could annoy the defence. A movable part of the front of the tower suddenly let fall upon the opposite battlements, at once opened a door and formed a bridge, by which the besiegers could make a rush upon the walls and effect a lodgment if successful, or retreat if unsuccessful to their own party.

Such a tower was constructed by Richard I. in Cyprus, as part of his preparation for his Crusade. An illustration of a tower thus opposed to a castle—not a very good illustration—is to be found in the Royal MS., 16 G. VI., at folio 278 v. Another, a great square tower, just level with the opposing battlements, with a kind of sloping roof to ward off missiles, is shown in the MS. *Chroniques d'Angleterres* (Royal 16, E. IV.), which was illuminated for Edward IV. Again, at f. 201 of the same MS., is another representation of wooden towers opposed to a city.

If the besieged could form a probable conjecture as to the point of the walls towards which the movable tower, whose threatening height they saw gradually growing at a bow-shot from their walls, would be ultimately directed, they sometimes sent out under cover of night and dug pitfalls, into which, as its huge bulk was rolled creaking forward, its fore wheels might suddenly sink, and so the machine fall forward, and remain fixed and useless. As it approached, they also tried to set it on fire by missiles tipped with combustibles. If it fairly attained its position, they assailed every loop and crevice in it with arrows and crossbow bolts, and planted a strong body of men-at-arms on the walls opposite to it, and in the neighbouring towers, to repel the "boarders" in personal combat. A bold and enterprising captain did not always wait for the approach of these engines of assault, but would counter-work them as he best could from the shelter of his walls. He would sometimes lower the drawbridge, and make a sudden sally upon the unfinished tower or the advancing sow, beat off the handful of men who were engaged about it, pile up the fragments and chips lying about, pour a few pots of oil or tar over the mass, and set fire to it, and return in triumph to watch from his battlements how his fiery ally would, in half an hour, destroy his enemy's work of half a month. In the early fourteenth century MS. Add. 10,294, at fol. 740, we have a small picture of a fight before a castle or town, in which we see a column of men-at-arms crossing the drawbridge on such an expedition. And again, in the plates in which Hans Burgmaier immortalised the events of the reign of the Emperor Maximilian, a very artistic representation of a body of men-at-arms, with their long lances, crowding through the picturesque gate and over the drawbridge, brings such an incident vividly before us.

The besiegers on their part did not neglect to avail themselves of such shelter as they could find or make from the shot and from the sallies of the enemy, so as to equalise as much as practicable the conditions of the contest. The archers of the castle found shelter behind the merlons of the battlements, and had the windows from which they shot screened by movable shutters; as may be seen in the next woodcut of the assault on a castle. It would have put the archers of the assailants at a great disadvantage if they had had to stand out in the open space, exposed defenceless to the aim of the foe; all neighbouring trees which could give shelter were, of course, cut down, in order to reduce them to this defenceless condition, and works were erected so as to command every possible coigne of vantage which the nooks and angles of the walls might have afforded. But the archers of the besiegers sought to put themselves on more equal terms with their opponents by using the *pavis* or *mantelet*. The pavis was a tall shield, curved so as partly to envelop the person of the bearer, broad at the top and tapering to the feet. We sometimes see cross-bowmen carrying it slung at their backs (as in Harl. 4,379, and Julius E. IV., f. 219, engraved on p. 294), so that after discharging a shot they could turn round and be sheltered by the great shield while they wound up their instrument for another shot. Sometimes this shield seems to have been simply three planks of wood nailed together, which stood upright on the ground, and protected the soldier effectively on three sides. There are illustrations of it in the MS. Royal 20 C vii. (temp. Rich. II.), at f. 19, f. 24 v., and f. 29 v., and in the MS. Harl. 4,382, f. 133 v. and f. 154 v. The mantelet was a shield still more ample, and capable of being fixed upright by a prop, so that

Use of the Pavis, etc.

it formed a kind of little movable fort which the bowman, or man-at-arms, could carry out and plant before the walls, and thence discharge his missiles, or pursue any other operation, in comparative safety from the smaller artillery of the enemy. The most interesting example which we have met of the employment of the pavis and mantelet, is in a picture in the Harl. MS. 4,425, at f. 133. The woodcut on the previous page represents only a portion of the picture, the whole of which is well worth study. The reader will see at once that we have here the work of a draughtsman of far superior skill to that of the limners of the rude illuminations which we have previously given. The background really gives us some adequate idea of the appearance of an Edwardian castle with its barbican and drawbridge, its great tower with the heads of the defenders just peeping over the battlements. We must call attention to the right-hand figure in the

Cannon and Mortar.

foreground, who is clad in a *pourpoint*, one of the quilted armours which we have formerly described, because it is the best illustration of this species of armour we have met with. But the special point for which we give the woodcut here, is to illustrate the use of the mantelet. It will be seen—though somewhat imperfectly, from the fragment of the engraving introduced—that these defences have been brought up to the front of the attacking party in such numbers as to form an almost continuous wall, behind which the men-at-arms are sheltered; on the right are great fixed mantelets, with a hole in the middle of each, through which the muzzle of a gun is thrust; while the cannoniers work their guns as behind the walls of a fort.

Similar movable defences, variously constructed, continued to be used down to a very late period. For example, in some large plans of the array of the army of Henry VIII., preserved in the British Museum (Cottonian MS., Augustus III., f. 1 v.), the cannon are flanked by huge mantelets of timber, which protect the cannoniers. In the one engraved between pp. 454 and 455, we see a representation of the commencement of the battle, showing some of the mantelets overthrown by the assault of soldiers armed with poleaxes. In modern warfare the sharpshooter runs out into the open, carrying a sand-bag by way of pavis, behind which he lies and picks off the enemy, and the artillery throw up a little breastwork, or mantelet, of sand-bags.

Sometimes the besieging army protected itself by works of a still more permanent kind. It threw up embankments with a pallisade at top, or sometimes constructed a breastwork, or erected a fort, of timber. For example, in the Royal MS. 14 E. IV., at f. 14, we have a picture of an assault upon a fortified place, in which the besiegers have strengthened their position by a timber breastwork. It is engraved at p. 443; the whole picture is well worth study. Again, in the Cottonian MS., Augustus V., at folio 266, is a camp with a wooden fence round it.

An army in the field often protected its position in a similar way. So far back as the eleventh century the historians tell us that William the Conqueror brought over a timber fort with him to aid his operations. The plan of surrounding the camp with the waggons and baggage of the army is perhaps one of the most primitive devices of warfare, and we find it used down to the end of the period which is under our consideration. In the MS. already mentioned, Augustus III., on the reverse of folio 4, is a picture of an army of the time of Henry VIII. encamped by a river, and enclosed on the open sides by the baggage, and by flat-bottomed boats on their carriages, which we suppose have been provided for the passage of the stream.

The siege of Bedford Castle, as described by Roger Wendover, in the year 1224, gives a good historical instance of the employment of these various modes of attacking a stronghold at that period. The castle was being held against the king, who invested it in person. Two towers of wood were raised against the walls, and filled with archers; seven mangonels cast ponderous stones from morning to night; sappers approached the walls under the cover of the cat. First the barbican, then the outer bailey was taken. A breach in the second wall soon after gave the besiegers admission to the inner bailey. The donjon still held out, and the royalists proceeded to approach it by means of their sappers. A sufficient portion of the foundations having been removed, the stancheons were

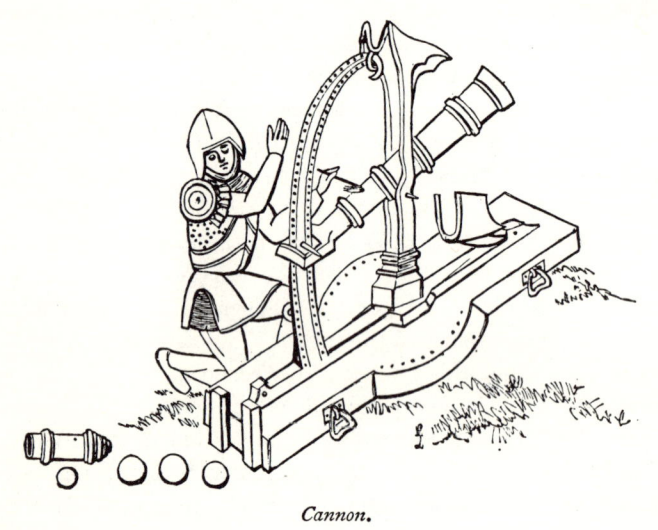

Cannon.

set on fire, one of the angles sank deep into the ground, and a wide rent laid open the interior of the keep. The garrison now planted the royal standard on the walls, and sent the women to implore mercy. But a severe example was made of the defenders, in order to strike terror among the disaffected in other parts of the realm.*

Among the occasional warlike contrivances, stinkpots were employed to repel the enemy, and the Greek fire was also occasionally used. A representation of the use of stinkpots, and also of the mode of using the

---

* Hewitt's "Ancient Armour," i. 361.

Greek fire, may be seen in the Royal MS. 18 E. V., at f. 207 (date 1473 A.D).

Those more terrible engines of war which ultimately revolutionised the whole art of warfare, which made the knight's armour useless, and the trebuchet and arbalest the huge toys of an unscientific age, were already introduced; though they were yet themselves so immature, that for a time military men disputed whether the old long bow or the new fire-arm was the better weapon, and the trebuchet still held its place beside the cannon. In the old illuminations we find mediæval armour and fire-arms together in incongruous conjunction. The subject of the use of gunpowder is one of so much interest, that it deserves to be treated in a separate chapter.

CHAPTER VII.

ARMOUR OF THE FIFTEENTH CENTURY.

IN former papers we have seen the characteristic feature of the armour of Saxon, Norman, and Early English times, down to the latter part of the thirteenth century, was that of mail armour —*i.e.* composed of rings sewn upon garments of something like the ordinary shape—tunic, hose, and hood—or linked together into the shape of such garments. The fourteenth century was a period of transition from mail armour to plate. First it was found convenient to protect the elbow and knee with conical caps made out of a plate of steel; then the upper arm and fore arm, the thigh and leg, were encased in separate pieces of armour made to fit to the limbs; in place of the old helmet worn over the mail hood, a globular bascinet of plate was used, with a fringe of mail attached to it, falling over the shoulders; in place of the hauberk of mail, a globular plate to protect the breast, and another the back, connected at the sides, with a deep skirt of mail attached to them, falling over the hips. In the old days of mail armour a flowing surcoat was worn over it, to protect it from wet, dust, and the heat of the sun; in the fourteenth century the body-armour was covered with a close-fitting jupon of rich material and colour, embroidered with the arms of the wearer, and girded by a rich enamelled horizontal belt.

The characteristic of the armour of the fifteenth century was that it consisted of a complete suit of plate; the fringe of the bascinet being replaced by a gorget of plate, the skirt of mail by horizontal over-lapping plates; and for some time no covering was worn over the armour, but the knightly vanity of the time delighted in the glittering splendour of the burnished steel. Later in the century, however, mail came again into considerable use, in short sleeves for the protection of the upper arm, and in skirts, which were doubtless found more convenient to the horseman than the solid plates of overlapping steel. It also seems to have been found practically inconvenient to dispense with some textile covering over the armour; and a considerable variety of such coverings was used according to the caprice of the wearer. Numerous diversified experiments in the construction of armour were tried, and we commonly find in pictures of the time a great variety of fashions, both of armour and weapons, brought together in the same troop of warriors. It is a matter of interest to the antiquary to trace out the rise of all these various fashions and to determine when they went out of fashion again; but for our present purpose it is enough to point out the salient features of the military costume of the century, and, as varieties are brought before us in the illustrations from ancient MSS. which we proceed to introduce to our readers, to point out their meaning and interest. Let us begin, then, with a picture which will afford us, in the left-hand figure, a typical illustration of the complete plate-armour of the century, and proceed to describe the various pieces of which it is composed. His head is protected by a bascinet of steel, without visor to protect the face, though the picture represents him as actually engaged in the thick of a battle; but the steel gorget is brought up so as to protect the lower part of the face. It is not unfrequent to find the knights of this period with the face similarly exposed. Probably the heat and the difficulty of breathing caused by the visor were considered to outweigh the additional safety which it afforded. The neck is protected by a gorget of plate; and instead of the globular breastplate and skirt of mail worn under the gay jupon of the fourteenth century, the body is cased in two pairs of plates, which open with hinges at the sides, the lower plates coming to a point at the back and breast. In this illustration the whole suit of armour presents an unrelieved surface of burnished steel, the outlines of the various pieces of armour being marked by a narrow line of gold. But it was very usual for one of the two breastplates to be covered with silk or velvet embroidered. This will be seen in the armour of the archer from the same picture, in which the upper plate is covered with blue, powdered with gold spots arranged in trefoils. So in the woodcut on p. 399 the upper breastplate of the knight nearest to the spectator is blue with gold spots, while in the further knight the upper plate is red. Turning again to the knight before us, his shoulders are protected by pauldrons. These portions of the armour differ much in different examples; they were often ridged, so as to prevent a blow from glancing off to the neck, and sometimes they have a kind of standing collar to protect the neck from a direct stroke. Sometimes the pauldron of the left

Man-at-Arms and Archer of the Fifteenth Century.

shoulder is elaborately enlarged and strengthened to resist a blow, while the right shoulder is more simply and lightly armed, so as to offer as little hindrance as possible to the action of the sword arm. The upper arm is protected by brassarts, and the fore arm by vambraces, the elbows by coudières, while the gussets at the armpit and elbow are further guarded by roundels of plate. It will be seen that the gauntlets are not divided into fingers, but three or four plates are attached, like the plates of a lobster, to the outside of a leathern gauntlet, to protect the hand without interfering with the tenacity of its grasp of the weapon. The lower part of the body is protected by a series of overlapping plates, called taces. In most of the examples which we give of this period, the taces have a mail skirt or fringe attached to the lowest plate. Sometimes the taces came lower down over the thighs and rendered any further defence unnecessary; sometimes, as in the example before us, separate plates, called tuilles, were attached by straps to the lowest tace, so as to protect the front of the thigh without interfering with the freedom of motion. The legs are cased in cuissarts and jambarts, and the knee protected by genouillières; and as the tuilles strengthen the defence of the thigh, the shin has an extra plate for its more efficient defence. The feet seem in this example to be simply clothed with shoes, like those of the archer, instead of being defended by pointed sollerets of overlapping plates, like those seen in our other illustrations.

It will be noticed that in place of the broad military belt of the fourteenth century, enriched with enamelled plates, the sword is now suspended by a narrow strap, which hangs diagonally across the body.

The knight is taken from a large picture in the MS. *Chroniques d'Angleterre* (Royal 14, E. IV., f. 192 v.), which represents a party of French routed by a body of Portuguese and English. In front of the knight lies his horse pierced with several arrows, and the dismounted rider is preparing to continue the combat on foot with his formidable axe. The archer is introduced from the same picture, to show the difference between his half armour and the complete panoply of the knight. In the archer's equipment the body is protected by plates of steel and a skirt of mail, the upper arm by a half-sleeve of mail, and the head by a visored helmet; but the rest of the body is unarmed.

Our next illustration is from a fine picture in the same MS. (at f. ccxv.), which represents how the Duke of Lancaster and his people attacked the forts that defended the harbour of Brest. The background represents a walled and moated town—Brest—with the sea and ships in the distance; on the left of the picture the camp of the duke, defended by cannon; and in the foreground a skirmish of knights. It is a curious illustration of the absence of rigid uniformity in the military equipment of these times, that each suit of armour in this picture differs from every other; so that this one picture supplies the artist with fourteen or fifteen different examples of military costume, all clearly delineated with a gorgeous effect of colouring. Some of these suits are sufficiently represented in others of our illustrations. We have again selected one which stands in contrast with all the rest from the absence of colour; most of the others have the upper breastplate coloured, and the helmet unvisored, or with the visor raised. This gives us a full suit of armour unrelieved by colour,

Knight of the Fifteenth Century.

except in the helmet-feather, sword-belt, and sheath, which are all gilt. The unusual shape of the helmet will be noticed, and it will be seen that there is a skirt or fringe of mail below the taces. The horse is a grey, with trappings of red and gold, his head protected by a steel plate. In the cut on p. 403 one of the horses will be found to have the neck also defended by overlapping plates of steel. The shape of the deep military saddle is also well seen in this illustration.

The next woodcut is also only a part of a large picture which forms the frontispiece of the second book of the same MS. (f. lxii.). It represents a sally of the garrison of Nantes on the English, who are besieging it. Like the preceding picture, it is full of interesting examples of different armours. Our illustration selects several of them. The knight nearest to us has the upper plate of his breastplate covered with a blue covering powdered with gold spots, and riveted to the steel plate beneath by

Group of English Knights and French Men-at-Arms.

the two steel studs on the shoulder-blades. Between the series of narrow taces and the vandyked fringe of mail is a skirt of blue drapery, which perhaps partially hides the skirt of mail, allowing only its edge to appear. The gorget is also of mail; and the gusset of mail at the armpit is left very visible by the action of the arm. The further knight has his upper breastplate and skirt red. The horses are also contrasted in colour; the nearer horse is grey, with red and gold trappings; the further horse black, with blue and gold trappings. The man-at-arms who lies prostrate under the horse-hoofs is one of the garrison, who has been pierced by the spear whose truncheon lies on the ground beside him. His equipment marks him out as a man of the same military grade as the archer on p. 396, though the axe which he wields indicates that he is a man-at-arms. His body-armour is covered by a surcoat of blue, laced down the front; he wears a gorget and skirt of mail. His feet, like those of the men on p. 396, seem not to be covered with armour, and his hands are undefended by gloves.

The unarmed man on the left is one of the English party, in ordinary civil costume, apparently only a spectator of the attack. His hose are red, his long-pointed shoes brown, his short-skirted but long-sleeved gown is blue, worn over a vest of embroidered green and gold, which is seen at the sleeves and the neck; the cuffs are red, and he wears a gold chain and gilded sword-belt and sheath, and carries a walking staff. The contrast which he affords to the other figures adds interest and picturesqueness to the group.

The illustration on the next page from the Royal MS., 18 E. V., f. 310 v., forms the frontispiece to a chapter of Roman History, and is a mediæval representation of no less a personage than Julius Cæsar crossing the Rubicon. The foremost figure is Cæsar. He is in a complete suit of plate-armour; over his armour he wears a very curious drapery like a short tabard without sleeves; it is of a yellow brown colour, but of what material it is not possible to determine. There is great diversity in the fashion of the surcoat worn over the armour at this time. One variety is seen in the fallen man-at-arms in the preceding woodcut; and a similar surcoat, loosely fastened by three or four buttons down the front, instead of tightly laced all the way down, is not uncommon. In another picture, a knight in full plate-armour wears a short gown, with hanging sleeves, of the ordinary civilian fashion, like that worn by the gentleman on the left-hand side of the preceding cut. Out of a whole troop of Roman soldiers who follow Cæsar, we have taken only two as sufficient for our purpose of showing varieties of equipment. The first has the fore arm protected by a vambrace, but instead of pauldrons and brassarts the shoulders and arms are protected by sleeves of mail. The taces also are short, with a deep skirt of mail below them. The head defence looks in the woodcut like one of the felt hats that knights frequently wore when travelling, to relieve the head of the weight of the helmet, which was borne behind by a squire; but it is coloured blue, and seems to be of steel, with a white bandeau round it. The reader will notice the "rest" in which the lance was laid

Julius Cæsar crossing the Rubicon.

to steady it in the charge, screwed to the right breast of the breastplate; he will notice also the long-pointed solleret, the long neck of the spur, and the triangular stirrup, and the fashion of riding with a long stirrup, the foot thrust home into the stirrup, and the toe pointed downwards. The third figure wears a gorget with a chin-piece, and a visored bascinet; the whole of his body armour is covered by a handsome pourpoint, which is red, powdered with gold spots; the pauldrons are of a different fashion from those of Cæsar, and the coudière is finished with a spike.

The next woodcut does less justice than usual to the artistic merits of the illumination from which it is taken. It is from a fine MS. of the Romance of the Rose (Harl. 4,925, folio cxxx. v.); the figures are allegorical. The great value of the painting is in the rounded form of the breastplates and helmets, and the play of light and shade, and variety of

Allegorical Figures.   *A Knight at the hall-door.*

tint, upon them; the solid heavy folds of the mail skirts and sleeves are also admirably represented; and altogether the illuminations of this MS. give an unusually life-like idea of the actual pictorial effect of steel armour and the accompanying trappings. The arms and legs of these two figures are unarmed; those of the figure in the foreground are painted red, those of the other figure blue; the shield is red, with gold letters. The deep mail skirts, with taces and tuilles, were in common wear at the close of the fifteenth century, and on into the sixteenth.

The little woodcut of a knight at the hall-door illustrates another variety of skirt; in place of taces and mail skirt, we have a skirt covered with overlapping plates, probably of horn or metal. This knight wears gloves of leather, undefended by armour.

The last illustration in this chapter is from the valuable MS. Life and Acts of Richard Beauchamp, Earl of Warwick (Julius E. IV.), from which we shall hereafter give some other more important subjects. The

The Duke of Gloucester and the Earl of Warwick.

present is part of a fight before Calais, in which Philip Duke of Burgundy was concerned on one side, and Humphrey Duke of Gloucester, Richard Earl of Warwick, and Humphrey Earl of Stafford on the other. In the background of the picture is a view of Calais, with its houses, walls, and towers, washed by the sea. The two figures are taken from the foreground of the battle-scene, which occupies the major part of the picture. The helmets, it will be seen, are iron hats with a wide brim which partially protects the face; they have a considerable amount of ornament about them. Both warriors are armed in a single globular breastplate (the combination of two plates went out of fashion towards the end of the fifteenth century); one has short taces and a deep mail skirt, the other has deeper taces and tuilles besides. The knight on the left side has his left shoulder protected by a pauldron, which covers the shoulder and partially overlaps the breastplate, and has a high collar to protect the neck and face from a sweeping horizontal blow. It will be seen that the sollerets have lost the long-pointed form, though they have not yet reached the broad-toed shape which became fashionable with Henry VIII. The equipment of the horses deserves special examination. They are fully caparisoned, and armed on the face and neck, with plumes of feathers and magnificent bridles; it will be seen, also, that the point of the saddle comes up very high, and is rounded so as partly to enclose the thigh, and form a valuable additional defence. At a period a little later, this was developed still further in the construction of the tilting saddles, so as to make them a very important part of the system of defence.

How perfect the armour at length became may be judged from the fact that in many battles very few of the completely armed knights were killed—sometimes not one; their great danger was in getting unhorsed and ridden over and stifled in the press. Another danger to the unhorsed knight is pointed out in a graphic passage of the History of Philip de Comines, with which we will conclude this chapter. After one of the battles at which he was himself present, he says: "We had a great number of stragglers and servants following us, all of which flocked about the men-of-arms being overthrown, and slew the most of them. For the greatest part of the said stragglers had their hatchets in their hands, wherewith they used to cut wood to make our lodgings, with the which hatchets they brake the vizards of their head-pieces and then clave their heads; for otherwise they could hardly have been slain, they were so surely armed, so that there were ever three or four about one of them."

It is not necessary to infer that these unfortunate men-at-arms who were thus cracked, as if they were huge crustaceans, were helpless from wounds, or insensible from their fall. It was among the great disadvantages of plate-armour, that when a man was once in it he could not get out again without help; nay, he was sometimes so securely fastened in it that the aid must come in the shape of an armourer's tools; and the armour was sometimes so cumbrous that when he was once down he could not get up again—a castle of steel on his war-horse, a helpless log when overthrown.

CHAPTER VIII.

THE KNIGHT'S EDUCATION.

THE manner of bringing up a youth of good family in the Middle Ages was not to send him to a public school and the university, nor to keep him at home under a private tutor, but to put him into the household of some nobleman or knight of reputation to be trained up in the principles and practices of chivalry.* First, as a page, he attended on the ladies of the household, and imbibed the first principles of that high-bred courtesy and transcendental devotion to the sex which are characteristic of the knight. From the chaplain of the castle he gained such knowledge of book-learning as he was destined to acquire—which was probably more extensive than is popularly supposed. He learnt also to sing a romance, and accompany himself on the harp, from the chief of the band of minstrels who wore his lord's livery. As a squire he came under the more immediate supervision of his lord; was taught by some experienced old knight or squire to back a horse and use his weapons; and was stirred to emulation by constant practice with his fellow-squires. He attended upon his lord in time of peace, carved his meat and filled his cup, carried his shield or helmet on a journey, gave him a fresh lance in the tournament, raised him up and remounted him when unhorsed, or dragged him out of the press if wounded; followed him to battle, and acted as subaltern officer of the troop of men-at-arms who followed their lord's banner.

It is interesting to see how the pictures in the illuminated MSS. enable us to follow the knight's history step by step. In the following woodcut we

---

* For much curious detail on this subject see "The Babee's Book," published by the Early English Text Society.

see him as a child in long clothes, between the knight his father, and his lady mother, who sit on a bench with an embroidered *banker* * thrown over its seat, making an interesting family group.

The woodcut on the next page shows us a group of pages imbibing chivalrous usages even in their childish sports, for they are "playing at jousting." It is easy to see the nature of the toy. A slip of wood forms the foundation, and represents the lists; the two wooden knights are movable on their horses by a pin through the hips and saddle; when pushed together in mimic joust, either the spears miss, and the course must be run again, or each strikes the other's breast, and one or other gives way at the shock, and is forced back upon his horse's back, and is vanquished. This illustration is from Hans Burgmair's famous illustrations of the life of the Emperor Maximilian. A similar illustration is given in Strutt's "Sports and Pastimes." A third picture, engraved in the *Archæological Journal*, vol. ii. p. 173, represents a squire carving before his lord at a high feast, and illustrates a passage in Chaucer's description of his squire among the Canterbury Pilgrims, which we here extract (with a few verbal alterations, to make it more intelligible to modern ears) as a typical picture of a squire, even more full of life and interest than the pictorial illustrations:—

"With him ther was his son, a younge squire,
A lover and a lusty bacheler;

---

* A cover for a bench.

His lockes crull as they were laide in presse,
Of twenty yere of age he was I guess.
Of his stature he was of ever. lengthe,
And wonderly deliver, and grete of strengthe.
He hadde be some time in chevachie,
In Flanders, in Artois, and in Picardie,
And borne him wel, as of so litel space,
In hope to standen in his ladies grace.
Embroidered was he, as it were a mede
Alle ful of freshe flowres, white and rede.
Singing he was or floyting alle the day,
He was as freshe as is the moneth of May.

Short was his gowne, with sleves long and wide,
Wel coude he sitte on hors, and fayre ride.
He coude songes make, and wel endite,
Juste and eke dance, and wel poutraie and write.
So hot he loved that by nightertale
He slep no more than doth a nightingale.
Curteis he was, lowly and servisable,
And carf before his fader at the table."

Young noblemen and eldest sons of landed gentlemen were made knights, as a matter of course, when they had attained the proper age. Many others won for themselves this chivalric distinction by their deeds of arms in the field, and sometimes in the lists. The ceremony was essentially a religious one, and the clergy used sometimes to make a knight. In the Royal 14. E. IV. f. 89, we see a picture of Lancelot being made a knight, in which an abbess even is giving him the accolade by a stroke of the hand. But usually, though religious ceremonies accompanied the initiation, and the office for making a knight still remains in the Roman Office Book, some knight of fame actually conferred "the high order of knighthood." It was not unusual for young men of property who were entitled to the honour by birth and heirship to be required by the king to assume it, for the sake of the fine which was paid to the crown on the occasion. Let us here introduce, as a pendant to Chaucer's portrait of the squire already given, his equally beautiful portrait of a knight; not a young knight-errant, indeed, but a grave and middle-aged warrior, who has seen hard service, and is valued in council as well as in field:—

> "A knight ther was, and that a worthy man,
> That from the time that he firste began
> To riden out, he loved chivalry,
> Trouthe and honour, fredom and curtesie.
> Ful worthie was he in his lorde's werre,
> And thereto hadde he ridden, no man ferre,
> As wel in Christendom as in Hethenesse,
> And ever honoured for his worthinesse.
>   At Alesandre he was when it was wonne,
> Ful oftentime he hadde the bord begonne,
> Aboven all nations in Pruce.
> * * * * * *
> At many a noble army hadde he be,
> At mortal batailles had he been fiftene,
> And foughten for our faith in Tramisene
> In listes thries, and ever slaine his fo.
> * * * * * *
> And tho that he was worthy he was wise,
> And of his port as meke as is a mayde;
> He never yet no vilanie had sayde
> In alle his lif unto any manere wyht.
> He was a very parfit gentle knight.
>   But for to tellen you of his arraie,
> His hors was good, but he was not gaie;

> Of fustian he wered a jupon,
> All besmotred with his habergeon.
> For he was late ycom fro his viage,
> And wente for to don his pilgrimage."

Men who are in the constant habit of bearing arms are certain to engage in friendly contests with each other; it is the only mode in which they can acquire skill in the use of their weapons, and it affords a manly pastime. That such men should turn encounters with an enemy into trials of skill, subject to certain rules of fairness and courtesy, though conducted with sharp weapons and in deadly earnest, is also natural.* And thus we are introduced to a whole series of military exercises and encounters, from the mere holiday pageant in which the swords are of parchment and the spears headless, to the wager of battle, in which the combatants are clad in linen, while their weapons are such as will lop off a limb, and the gallows awaits the vanquished.

Homer shows us how the Greek battles were little else than a series of single combats, and Roman history furnishes us with sufficient examples

---

* In illustration of the way in which actual warfare was sometimes treated as if it were a chivalrous trial of skill, take the following anecdote from Froissart; on the occasion when the French had bribed Amery de Puy, the governor, to betray Calais, and fell into the ambush which Edward III. set for them, and the king himself fought under the banner of Sir Walter Murray:—" The Kyng lyht on the Lord Eustace of Rybemount, who was a strong and a hardy knyht; there was a long fyht bytwene hym and the kyng that it was joy to beholde them. . . . . The knight strake the kyng the same day two tymes on his knees; but finally the kynge himself toke hym prisoner, and so he yelded his sword to the kyng and sayd, Sir Knyght, I yeled me as your prisoner, he knewe not as then that it was the kyng." In the evening the king gave a supper in the castle, at which the French prisoners sat as guests; and, "when supper was done and the tables take away, the kyng taryed styll in the hall with his knyghtes and with the Frenchmen, and he was bare-heeded, savyng a chapelet of fyne perles that he ware on his heed. Than the kyng went fro one to another of the Frenchmen. . . . . Than the kyng come to Sir Eustace of Rybamont, and joyously to hym he said, 'Sir Eustace, ye are the knyht in the worlde that I have sene moost valyant assayle his ennemyes and defende hymselfe, nor I never founde knyght that ever gave me so moche ado, body to body, as ye have done this day; wherefore I give you the price above all the knyghtes of my court by ryht sentence.' Then the kyng took the chapelet that was upon his heed, beying bothe faire, goodly, and ryche, and sayd, 'Sir Eustace, I gyve you this chapelet for the best doar in armes in this journey past of either party, and I desire you to bere it this yere for the love of me; say whersover ye come that I dyd give it you; and I quyte you your prison and ransom, and ye shall depart to-morowe if it please you.'"

of such combats preluding the serious movements of opposing armies, and affording an augury, it was believed, of their issue. Sacred history supplies us with examples of a similar kind. In the story of Goliath we have the combat of two champions in the face of the hosts drawn up in battle array. A still more striking incident is that where Abner and the servants of Ishbosheth, and Joab and the servants of David, met accidentally at the pool of Gibeon. " And they sat down the one on the one side of the pool, and the other on the other. And Abner said to Joab, Let the young men now arise and play before us. And Joab said, Let them arise." So twelve men on each side met, " and they caught every one his fellow by the head, and thrust his sword in his fellow's side, so they fell down together." And afterwards the lookers-on took to their arms, and "there was a very sore battle that day; and Abner was beaten, and the men of Israel, before the servants of David."*

Our own history contains incidents enough of the same kind, from Tailefer the minstrel-warrior, who rode ahead of the army of Duke William at Hastings, singing the song of Roland and performing feats of dexterity in the use of horse and weapons, and then charging alone into the ranks of the Saxon men, down to the last young aide-de-camp who has pranced up to the muzzle of the guns to "show the way" to a regiment to which he had brought an order to carry a battery.

In the Middle Ages these combats, whether they were mere pageants † or sportive contests with more or less of the element of danger, or were waged in deadly earnest, were, in one shape or other, of very common occurrence, and were reduced to system and regulated by legislation.

When only two combatants contended, it was called jousting. If only a friendly trial of skill was contemplated, the lances were headed with a small coronal instead of a sharp point; if the sword were used at all it was with

---

* 2 Samuel ii.
† Such as that which took place at Windsor Park in the sixth year of Edward I., for which, according to a document in the Record Office at the Tower (printed in the "Archæologia," vol. xvii. p. 297), it appears that the knights were armed in a tunic and surcoat, a helmet of leather gilt or silvered, with crests of parchment, a wooden shield, and a sword of parchment, silvered and strengthened with whalebone, with gilded hilts.

the edge only, which would very likely inflict no wound at all on a well-armed man, or at most only a flesh wound, not with the point, which might penetrate the opening of the helmet or the joints of the armour, and inflict a fatal hurt. This was the *joute à plaisance.* If the combatants were allowed to use sharp weapons, and to put forth all their force and skill against one another, this was the *joute à l'outrance,* and was of common enough occurrence.

When many combatants fought on each side, it was called a tournament. Such sports were sometimes played in gorgeous costumes, but with weapons of lath, to make a spectacle in honour of a festal occasion. Sometimes the tournament was with bated weapons, but was a serious trial of skill and strength. And sometimes the tournament was even a mimic battle, and then usually between the adherents of hostile factions which sought thus to gratify their mutual hatreds, or it was a chivalrous incident in a war between two nations.

With these general introductory remarks, we shall best fulfil our purpose by at once proceeding to bring together a few illustrations from ancient sources, literary and pictorial, of these warlike scenes.

A MS. in the Egerton Collection, in the British Museum, gives us a contemporary account of the mode in which it was made known to knights ambitious of honour and their ladies' praise when and where opportunities of winning them were to be found. The heralds-at-arms of the king, or lord, or noble, or knight, or lady who designed to give a joust, went forth on horseback to castle and town, and sometimes from court to court of foreign countries, clad in their gay insignia of office, attended by a trumpeter; and in every castle court they came to, and at every market cross, first the trumpeter blew his blast and then the herald-at-arms made his proclamation as follows:—"Wee herawldes of armes beryng shields of devise, here we yeve in knowledge unto all gentilmen of name and of armys, that there bee VI gentilmen of name and of armes that for the gret desire and woorship that the seide VI gentilmen have, have taken upon them to bee the third day of May next coomyng before the high and mighty redowtid ladyes and gentilwoomen in this high and most honourable court. And in their presence the seide six gentilmen there to appear at IX of the clock before noone, and to juste aginst all coomers without, the seide day unto VI of the clok at aftir noone, and then, by the advyse of the seide ladyes and gentel women, to give unto the best juster withoute * a dyamaunde of xl^{li}, and unto the nexte beste juster a rubie of xx^{li}, and to the third well juster a saufir of x^{li}. And on the seide day there beyng officers of armys shewyng their mesure of theire speris garneste, that is, cornal, vamplate, and grapers all of acise, that they shall just with. And that the comers may take the length of the seide speirs with the avise of the seide officers of armes that shall be indifferent unto all parties unto the seide day." †

Then we have a description of the habiliments required for a knight's equipment for such an occasion, which includes a suit of armour and a horse with his trappings; an armourer with hammer and pincers to fasten the armour; two servants on horseback well beseen, who are his two squires; and six servants on foot all in one suit.

As the day approaches knights and ladies begin to flock in from all points of the compass. Some are lodged in the castle, some find chambers in the neighbouring town, and some bring tents with them and pitch them under the trees in the meadows without the castle. At length the day has arrived, and the knights are up with sunrise and bathe, and then are carefully armed by their squires and armourers. This is so important a matter that it is no wonder we find several minute descriptions of the way in which every article of clothing and armour is to be put on and fastened, illustrated with pictures of the knight in the several stages of the process. Two such descriptions with engravings are given in the twenty-ninth volume of the " Archæologia," taken from the work of a master of fence, of date 1400. Another description, "How a man shall be armyed at his ease when he shall fight on foot," is given in the Lansdowne MS. under our notice. The same description is given in the tenth volume of the *Archæological Journal*, p. 226, from a MS. in the possession of Lord Hastings of the date of Henry VI., accompanied by an engraving from an illumination in the MS. showing the knight with his legs fully armed, his body clothed in the under-

---

* *i.e.*, of the strangers. The challengers are afterwards called the gentlemen within.

† For other forms of challenge, and some very romantic challenges at full length, see the Lansdowne MS. 285.

Preliminaries of a Combat.

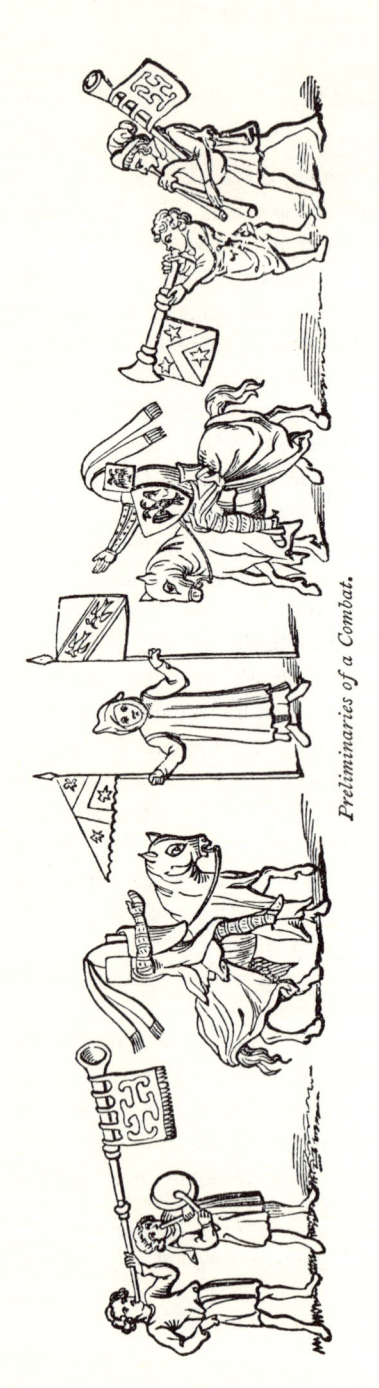

Termination of the Combat.

garment on which the gussets of mail are sewed, while the rest of his armour and his weapons are arranged on a bench beside him. The weapons are a glaive and a pole-axe, which were the usual weapons assigned to the combatants in serious duels on foot. When all is ready, and the company are assembled, the MS. tells us what next takes place:—
"The VI gentilmen must come into the felde unharnsyd, and their helmys borne before them, and their servants on horseback berying either of them a spere garneste, that is the VI speres which the seide VI servaunts shall ride before them into the felde, and as the seide VI gentilmen be coomyn before the ladyes and gentilwoomen. Then shall be sent an herowde of armys up unto the ladyes and gentilwoomen, saying on this wise: High and mighty, redowtyd, and right worchyfull ladyes and gentilwoomen, theis VI gentilmen hav coome into your presence and recommende them all unto your gode grace in as lowly wise as they can, besechyng you for to geve unto the iii best justers without a diamonde, and a rubie, and a saufir unto them that ye think best can deserve it. Then this message is doone. Then the VI gentilmen goth into the tellwys* and doth on their helmys."

Then comes the jousting. Probably, first of all, each of the six champions in turn runs one or more courses with a stranger knight; then, perhaps, they finish by a miniature tournament, all six together against six of the strangers. Each strange knight who comes into the field has to satisfy the officer-at-arms that he is a "gentilman of name and of arms," and to take oath that he has no secret weapons or unfair advantage. The woodcut represents this moment of the story. This being ascertained, they take their places at the opposite ends of the lists, the presiding herald cries to let go, and they hurl together in the midst, with a clang of armour, and a crash of broken spears, amidst the shouts of the spectators and the waving of kerchiefs and caps. If the course be successfully run, each breaks his lance full on the breastplate or helm of his adversary, but neither is unhorsed; they recover their steeds with rein and spur, and prance away

---

* Probably the tilt-house (the shed or tent which they have in the field at one end of the lists).

amidst applause. If one knight is unhorsed, or loose his stirrup, he is vanquished, and retires from the game. If the jousting were not the mere sport which the MS. puts before us, but were a *joute à l'outrance*, the next woodcut represents a very probable variation in this point of the game.

At length, when all have run their courses, the MS. resumes its directions: "And when the heraldes cry *à lôstel! à lôstel!* then shall all the

Spectators of a Tournament.

VI. gentlemen within unhelme them before the seide ladies, and make their obeisaunce, and goo home unto their lodgings and change them." Then, continues the MS.: "The gentilmen* without comyn into the presence of the ladies. Then comys foorth a lady by the advise of all the ladyes and gentilwomen, and gives the diamounde unto the best juster withoute, saying

---

* The Lansdowne MS. says "gentlewomen," an obvious error; it is correctly given as above in the Hastings MS.

in this wise:—'Sir, theis ladyes and gentilwomen thank you for your disporte and grete labour that ye have this day in their presence. And the saide ladyes and gentilwomen seyn that ye have best just this day; therefore the seide ladyes and gentilwomen geven you this diamounde, and send you much joy and worship of your lady.' Thus shall be doone with the rubie and with the saufre unto the other two next the best justers. This doon, then shall the heralde of armys stande up all on hygh, and shall sey withall in high voice:—'John hath well justed, Ric. hath justed better, and Thomas hath justed best of all.' Then shall he that the diamound is geve unto take a lady by the hande and bygene the daunce, and when the ladyes have dauncid as long as them liketh, then spyce wyne and drynk, and then avoide."*

The last woodcut, greatly reduced from one of the fine tournament scenes in the MS. history of the Roi Meliadus, already several times quoted in this work, shows the temporary gallery erected for the convenience of the ladies and other spectators to witness the sports. The tent of one of the knights is seen in the background, and an indication of the hurly-burly of the combat below. A larger illustration of a similar scene from this fine MS. will be given hereafter.

The next woodcut is from the MS. Life and Acts of Richard Beauchamp, Earl of Warwick (Julius E. IV., folio 217). It represents "howe a mighty Duke chalenged Erle Richard for his lady sake, and in justyng slewe the Duke and then the Empresse toke the Erle's staff and bear from a knight shouldre, and for great love and fauv^r she sette it on her shouldre. Then Erle Richard made one of perle and p'cious stones, and offered her that, and she gladly and lovynglee reseaved it." The picture shows the Duke and Earl in the crisis of the battle. It would seem from the pieces of splintered spears, which already lie on the ground, that a previous course had been run with equal fortune; but in this second course the doughty Earl has just driven his lance half a yard through his unfortunate chal-

---

* Dugdale, in his "History of Warwickshire," gives a curious series of pictures of the famous combat between John Astle and Piers de Massie in the year 1438, showing the various incidents of the combat.

lenger's breast. In the background we see the Emperor Sigismund, and the Empress taking the Earl's badge from the neck of the Earl's knight. The whole incident, so briefly told and so naïvely illustrated, is very characteristic of the spirit of chivalry. As we close the page the poor

How a mighty Duke fought Earl Richard for his Lady's sake.

nameless Duke's life-blood seems to be smeared, not only over his own magnificent armour, but over the hand of the Empress and the Emperor's purple who presided over the scene; and while we seem to hear the fanfaronade with which the trumpeters are cracking their cheeks, we hear mingling with it the groan of the mighty Duke thus slain "for his lady sake."

A whole chapter might be well dedicated to the special subject of judicial combats. We must, however, content ourselves with referring the reader to authorities both literary and artistic, and to some anecdotes illustrative of the subject. In the Lansdowne MS. 285, copied for Sir John Paxton, will be found directions for the complete arming of a man who is to engage on foot in a judicial combat, with a list of the things, such as tent, table, chair, &c., which he should take into the field with him. The same MS. contains (article 8) the laws of the combat—"the ordinance and forme of fighting within listes," as settled by Thomas Duke of Gloucester, Constable of England, in the time of Richard II. Also in Tiberius E. VIII. there are directions for making a duel before the king. There are other similar documents in the same book, *e.g.* Of the order of knighthood, justs and prizes to be given thereat: The Earl of Worcester's orders for jousts and triumphs: Declaration of a combat within lists. The MS. Tiberius B. VIII. contains the form of benediction of a man about to fight, and of his shield, club, and sword. For a picture of a combat on foot in lists see Royal 16 E. IV. (MS. "Chronique d'Angleterre," written for King Edward IV.) at f. 264.* In the "Archæologia," vol. xxix., p. 348-361, will be found a paper on Judicial Duels in Germany, with a series of curious drawings of about the year 1400 A.D., representing the various phases of the combat. Plate 31, fig. 5, shows the combatant in the act of being armed; fig. 6, receiving Holy Communion in church before the combat. Plate 32, fig. 2, the oath in the lists, the combatant seated armed in an arm-chair with his attendants about him, his weapons around, and—ominously enough—a bier standing by, covered with a pall, ready to carry him off the ground if slain. Plate 34, fig. 2, shows the vanquished actually being laid in his coffin; and fig. 3 shows the victor returning thanks in church for his victory. Plate 37 is another series of subjects showing the

---

* The Harleian MS. No. 69, is a book of certain triumphs, containing proclamations of tournaments, statutes of arms for their regulation, and numerous other documents relating to the subject. From folio 20 and onwards are given pictures of combats; folio 22 v. represents spear-play at the barriers; folio 23, sword-play at the barriers, &c.

different positions of attack and defence with the pole-axe. Several very good and spirited representations of these duels of the time of our Henry VIII. may be found in the plates of Hans Burgmaier's Der Weise Könige.

As an example of the wager of battle we will take an account of one related by Froissart between a squire called Jaques de Grys and a knight, Sir John of Carougne. It is necessary to the understanding of some of the incidents of the narrative to state what was the origin of the duel. The knight and the squire were friends, both of the household of the Earl of Alençon. Sir John de Carougne went over sea for the advancement of his honour, leaving his lady in his castle. On his return his lady informed him that one day soon after his departure his friend Jaques de Grys paid a visit to her, and made excuses to be alone with her, and then by force dishonoured her. The knight called his and her friends together, and asked their counsel what he should do. They advised that he should make his complaint to the Earl. The Earl called the parties before him, when the lady repeated her accusation; but the squire denied it, and called witnesses to prove that at four o'clock on the morning of the day on which the offence was stated to have been committed he was at his lord the Earl's house, while the Earl himself testified that at nine o'clock he was with himself at his levée. It was impossible for him between those two hours—that is, four hours and a half—to have ridden twenty-three leagues. "Whereupon the Erl sayd to the lady that she dyd but dreame it, wherefore he wolde maynteyne his squyre, and commanded the lady to speke noe more of the matter. But the knyght, who was of great courage, and well trusted and byleved his wife, would not agree to that opinion, but he wente to Parys and shewed the matter there to the parlyament, and there appeled Jaques de Grys, who appered and answered to his appele." The plea between them endured more than a year and a half. At length " the parlyament determined that there shold be batayle at utterance between them. . . . And the Kynge sent to Parys, commandynge that the journey and batayle bytwene the squyer and the knight sholde be relonged tyl his comynge to Parys: and so his commaundement was obeyed. . . .

"Then the lystes were made in a place called Saynt Katheryne, behynde the Temple. There was so moche people that it was mervayle to beholde; and on the one syde of the lystes there was made grete scaffoldes, that the lordes myght the better se the battayle of the ij champions; and so they bothe came to the felde, armed at all places, and there eche of them was set in theyr chayre." *

"The Erle of Saynt Poule governed John of Carougne, and the Erle of Alanson's company with Jaques de Guys. And when the knyght entered into the felde, he came to his wyfe who was there syttinge in a chayre, covered in blacke, and he seyd to her thus,—Dame, by your enformacyon and in your quarele I do put my lyfe in adventure as to fyght with Jaques le Grys; ye knowe if the cause be just and true. Syr, sayd the lady, it is as I have sayd; wherfore ye may fyght surely, the cause is good and true. With those wordes the knyghte kyssed the lady and toke her by the hande, and then blessyd her, and so entered into the felde. The lady sate styll in the blacke chayre in her prayers to God and to the Vyrgyne Mary, humbly prayenge them, by theyr specyall grace, to sende her husbande the vyctory accordynge to the ryght he was in. The lady was in grete hevynes, for she was not sure of her lyfe; for yf her husbande sholde have been discomfyted she was judged without remedy to be brente and her husbande hanged. I cannot say whether she repented her or not yt the matter was so forwarde, that bothe she and her husbande were in grete peryle; howbeit fynally she must as then abyde the adventure. Then these two champyons were set one agaynst another, and so mounted on theyr horses and behaved them nobly, for they knew what pertayned to deades of armes. There were many lordes and knyghtes of France that were come thyder to se that batayle: ye two champyons parted at theyr first metyng, but none of them dyd hurte other; and upon the justes they lyghted on foote to performe their batayle, and soe fought valyauntly; and fyrst John of Carougne was hurt in the thyghe, whereby al his friendes were in grete fear; but after that he fought so valyauntly that he bette

* In the picture given by Dugdale of the combat between John Astle and Piers de Massie, the combatants are represented each sitting in his chair—a great carvad chair, something like the coronation chair in Westminster Abbey.

down his adversary to the erthe, and thruste his sworde in his body, and so slew hym on the felde; and then he demaunded yf he had done his devoyre or not; and they answered that he had valyauntly acheved his batayle. Then Jaques le Grys was delyvered to the hangman of Parys, and he drew him to the gybet of Mount Faucon and there hanged hym up. Then John of Carougne came before the Kynge and kneeled downe and ye Kynge made hym to stand up before hym, and the same day the kynge caused to be delyvered to hym a thousand frankes, and reteyned hym to be of his chambre with a pencyon of ij hundred poundes by the yere durynge the term of his lyfe; then he thanked the Kynge and the lordes, and wente to his wyfe and kyssed her, and then they wente togyder to the churche of Our Lady in Parys, and made theyr offerynge and then retourned to theyr lodgynges. Then this Syr John of Carougne taryed not long in France, but wente to vysyte the Holy Sepulture."

CHAPTER IX.

ON TOURNAMENTS.

THE romances, confirmed as they are by such documents as we have referred to in our last paper, may be taken as perfectly safe authorities on all that relates to the subject of tournaments, and they seize upon their salient features, and offer them in a picturesque form very suitable to our purpose. We will take all our illustrations, as in former chapters, from Malory's " History of Prince Arthur."

Here is a statement of the way in which a tournament was arranged and published: "So it befel, that Sir Galahalt the haughty Prince was lord of the country of Surluse, whereof came many good knights. And this noble prince was a passing good man of arms, and ever he held a noble fellowship together. And he came unto King Arthur's court, and told him all his intent, how he would let do cry a justs in the country of Surluse, the which country was within the lands of King Arthur, and that he asked leave for to let cry a justs. 'I will well give you leave,' said King Arthur, 'but wot you well that I may not be there.' So in every good town and castle of this land was made a cry, that in the country of Surluse Sir Galahalt the haughty prince should make justs that should last eight days, and how the haughty prince, with the help of Queen Guenever's knights, should just against all manner of men that would come. When the cry was known kings, princes, dukes, and earls, barons, and many noble knights made them ready to be at that justs."

So we read in another place how as Sir Tristram was riding through the country in search of adventures, " he met with pursevants, and they told him that there was made a great cry of a tournament between King

Carados of Scotland and the King of Northgales, and either should just against other at the Castle of Maidens. And these pursevants sought all the country for the good knights, and in especial King Carados let seek for Sir Launcelot, and the King of Northgales let seek for Sir Tristram." Then we find how all the reckless knights-errant suddenly become prudent, in order to keep themselves fresh and sound for this great tournament. Thus : " Sir Kay required Sir Tristram to just ; and Sir Tristram in a manner refused him, because he would not go hurt nor bruised to the Castle of Maidens ; and therefore he thought to have kept him fresh and to rest him." But his prudence was not proof against provocation, for when Sir Kay persisted, he rode upon him and " smote down Sir Kay, and so rode on his way." So Sir Palomides said, " Sir, I am loth to do with that knight, and the cause why for as to-morrow the great tournament shall be, and therefore I will keep me fresh, by my will." But being urged he consented : " Sir, I will just at your request, and require that knight to just with me, and often I have seen a man have a fall at his own request ;" a sage reflection which was prophetic. It was Sir Launcelot in disguise whom he was moved thus to encounter ; and Sir Launcelot " smote him so mightily that he made him to avoid his saddle, and the stroke brake his shield and hawberk, and had he not fallen he had been slain."

No doubt a great company would be gathered on the eve of the tournament, and there would be much feasting and merriment, and inquiry what knights were come to just, and what prospects had this man and the other of honour and lady's grace, or of shame and a fall. Here is such an incident :—" Then Sir Palomides prayed Queen Guenever and Sir Galahalt the haughty prince to sup with him, and so did both Sir Launcelot and Sir Lamorake and many good knights ; and in the midst of their supper in came Sir Dinadan, and he began to rail. ' Well,' said Sir Dinadan unto Sir Launcelot, ' what the devil do you in this country, for here may no mean knights win no worship for thee ; and I ensure thee that I shall never meet thee no more, nor thy great spear, for I may not sit in my saddle when that spear meet me ; I shall beware of that boisterous spear that thou bearest.' Then laughed Queen Guenever and the haughty prince that they might not sit at table. Thus they made great joy till the morrow ; and then they heard mass, and blew to the field. And Queen Guenever and all their estates were set, and judges armed clean with their shields for to keep the right."

State Carriage of the Fourteenth Century.

It would take up too much space to transcribe the account of the tournament; the romancers and chroniclers dwell on every stroke, and prolong the narrative through page after page. We leave the reader to imagine to himself the crowd of meaner knights " hurtling together like wild boars," and " lashing at each other with great strokes"; and can only tell one or two unusual deeds which caused most talk among the knights and ladies, and supplied new matter for the heralds and minstrels to record. How Sir Launcelot rushed against Sir Dinadan with the " boisterous spear" he had deprecated, and bore him back on his horse croup, that he lay there as dead, and had to be lifted off by his squires; and how Sir Lamorake struck Sir Kay on the helm with his sword, that he swooned in the saddle; and how Sir Tristram avoided Sir Palomides' spear, and got him by the neck with both his hands, and pulled him clean out of his saddle, and so

Cabriolet of the Fourteenth Century.

bore him before him the length of ten spears, and then, in the presence of them all, let him fall at his adventure; " until at last the haughty prince cried ' Hoo!' and then they blew to lodging, and every knight unarmed him and went to the great feast." We may, however, quote one brief summary of a tournament which gives us several pictures worth adding to our story :—" Sir Launcelot mounted his horse and rode into a forest and held no high way. And as he looked afore him he saw a fair plain, and beside that plain stood a fair castle, and before that castle were many pavilions of silk and of divers hue; and him seemed that he saw there five hundred knights riding on horseback; and there was two parties; they that were of the castle were all in black, their horses and their trappings black; and they that were without were all upon white horses with white trappours. And every each hurled to other, whereof Sir Launcelot marvelled greatly. And at the last him thought that they of the castle were put unto the worst; and then thought Sir Launcelot for to help the weaker part in increasing of his chivalry. And so Sir Launcelot thrust in among the parties of the castle, and smote down a knight, both horse and man, to the earth: and then he rushed here and there and did marvellous deeds of arms; but always the white knights held them nigh about Sir Launcelot, for to weary him and win him. And at the last, as a man may not ever endure, Sir Launcelot waxed so faint of fighting, and was so weary of great deeds, that he might not lift up his arms for to give one stroke."

Now for some extracts to illustrate the prize of the tournament: "Turn we unto Ewaine, which rode westward with his damsel, and she brought him there as was a tournament nigh the march of Wales. And at that tournament Sir Ewaine smote down thirty knights, wherefore the prize was given him, and the prize was a jerfawcon and a white steed trapped with a cloth of gold." Sir Marhaus was equally fortunate under similar circumstances:—" He departed, and within two days his damsel brought him to where as was a great tournament, that the Lady de Vaux had cried; and who that did best should have a rich circlet of gold worth a thousand besants. And then Sir Marhaus did so nobly that he was renowned to have smitten down forty knights, and so the circlet of gold was rewarded to him."

Again:—" There was cried in this country a great just three days. And all the knights of this country were there, and also the gentlewomen. And who that proved him the best knight should have a passing good sword and a circlet of gold, and the circlet the knight should give to the fairest lady that was at those justs. And this knight Sir Pelleas was the best knight that was there, and there were five hundred knights, but there was never man that Sir Pelleas met withal but that he struck him down or else from his horse. And every day of the three days he struck down twenty knights; therefore they gave him the prize. And forthwithal he went there as the Lady Ettarde was, and gave her the circlet, and said

A Tournament.

openly that she was the fairest lady that was there, and that he would prove upon any knight that would say nay."

The accompanying woodcut is a reduced copy of the half of one of the many tournament scenes which run along the lower part of the double page of the MS. romance of "Le Roi Meliadus," already so often alluded to. They are, perhaps, the most spirited of all the contemporary pictures of such scenes, and give every variety of incident, not out of the imagination of a modern novelist, but out of the memory of one who had frequented deeds of arms and noted their incidents with an artist's eye.

For an actual historical example of the tournament in which a number of knights challengers undertake to hold the field against all comers, we will take the passage of arms at St. Inglebert's, near Calais, in the days of Edward III., because it is very fully narrated by Froissart, and because the splendid MS. of Froissart in the British Museum (Harl. 4,379) supplies us with a magnificent picture of the scene. Froissart tells that it happened in this wise :—" In ye dayes of King Charles there was an Englisshe knyght called Sir Peter Courteney, a valyaunt knight in armes, came out of Englande into Fraunce to Paris, and demanded to do armes with Sir Guy of Tremoyle * in the presence of the king or of suche as wolde se them. Sir Guy wolde not refuce his offre, and in the presence of the kyng and of other lordes they were armed on a daye and ran togeyder one course ; and then the kyng wolde not suffre them to ryn agayne togeyther, wherwith the English knyght was ryt evyl content, for, as he shewed, he wolde have furnysshed his chalenge to the uttrance ; but he was apeased with fayre wordes, and it was sayde to hym that he had done ynough and ought to be content therewith. The kyng and the duke of Burgoyne gave hym fayre gyftes and presentes. Than he returned agayne towardes Calays, and the lorde of Clary, who was a friscay and a lusty knyght, was charged to convey hym." One night they lodged at Lucen, where lived the Countess of St. Paul, sister to King Richard of England, whose first wife had been a cousin of Sir Peter's, and who therefore received them gladly. In the course of the evening the countess asked Sir Peter

---

* Tremouille.

whether he was content with the entertainment he had met with in France. Whereupon the knight complained of the interruption of his combat, swore he should say wherever he went that he could find none in France to do armes with him; that had a French knight, for example the Lord of Clary then present, come into England and desired to do armes, he would have found enough to answer his challenge. The Lord of Clary having Sir Peter then placed under his safe conduct by the king, held his tongue till he had brought him within the English territory about Calais; then he challenged Sir Peter, and next day they met. "Then they toke their speares with sharpe heades wel fyled, and spurred their horses and rune togeyder. The fyrst course fayled, wherwith they were bothe sore displeased. At the seconde juste they mette so togeyder, that the Lord of Clary struke the Englysshe knyght throughe the targe and throughe the shoulder a handfull, and therwith he fell from his horse to the erthe. . . . Then the Lord of Clary departed with his company, and the Englysshemen led Sir Peter Courtney to Calays to be healed of his hurtes."

This incident stirred up several young French knights to undertake some feat of arms. "There was thre gentylmen of highe enterprise and of great valure, and that they well shewed as ye shall here. Fyrst there was the yonge Sir Bouciquaut, the other Sir Raynold of Roy, and the thirde the Lorde of Saynt Pye. These thre knyghtes were chamberleyns with the kyng, and well-beloved of hym. These thre being at Mountpellier among the ladyes and damosels, they toke on them to do armes on the fronter beside Calais the next somer after . . . abyding all knyghtes and squiers straungers the terme of xxx dayes whosoever wolde justè with them in justes of peace or of warre. And because the enterprise of these thre knyghtes seemed to the French kyng and his counsalye to be an high enterprice, then it was said to them that they shulde putte it into writyng, because the kyng wolde se the artycles thereof, that if they were to high or to outraygous that the kyng might amende them; bycause the kyng nor his counsalye wolde not sustayne any thynge that shoulde be unresonable. These thre knyghtes answered and said, 'It is but reson that we do this; it shall be done.' Then they toke a clerk and caused him to write as forthwith:—'For the great desyre that we have to come to the knowledge of noble gentlemen, knights and squires, straungers as well of the realme of France, as elsewhere of farre countreys, we shall be at Saynt Inglebertes, in the marches of Calays, the twenty day of the month of May next commying, and there contynewe thirtye dayes complete, the Frydayes onely excepte ; and to delyver all manner of knyghtes and squyers, gentlemen, straungers of any manner of nacyon whatsoever they be, that wyll come thyder for the breakynge of fiyve speares, outher sharpe or rokettes at their pleasure,'" &c.

The challenge was "openly declared and publyshed, and especially in the realme of Englande," for it was in truth specially intended at English knights, and they alone appear to have accepted the challenge. "For in England knyghtes and squiers were quyckened to the mater, and ware in gret imagynacions to know what they might best do. Some said it shulde be greatly to their blame and reproche such an enterprise taken so nere to Calays without they passed the see and loke on those knyghtes that shulde do arms there. Such as spake most of the mater was, first, Syr Johan of Holande Erle of Huntyngdon, who had great desyre to go thyder, also Sir Johan Courtney . . . and dyvers others, more than a hundred knyghtes and squiers, all then sayed, 'Let us provyde to go to Calays, for the knyghtes of Fraunce hath not ordayned that sporte so nere our marches but to the entent to see us there; and surely they have done well and do lyke good companions, and we shall not fayle them at their busynes.' This mater was so publisshed abrode in Englande, that many such as had no desyn to do dedes of armes ther on self, yet they sayd they wolde be there to loke on them that shulde. So at the entryng in of ye joly fresshe month of May these thre young knyghtes of Fraunce come to the Abbay of Saynt Ingilbertes, and they ordayned in a fayre playne between Calays and Saynt Ingilbertes thre fresh grene pavilyons to be pyght up, and at the entre of every pavylyon there hanged two sheldes with the armes of the knyghtes, one shelde of peace, another of warre ; and it was ordayned that such as shulde ryn and do dedes of armes shulde touche one of the sheldes or cause it to be touched. And on the xxi day of the moneth of May, accordyng as it had been publisshed, there the French knyghtes were redy in the place to furnish their enterprise. And the same day knyghtes and squiers issued out of Calays, suche as wolde just, and also such other as had pleasure to regarde that sporte; and they came to the place appoynted and drew all on the one parte: the place to juste in was fayre green and playne. Sir Johan Hollande first sent to touche the shelde of warre of Syr Bociquaut, who incontinent issued out of his pavylyon redy mounted, with shelde and speare: these two knyghtes drew fro other a certayne space, and when each of them had well advysed other, they spurred their horses and came together rudely, and Bociquaut struke the Erle of Huntingdon through the shelde, and the speare head glente over his arme and dyd hym no hurt; and so they passed further and turned and rested at their pease. This course was greatly praysed. The second course they met without any hurt doygne; and the third course their horses refused and wolde not cope." And so Froissart goes on to describe, in page after page, how the English knights, one after another, encountered the three challengers with various fortune, till at last "they ran no more that day, for it was nere night. Then the Englysshmen drew togeder and departed, and rode to Calays, and there devysed that night of that had been done that day; in likewyse the Frenchmen rode to Saint Ingilbertes and communed and devysed of yt had been done ye same day." "The Tuesday, after masse, all suche as shulde just that day or wolde gyve the lookyng on, rode out of Calis and came to the place appoynted, and the Frenchmen were redy there to recyve them: the day was fayre and hot." And so for four days the sports continued. In many cases the course failed through fault of horse or man; the commonest result of a fair course was that one or both the justers were unhelmed; a few knights were unhorsed; one knight was wounded, the spear passing through the shield and piercing the arm, where "the spere brake, and the trunchon stucke styll in the shelde and in the knyhte's arme; yet for all yt the knyght made his turn and came to his place fresshly."

The illuminator has bestowed two large and beautiful pictures on this famous deed of arms. One at folio 230 represents the knights parading round the lists to show themselves before the commencement of the sports. Our woodcut on page 434 is reduced from another picture at folio 43, which represents the actual combat. There are the three handsome pavilions of the knights challengers, each with its two shields—the shield of peace and the shield of war—by touching which each juster might indicate whether he chose to fight "in love or in wrath." There are the galleries hung with tapestries, in which sit the knights and ladies "as had pleasure to regard that sporte." There are the groups of knights, and the judges of the field; and there in the foreground are two of the gallant knights in full career, attended by their squires.

It will be interesting to the artist to know something of the colours of the knightly costumes. The knight on this side the barrier has his horse trapped in housings of blue and gold, lined with red, and the bridle to match; the saddle is red. The knight is in armour of steel, his shield is emblazoned *or*, three hearts *gules*; he bears as a crest upon his helmet two streamers of some transparent material like lawn. His antagonist's horse is trapped with red and gold housings, and bridle to match. He wears a kind of cape on his shoulders of cloth of gold; his shield is blue. Of the knights on the (spectator's) left of the picture, one has horse trappings of gold and red embroidery lined with plain red, his shield yellow (not gold) with black bearings; another has blue and gold trappings, with shield red, with white bearings. Of the knights on the right, one has horse-trappings blue and gold laced with red, and shield red and white; the other trappings red and gold, shield yellow. The squires are dressed thus: the limbs encased in armour, the body clothed in a jupon, which is either green embroidery on red ground or red embroidery on green ground. The pavilions are tinted red, with stripes of a darker red. The shields of the challengers are—on the left tent, *azure*, three hearts *argent;* on the middle, *vert*, three hearts *or;* on the right, *or*, three hearts *gules*.

We have drawn upon the romancer and the historian to illustrate the subject; we have cited ancient documents, and copied contemporary pictures; we will call upon the poet to complete our labour. Chaucer, in the Knight's Tale, gives a long account of a just *à l'outrance* between Palamon and Arcite and a hundred knights a-side, which came to pass thus: Palamon and Arcite, two cousins and sworn brothers-in-arms, had the

The Feat of Arms at St. Inglebert's.

misfortune both to fall in love with Emily, the younger sister of Ipolyta, the Queen of Theseus Duke-regnant of Athens. Theseus found the two young men, one May morning, in the wood engaged in a single combat.

> "This Duke his courser with his spurres smote,
> And at a start he was betwixt them two,
> And pulled out his sword and cried Ho!
> No more, up pain of losing of your head."

After discovering the cause of their enmity, the Duke ordained that that day fifty weeks each should bring a hundred knights ready to fight in the lists on his behalf—

> "And whether he or thou
> Shall with his hundred as I speak of now
> Slay his contrary or out of listes drive,
> Him shall I given Emilie to wive."

Each of the rivals rode through the country far and near during the fifty weeks, to enlist valiant knights to make up his hundred; and on the eve of the appointed day each party rode into Athens; and, says Chaucer, " never did so small a band comprise so noble a company of knights " :—

> "For every wight that loved chevalrie,
> And wolde, his thankes, have a lasting name,
> Hath praied that he might ben of that game,
> And well was he that thereto chosen was."

And the poet goes on with this testimony to the chivalrous feeling of his own time :—

> "For if there fell to-morrow such a case,
> Ye knowen well that every lusty knyght
> That loveth par amour, and hath his might,
> Were it in Engleland or elleswhere,
> They wolde, hir thankes, willen to be there."

At length the day arrives :—

> "Gret was the feste in Athens thilke day.
> *   *   *
> And on the morrow when the day gan spring,
> Of horse and harness, noise and clattering
> There was in all the hostelries about :
> And to the palace rode there many a rout
> Of lordes upon stedes and palfries.
> There mayst thou see devising of harness

> So uncouth and so riche, and wrought so well,
> Of goldsmithry, of brouding, and of steel;
> The shieldes bright, testeres, and trappours;
> Gold-hewen helms, hawberks, cote-armures;
> Lordes in parements on their coursers,
> Knyghts of retenue and eke squires,
> Nailing the speares and helms buckeling,
> Gniding of shields with lainers lacing;
> There, as need is, they were nothing idle.
> The foaming steedes on the golden bridle
> Gnawing, and fast the armourers also
> With file and hammer pricking to and fro;
> Yeomen on foot, and commons many a one,
> With shorte staves thick as they may gon;
> Pipes, trompes, nakeres, and clariouns,
> That in the battaille blowen bloody sounes.
> The palais full of people up and down.
>   *   *   *
> Duke Theseus is at a window sette,
> Arraied right as he were a god in throne;
> The people presseth thitherward full soon
> Him for to see, and do him reverence,
> And eke to hearken his heste and his sentence.
> An herauld on a scaffold made an O *
> Till that the noise of the people was ydo;
> And when he saw the people of noise all still,
> Thus shewed he the mighty Dukes will."

The Duke's will was, that none of the combatants should use any shot (*i.e.* any missile), or poleaxe, or short knife, or short pointed sword, but they were to run one course with sharp spears and then—

> "With long sword or with mace to fight their fill."

However, any one who was forcibly drawn to a stake—of which one was planted at each end of the lists—should be *hors de combat;* and if either of the leaders was slain or disabled or drawn to the stake, the combat should cease.

> "Up goe the trumpets and the melodie
> And to the listes rode the compaynie.
> By ordinance throughout the city large
> Hanged with cloth of gold, and not with serge.
>   *   *   *
> And thus they passen through the citie

---

* "Oyez!" or perhaps "Ho!"

> And to the listes comen they be-time
> It was not of the day yet fully prime,
> When set was Theseus full rich and high,
> Ipolita the queen and Emilie,
> And other ladies in degrees about,
> Unto the seates presseth all the rest."

Then Arcite and his hundred knights enter through the western side of the lists under a red banner, and Palamon and his company at the same moment, under a white banner, enter by the eastern gates.

> "And in two ranges fayre they hem dresse,
> When that their names read were every one,
> That in their number guile were there none.
> Then were the gates shut, and cried was loud,
> 'Do now your devoir, young knyghtes proud.'
> The herauldes left there pricking up and down;
> Then ringen trompes loud and clarioun;
> There is no more to say, but east and west,
> In go the speres quickly into rest,
> In goeth the sharpe spur into the side;
> There see men who can juste and who can ride;
> There shiver shafts upon sheldes thick,
> He feeleth through the herte-spoon the prick.
> Up springen speres, twenty foot in hyhte,
> Out go the swords as the silver bright
> The helmes they to-hewen and to-shred;
> Out bursts the blood with sterne streames red.
> With mighty maces the bones they to-brest.
> He through the thickest of the throng gan thrust,
> There stumble steedes strong, and down goth all.
> He rolleth under foot as doth a ball!
> He foineth on his foe with a truncheon,
> And he him hurteth, with his horse adown;
> He through the body is hurt and sith ytake,
> Maugre his head, and brought unto the stake."

At last it happened to Palamon—

> "That by the force of twenty is he take
> Unyolden, and drawen to the stake.
> And when that Theseus had seen that sight,
> Unto the folk that foughten thus eche one
> He cried 'Ho! no more, for it is done!'
> The troumpors with the loud minstralcie,

> The herauldes that so loude yell and crie,
> Been in their joy for wele of Don Arcite.
>   *   *   *
> This fierce Arcite hath off his helm ydone,
> And on a courser, for to show his face,
> He pusheth endilong the large place,
> Looking upward upon this Emilie,
> And she towards him cast a friendly eye;"

when, alas! his horse started, fell, and crushed the exulting victor, so that he lay bruised to death in the listes which had seen his victory. After a decent time of mourning, by Theseus's good offices, Emily accepts her surviving lover:

> "And thus with alle blisse and melodie
> Hath Palamon ywedded Emelie."

The two curious woodcuts * on pages 425 and 426 show the style of carriage associated—grotesquely associated, it seems to our eyes—with the armour and costume of the Middle Ages. No. 1 might represent Duke Theseus going in state through the streets of Athens, hung with tapestry and cloth of gold, to the solemn deed of arms of Palamon and Arcite. No. 2 may represent to us the merry Sir Dinadan driving to the tournament of the Castle of Maidens.

---

* From Mr. Wright's "Domestic Manners and Customs of the Middle Ages."

CHAPTER X.

MEDIÆVAL BOWMEN.

THE archers of England were so famous during the Middle Ages that we feel special interest in knowing something about them. As early as the Conquest we find the Norman archers giving the invader a great advantage over the Saxons, who had not cultivated this arm with success. Their equipment and appearance may be seen in the Bayeux tapestry; most of them are evidently unarmed, but some are in armour like that of the men-at-arms. Usually the quiver hangs at the side; yet occasionally at the back, so that the arrows are drawn out over the shoulder; both fashions continued in later times. In one case, at least, an archer, in pursuit of the flying Saxons, is seen on horseback; but it may be doubted whether at this period, as was the case subsequently, some of the archers were mounted, or whether an archer has leaped upon a riderless horse to pursue the routed enemy. The bow was of the simplest construction, not so long as it afterwards became; the arrows were barbed and feathered. Each archer—in later times, at least—commonly carried two dozen arrows "under his belt." He also frequently bore a stake sharpened at both ends, so that in the field, when the front ranks fixed their stakes in the ground with their points sloping outward, and the rear rank fixed theirs in the intermediate spaces, they formed a *cheval de frise* against cavalry, and, with the flanks properly cared for, they could hold their ground even against the steel-clad chivalry. Latterly also the archers were sometimes protected by a great movable shield; this they fixed upright by a rest, and behind it were sheltered from the adverse bowmen. The archer also carried a sword, so that he could defend himself, if attacked, hand to hand; or act on the offensive with the main body of foot when his artillery was expended. By the twelfth century there are stories on record which show that the English bowmen had acquired such skill as to make their weapon a very formidable one. Richard of Devizes tells us that at the siege of Messina the Sicilians were obliged to leave their walls unmanned, "because no one could look abroad but he would have an arrow in his eye before he could shut it."

In the thirteenth century the archer became more and more important. He always began the battle at a distance, as the artillery do in modern warfare, before the main bodies came up to actual hand-to-hand fighting. We find in this century a regular use of mounted corps of bowmen and cross-bowmen; and the knights did not scorn to practise the use of this weapon, and occasionally to resort to it on a special occasion in the field. Some of the bowmen continue to be found, in the MS. illustrations, more or less fully armed, but the majority seem to have worn only a helmet of iron, and perhaps half armour of leather, or often nothing more than a woollen jerkin.

The cross-bow, or arbalest, does not appear to have been used in war until the close of the twelfth century. It was not equal to the long-bow in strong and skilful hands, because a powerful and skilful bowman, while he could probably send his shaft with as much force as a cross-bow, could shoot half-a-dozen arrows while the cross-bow was being wound up to discharge a second bolt; but still, once introduced, the mechanical advantage which the cross-bow gave to men of ordinary strength and of inferior skill caused it to keep its ground, until the invention of fire-arms gradually superseded both long-bow and arbalest. The bow of the cross-bow seems to have been usually of steel; some of them were strung by putting the foot into a loop at the end of the stock, and pulling the cord up to its notch by main force: an illustration of this early form appears in the arbalester shooting from the battlement of the castle in the early fourteenth-century illumination on p. 381, and another at p. 382; but the more powerful bows required some mechanical assistance to bring the string to its place. In a picture in the National Gallery of the Martyrdom of St. Sebastian, by Antonio Pollajuolo, of Florence, A.D. 1475, an arbalester has a cord attached to his belt, and a pulley running on it, with a hook to catch the bow-string, so that, putting his foot into the loop at the end of the stock, looping the end of the cord on to a hook at its butt, and catching the bow-string by the pulley, he could, by straightening himself, apply the whole force of his body to the stringing of his weapon. More frequently, however, a little winch was used, by which the string was wound into its place with little expenditure of strength. One of the men in the cut on the next page is thus stringing his bow, and it is seen again in the cut on p. 449. The arrow shot by the cross-bow was called a bolt or quarrel; it was shorter and stouter than an ordinary arrow, with a heavier head. The arbalester seems to have carried fifty bolts into the field with him; the store of bolts was carried by waggons which followed the army.

We have already said that there were, from the thirteenth century, bodies of mounted arbalesters. But the far larger proportion of archers, of both arms, were footmen, who were usually placed in front of the array to commence the engagement.

The arbalest, however, was more used on the Continent than in England; and hence the long-bow came to be especially considered the national arm of the English, while the Genoese became famous as arbalesters. The superior rapidity of fire gave the English archer the same advantage over his foemen that the needle-gun gave to the Prussians in the late war.

Later on, in the fourteenth century, the battle seems to have been usually begun by the great machines for throwing stones and darts which then played the part of modern cannon, while the bowmen were placed on the flanks. Frequently, also, archers were intermixed with the horsemen, so that a body of spearmen with archers among them would play the part which a body of dragoons did in more modern warfare, throwing the opposing ranks into confusion with missiles, before charging upon them hand to hand.

In the fourteenth century the bow had attained the climax of its reputation as a weapon, and in the French wars many a battle was decided by the strength and skill and sturdy courage of the English bowmen. Edward III. conferred honour on the craft by raising a corps of archers of the King's Guard, consisting of 120 men, the most expert who could be found in the kingdom. About the same period the French kings enrolled from their allies of Scotland the corps of Scottish Archers of the Guard, who were afterwards so famous.

We have already given a good illustration of the long-bowman from the Royal MS. 14, E. IV., a folio volume illustrated with very fine pictures executed for our King Edward IV. From the same MS. we now take an illustration of the cross-bow. The accompanying cut is part of a larger picture which represents several interesting points in a siege. On the right is a town surrounded by a moat; the approach to the bridge over the moat

Bowmen and Arbalesters.

is defended by an outwork, and the arbalesters in the cut are skirmishing with some bowmen on the battlements and angle-turrets of this outwork. On the left of the picture are the besiegers. They have erected a wooden castle with towers, surrounded by a timber breast-work. In front of this breast-work is an elaborate cannon of the type of that represented in the cut on page 392. At a little distance is a battery of one cannon elevated on a wooden platform, and screened by a breast-work of basket-work, which was a very usual way of concealing cannon down to the time of Henry VIII.

The man on the right of the cut wears a visored helmet, but it has no amail; his body is protected by a skirt of mail, which appears at the shoulders and hips, and at the openings of his blue surcoat; the legs are in brown hose, and the feet in brown shoes. The centre figure has a helmet and camail, sleeves of mail, and iron breastplate of overlapping plates; the upper plate and the skirt are of red spotted with gold; his hose and shoes are of dark grey. The third man has a helmet with camail, and the body protected by mail, which shows under the arm, but he has also

Arbalesters.

shoulder-pieces and elbow-pieces of plate; his surcoat is yellow, and his hose red. The artist has here admirably illustrated the use of the cross-bow. In one case we see the archer stringing it by help of a little winch; in the next he is taking a bolt out of the quiver at his side with which to load his weapon; in the third we have the attitude in which it was discharged.

The illustration above, from a fourteenth-century MS. (Cott. Julius, E. IV.

f. 219), represents a siege. A walled town is on the right, and in front of the wall, acting on the part of the town, are the cross-bowmen in the cut, protected by great shields which are kept upright by a rest. The men seem to be preparing to fire, and the uniformity of their attitude, compared with the studied variety of attitude of groups of bowmen in other illustrations, suggests that they are preparing to fire a volley. On the left of the picture is sketched a group of tents representing the camp of the besiegers, and in front of the camp is a palisade which screens a cannon of considerable length. The whole picture is only sketched in with pen and ink.

The woodcut here given (Royal 14, E. IV. f. xiv.) forms part of a large and very interesting picture. In the middle of the picture is a castle with a bridge, protected by an advanced tower, and a postern with a drawbridge drawn up. Archers, cross-bowmen, and men-at-arms man the battlements. In front is a group of men-at-arms and tents, with archers and cross-bowmen shooting up at the defenders. On the right is a group of men-at-arms who seem to be meditating an attack by surprise upon the postern. On the left, opposed to the principal gate, is the timber fort shown in the woodcut. Its construction, of great posts and

Timber Fort.

thick slabs of timber strengthened with stays and cross-beams, is well indicated. There seem to be two separate works: one is a battery of two cannon, the cannon having wheeled carriages; the other is manned by archers. It is curious to see the mixture of arms—long-bow, cross-bow, portable fire-arm, and wheeled cannon, all used at the same time; indeed, it may be questioned whether the earlier fire-arms were very much superior in effect to the more ancient weapons which they supplanted. No doubt many an archer preferred the long-bow, with which he could shoot with truer aim than with a clumsy hand-gun; and perhaps a good catapult was only inferior to one of the early cannon in being a larger and heavier engine.

At fol. 1 v. of the same MS., a wooden tower and lofty breast-work have been thrown up in front of a town by the defenders as an additional protection to the usual stone tower which defends the approach to the bridge. The assailants are making an assault on this breast-work, and need ladders to scale it; so that it is evident the defenders stand on a raised platform behind their timber defence. See a similar work at f. xlviij., which is mounted with cannon.

The practice of archery by the commonalty of England was protected and encouraged by a long series of legislation. As early as Henry I. we find an enactment—which indicates that such accidents happened then as do unhappily in these days, when rifle-shooting is become a national practice—that if any one practising with arrows or with darts should by accident slay another, it was not to be punished as a crime. In the fourteenth century, when the archer had reached the height of his importance in the warfare of the time, many enactments were passed on the subject. Some were intended to encourage, and more than encourage, the practice by the commonalty of what had become the national arm. In 1363, and again in 1388, statutes were passed calling upon the people to leave their popular amusements of ball and coits and casting the stone and the like, on their festivals and Sundays, and to practise archery instead. "Servants and labourers shall have bows and arrows, and use the same the Sundays and holidays, and leave all playing at tennis or foot-ball, and other games called coits, dice, casting the stone, kailes, and other such inopportune games."

In 1482 a statute says that the dearness of bows has driven the people to leave shooting, and practise unlawful games, though the king's subjects are perfectly disposed to shoot; and it therefore regulates the price of bows. This crude legislation, of course, failed to remedy the evil, for if the bowyers could not sell them at a profit, they would cease to make them, or rather to import the wood of which they were made, since the best yew for bows came from abroad, English yew not supplying pieces sufficiently long without knots. Accordingly, in 1483, another statute required all merchants sending merchandise to England from any place from which bow-staves were usually exported, to send four bow-staves for every ton of merchandise, and two persons were appointed at each port to inspect the staves so sent, and mark and reject those which were not good and sufficient.

Still later the erection of butts was encouraged in every parish to prevent the accidents which the statute of Henry I. had directed justice to wink at; and traces of them still remain in the names of places, as in Newington Butts; and still more frequently in the names of fields, as the "butt-field."

Our history of ancient artillery would be imperfect without a few words on the modern artillery of metal balls propelled from hollow tubes by the explosive force of gunpowder, which superseded the slings and bows and darts, the catapults and trebuchets and mangonels and battering-rams, which had been used from the beginning of warfare in the world, and also drove out of use the armour, whether of leather, bone, or steel, which failed to pay in security of person against shot and cannon-ball for its weight and encumbrance to the wearer. A good deal of curious inquiry has been bestowed upon the origin of this great agent in the revolution of modern warfare. The Chinese and Arabs are generally regarded as the first inventors of gunpowder; among Europeans its invention has been attributed to Marcus Graecus, Albertus Magnus, Barthold Schwaletz, and Roger Bacon.

The first written evidence relating to the existence of cannon is in the ordinances of Florence, in the year 1326, wherein authority is given to the Priors Gonfalionieri and twelve good men to appoint persons to superintend the manufacture of cannons and iron balls for the defence of the Commune Camp and territory of the Republic. J. Barbour, the poet, is usually quoted as an authority for the use of cannon "crakeys of war," by Edward III., in his Scottish campaign, in the year 1327. But since Barbour was not born till about that year, and did not write till 1375, his authority was not contemporary and may be doubted, especially since there is strong negative evidence to the contrary: *e. g.* that all the army accounts of this campaign still remain, and no mention of guns or gunpowder is to be found in them. In 1338, however, there is unquestionable evidence that cannon of both iron and brass were employed on board English ships of war. In an inventory of things delivered that year by John Starling, formerly clerk of the king's vessels, to Helmyng, keeper of the same, are noted "un canon de fer ov ii chambers, un autre de bras ove une chamber, iii canons de fer of v chambres, un handgonne," &c. In explanation of the two and five chambers, it appears that these earliest cannon were breechloaders, and each cannon had several movable chambers to contain the charges. The same year, 1338, gives the first French document relating to cannon. It is doubly interesting; first because it relates to the provision made for an expedition against Southampton in that year, and secondly because it was a curious attempt to combine the cannon and the arbalest, in other words, to make use of the force of gunpowder for propelling the old short quarrel. It was an iron fire-arm provided with forty-eight bolts (carreaux) made of iron and feathered with brass. We learn that a tube received the arrow, which was wrapped round with leather at the butt to make it fit closely, and this tube fitted to a box, or chamber, which contained the charge and was kept in its place by a wedge.* In 1339 it is recorded that the English used cannon at the siege of Cambray. In 1346 experiments on improved cannon were made by Peter of Bruges, a famous maker, before the consuls of Tournay. At the siege of Calais, in 1347, the English built a castle of wood, and armed it with bombards. In the household expenses of Edward III., commencing 1344, are payments to "engyners lvii., artillers vi., gunners vi.," who each received sixpence a day.

The date of the first appearance of cannon in the field is still disputed;

---

* "Ancient Cannon in Europe," by Lieut. Brackenbury.

some say they were used at Crecy in the year 1346. Certainly, in 1382, the men of Ghent carried guns into the field against the Brugeois; and at the combat of Pont-de-Comines, in the same year, we read *bombardes portatives* were used.

We have already given several illustrations of cannon. Siege cannon for throwing heavy balls which did not need very great accuracy of aim;

Long-bow, Arquebus, Cannon, and Greek Fire.

soon superseded entirely the more cumbrous military engines which were formerly used for the same purpose. But hand-guns were not at first so greatly superior to bows, and did not so rapidly come into exclusive use. And yet a good deal of inventive ingenuity was bestowed upon their improvement and development. The "Brown Bess" of our great continental war was a clumsy weapon after all, and it may fairly be doubted whether a regiment armed with it could have stood against a row of Robin

Hood's men with their long-bows. It was really left to our day to produce a portable fire-arm which would fire as rapidly, as far, and with as accurate an aim as Robin Hood's men could shoot their cloth-yard shafts six hundred years ago; and yet it is curious to find some of the most ingenious inventions of the present day anticipated long since: there are still preserved in the Tower armoury breech-loaders and revolving chambers and conical shot of the time of Henry VIII.

The woodcut on the preceding page, which is from the MS. Royal 14, E. IV., contains several figures taken from one of the large illuminations that adorn the MS.; it affords another curious illustration of the simultaneous use of various forms of projectiles. On the right side is an archer, with his sheaf at his belt and his sword by his side. On the left is a man-at-arms in a very picturesque suit of complete armour, firing a hand-gun of much more modern form than those in the former woodcut. A small wheeled cannon on the ground shows the contemporary form of that arm, while the pikes beside it help to illustrate the great variety of weapons in use. The cross-bowman here introduced is from the same illumination; he is winding up his weapon with a winch, like the cross-bowman on p. 442; his shield is slung at his back.

Cross-bow.

But we have specially to call attention to the two men who are throwing shells, which are probably charged with Greek fire. This invention, which inspired such terror in the Middle Ages, seems to have been discovered in the east of Europe, and to have been employed as early as the seventh century. We hear much of its use in the Crusades, by the Greeks, who early possessed the secret of its fabrication. They used it either by ejecting it through pipes to set fire to the shipping or military engines, or to annoy and kill the soldiers of the enemy; or they cast it to a distance by means of vessels charged with it affixed to javelins; or they hurled larger vessels by means of the great engines for casting stones; or they threw the fire by hand in a hand-to-hand conflict; or used hollow maces charged with it, which were broken over the person of the enemy, and the liquid fire poured down, finding its way through the crevices of his armour. It was, no doubt, a terrible sight to see a man-at-arms or a ship wrapped in an instant in liquid flames; and what added to the terror it inspired was that the flames could not be extinguished by water or any other available appliance. On the introduction of the use of gunpowder in European warfare, Greek fire seems also to have been experimented

Battering-ram.

upon, and we find several representations of its use in the MS. drawings, where it is chiefly thrown by hand to set fire to shipping; in the present example, however, it is used in the field.

Lastly, in the above cut we give a representation of the battering-ram from an interesting work which illustrates all the usual military engines.* It contains curious contrivances for throwing up scaling-ladders and affixing

---

* See also Viollet le Duc's "Dictionary of Architecture."

them to the battlements, from which the inventors of our fire-escapes may have borrowed suggestions; and others for bridging wide moats and rivers with light scaffolding, which could be handled and fixed as easily and quickly as the scaling-ladders. The drawing of the ram only indicates that the machine consists of a heavy square beam of timber, provided, probably, with a metal head, which is suspended by a rope from a tall frame, and worked by manual strength. The cut is especially interesting as an illustration of the style of armour of the latter part of the fifteenth century. It gives the back as well as the front of the figure, and also several varieties of helmet.

CHAPTER XI.

FIFTEENTH CENTURY ARMOUR.

AS the fifteenth century advanced the wars of the Roses gave urgent reason for attention to the subject of defensive armour; and we find, accordingly, that the fashions of armour underwent many modifications, in the attempt to give the wearer more perfect protection for life and limb. It would be tedious to enter into the minute details of these changes, and the exact date of their introduction; we must limit ourselves to a brief history of the general character of the new fashions. The horizontal bands of armour called *taces*, depending from the corslet, became gradually narrower; while the pieces which hung down in front of the thighs, called *tuilles*, became proportionately larger. In the reigns of Richard III. and Henry VII. the knightly equipment reached its strangest forms. Besides the usual close-fitting pieces which protected the arms, the elbow-piece was enlarged into an enormous fan-like shape that not only protected the elbow itself, but overlapped the fore arm, and by its peculiar shape protected the upper arm up to the shoulder. The shoulder-pieces also were strengthened, sometimes by several super-imposed overlapping plates, sometimes by hammering it out into ridges, sometimes by the addition of a *passe garde*—a kind of high collar which protected the neck from a sweeping side blow. The breast-plate is globular in shape, and often narrow at the waist; from it depend narrow *taces* and *tuilles*, and under the *tuilles* we often find a deep skirt of mail. When broad-toed shoes came into fashion, the iron shoes of the knight followed the fashion; and at the same time, in place of the old gauntlet in which the fingers were divided, and each finger protected by several small plates of metal, the leather glove was now furnished at the back of the hand with three or four broad over-lapping plates, like those of a lobster, each of which stretched across the whole hand. These alterations may have added to the strength of the armour, but it was at the cost of elegance of appearance. A suit of armour embossed with ornamental patterns, partially covered with a blue mantle, may be seen in the fifteenth-century Book of Hours, Harl. 5,328, f. 77.

In the time of Henry VIII., in place of the *taces* and *tuilles* for the defence of the body and thighs, a kind of skirt of steel, called *lamboys*, was introduced, which was fluted and ribbed vertically, so as to give it very much the appearance of a short petticoat. Henry VIII. is represented in this costume in the equestrian figure on his great seal. And a suit of armour of this kind, a very magnificent one, which was presented to the king by the Emperor Maximilian on the occasion of his marriage to Katharine of Arragon, is preserved in the Tower armoury. A good sketch of a suit of this kind will be seen in one of the pikemen—the fifth from the right hand—in the nearest rank of the army in the engraving of King Henry VIII.'s army, which faces page 455. The armour of this reign was sometimes fashioned in exact imitation of the shape of the ordinary garments of a gentleman of the time, and engraved and inlaid in imitation of their woven or embroidered ornamentation.

In the tournament armour of the time the defences were most complete, but unwieldy and inelegant. The front of the saddle had a large piece of armour attached, which came up to protect the trunk, and was bent round to encase each thigh. A clearly drawn representation of this will be found in a tilting scene in the illumination on f. 15 v. of the MS. Add. 24,189, date *circa* 1400 A.D. There are several examples of it in the Tower armoury. The shield was also elaborately shaped and curved, to form an outer armour for the defence of the whole of the left side. Instead of the shield there was sometimes an additional piece of armour, called the *grand garde*, screwed to the breastplate, to protect the left side and shoulder; while the great spear had also a piece of armour affixed in front of the grasp, which not only protected the hand, but was made large enough to make a kind of shield for the right arm and breast. There was also sometimes a secondary defence affixed to the upper part of the breast-plate, which stood out in front of the face. These defences for thigh and breast will be observed in the woodcut of the "playing at tournament," on p. 408; and in the combat of the Earl of Warwick, p. 418, will be seen how the *grande garde* is combined with the *volante* piece which came in front of the face. Behind such defences the tilter must have been almost invulnerable. On the other hand, his defences were so unwieldy that he must have got into his saddle first, and then have been packed securely

Combat on Foot.

into his armour; and when there, he could do nothing but sit still and hold his spear in rest—it seems impossible for him even to have struck a single sword stroke. James I.'s remark on armour was especially true of such a suit: "It was an admirable invention which preserved a man from being injured, and made him incapable of injuring any one else."

There are several very good authorities for the military costume of the reign of Henry VIII. easily accessible to the student and artist. The roll preserved in the College of Arms which represents the tournament held at Westminster, A.D. 1510, in honour of the birth of the son of Henry and Katharine of Arragon, has been engraved in the "Vetusta Monumenta." The painting of the Field of the Cloth of Gold at Hampton Court is another contemporary authority full of costumes of all kinds. The engravings of Hans Burgmaier, in the *Triumphs of Maximilian* and the *Weise Könige* contain numerous authorities very valuable for the clearness and artistic skill with which the armour is depicted. We have given an illustration, on the preceding page, reduced from one of the plates of the latter work, which represents a combat of two knights, on foot. The armour is partly covered by a surcoat; in the left-hand figure it will be seen that it is fluted. The shields will be noticed as illustrating one of the shapes then in use.

But our best illustration is from a contemporary drawing in the British Museum (Aug. III., f. 4), which represents Henry VIII.'s army, and gives us, on a small scale, and in very sketchy but intelligible style, a curious and valuable picture of the military equipment of the period. We have two armies drawn up in battle array, and the assault is just commenced. The nearer army has its main body of pikemen, who, we know from contemporary writers, formed the main strength of an army at this time, and for long after. In front of them are two lines of arquebusiers. Their front is protected by artillery, screened by great *mantelets* of timber. The opposing army has similarly its main body of pikemen, and its two lines of arquebusiers; the first line engaged in an assault upon the enemy's artillery. On the left flank of its main body is the cavalry; and there seems to be a reserve of pikemen a little distance in the rear, behind a rising ground. Tents pitched about a village represent the head-quarters of the army, and baggage waggons on the left of the picture show that the artist has overlooked nothing. A fortress in the distance seems to be taking part in the engagement with its guns.

There are other similar pictures in the same volume, some of which supply details not here given, or not so clearly expressed. At folio 1 are two armies, each with a van of musketeers three deep, a main body of pikemen eleven deep, and a third line of musketeers three deep. The cavalry are more distinctly shown than in the picture before us, as being men-at-arms in full armour, with lances. At folio 3 the drummers, fifers, and baggage and camp followers are shown.

In the *Weise Könige*,* on plate 44, is a representation of a camp surrounded by the baggage waggons; on plates 91 and 96 a square fort of timber in the field of battle; on plates 57, 84, &c., are cannons surrounded by mantelets, some of wicker probably filled with earth; on plate 60 is a good representation of a column of troops defiling out of the gate of a city.

The following account, from Grafton's Chronicle, of the array in which Henry VIII. took the field when he marched to the siege of Boulogne, will illustrate the picture:—

"The xxj. day of July (1513), when all thinges by counsayle had bene ordered concernyng the order of battaile, the king passed out of the town of Calice in goodly array of battaile, and toke the field. And notwithstandyng that the forewarde and the rerewarde of the kinges great armye were before Tyrwin, as you have heard, yet the king of his own battaile made three battailes after the fassion of the warre. The Lord Lisle, marshall of the hoste, was captain of the foreward, and under him three thousand men; Sir Rychard Carew, with three hundred men, was the right-hand wing to the foreward; and the Lord Darcy, with three hundred men, was wing on the left hande; the scowrers and fore-ryders of this battaile were the Northumberland men on light geldings. The Erle of Essex was lieutenaunt-generall of the speres, and Sir John Pechy was vice-governour of the horsemen. Before the king went viij. hundred Almaynes, all in a plump by themselves. After them came the standard with the red dragon, next the banner of our ladie, and next after the banner of the Trinitie: under the same were all the kinges housholde servauntes. Then went the banner of the armes of Englande, borne by Sir Henry Guilforde, under which banner was the king himselfe, with divers noblemen and others, to the number of three thousand men. The Duke of Buckyngham, with sixe hundred men, was on the kinges left

---

* The British Museum does not possess this fine work, but a copy of it is accessible to the public in the Library of the South Kensington Museum.

hande, egall with the Almaynes; in like wise on the right hande was Sir Edward Pournynges, with other sixe hundred men egall with the Almaynes. The Lord of Burgoynie, with viij. hundred men, was wing on the right hande; Sir William Compton, with the retinue of the Bishop of Winchester, and Master Wolsey, the king's almoner,* to the number of viij.

Pikeman.

hundred, was in manner of a rereward. Sir Anthony Oughtred and Sir John Nevell, with the kinges speres that followed, were foure hundred; and so the whole armie were xj. thousand and iij. hundred men. The Mayster of the Ordinaunce set forth the kinges artillerie, as fawcons,

---

* Afterwards cardinal.

slinges, bombardes, cartes with powder, stones, bowes, arrowes, and suche other thinges necessary for the fielde; the whole number of the carriages were xiij. hundreth; the leaders and dryvers of the same were xix hundreth men; and all these were rekened in the battaile, but of good fightyng men there were not full ix. thousande. Thus in order of battayle the king rode to Sentreyla."

A little after we have a description of the king's camp, which will illustrate the other pictures above noted.

"Thursedaie, the fourth daye of Auguste, the king, in good order of battaile, came before the city of Tyrwyn, and planted his siege in most warlike wise; his camp was environed with artillerie, as fawcons, serpentines, crakys, hagbushes, and tryed harowes, spien trestyles, and other warlike defence for the savegard of the campe. The king for himselfe had a house of timber, with a chimney of iron; and for his other lodgings he had great and goodlye tents of blewe waterworke, garnished with yellow and white, and divers romes within the same for all officers necessarie. On the top of the pavalions stoode the kinges bestes, holding fanes, as the lion, the dragon, the greyhound, the antelope, the Done Kowe.* Within, all the lodginge was paynted full of the sunnes rising: the lodginge was a hundred xxv. foote in length."

At folio 5 of the MS. already referred to (Aug. III.) is a connected arrangement of numerous tents, as if to form some such royal quarters. But at folio 8 are two gorgeous *suites* of tents, which can hardly have been constructed for any other than a very great personage. One *suite* is of red, watered, with gold ornamentation; the other is of green and white stripes (or rather gores), with a gilded cresting along the ridge, and red and blue fringe at the eaves.

Our next engravings are from coloured drawings at f. 9, in the same MS., and respectively represent very clearly the half-armour worn by the pikeman and the arquebusier, and the weapons from which they took their name.

In the reign of Elizabeth and James I. armour was probably very little worn; but every country knight and esquire possessed a suit of armour,

---

* Dun Cow.

which usually hung in his hall over his chair of state, surrounded by corslets and iron hats, pikes and halberts, cross-bows and long-bows, wherewith to arm his serving-men and tenants, if civil troubles or foreign invasion should call the fighting-men of the country into the field.* The

Arquebusier.

knights and esquires of these times are also commonly represented in armour, kneeling at the prayer-desk, in their monumental effigies. The

---

* "He is so hung round," says Truewit, in Ben Jonson's *Epicœne*, "with pikes, halberds, petronels, calivers, and muskets, that he looks like a justice of peace's hall." Clement Sysley, of Eastbury House, near Barking, bequeathed in his will the "gonnes, pikes, cross-bows, and other weapons, to Thomas Sysley, to go with the house, and remain as standards for ever in Eastbury Hall."

fashion of the armour differs from that of preceding reigns. The elaborate ingenuities of the latter part of the fifteenth century have been dispensed with, and the extravagant caprices also by which the armour of Henry VIII.'s time imitated in steel the fashion of the ordinary costume of the day are equally abandoned. The armour is simply made to fit the breast, body, arms, and legs; the thighs being protected by a modification of the *tuilles* in the form of a succession of overlapping plates (*tassets* or *cuisses*) which reach from the corslet to the knee.

The civil war of the Great Rebellion offers a tempting theme, but we must limit ourselves to the notice that few, except great noblemen when acting as military leaders, ever wore anything like a complete suit of armour. A beautiful suit, inlaid with gold, which belonged to Charles I., is in the Tower armoury. But knights are still sometimes represented in armour in their monumental effigies. A breast and back-plate over a leather coat, and a round iron cap, were commonly worn both by cavalry and infantry.

In the time of Charles II. and James II., and William and Mary, officers still wore breastplates, and military leaders were sometimes painted in full armour, though it may be doubted whether they ever actually wore it. As late as the present century, officers, in some regiments at least, wore a little steel gorget, rather as a distinction than a defence. But even yet our horse-guards remain with their breast and back-plates and helmets, and their thick leather boots, to show us how bright steel and scarlet, waving plumes and embroidered banners, trained chargers and gay trappings, give outward bravery and chivalric grace to the holiday aspect of the sanguinary trade of war.

THE MERCHANTS OF THE MIDDLE AGES.

CHAPTER I.

THE BEGINNINGS OF BRITISH COMMERCE.

IN the remotest antiquity, before European civilisation dawned in Greece, Britain was already of some commercial importance. In those days, before the art of tempering iron was discovered, copper occupied the place which iron now fills. But an alloy of tin was requisite to give to copper the hardness and edge needed to fit it for useful tools for the artisan, for arrow and spear heads for the hunter, and for the warrior's sword and shield; and there were only two places known in the world where this valuable metal could be obtained—Spain and Britain. For ages the Phœnician merchants and their Carthaginian colonists had a monopoly of this commerce, as they only had the secret of the whereabouts of the "Isles of Tin." It is very difficult for us to realise to ourselves how heroic was the daring of those early adventurers. We, who have explored the whole earth, and by steam and telegraph brought every corner of it within such easy reach; we, to whom it is a very small matter to make a voyage with women and children to the other side of the world; we, who walk down to the pier to see the ships return from the under world, keeping their time as regularly as the Minster clock—we cannot comprehend what it was to them, to whom the tideless sunny Mediterranean was "The Great Sea," about which they groped cautiously from one rocky headland to another in fine weather, and laid up in harbour for the winter; to whom the Pillars of Hercules were the western boundary of the world, beyond which the weird ocean with its great tides and mountain-waves stretched without limit towards the sunset; we cannot comprehend the heroic daring of the men who, in those little ships, without compass, came from the easternmost shores of the Great Sea, ventured through its western portal into this outer waste, and steered boldly northwards towards the unknown regions of ice and darkness.

Our readers will remember that Strabo tells us how, when Rome became the rival of Carthage, the Romans tried to discover the route to these mysterious islands. He relates how the master of a Carthaginian vessel, finding himself pursued by one whom the Romans had appointed to watch him, purposely ran his vessel aground, and thus sacrificing ship and cargo to the preservation of the national secret, was repaid on his return out of the public treasury.

The trade, which included lead and hides as well as tin, when it left the hands of the Phœnicians, did not, however, fall into those of the Romans, but took quite a different channel. The Greek colony of Marseilles became then the emporium from which the world was supplied; but the scanty accounts we have received imply that it was not conveyed there direct on ship-board, but that the native ships and traders of the Gallic towns on the coasts of the Continent conveyed the British commerce across the Channel, and thence transported it overland to Marseilles.

The Britons, however, had ships, and it is interesting to know of what kind were the prototypes of the vast and magnificent vessels which in later days have composed the mercantile navy of Great Britain. They were a kind of large basket of wickerwork, in shape like a walnut shell, strengthened by ribs of wood, covered on the outside with hides.* Such constructions seem very frail, but they were capable of undertaking considerable voyages. Pliny quotes the old Greek historian Timæus as affirming that the Britons used to make their way to an island at the distance of six

---

* A sketch illustrating their construction may be found in Witsen's "Sheeps Bouw." Appendix, Plate 10.

days' sail in boats made of osiers and covered with skins. Solinus states that in his time the communication between Britain and Ireland was kept up on both sides by means of these vessels. Two passages in Adamson, quoted by Macpherson,* tell us that the people sailed in them from Ireland as far as Orkney, and on one occasion we hear of one of these frail vessels advancing as far into the Northern Ocean as fourteen days with full sail before a south wind. The common use of such vessels, and the fact of this intercommunication between England and Ireland and the islands farther north, seem to imply, at least, some coasting and inter-insular traffic: ships are the instruments either of war or commerce.

The invasion of Julius Cæsar opened up the island to the knowledge of the civilised world, and there are indications that in the interval of a hundred years between his brief campaign and the actual conquest under Claudius, a commerce sprang up between the south and south-east of Britain and the opposite coasts of the Continent. In this interval the first British coinage was struck, and London became the chief emporium of Britain. When the island became a province of the Roman empire, active commercial intercourse was carried on between it and the rest of the empire. Its chief production was corn, of which large quantities were exported, so that Britain was to the northern part of the empire what Sicily was to the southern. Besides, the island exported cattle, hides, and slaves; British hunting dogs were famous, and British oysters and pearls. The imports would include all the articles of convenience and luxury used by the civilised inhabitants. We do not know with certainty whether this foreign commerce was carried on by British vessels or not. History has only preserved the record of the military navy. But when we know that the British fleet, which had been raised to control the piratical enterprises of the Saxons and Northmen, was so powerful that its admiral, Carausius, was able to seize upon a share of the empire, and that his successor in command, Allectus, was able, though for a shorter period, to repeat the exploit, we may conclude that the natives of the island must have acquired considerable knowledge and experience of maritime affairs, and were very

---

* "History of Commerce."

likely to turn their acquirements in the direction of commerce. Many of the representations of Roman ships, to be found in works on Roman antiquities, would illustrate this part of the subject; we may content ourselves with referring the reader to a representation, in Witsen's "Sheeps Bouw," of a Roman ship being laden with merchandise: a half-naked porter is just putting on board a sack, probably of corn, which is being received by a man in Roman armour.; it brings the salient features of the trade at once before our eyes.

The Saxon invasion overwhelmed the civilisation which was then widely spread over Britain; and of the history of the country for a long time after that great event we are profoundly ignorant.

It appears that the Saxons after their settlement in England completely neglected the sea, and it was not until the reign of Alfred, towards the end of the ninth century, that they again began to build ships, and not until some years later that foreign commerce was carried on in English vessels. In these later Saxon times, however, considerable intercourse took place with the Continent. There was a rage among Saxon men, and women too, for foreign pilgrimages; and thousands of persons were continually going and coming between England and the most famous shrines of Europe, especially those of Rome, the capital city of Western Christendom. Among these travellers were some whose object was traffic, probably in the portable articles of jewellery for which the Saxon goldsmiths were famous throughout Europe. It seems probable that some of these merchants were accustomed to adopt the pilgrims' character and habit in order to avail themselves of the immunities and hospitalities accorded to them; and, perhaps, on the other hand, some of those whose first object was religion, carried a few articles for sale to eke out their expenses. This, probably, is the explanation of the earliest extant document bearing on Saxon commerce, which is a letter from the Emperor Charlemagne to Offa, King of the Mercians, in which he says: "Concerning the strangers, who, for the love of God and the salvation of their souls, wish to repair to the thresholds of the blessed Apostles, let them travel in peace without any trouble; nevertheless, if any are found among them not in the service of religion, but in the pursuit of gain, let them pay the established duties at the proper places. We also will that merchants shall have lawful protection in our kingdom; and if they are in any place unjustly aggrieved, let them apply to us or our judges, and we shall take care that ample justice be done them." The latter clause seems clearly to imply that English merchants in their acknowledged character were also to be found in the dominions of the great Emperor.

The next notice we find of Saxon foreign commerce is equally picturesque, and far more important. It is a law passed in the reign of King Athelstan, between 925 and 950, which enacts that every merchant who shall have made three voyages over the sea in a ship and cargo of his own should have the rank of a thane, or nobleman. It will throw light upon this law, if we mention that it stands side by side with another which gives equally generous recognition to success in agricultural pursuits: every one who had so prospered that he possessed five hides of land, a hall, and a church, was also to rank as a thane.

The law indicates the usual way in which foreign commerce was carried on by native merchants. The merchant owned his own ship, and laded it with his own cargo, and was his own captain, though he might, perhaps, employ some skilful mariner as his ship-master; and, no doubt, his crew was well armed for protection from pirates. In these days a ship is often chartered to carry a cargo to a particular port, and there the captain obtains another cargo, such as the market affords him, to some other port, and so he may wander over the world in the most unforeseen manner before he finds a profitable opportunity of returning to his starting-place. So, probably, in those times the spirited merchant would not merely oscillate between home and a given foreign point, but would carry on a traffic of an adventurous and hazardous but exciting kind, from one of the great European ports to another.

From a volume of Saxon dialogues in the British Museum (Tiberius, A. III.), apparently intended for a school-book, which gives information of various kinds in the form of question and answer, Mr. S. Turner quotes a passage that illustrates our subject in a very interesting way. The merchant is introduced as one of the characters, to give an account of his occupation and way of life. "I am useful," he says, "to the king and to ealdormen, and to the rich, and to all people. I ascend my ship with my merchandise, and sail over the sea-like places, and sell my things, and buy dear things which are not produced in this land, and I bring them to you here with great danger over the sea; and sometimes I suffer shipwreck with the loss of all my things, scarcely escaping myself." The question, "What do you bring us?" demands an account of the imports, to which he answers, "Skins, silks, costly gems, and gold; various garments, pigment, wine, oil, ivory, and onchalcus (perhaps brass); copper, tin, silver, glass, and such like." The author has omitted to make his merchant tell us what things he exported, but from other sources we gather that they were chiefly wool, slaves, probably some of the metals, viz., tin and lead, and the goldsmith's work and embroidery for which the Saxons were then famous throughout Europe. The dialogue brings out the principle which lies at the bottom of commerce by the next question, "Will you sell your things here as you bought them there?" "I will not, because what would my labour profit me? I will sell them here, dearer than I bought them there, that I may get some profit to feed me, my wife, and children." For the silks and ivory, our merchant would perhaps have to push his adventurous voyage as far as Marseilles or Italy. Corn, which used to be the chief export in British and Roman times, appears never to have been exported by the Saxons; they were a pastoral, rather than an agricultural, people. The traffic in slaves seems to have been regular and considerable. The reader will remember how the sight of a number of fair English children exposed for sale in the Roman market-place excited Gregory's interest, and led ultimately to Augustine's mission. The contemporary account of Wolfstan, Bishop of Worcester, at the time of the Conquest, speaks of similar scenes to be witnessed in Bristol, from which port slaves were exported to Ireland—probably to the Danes, who were then masters of the east coast. "You might have seen with sorrow long ranks of young people of both sexes, and of the greatest beauty, tied together with ropes, and daily exposed to sale: nor were these men ashamed—O horrid wickedness—to give up their nearest relations, nay their own children, to slavery." The good bishop induced them to abandon the trade, "and set an example to all the rest of England to do the same." Nevertheless, William of

Malmesbury, who wrote nearly a century later, says that the practice of selling even their nearest relations into slavery had not been altogether abandoned by the people of Northumberland in his own memory.

Already, on the death of Ethelbert, in 1016, the citizens of London had arrived at such importance, that, in conjunction with the nobles who were in the city, they chose a king for the whole English nation, viz., Edmund Ironside; and again on the death of Canute, in 1036, they took a considerable part in the election of Harold. At the battle of Hastings the burgesses of London formed Harold's body-guard. A few years previously, Canute, on his pilgrimage to Rome, met the Emperor Conrade and other princes, from whom he obtained for all his subjects, whether merchants or pilgrims, exemption from the heavy tolls usually exacted on the journey to Rome.

During the peaceful reign of Edward the Confessor a much larger general intercourse seems to have sprung up with the Continent, and the commerce of England to have greatly increased. For this we have the testimony of William of Poictiers, William the Conqueror's chaplain, who says, speaking of the time immediately preceding the Conquest, "The English merchants to the opulence of their country, rich in its own fertility, added still greater riches and more valuable treasures. The articles imported by them, notable both for their quantity and their quality, were to have been hoarded up for the gratification of their avarice, or to have been dissipated in the indulgence of their luxurious inclinations. But William seized them, and bestowed part on his victorious army, and part on the churches and monasteries, while to the Pope and the Church of Rome he sent an incredible mass of money in gold and silver, and many ornaments that would have been admired even in Constantinople."

We are not able to give any authentic contemporary illustration of the shipping of this period. Those which are given by Strutt are not really representations of the ships of the period: Byzantine Art still exercised a powerful influence over Saxon Art, and the illuminators frequently gave traditional forms; and the ships introduced by Strutt, though executed by a Saxon artist, are probably copied from Byzantine authorities. The Bayeux tapestry is probably our earliest trustworthy authority for a British ship, and it gives a considerable number of illustrations of them, intended to represent in one place the numerous fleet which William the Conqueror gathered for the transport of his army across the Channel; in another place the considerable fleet with which Harold hoped to bar the way. The one we have chosen is the duke's own ship; it displays at its mast-head the banner which the Pope had blessed, and the trumpeter on the high poop is also an evidence that it is the commander's ship. In the present case

William the Conqueror's Ship.

the trumpeter is known, from contemporary authority, to have been only wood gilded; but in many of the subsequent illustrations we shall also find a trumpeter, or usually two, who were part of the staff of the commander, and perhaps were employed in signalling to other ships of the fleet.

The Conquest checked this thriving commerce. William's plunder of the Saxon merchants, which was probably not confined to London, must have gone far to ruin those who were then engaged in it; the general depression of Saxon men for a long time after would prevent them or others from reviving it; and the Normans themselves were averse from mercantile pursuits. In the half-century after the Conquest we really know little or nothing of the history of commerce. The charters of the first Norman kings make no mention of it. Stephen's troubled reign must have been very unfavourable to it. Still foreign merchants would seek a market where they could dispose of their goods, and the long and wise reign of Henry II. enabled English commerce, not only to recover, but to surpass its ancient prosperity. An interesting account of London, given by William FitzStephen, about 1174, in the introduction to a Life of à Becket, gives much information on our subject: he says that "no city in the world sent out its wealth and merchandise to so great a distance," but he does not enumerate the exports. Among the articles brought to London by foreign merchants he mentions gold, spices, and frankincense from Arabia; precious stones from Egypt; purple cloths from Bagdad; furs and ermines from Norway and Russia; arms from Scythia; and wines from France. The citizens he describes as distinguished above all others in England for the elegance of their manners and dress, and the magnificence of their tables. There were in the city and suburbs thirteen large conventual establishments and 120 parish churches. He adds that the dealers in the various sorts of commodities, and the labourers and artizans of every kind, were to be found every day stationed in their several distinct places throughout the city, and that a market was held every Friday in Smithfield for the sale of horses, cows, hogs, &c.; the citizens were distinguished from those of other towns by the appellation of barons; and Malmesbury, an author of the same age, also tells us that from their superior opulence, and the greatness of the city, they were considered as ranking with the chief people or nobility of the kingdom.

The great charter of King John provided that all merchants should have protection in going out of England and in coming back to it, as well as while residing in the kingdom or travelling about in it, without any impositions or payments such as to cause the destruction of their trade. During the thirteenth century, it seems probable that much of the foreign commerce of the country was carried on by foreign merchants, who imported chiefly articles of luxury, and carried back chiefly wool, hides, and leather, and the metals found in England. But there were various enactments to prevent foreign merchants from engaging in the domestic trade of the country. In the fourteenth century commerce received much attention from government, and many regulations were made in the endeavour to encourage it, or rather to secure as much of its profits as possible to English, and leave as little as possible to foreign, merchants. Our limits do not allow us to enter into details on the subject, and our plan aims only at giving broad outside views of the life of the merchants of the Middle Ages.

Let us introduce here an illustration of the ships in which the commerce was conducted. Perhaps the only illustration to be derived from the MS. illuminations of the thirteenth century is one in the Roll of St. Guthlac, which is early in the century, and gives a large and clear picture of St. Guthlac in a ship with a single mast and sail, steered by a paddle consisting of a pole with a short cross handle at the top, like the poles with which barges are still punted along, and expanding at bottom into a short spade-like blade. Some of the seals of this century also give rude representations of ships: one of H. de Neville gives a perfectly crescent-shaped hull with a single mast supported by two stays; that of Hugo de Burgh has a very high prow and stern, which reminds us of the build of modern *prahus*. Another, of the town of Monmouth, has a more artistic representation of a ship of similar shape, but the high prow and stern are both ornamented with animals' heads, like the prow of William the Conqueror's ship. The Psalter of Queen Mary, which is of early fourteenth-century date, gives an illustration of the building of Noah's ark, which is a ship of the shape found in the Bayeux tapestry, with a sort of house within it. The illustration we give opposite from the Add. MS. 3,983, f. 6, was also executed early in the fourteenth century, and though rude it is valuable as one of the earliest examples of a ship with a rudder of the modern construction; it also clearly indicates the fact that these early vessels used oars as well as sails. The usual mode of steering previous to, and for some time subsequent to, this time was with a large broad oar at the ship's counter, worked in a noose of rope (a *gummet*) or through a hole in a piece of wood attached to the vessel's side. The first mode will be found illustrated in the Add. MS. 24,189, at f. 30, and the second at f. 5 in the same MS. The men of this period were not insensible to the value of a means of propelling a vessel independently of the wind; and employed human

A Ship, Early Fourteenth Century.

muscle as their motive power. Some of the great trading cities of the Mediterranean used galleys worked by oars, not only for warfare, but for commercial purposes: *e.g.* in 1409 A.D., King Henry granted to the merchants of Venice permission to bring their carracks, galleys, and other vessels, laden with merchandise, to pass over to Flanders, return and sell

472 *The Merchants of the Middle Ages.*

their cargoes without impediment, and sail again with English merchandise and go back to their own country.

A very curious and interesting MS. (Add. 27,695) recently acquired by

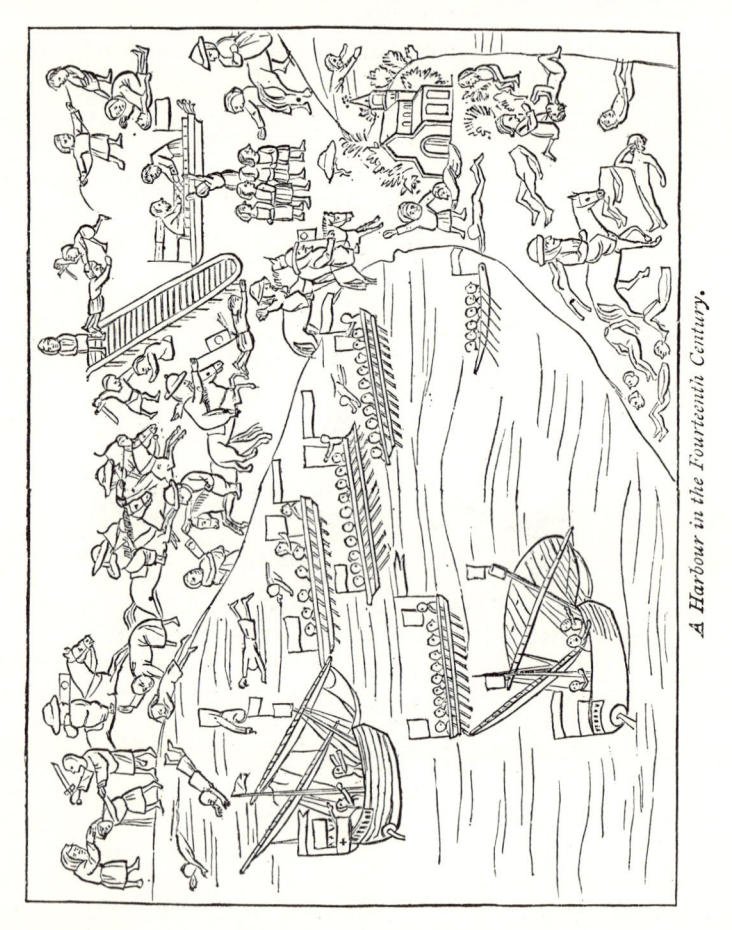

A Harbour in the Fourteenth Century.

the British Museum, which appears to be of Genoese Art, and of date about A.D. 1420, enables us to give a valuable illustration of our subject. It occupies the whole page of the MS.; we have only given the lower half, of the size of the original. It appears to represent the siege of Tripoli. The city is in the upper part of the page; our cut represents the harbour and a suburb of the town. It is clearly indicated that it is low water, and

An Early Representation of the Whale Fishery.

the high-water mark is shown in the drawing by a different colour. Moreover, a timber pier will be noticed, stretching out between high and low-water mark, and a boat left high and dry by the receding tide. In the harbour are ships of various kinds, and especially several of the galleys of which we have spoken. The war-galley may be found fully illustrated in Witsen's "Sheep's Bouw," p. 186.

The same MS., in the lower margin of folio 9 v., has an exceedingly interesting picture of a whaling scene, which we are very glad to introduce as a further illustration of the commerce and shipping of this early period. It will be seen that the whale has been killed, and the successful adventurers are "cutting out" the blubber very much after the modern fashion.

CHAPTER II.

THE MERCHANT NAVY.

THE history of the merchant navy in the Middle Ages is very much mixed up with that of the military navy.

In the time of the earlier Norman kings we seem not to have had any war-ships. The king had one or two ships for his own uses, and hired or impressed others when he needed them; but they were only ships of burden, transports by which soldiers and munitions of war were conveyed to the Continent and back, as occasion required. If hostile vessels encountered one another at sea, and a fight ensued, it seems to have been a very simple business: the sailors had nothing to do with the fighting, they only navigated the ships; the soldiers on board discharged their missiles at one another as the ships approached, and when the vessels were laid alongside, they fought hand to hand. The first ships of war were a revival of the classical war-galleys. We get the first clear description of them in the time of Richard I., from Vinesauf, the historian of the second Crusade. He compares them with the ancient galleys, and says the modern ones were long, low in the water, and slightly built, rarely had more than two banks of oars, and were armed with a "spear" at the prow for "ramming." Gallernes were a smaller kind of galleys with only one bank of oars.

From this reign the sovereign seems to have always maintained something approaching to a regular naval establishment, and to have aimed at keeping the command of the narrow seas. In the reign of John we find the king had galleys and galliases, and another kind of vessels which were probably also a sort of galley, called "long ships," used to guard the coasts, protect the ports, and maintain the police of the seas.

The accompanying drawing, from one of the illuminations in the

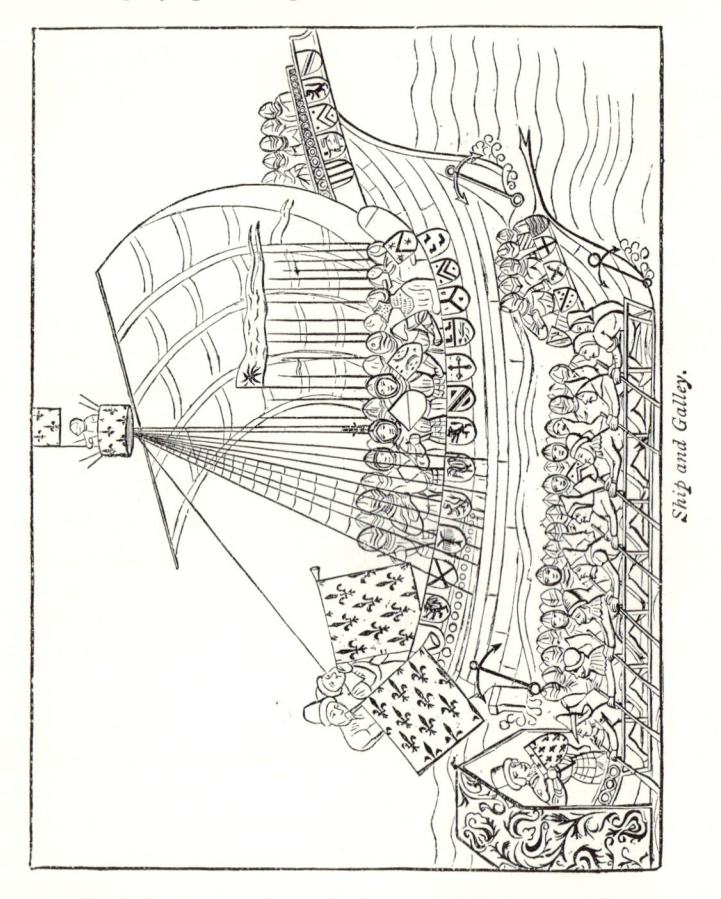

Ship and Galley.

famous MS. of Froissart's Chronicle, in the British Museum (Harl. 4,379), is perhaps one of the clearest and best contemporary illustrations we have of these mediæval galleys. It will be seen that it consists of a long low open boat, with outrigger galleries for the rowers, while the hold is left free for merchandise, or, as in the present instance, for men-at-arms. It has a forecastle like an ordinary ship; the shields of the men-at-arms who occupy it are hung over the bulwarks; the commander stands at the stern under a pent-house covered with tapestry, bearing his shield, and holding his leader's truncheon. A close examination of the drawing seems to show that there are two men to each oar; we know from other sources that several men were sometimes put to each oar. The difference in costume between the soldiers and the sailors is conspicuous. The former are men-at-arms in full armour—one on the forecastle is very distinctly shown; the sailors are entirely unarmed, except the man at the stroke-oar, probably an officer, who wears an ordinary hat of the period, the rest wear the hood drawn over the head. The ship in the same illustration is an ordinary ship of burden, filled with knights and men-at-arms; the trumpeters at the stern indicate that the commander of the fleet is on board this ship; he will be seen amidships, with his visor raised and his face towards the spectator, with shield on arm and truncheon in hand.

If the reader is curious to see illustrations of the details of a naval combat, there are a considerable number to be found in the illuminated MSS.; as in MS. Nero, D. iv., at folio 214, of the latter part of the thirteenth century; in some tolerably clearly drawn in the "Chronique de S. Denis" (Royal, 20, cvii.), of the time of our Richard II., at folio 18, and again at folio 189 v. Other representations of ships occur at folios 25, 26 v., 83, 136 v. (a bridge of boats), 189 v., and 214 of the same MS.

These ships continued to a late period to be small compared with our notion of a ship, and most rude in their arrangements. They were great undecked boats, with a cabin only in the bows, beneath the raised platform which formed the forecastle; and the crew of the largest ships was usually from twenty-five to thirty men. An illumination in the MS. of Froissart's Chronicle (Harl. 4,379), folio 104 v., shows a ship, in which a king and his suite are about to embark, from such a point of view that we see the interior of the ship in the perspective, and find that there is a cabin only in the prow. The earliest notice of cabins occurs in the year A.D. 1228, when a ship was sent to Gascony with some effects of the king's, and 4s. 6d. was paid for making a chamber in the same ship for the king's wardrobe, &c. In A.D. 1242 the king and queen went to

Ship of Richard Earl of Warwick.

Gascony; and convenient chambers were ordered to be built in the ship for their majesties' use, which were to be wainscoted—like that probably in Earl Richard of Warwick's ship in the present woodcut. This engraving, taken from Rouse's MS. Life of Richard Beauchamp, Earl of Warwick (British Museum, Julius, E. IV.), of the latter part of the fourteenth century, gives a very clear representation of a ship and its boat. The earl is setting out on his pilgrimage to the Holy Land. In the foreground we see him with his pilgrim's staff in hand, stepping into the boat which is to carry him to his ship lying at anchor in the harbour. The costume of the sailors is illustrated by the men in the boat. The vessel is a ship of burden, but such a one as kings and great personages had equipped for their own uses; resembling an ordinary merchant-ship in all essentials, but fitted and furnished with more than usual convenience and sumptuousness. In Earl Richard's ship the sail is emblazoned with his arms, and the pennon, besides the red cross of England, has his badges of the bear and ragged staff; the ragged staff also appears on the castle at the mast-head. The castle, which all ships of this age have at the stern, is in this case roofed in and handsomely ornamented, and no doubt formed the state apartment of the earl. There is also a castle at the head of the ship, though it is not very plainly shown in the drawing. It consists of a raised platform, the round-headed entrance to the cabin beneath it is seen in the picture; the two bulwarks also which protect it at the sides are visible, though their meaning is not at first sight obvious. A glance at the forecastle of the other ships in our illustrations will enable the reader to understand its construction and use. Besides the boat which is to convey the earl on board, another boat will be seen hanging at the ship's quarter.

The next woodcut is taken from the interesting MS. in the British Museum (Add. 24,189, f. 3 v.), from which we have borrowed other illustrations, containing pictures of subjects from the travels of Sir John Mandeville. We have introduced it to illustrate two peculiarities: the first is the way of steering by a paddle passed through a gummet of rope, still, we see, in use in the latter part of the fourteenth century, long after the rudder had been introduced; and the use of lee-boards to obviate the lee-way of the ship, and make it hold its course nearer to the wind. The high, small, raised castle in the stern is here empty, and the forecastle is curiously defended by a palisade, instead of the ordinary bulwarks.

480   *The Merchants of the Middle Ages.*

Another representation of the use of lee-boards occurs at folio 5 of the same MS.

But though the royal navy was small, as we have said, in case of need there was a further naval force available. The ancient ports of Kent and Sussex, called the Cinque Ports, with their members (twelve neighbouring ports incorporated with them), were bound by their tenure, upon forty days' notice, to supply the king with fifty-seven ships, containing twenty-

Sir J. Mandeville on his Voyage to Palestine.

one men and a boy in each ship, for fifteen days, once in the year, at their own expense, if their service was required. Thus *e.g.* a mandate of the 18th Rich. II., addressed to John de Beauchamp, Constable of Dover Castle, and Warden of the Cinque Ports, after reciting this obligation, requires fifty-seven ships, each having a master and twenty men well armed and arrayed to meet him at Bristol; stating further, that at the expiration of the fifteen days the ships and men should be at the king's own charges and pay, so long as he should have the use of them, viz., the master of each ship to have 6*d.*, the constable 6*d.*, and each of the other men 3*d.*, per day.

In the year A.D. 1205 we have a list of royal galleys and vessels of war ready for service; and it is instructive to see where they were stationed: there were at London 5, Newhaven 2, Sandwich 3, Romney 4, Rye 2, Winchelsea 2, Shoreham 5, Southampton 2, Exeter 2, Bristol 3, Ipswich 2, Dunwich 5, Lyme 5, Yarmouth 3, in Ireland 5, at Gloucester 1—total 51; and the Cinque Ports furnished 52; so that there were ready for sea more than 100 galleys or "men-of-war."

If the occasion required a greater force than that which the Cinque Ports were required to furnish, the king was at liberty to issue his royal mandate, and impress merchant ships.. Thus, in May, 1206 A.D., the Barons of the Cinque Ports were commanded to be at Portsmouth by a certain date with all the service they owed; and writs were also issued to all such merchants, masters, and seamen, as might meet the king's messengers on the sea, to repair to Portsmouth, and enter the king's service; and the royal galleys were sent to cruise at sea to arrest ships and send them in. Again, in A.D. 1442, the Commons in Parliament stated the necessity of having an armed force upon the sea, and pointed out the number of ships and men that it would be proper to employ: viz., eight ships with fore-stages carrying 150 men each, and that there should be attendant upon each ship a barge carrying eighty men, and a balynfer carrying forty men; and that four spynes, or pinnaces, carrying twenty-five men each, would be necessary. The Commons also pointed out the individual ships which it recommended to be obtained to compose this force: viz., at Bristol the *Nicholas of the Tower*, and *Katherine of Burtons;* at Dartmouth the Spanish ship that was the Lord Poyntz's, and Sir Philip Courtenay's great ship. In the port of London two great ships, one called *Trinity*, and the other *Thomas*. At Hull a great ship called Taverner's, the name *Grace-dieu.* At Newcastle a great ship called *The George.* They also state where the barges, balynfers, and pinnaces may be obtained. Some of these may have been royal ships, but not all of them. Of the

Grace-dieu of Hull, we know from Rymer (xi., 258) that John Taverner of Hull, mariner, having made a ship as large as a great carrack, or larger, had granted to him that the said ship, by reason of her unusual magnitude, should be named the *Grace-dieu* carrack, and enjoy certain privileges in trade.

On a great emergency, a still more sweeping impressment of the mercantile fleet was made : *e.g.*, Henry V., in his third year, directed Nicholas Manslyt, his sergeant-at-arms, to arrest all ships and vessels in every port in the kingdom, of the burden of twenty tons and upwards, for the king's service ; and Edward IV., in his fourteenth year, made a similar seizure of all ships of over sixteen tons burden. On the other hand, the king hired out his ships to merchants when they were not in use. Thus, in 1232 A.D., John Blancboilly had the custody of King Henry III.'s great ship called the *Queen*, for his life, to trade wherever he pleased, paying an annual rent of eighty marks ; and all his lands in England were charged with the fulfilment of the contract. In 1242 directions were given to surrender the custody of the king's galleys in Ireland to the sailors of Waterford, Drogheda, and Dungaroon, to trade with in what way they could, taking security for their rent and restoration.

The royal ships, however, maintained the police of the seas very inefficiently, and a *petite guerre* seems to have been carried on continually between the ships of different countries, and even between the ships of different seaports ; while downright piracy was not at all uncommon. When these injuries were inflicted by the ships of another nation, the injured men often sought redress through their own government from the government of the people who had injured them, and the mediæval governments generally took up warmly any such complaints. But the merchants not unfrequently took the law into their own hands. In the twelfth century, *e.g.*, it happened to a merchant of Berwick, Cnut by name, that one of his ships, having his wife on board, was seized by a piratical Earl of Orkney, and burnt. Cnut spent 100 marks in having fourteen stout vessels suitably equipped to go out and punish the offender. And so late as 1378 a sort of private naval war was carried on between John Mercer, a merchant of Perth, and John Philpott of London. Mercer's father had for some time given assistance to the French by harassing the merchant ships of England; and in 1377, being driven by foul weather on the Yorkshire coast, he was caught, and imprisoned in Scarborough Castle. Thereupon the son carried on the strife. Collecting a little fleet of Scottish, French, and Spanish ships, he captured several English merchantmen off Scarborough, slaying their commanders, putting their crews in chains, and appropriating their cargoes. Philpott, the mayor of London, at his own cost, collected a number of vessels, put in them 1,000 armed men, and sailed for the north. Within a few weeks he had retaken the captured vessels, had effectually beaten their captors, and, in his turn, had seized fifteen Spanish ships laden with wine, which came in his way. On his return to London he was summoned before the council to answer for his conduct in taking an armed force to sea without the king's leave. But he boldly told the council: "I did not expose myself, my money, and my men to the dangers of the sea that I might deprive you and your colleagues of your knightly fame, nor that I might win any for myself, but in pity for the misery of the people and the country, which from being a noble realm with dominion over other nations, has through your supineness become exposed to the ravages of the vilest race, and since you would not lift a hand in its defence, I exposed myself and my property for the safety and deliverance of our country."

The ships of the Cinque Ports seem to have been at frequent feud with those of the other ports of the kingdom (see Matthew Paris under A.D. 1242). For example, in 1321 Edward II. complained of the great dissension and discord which existed between the people of the privileged Cinque Ports and the men and mariners of the western towns of Poole, Weymouth, Melcombe, Lyme, Southampton, &c.; and of the homicide, depredation, ship-burning, and other evil acts resulting therefrom. But in place of taking vigorous measures to repress these disorders, the king did not apparently find himself able to do more than issue a proclamation against them.

When so loose a morality prevailed among seafaring men, and the police of the seas was so badly maintained, it follows almost as a matter of course that piracy should flourish. The people of Brittany, and especially the men of St. Malo, at one time were accustomed to roam the sea as the old sea-kings did, plundering merchant-ships, making descents on the coasts of England, exacting contributions and ransoms from the towns. In the time of Alfred it would seem by one of his laws as if English vessels sometimes pillaged their own coasts.*

About the year 1242 a Sir William de Marish, who was accused of murder and treason, took refuge in the Isle of Lundy, whence he robbed the merchantmen passing to and fro, and made descents on the coast. He was building a galley in which to carry on his piracies when he was taken and hanged.

The spirit that lingered to very recent times among the "wreckers" of remote spots on our coast seems to have prevailed largely in the days of which we are writing. A foreigner was regarded as a "natural enemy," and his ships and goods as a legitimate prize, when they could be seized with impunity. So in 1227 A.D. we find a mariner named Dennis committed to Newgate for being present when a Spanish ship was plundered and her crew slain at Sandwich. In the same year the inhabitants of some towns in Norfolk were accused of robbing a Norwegian ship. And, to give a later example, in 1470 some Spanish merchants applied to King Edward IV. for compensation for the loss of seven vessels, alleged to have been piratically taken from them by the people of Sandwich, Dartmouth, Plymouth, and Jersey. Yet there is a Saxon law as early as King Ethelred, which gives immunities to merchant ships, even in time of war, which the Council of Paris a few years ago hardly equalled:—"If a merchant ship, even if it belonged to an enemy, entered any port in England, she was to have 'frith,' that is peace, and freedom from molestation, provided it was not driven or chased into port; but even if it were chased, and it reached any frith burgh, and the crew escaped into the burgh, then the crew and whatever they brought with them were to have 'frith.'"

The shipping of the time of Henry VIII. is admirably illustrated in Holbein's famous painting at Hampton Court. The great vessel of his reign, the *Henri Grace à Dieu*, is also illustrated in the *Archæologia*. Both

---

* Sir Harris Nicholas' "History of the British Navy," vol. i. p. 21.

these subjects are so well-known, or so easily accessible, that we do not think it necessary to reproduce them here. In the MS. Aug. 1, will be found a large size drawing of a galley intended to be built for King Henry VIII.

The discovery of the sea-passage to India, and of the new world, opened up to commerce a new career of heroic adventure and the prospect of fabulous wealth. England was not backward in entering upon this course. In truth, although Sebastian Cabot was not an Englishman by birth, we claim the honour of his discoveries for England, inasmuch as he was resident among us, and was fitted out from Bristol, at the cost of English merchants, on his voyages of discovery. It was in this career—which was part discover, party conquest, part commerce—that our Hawkinses, and Drakes, and Frobishers, and Raleighs were trained. And besides those historic names, there were scores of men who fitted out ships and entered upon the roads these pioneers had opened up, and completed their discoveries, and created the commerce whose possibility they had indicated.

The limitation of our subject to the mediæval period forbids us to enter further upon this tempting theme. But we may complete our brief series of illustrations of merchant shipping by giving a picture of one of the gallant little ships—little, indeed, compared with the ships which are now employed in our great lines of sea-traffic—in which those heroes accomplished their daring voyages. The woodcut is a reproduction from the frontispiece of one of Hulsius' curious tracts on naval affairs, and represents the ship *Victoria*, in which Magellan sailed round the world, passing through the straits to which he gave his name. The epitaph that the author has subjoined to the engraving tells briefly the story of the famous ship :—

> "Prima ego velivolvis ambivi cursibus orbem
> Magellane novo te duce ducta freto.
> Ambivi meritoque dicor *Victoria :* Sunt mihi
> Vela, alæ, precium, gloria, pugna, mare."

The ship, it will be seen, is not very different in general features from those of the Middle Ages which we have been considering. It has the high prow and stern with their castles, it has shields outside the bulwarks, in imitation of the way in which, as we have seen in former illustrations,

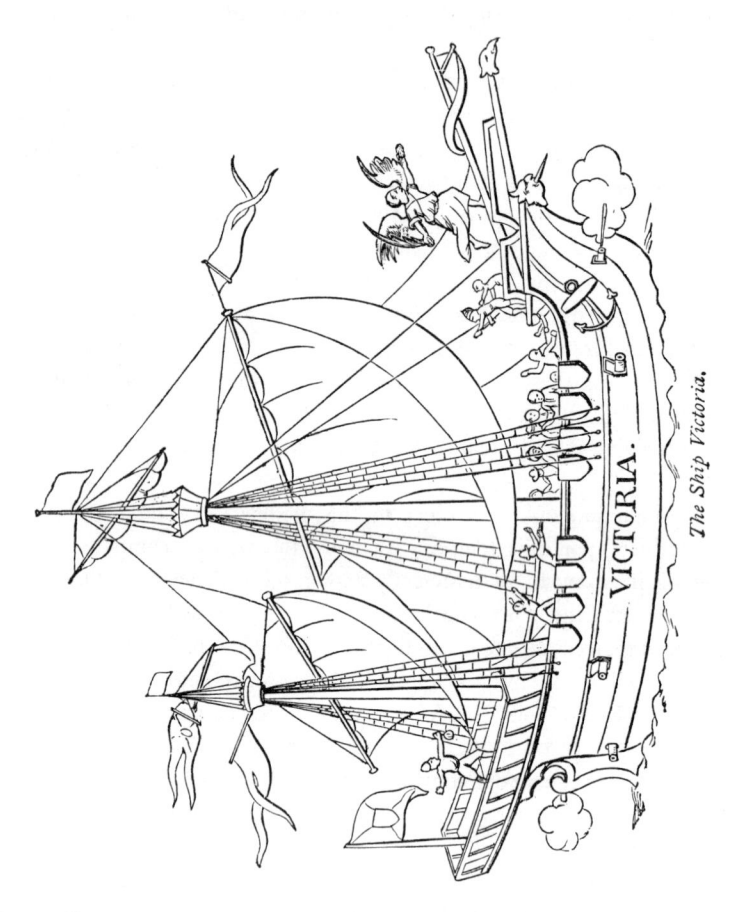

The Ship Victoria.

the mediæval men-at-arms hung their shields over the bulwark of the ship in which they sailed. But it has decks (apparently two), and is armed with cannon at the bows and stern.

CHAPTER III.

THE SOCIAL POSITION OF THE MEDIÆVAL MERCHANTS.

THOUGH the commerce of England has now attained to such vast dimensions, and forms so much larger a proportion of the national wealth and greatness than at any former period, yet we are inclined to think that, in the times of which we write, the pursuit of commerce held a higher and more honourable place in the esteem of all classes than it does with us.

It is true that one class was then more distinctly separated from another, by costume and some external habits of life; the knight and the franklin, the monk and the priest, the trader and the peasant, always carried the badges of their position upon them; and we, with our modern notions, are apt to think that the man who was marked out by his very costume as a trader must have been "looked down upon" by what we call the higher classes of society. No doubt something of this feeling existed; but not, we think, to the same extent as now. Trade itself was not then so meanly considered. Throughout the Middle Ages the upper classes were themselves engaged in trade in various ways. In the disposal of the produce of his estates the manorial lord engaged in trade, and purchased at fairs and markets the stores he needed for himself and his numerous dependants. Noblemen and bishops, abbots and convents, nay kings themselves, in the fourteenth and fifteenth centuries, had ships which, commanded and manned by their servants, traded for their profit with foreign countries. In the thirteenth century the Cistercian monks had become the greatest wool-merchants in the kingdom. In the fifteenth century Edward IV. carried on a considerable commerce for his own profit. Just as now, when noblemen and gentlemen commonly engage in agriculture, and thus farming comes to be considered less vulgar than trade, so, then, when dignified ecclesiastics, noblemen, and kings engaged in trade, it must have helped to soften caste prejudices against the professional pursuit of commerce.*

A considerable number of the traders of the fourteenth and fifteenth centuries were cadets of good families. Where there were half a dozen sons in a knightly family, the eldest succeeded to the family estate and honours: of the rest, one might become a lawyer; another might have a religious vocation, and, as a secular priest, take the family living, or obtain a stall in the choir of the neighbouring monastery; a third might prefer the profession of arms, and enter into the service of some great lord or of the king, or find employment for his sword and lance, and pay for himself and the dozen men who formed the " following of his lance," in the wars which seldom ceased in one part of Europe or another; another son might engage in trade, either in a neighbouring town or in one of the great commercial cities of the time, as Bristol, Norwich, or London.†

The leading men of the trading class stood side by side with the leading men of the other classes. They were consulted by the king on the affairs of the kingdom, were employed with bishops and nobles on foreign embassies, were themselves ennobled. And the greatness which men attain in any class reflects honour on the whole class. The Archbishop of Canterbury's high position gives social consideration to the poor curate, who may one day also be archbishop; and the Lord Chancellor's to the now briefless barrister who may attain to the woolsack. The great free

---

* In our own day we see the scorn of trade being rapidly softened down. Many of our commercial houses are almost as important as a department of State, and are conducted in much the same way. The principals of these houses are often considerable landholders besides, have been educated at the public schools and universities, and are frankly received as equals in all societies. On the other hand, the nobility are putting their younger sons into trade. At this moment, we believe, the brother-in-law of a princess of England is in a mercantile house.

† *Avarice*, in "Piers Ploughman's Vision," v. 255, says:—

"I have ymade many a knyht both mercer and draper
That payed nevere for his prentishode not a paire of gloves."

towns of the German Empire reflected honour on every town of Europe; and the merchant princes of Venice and Florence and the Low Countries on the humblest member of their calling.

But what, perhaps, more than anything else tended to maintain the social consideration of traders, was their incorporation into wealthy and powerful guilds; and the civil freedom and political weight of the towns. The rather common-looking man, in a plain cloth gown and flat cap, jogging along the high road on a hack, with great saddle-bags, is not to be compared in appearance with the knight who prances past him on a spirited charger, with a couple of armed servants at his heels; and the trader pulls his horse to the side of the road, and touches his bonnet as the cavalcade passes him in a cloud of dust; but the knight glances at his fellow-traveller's hood as he passes, and recognises in him a member of the great Guild of Merchants of the Staple, and returns his courtesy. The nobleman, jostling at court against a portly citizen in a furred gown with a short dagger and inkhorn at his belt, sees in him an alderman of one of those great towns by whose help the king maintains the balance of power against the feudal aristocracy. Yet, after all, why should the merchant be "a rather common-looking man," and the alderman a "portly citizen"? We are all apt to let our sober sense be fooled by our imagination. Thus we are apt to have in our minds abstract types of classes of men: our ideal knight is gallant in bearing, gay in apparel, chivalrous in character; while our ideal merchant is prosaic and closefisted in character, plain and uncourtly in manner and speech. A moment's thought would be enough to remind us that Nature does not anticipate or adapt herself to class distinctions: the knight and the merchant, we have seen, might be brothers, reared up in the same old manor-house; and the elder son might be naturally a clown, though fortune made him Sir Hugh; while the cadet might be full of intelligence and spirit, dignified and courteous, though fortune had put a flat cap instead of a helmet on his head, and a pen instead of a lance into his hand.

Our plan limits us to mere glances at the picturesque outside aspect of things. Let us travel across England, and see what we can learn on our subject from the experiences of our journey. A right pleasant journey, too, in the genial spring-time or early summer. It must be taken on horse-back; for, though sometimes we shall find ourselves on a highway between one great town and another, yet, for the most part, our road is along bridle-paths, across heath and moor; through miles of "greenwood;" across fords; over wide unenclosed wolds and downs dotted with sheep; through valleys where oxen feed in the deep meadow-land; with comparatively little arable, covered with the green blades of rye and barley, oats, and a little wheat—

> "Long fields of barley and of rye,
> That clothe the wold and meet the sky."

Now and then we ride through a village of cottages scattered about the village-green; and see, perhaps, the parish-priest, in cassock and biretta, coming out of the village-church from his mass. Further on we pass the moated manor-house of a country knight, or the substantial old timber-built house of a franklin, with the blue wood-smoke puffing in a volume out of the louvre of the hall, and curling away among the great oak-trees which overshadow it. We may stay there and ask for luncheon, and be sure of a hearty welcome: Chaucer tells us,

> "His table dormant in the hall alway
> Stands ready covered, all the longe day."

Then a strong castle comes in sight on a rising ground, with its picturesque group of walls and towers, and the donjon-tower rising high in the midst, surmounted by the banner of its lord. We seek out the monasteries for their hospitable shelter at nights: they are the inns of mediæval England; and we gaze in admiration as we approach them and enter their courts. From outside we see a great enclosure-wall, over which rise the clerestories and towers of a noble minster-church; and when we have entered through the gate-house we find the cloister court, with its convent buildings for the monks, and another court of offices, and the guest-house for the entertainment of travellers, and the abbot's-house—a separate establishment, with a great hall and chambers and chapel, like the manor-house of a noble; so that, surrounded by its wall, with strong entrance-towers, the monastery looks like a great castle or a little town; and we doff our hats to the dignified-looking monk who is ambling out of the great gate on his mule, as to the representative of the noble community which has erected so grand a house, and maintains there its hospitalities and charities, schools and hospitals, and offers up, seven times a day in the choir, a glorious service of praise to Almighty God, and of prayer for the welfare of His church and people. But from time to time, also, we approach and ride through the towns, which are studded as thickly over the land as castles or monasteries. Each surrounded by a fair margin of common meadow-land, out of which rise the long line of strong walls with angle towers, with picturesque machicolations and overhanging pent-houses; and the great gate-towers with moat, drawbridge, and barbican. Over the wall numerous church-towers and spires are seen rising from a forest of gables, making a goodly show. We enter, and find wide streets of handsome picturesque houses, with abundance of garden and orchard ground behind them, and guildhalls and chapels, the head-quarters of the various guilds and companies. The traders are wealthy, and indulge in conveniences which are rare in the franklin's house, and even the lord's castle; and live a more refined mode of life than the old rude, if magnificent, feudal life. Look at the extent of the town, at its strong defences; estimate the wealth it contains; think of the clannish spirit of its guilds; see the sturdy burghers, who turn out at the sound of the town-bell, in half armour, with pike and bow, to man the walls; consider the chiefs of the community, men of better education, wider experience of the world, deeper knowledge of political affairs, than most of their countrymen, many of them of the "gentleman" class by birth and breeding, men of perfect self-respect, and of high public spirit. If our journey terminates at one of the seaports, as Hull, or Lynn, or Dover, or Hythe, or Bristol, we find—in addition to the usual well-walled town, with houses and noble churches and guildhalls—a harbour full of merchant-ships, and exchanges full of foreign merchants; and we soon learn that these are the links which join England to the rest of the world in a period of peace, and enable her in time of war to make her power felt beyond the seas. Many of these towns have inherited their walls and their civic freedom from Roman times: they stood like islands amid the flood of the Saxon invasion; they received their charters from Norman kings, and maintained them against Norman barons. Each of them is a little republic amidst the surrounding feudalism; each citizen is a freeman, when everybody else is the sworn liege-man of some feudal lord.

These experiences of our ride across England will have left their strong impressions on our minds. The castles will have impressed our minds with a sense of the feudal power and chivalric state of the territorial class; and

Entry of Queen Isabel of Bavaria into Paris, A.D. 1389.

the monasteries with admiration of the grandeur and learning and munificence and sanctity of the religious orders; and the towns with a feeling of solid respect for the wealth and power and freedom and civilisation of the trader class of the people.

Our first illustration forms part of a large picture in the great Harleian MS. of Froissart's Chronicle (Harl. 2,397, f. 3), and represents Isabel of

Bavaria, Queen of Charles VII., making her entry into Paris attended by noble dames and lords of France, on Sunday, 20th of August, in the year of our Lord 1389. There was a great crowd of spectators, Froissart tells us, and the *bourgeois* of Paris, twelve hundred, all on horseback, were ranged in pairs on each side of the road, and clothed in a livery of gowns of baudekyn green and red. The Queen, seated in her canopied litter, occupies the middle of the picture, in robe and mantle of blue powdered with *fleur-de-lis*, three noblemen walking on each side in their robes and coronets. The page and ladies, who follow on horseback, are not given in our woodcut. The Queen has just arrived at the gate of the city; through the open door may be seen a bishop (? the Archbishop of Paris) in a cope of blue powdered with gold *fleur-de-lis*, holding a gold and jewelled box, which perhaps contains the chrism for her coronation. On the wall overlooking the entrance is the king with ladies of the court, and perched on the angle of the wall is the court jester in his cap and bauble. On the left of the picture are the burgesses of Paris; their short gowns are of green and red as described; the hats, which hang over their shoulders, are black. On the opposite side of the road (not represented in the cut) is another party of burgesses, who wear their hats, the bands falling on each side of the face. In the background are the towers and spires of the city, and the west front of Notre-Dame, rising picturesquely above the city-wall.

Some of the merchant-princes of the Middle Ages have left a name which is still known in history, or popular in legend. First, there is the De la Pole family, whose name is connected with the history of Hull. Wyke-upon-Hull was a little town belonging to the convent of Selby, when Edward III. saw its capabilities and bought it of the monks, called it Kingston-upon-Hull, and, by granting trading and civil privileges to it, induced merchants to settle there. De la Pole, a merchant of the neighbouring port of Ravensern, was one of the earliest of these immigrants; and Hull owes much of its greatness to his commercial genius and public spirit. Under his inspiration bricks were introduced from the Low Countries to build its walls and the great church: much of the latter yet remains. He rose to be esteemed the greatest merchant in England. Edward III. honoured him by visiting him at his house in Hull, and in time made him Chief Baron of his Exchequer, and a Knight Banneret. In the following reign we find him engaged, together with the most distinguished men in the kingdom, in affairs of state and foreign embassies. His son, who also began life as a merchant at Hull, was made by Richard II. Earl of Suffolk and Lord Chancellor. In the end a royal alliance raised the merchant's children to the height of power; and designs of a still more daring ambition at length brought about their headlong fall and ruin.

William Cannynges, of Bristol, was another of these great merchants. On his monument in the magnificent church of St. Mary Redcliffe, of which he was the founder, it is recorded that on one occasion Edward IV. seized shipping of his to the amount of 2,470 tons, which included ships of 400, 500, and even 900 tons.

Richard Whittington, the hero of the popular legend, was a London merchant, thrice Lord Mayor. He was not, however, of the humble origin stated by the legend, but a cadet of the landed family of Whittington, in Gloucestershire. What is the explanation of the story of his cat has not been satisfactorily made out by antiquaries. Munificence was one of the characteristics of these great merchants. De la Pole, we have seen, built the church at Hull; Cannynges founded one of the grandest parish churches yet remaining in all England; Whittington founded the College of the Holy Spirit and St. Mary, a charitable foundation which has long ceased to exist. Sir John Crosby was an alderman of London in the reign of Edward IV., and allied his family with the highest nobility. His house still remains in Bishopsgate, the only one left of the great city-merchants' houses: Stowe describes it as very large and beautiful, and the highest at that time in London. Richard III. took up his residence and received his adherents there, when preparing for his usurpation of the crown.

Monuments remaining to this day keep alive the memory of other great merchants, which would otherwise have perished. In the series of monumental brasses, several of the earliest and most sumptuous are memorials of merchants. There was an engraver of these monuments living in England in the middle of the fourteenth century, whose works in that style of art have not been subsequently surpassed: Gough calls him the "Cellini of the fourteenth century." He executed a grand effigy for Thomas Delamere, abbot of St. Alban's Abbey; and the same artist executed two designs, no less sumptuous and meritorious as works of art, for two merchants of the then flourishing town of Lynn, in Norfolk. One is to Adam de Walsokne, "formerly burgess of Lynn," who died in 1349 A.D., and Margaret his wife; it contains very artistically drawn effigies of the two persons commemorated, surmounted by an ornamental canopy on a diapered field. The other monumental brass represents Robert Braunche, A.D. 1364, and his two wives. A feature of peculiar interest in this design is a representation, running along the bottom, of an entertainment which Braunche, when mayor of Lynn, gave to King Edward III. There was still a third brass at Lynn, of similar character, of Robert Attelathe—now, alas! lost. Another monument, apparently by the same artist, exists at Newark, to the memory of Alan Fleming, a merchant, who died in 1361 A.D.

Hundreds of churches yet bear traces of the munificence of these mediæval traders. The noble churches which still exist in what are now comparatively small places, in Lincolnshire, Norfolk, and Suffolk, are monuments of the merchants of the staple who lived in those eastern counties; and monuments, and merchants' marks, and sometimes inscriptions cut in stone or worked in flint-work in the fabrics themselves, afford data from which the local antiquary may glean something of their history. Many interesting traces of mediæval traders' houses remain too in out-of-the-way places, where they seem quite overlooked. The little town of Coggeshall, for example, is full of interesting bits of domestic architecture—the traces of the houses of the "Peacockes" and other families, merchants of the staple and clothmakers, who made it a flourishing town in the fifteenth century; the monumental brasses of some of them remain in the fine perpendicular church, which they probably rebuilt. Or, to go to the other side of the kingdom, at the little town of Northleach, among the Cotswold Hills, is a grand church, with evidences in the sculpture and monuments that the wool-merchants there contributed largely to its building. It contains an interesting series of small monumental brasses, which preserve their names and costumes, and those of their wives and children; and the merchants' marks which were painted on their woolpacks appear here as honourable badges on their monuments. There are traces of their old houses in the town.

A general survey of all these historical facts and all these antiquarian remains will confirm the assertion with which we began this chapter, that at least from the early part of the fourteenth century downwards, the mediæval traders earned great wealth and spent it munificently, possessed considerable political influence, and occupied an honourable social position beside the military and ecclesiastical orders.

We must not omit to notice the illustrations which our subject may derive from Chaucer's ever-famous gallery of characters. Here is the merchant of the Canterbury cavalcade of merry pilgrims :—

> "A merchant was there with a forked beard,
> In mottély, and high on horse he sat,
> And on his head a Flaundrish beaver hat,
> His bote's clapsed fayre and fetisly,*
> His reasons spake he full solempnely,
> Sounding alway the increase of his winning,
> He would the sea were kept, for any thing,
> Betwixen Middleburgh and Orewell.
> Well could he in exchanges sheldes † sell,
> This worthy man full well his wit beset;
> There weste no wight that he was in debt,
> So steadfastly didde he his governance
> With his bargeines and with his chevisance,‡
> Forsooth he was a worthy man withal;
> But, sooth to say, I n'ot how men him call." §

Of the trader class our great author gives us also some examples :—

> "An haberdasher and a carpenter,
> A webber, a dyer, and a tapiser,
> Were all yclothed in one livery,
> Of a solempne and great fraternitie,
> Full fresh and new their gear y-piked was
> Their knives were ychaped, not with brass.
> But all with silver wrought full clene and well,
> Their girdles and their pouches every deal.

* Neatly, properly.   † Shields, *i.e. écus*, French crowns.
‡ Agreement for borrowing money.   § Know not his name.

> Well seemed each of them a fair burgess
> To sitten in a gild-hall on the dais.
> Each one for the wisdom that he can,
> Was likely for to be an alderman.
> For chattles hadden they enough and rent,
> And eke their wives would it well assent,
> And elles certainly they were to blame,
> It is full fair to be ycleped madame,
> And for to go to vigils all before,
> And have a mantle royally upbore."

The figures on the next page from a monument to John Field, Alderman of London, and his son, are interesting and characteristic. Mr. Waller, from whose work on monumental brasses the woodcut is taken, has been able to discover something of the history of Alderman Field. John Field, senior, was born about the beginning of the fifteenth century, but nothing is known of his early life. In 1449 he had clearly risen to commercial eminence in London, since he was in that year appointed one of fifteen commissioners to treat with those of the Duke of Burgundy concerning the commercial interests of the two countries in general, and specially to frame regulations for the traffic in wool and wool-fells brought to the staple at Calais. Of these commissioners five were of London, three of Boston, three of Hull, and one of Ipswich. These names, says Mr. Waller, probably comprise the chief mercantile wealth and intelligence in the eastern ports of the kingdom at this period. In 1454 he was made sheriff, and subsequently was elected alderman, but never served the office of mayor; which, says the writer, may be accounted for by the fact that in the latter part of his life he was afflicted with bodily sickness, and on that ground in 1463 obtained a grant from the then lord mayor, releasing him from all civic services. The alderman acquired large landed estates in Kent and Hertfordshire, in which he was succeeded by his eldest son John, the original of the second effigy, who only survived his father the short term of three years.

The brasses have been inlaid with colour; the alderman's gown of the father with red enamel, and its fur-lining indicated by white metal; the tabard of arms of the son is also coloured according to its proper heraldic blazoning—*gules*, between three eagles displayed *argent, guetté de sangue*, a fesse *or*. The unfinished inscription runs, "Here· lyeth John Feld, sometyme alderman of London, a merchant of the stapull of Caleys, the which deceased the xvj day of August, in the yere of our Lord God mcccclxxiiij. Also her' lyeth John his son, squire, yᵉ which deceased yᵉ iiij day of May yᵉ yere of" .... The monumental slab is ornamented

Monumental Brass of Alderman Field and his Son, A.D. 1474.

with four shields of arms: the first of the city of London, the second of the merchants of the staple, the third bears the alderman's merchant's-mark, and the fourth the arms which appear on the tabard of his son, the esquire, to whom, perhaps, they had been specially granted by the College of Arms. The father's costume is a long gown edged with fur, a leather girdle from which hang his gypcire (or purse) and rosary, over which is worn his alderman's gown. The son wears a full suit of armour of the time of Edward IV., with a tabard of his arms. The execution of the brass is unusually careful and excellent.

The third woodcut, from the Harleian MS. 4,379, f. 64, represents the execution, in Paris, of a famous captain of robbers, Aymerigol Macel.

An Execution in Paris.

The scaffold is enclosed by a hoarding; at the nearer corners are two friars, one in brown and one in black, probably a Franciscan and a Dominican; the official, who stands with his hands resting on his staff superintending the executioner, has a gown of red with sleeves lined with white fur, his bonnet is black turned up also with white fur. In the background are the timber houses on one side of the place, with the people looking out of their windows; a signboard will be seen standing forth from one of the houses. The groups of people in the distance and those in the foreground give the costumes of the ordinary dwellers in a fourteenth-century city. The man on the left has a pink short gown, trimmed with white fur; his hat, the two ends of a liripipe hanging over his shoulders, and his purse and his hose, are black. The man on his right has a long blue gown and red hat and liripipe; the man between them and a little in front, a brown long gown and black hat. The man on horseback on the left wears a very short green gown, red hose, and black hat; the footman on his left, a short green gown and red hat and liripipe; and the man on his left, a black jacket and black hat fringed. The man on horseback, with a foot-boy behind holding on by the horse's tail, has a pink long gown, black hat and liripipe, purse, and girdle; the one on the right of the picture, a long blue gown with red hat, liripipe, and purse. Just behind him (unhappily not included in the woodcut) is a touch of humour on the part of the artist. His foot-boy is stealing an apple out of the basket of an apple-woman, who wears a blue gown and red hood, with the liripipe tucked under her girdle; she has a basket of apples on each arm, and another on her head. Still further to the right is a horse whose rider has dismounted, and the foot-boy is sitting on the crupper behind the saddle holding the reins.

The last cut is taken from the painted glass at Tournay of the fifteenth century, and represents *marchands en gros*. This illustration of a warehouse with the merchant and his clerk, and the men and the casks and bales, and the great scales, in full tide of business, is curious and interesting.

Chaucer once more, in the "Shipman's Tale," gives us an illustration of our subject. Speaking of a merchant of St. Denys, he says:—

"Up into his countour house goth he,
To reken with himselvin, wel may be,
Of thilke yere how that it with him stood,
And how that he dispended had his good,
And if that he encreased were or non.
His bookes and his bagges many one
He layeth before him on his counting bord.
Ful riche was his tresor and his hord;

> For which ful fast his countour done he shet,
> And eke he n'olde no man shuld him let
> Of his accountes for the mene time;
> And thus he sat till it was passed prime."

Marchands en Gros, Fifteenth Century.

The counting-board was a board marked with squares, on which counters were placed in such a way as to facilitate arithmetical operations.

We have also a picture of him setting out on a business journey attended by his apprentice:—

"But so bifell this marchant on a day
Shope him to maken ready his array
Toward the town of Brugges for to fare
To byen there a portion of ware.
  * * * * *
The morrow came, and forth this marchant rideth
To Flaundersward, his prentis wel him gideth,
Til he came into Brugges merily.
Now goth this marchant fast and bisily
About his nede, and bieth and creanceth;
He neither playeth at the dis ne danceth,
But as a marchant shortly for to tell
He ledeth his lif, and ther I let him dwell."

CHAPTER IV.

MEDIÆVAL TRADE.

IT is difficult at first to believe it possible that the internal trade of mediæval England was carried on chiefly at great annual fairs for the wholesale business, at weekly markets for the chief towns, and by means of itinerant traders, of whom the modern pedlar is the degenerate representative, for the length and breadth of the country. In order to understand the possibility, we must recall to our minds how small comparatively was the population of the country. It was about two millions at the Norman Conquest, it had hardly increased to four millions by the end of the fifteenth century, it was only five millions in the time of William III. Nearly every one of our towns and villages then existed; but the London, and Bristol, and Norwich, and York of the fourteenth century; though they were relatively important places in the nation, were not one-tenth of the size of the towns into which they have grown. Manchester, and Leeds, and Liverpool, and a score of other towns, existed then, but they were mere villages; and the country population was thinly scattered over a half-reclaimed, unenclosed, pastoral country.

To begin with the fairs. The king exercised the sole power of granting the right to hold a fair. It was sought by corporations, monasteries, and manorial lords, in order that they might profit, first by the letting of ground to the traders who came to dispose of their wares, next by the tolls which were levied on all merchandise brought for sale, and on the sales themselves; and then indirectly by the convenience of getting a near market for the produce the neighbourhood had to sell, and for the goods it desired to buy.

504   *The Merchants of the Middle Ages.*

The annexed woodcut, from the MS. Add. 24,189, represents passengers paying toll on landing at a foreign port, and perhaps belongs in strictness to an earlier part of our subject. The reader will notice the

Passengers paying Toll.

picturesque custom-house officers, the landing-places, and the indications of town architecture. The next illustration, from painted glass at Tournay (from La Croix and Seré's "Moyen Age et la Renaissance") shows a group of people crossing the bridge into a town, and the collector levying the toll. The oxen and pigs, the country-wife on horseback, with a lamb laid over the front of her saddle, represent the country-people and their

Traders entering a Town.

farm-produce; the pack-horse and mule on the left, with their flat-capped attendant, are an interesting illustration of the itinerant trader bringing in his goods. The toll-collector seems to be, from his dress and bearing, a rather dignified official, and the countryman recognises it by touching his hat to him. The river and its wharves, and the boats moored alongside, and the indication of the town gates and houses, make up a very interesting sketch of mediæval life.

There were certain great fairs to which traders resorted from all parts of the country. The great fair at Nijni Novgorod, and in a lesser degree the fair of Leipsic, remain to help us to realise such gatherings as Bartholomew Fair used to be. Even now the great horse-fair at Horncastle, and the stock-fair at Barnet, may help us to understand how it answered the purpose of buyers and sellers to meet annually at one general rendezvous. The gathering into one centre of the whole stock on sale and the whole demand for it, was not only in other ways a convenience to buyers and sellers, but especially it regulated the general prices current of all vendibles, and checked the capricious variations which a fluctuating local supply and demand would have created in the then condition of the country and of commerce. The king sometimes, by capricious exercises of his authority in the subject of fairs, seriously interfered with the interests of those who frequented them—*e.g.* by granting license to hold a new fair which interfered with one already established; by licensing a temporary fair, and forbidding trade to be carried on elsewhere during its continuance. Thus in 1245 A.D. Henry II. proclaimed a fair at Westminster to be held for fifteen days, and required all the London traders to shut up their shops and bring their goods to the fair. It happened that the season was wet; few consequently came to the fair, and the traders' goods were injured by the rain which penetrated into their temporary tents and stalls. He repeated the attempt to benefit Westminster four years afterwards, with a similar result.

Of course when great crowds were gathered together for days in succession, and money was circulating abundantly, there would be others who would seek a profitable market besides the great dealers in woolfels and foreign produce. The sellers of ribbands and cakes would be there, purveyors of food and drink for the hungry and thirsty multitude, caterers for the amusement of the people, minstrels and jugglers, exhibitors of morality-plays and morrice-dancers, and still less reputable people. And so, besides the men who came for serious business, there would be a mob of pleasure-seekers also. The crowd of people of all ranks and classes from every part of the country, with the consequent variety of costume in material, fashion, and colour—the knight's helm and coat of mail, or embroidered *jupon* and plumed bonnet, the lady's furred gown and jewels, the merchant's sober suit of cloth, the minstrel's gay costume and the jester's motley, the monk's robe and cowl, and the peasant's smockfrock, continually in motion up and down the streets of the temporary canvas town, the music of the minstrels, the cries of the traders, the loud talk and laughter of the crowd —must have made up a picturesque scene, full of animation.

When the real business of the country had found other channels, the fairs still continued—and in many places still continue—as mere " pleasure-fairs ;" still the temporary stalls lining the streets, and the drinking-booths and shows, preserve something of the old usages and outward aspect, though, it must be confessed, they are dreary, desolate relics of what the mediæval fairs used to be. The fair was usually proclaimed by sound of trumpet, before which ceremony it was unlawful to begin traffic, or after the conclusion of the legal term for which the fair was granted. A court of *pie-poudre* held its sittings for the cognizance of offences committed in the fair. Many of our readers will remember the spirited description of such a fair in Sir Walter Scott's novel of " The Betrothed."

In the great towns were shops in which retail trade was daily carried on, but under very different conditions from those of modern times. The various trades seem to have been congregated together, and the trading parts of the town were more concentrated than is now the case ; in both respects resembling the bazaars of Eastern towns. Thus in London the tradesmen had shops in the Cheap, which resembled sheds, and many of them were simply stalls. But they did not limit themselves to their dealings there ; they travelled about the country also. The mercers dealt in toys, drugs, spices, and small wares generally; their stocks being of the same miscellaneous description as that of a village-shop of the present day. The station of the mercers of London was between Bow Church and Friday Street, and here round the old cross of Cheap they sold their goods at little standings or stalls, surrounded by those belonging to other trades. The trade of the modern grocer was preceded by that of the pepperer, which was often in the hands of Lombards and Italians, who dealt also in drugs and spices. The drapers were originally manufacturers of cloth; to drape meaning to make cloth. The trade of the fishmonger was divided into two branches, one of which dealt exclusively in dried fish, then a very common article of food. The goldsmiths had their shops in the street of Cheap; but fraudulent traders of their craft, and not members of their guild, set up shops in obscure lanes, where they sold goods of inferior metal. A list of the various trades and handicrafts will afford a general idea of the trade of the town. Before the 50th of Edward III. (1376 A.D.) the "mysteries" or trades of London, who elected the Common Council of the city, were thirty-two in number; but they were increased by an ordinance of that year to forty-eight, which were as follows:—grocers, masons, ironmongers, mercers, brewers, leather-dressers, drapers, fletchers, armourers, fishmongers, bakers, butchers, goldsmiths, skinners, cutlers, vintners, girdlers, spurriers, tailors, stainers, plumbers, saddlers, cloth-measurers, wax-chandlers, webbers, haberdashers, barbers, tapestry-weavers, braziers, painters, leather-sellers, salters, tanners, joiners, cappers, pouch-makers, pewterers, chandlers, hatters, woodmongers, fullers, smiths, pinners, curriers, horners.

As a specimen of a provincial town we may take Colchester. A detailed description of this town in the reign of Edward III. shows that it contained only 359 houses, some built of mud, others of timber. None of the houses had any but latticed windows. The town-hall was of stone, with handsome Norman doorway. It had also a royal castle, three or more religious houses—one a great and wealthy abbey—several churches, and was surrounded by the old Roman wall. The number of inhabitants was about three thousand. Yet Colchester was the capital of a large district of country, and there were only about nine towns in England of greater importance. In the year 1301 all the movable property of the town, including the furniture and clothing of the inhabitants, was estimated, for the purpose of a taxation, to be worth £518, and the details give us a curious picture of the times. The tools of a carpenter consisted of a broad axe, value 5*d*., another 3*d*., an adze 2*d*., a square 1*d*., a *noveyn* (probably a spokeshave) 1*d*., making the total value of his tools 1*s*. The tools and stock of a blacksmith were valued at only a few shillings, the highest being 12s. The stock-in-trade and household goods of a tanner were estimated at £9 17s. 10d. A mercer's stock was valued at £3, his household property at £2 9s. The trades carried on there were the twenty-nine following:— Baker, barber, blacksmith, bowyer, brewer, butcher, carpenter, carter, cobbler, cook, dyer, fisherman, fuller, furrier, girdler, glass-seller, glover, linen-draper, mercer and spice-seller, miller, mustard and vinegar seller, old clothes-seller, tailor, tanner, tiler, weaver,

A Goldsmith's Shop.

wood-cutter, and wool-comber. Our woodcut, from the MS. Add. 27,695, which has already supplied us with several valuable illustrations, represents a mediæval shop of a high class, probably a goldsmith's. The shopkeeper eagerly bargaining with his customer is easily recognised, the shopkeeper's clerk is making an entry of the transaction, and the customer's servant stands behind him, holding some of his purchases; flagons and cups and dishes seem to be the principal wares; heaps of money lie on the table, which is covered with a handsome tablecloth, and in the background are hung on a "perch," for sale, girdles, a hand-mirror, a cup, a purse, and sword.

Here, from " Le Pélerinage de la Vie Humaine," in the French National Library,* is another illustration of a mediæval shop. This is a mercer's, and the merceress describes her wares in the following lines:—

* From Mr. Wright's " Domestic Manners and Customs of the Middle Ages."

"Quod sche, 'Gene* I schal the telle
Mercerye I have to selle
In boystes,† soote oynementes,‡
Therewith to don allegementes §
To ffolkes which be not gladde,
But discorded and malade.
I have kyves, phylletys, callys,
At ffestes to hang upon walles;
Kombes no mo than nyne or ten,
Bothe for horse and eke ffor men;
Mirrours also, large and brode,
And ffor the syght wonder gode;
Off hem I have ffull greet plenté,
For ffolke that haven volunté
Byholde himselffe therynne.'"

In some provincial towns, as Nottingham, the names of several of the streets bear witness to an aggregation of traders of the same calling.

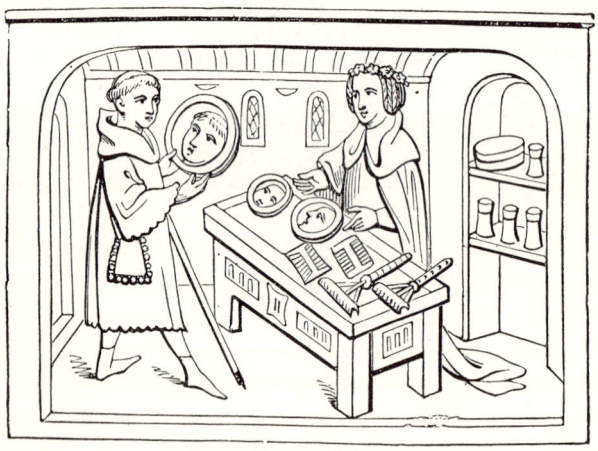

French National Library.

Bridlesmith Gate was clearly the street in which the knights and yeomen of the shire resorted for their horse-furniture and trappings, and in the open stalls of Fletcher Gate sheaves of arrows were hung up for sale to the green-coated foresters of neighbouring Sherwood. The only trace of

---

* If. † Boxes. ‡ Sweet ointments. § To give relief.

the custom we have left is in the butcheries and shambles which exist in many of our towns, where the butchers' stalls are still gathered together in one street or building.

But the greater part of the trade of the towns was transacted on market-days. Then the whole neighbourhood flocked in, the farmers to sell their farm produce, their wives and daughters with their poultry and butter and eggs for the week's consumption of the citizens, and to carry back with them their town-purchases. In every market-town there was usually a wide open space—the market-place—for the accommodation of this weekly traffic; in the principal towns were several market-places, appropriated to different kinds of produce: *e.g.* at Nottingham, besides the principal market-place—a vast open space in the middle of the town, surrounded by overhanging houses supported on pillars, making open colonnades like those of an Italian town—there was a "poultry" adjoining the great market, and a "butter-cross" in the middle of a small square, in which it is assumed the women displayed their butter. In an old-fashioned provincial market-town, the market-day is still the one day in the week on which the streets are full of bustle and the shops of business, while on the other days of the week the town stagnates; it must have been still more the case in the old times of which we write. In some instances there seems reason to think a weekly market was held in places which had hardly any claim to be called towns—mere villages, on whose green the neighbourhood assembled for the weekly market. Round the green, perhaps, a few stalls and booths were erected for the day; pedlars probably supplied the shop element; and artificers from neighbouring towns came in for the day, as in some of our villages now the saddler and the shoemaker and the watchmaker attend once a week to do the makings and mendings which are required. There are still to be seen in a few old-fashioned towns and remote country places market-crosses in the market-place or on the village-green. They usually consist of a tall cross of stone, round the lower part of whose shaft a penthouse of stone or wood has been erected to shelter the market-folks from rain and sun. There is such a cross at Salisbury; a good example of a village market-cross at Castle Combe, in Gloucestershire, one of wood at Shelford, in Cambridge-hire, and many others up and down the country, well worthy of being collected and illustrated by the antiquary before they are swept away. Our illustration, from the painted glass at Tournay, represents a market

A Market Scene.

scene, the women sitting on their low stools, with their baskets of goods displayed on the ground before them. The female on the left seems to be filling up her time by knitting; the woman on the right is paying her market dues to the collector, who, as in the cut on p. 505, is habited as a clerk. The background appears to represent a warehouse, where transactions of a larger kind are going on.

But the inhabitants of rural districts were not altogether dependent on a visit to the nearest market for their purchases. The pursuit of gain enlisted the services of numerous itinerant traders, who traversed the land in all directions, calling at castle and manor house, monastery, grange, and cottage; and by the tempting display of pretty objects, and the handy supply of little wants, brought into healthy circulation many a silver penny which would otherwise have jingled longer in the owner's *gypcire*, or rested in the hoard in the homely stocking-foot. An entry in that mine of curious information, the York Fabric Rolls, reveals an incident in the pedlar's mode of dealing. It is a presentation, that is, a complaint, made to the Archbishop by the churchwardens of the parish of Riccall, in Yorkshire, under the date 1519 A.D. They represent, in the dog-Latin of the time: "*Item, quod Calatharii (Anglice Pedlars), veniunt diebus festis in porticum ecclesiæ et ibidem vendunt mercimonium suum.*" That *Calatharii*—that is to say, Pedlars—come into the church-porch on feast-days, and there sell their merchandise. From another entry in the same records it seems that sometimes the chapmen congregated in such numbers that the gathering assumed the proportions of an irregular weekly market. Thus among the presentations in 1416, is one from St. Michael de Berefredo, St. Michael-le-Belfry, in the city of York, which states, "The parishioners say that a common market of vendibles is held in the churchyard on Sundays and holidays, and divers things and goods and rushes are exposed there for sale." The complaint is as early as the fourth century; for we find St. Basil mentioning as one abuse of the great church-festivals, that men kept markets at these times and places under colour of making better provision for the feasts which were kept thereat.

The presentation from Riccall carries us back into the old times, and enables us to realise a picturesque and curious incident in their primitive mode of life. A little consideration will enable us to see how such a practice arose, and how it could be tolerated by people who had at least so much respect for religion as to come to church on Sundays and holidays. When we call to mind the state of the country districts, half reclaimed, half covered with forest and marsh and common, traversed chiefly by footpaths and bridle-roads, we shall understand how isolated a life was led by the inhabitants of the country villages and hamlets, and farmhouses and out-lying cottages. It was only on Sundays and holidays that neighbours met together. On those days the goodman mounted one of his farm-horses, put his dame behind him on a pillion, and jogged through deep and miry ways to church, while the younger and poorer came sauntering along the footpaths. One may now stand in country churchyards on a Sunday afternoon, and watch the people coming in all directions, across the fields, under copse, and over common, climbing the rustic styles, crossing the rude bridge formed by a tree-trunk thrown over the sparkling trout-stream, till all the lines converge at the church porch. And one has felt that those paths—many of them ploughed up every year and made every year afresh by the feet of the wayfarer—are among the most venerable relics of ancient times. And here among the ancient laws of Wales is one which assures us that our conjecture is true : " Every habitation," it says, " ought to have two good paths (convenient right of road), one to its church, and one to its watering-place." Very pleasant in summer these church-paths to the young folks who saunter along them in couples or in groups, but very disagreeable in wet wintery weather, and difficult at all times to the old and infirm. Another presentation out of the York Fabric Rolls, gives us a contemporary picture of these church-paths, seen under a gloomy aspect : In A.D. 1472, the people of Haxley complain to the Archdeacon that they " inhabit so unresonablie fer from ther parisch cherche that the substaunce (majority) of the said inhabi-tauntes for impotensaye and feblenes, farrenes (farness=distance) of the way, and also for grete abundance of waters and perlouse passages at small brigges for peple in age and unweldye, between them and ther next parische cherche, they may not come with ese or in seasonable tyme at ther saide parische cherche as Cristen people should, and as they wold," and so they pray for leave and help for a chaplain of their own.

We must remember, too, that our ante-Reformation forefathers did not hold modern doctrines concerning the proper mode of observing Sundays and holydays. They observed them more in the way which makes us still call a day of leisure and recreation a "holiday;" they observed them all in much the same spirit as we still observe some of them, such as Christmas-day and Whitsuntide. When they had duly served God at *matins* and mass, they thought it no sin to spend the rest of the day in lawful occupations, and rather laudable than otherwise to spend it in innocent recreations. The Riccall presentation gives us a picture which, no doubt, might have been seen in many another country-place on a Sunday or saint-day. The pedlar lays down his pack in the church-porch —and we will charitably suppose assists at the service—and then after service he is ready to spread out his wares on the bench of the porch before the eyes of the assembled villagers and make his traffickings, ecclesiastical canons to the contrary notwithstanding, and so save himself many a weary journey along the devious ways by which his customers have to return in the evening to their scattered homes. The complaint of the churchwardens does not seem to be directed against the traffic so much as against its being conducted in the consecrated precincts. Let the pedlar transfer his wares to the steps of the village-cross, and probably no one would have complained; but then, though they who wanted anything might have sought him there, he would have lost the chance of catching the eye of those who did not want anything, and tempting them to want and buy—a course for which we must not blame our pedlar too much, since we are told it is the essence of commerce, on a large as on a small scale, to create artificial wants and supply them.

In the late thirteenth-century MS. Royal, 10 Ed. IV., are some illuminations of a mediæval story, which afford us very curious illustrations of a pedlar and his pack. At f. 149, the pedlar is asleep under a tree, and monkeys are stealing his pack, which is a large bundle, bound across and across with rope, with a red strap attached to the rope by which it is slung over the shoulder. On the next page the monkeys have opened the wrapper, showing that it covered a kind of box, and the mischievous creatures are running off with the contents, among which we can distinguish a shirt and some circular mirrors. On f. 150, the monkeys have conveyed their spoil up into the tree, and we make out a purse and belt, a musical pipe, a belt and dagger, a pair of slippers, a hood and gloves, and a mirror. On the

Pack-horses.

next page, a continuation of the same subject, we see a pair of gloves, a man's hat, a woman's head-kerchief; and again, on p. 151, we have, in addition, hose, a mirror, a woman's head-dress, and a man's hood. These curious illuminations sufficiently indicate the usual contents of a pedlar's pack.

In the Egerton MS., 1,070, of the fourteenth century, at f. 380, is a reresentation of the flight into Egypt, in which Joseph is represented carrying a round pack by a stick over the shoulder, which probably illustrates the usual mode of carrying a pack or a pedestrian's personal luggage. Other illustrations of the pedlar of the latter part of the fifteenth and sixteenth centuries will be found in the series of the Dance of Death.

A former illustration has shown us a pack-horse and mule, the means by which those itinerant traders chiefly carried their merchandise over the country. But some kinds of goods would not bear packing into ordinary bundles of the kind there shown; for such goods, boxes or trunks, slung on each side of a pack-saddle, were used. We are able to give an illustration of them from an ancient tapestry figured in the fine work on "Anciennes Tapisseries" by Achille Jubinal. It is only a minor incident in the background of the picture, but is represented with sufficient clearness. Another mode of carrying personal baggage is represented in the fifteenth-century MS. Royal, 15 E. V., where a gentleman travelling on horseback is followed by two servants, each with a large roll of baggage strapped to the croupe of his saddle. The use of pack-horses has not even yet (or had not a few years ago) utterly died out of England. The writer saw a string of them in the Peak of Derbyshire, employed in carrying ore from the mines. The occasional occurrence of the pack-horse as the sign of a roadside inn also helps to keep alive the remembrance of this primitive form of "luggage-train." Many of our readers may have travelled with a valise at their saddle-bow and a cloak strapped to the croupe; the fashion, even now, is not quite out of date.

CHAPTER V.

COSTUME.

WE have, in a former chapter, given some pictures from illuminated MSS., in illustration of the costume and personal appearance of the merchants of the Middle Ages; but they are on such a scale as not to give much characteristic portraiture—except in the example of the bourgeoise of Paris, in the illumination from Froissart, on page 492—and they inadequately represent the minute details of costume. We shall endeavour in this chapter to bring our men more vividly before the eye of the reader in dress and feature.

The "Catalogus Benefactorum" of St. Alban's Abbey, to which we have been so often indebted, will again help us with some pictures of unusual character. They are of the fourteenth century, and illustrate people of the burgess class who were donors to the abbey; the peculiarity of the representation is, that they are half-length portraits on an unusually large scale for MS. illuminations. When we call them portraits, we do not mean absolutely to assert that the originals sat for their pictures, and that the artist tried to make as accurate a portrait as he could; but it is probable that the donations were recorded and the pictures executed soon after the gifts were made, therefore, presumedly, in the lifetime of the donors. It is, moreover, probable that the artist was resident in the monastery or in the dependent town, and was, consequently, acquainted with the personal appearance of his originals; and in that case, even if the artist had not his subjects actually before his eyes at the time he painted these memorials, it is likely that he would, at least from recollection, give a general *vraisemblance* to his portrait. The faces are very dissimilar, and all have a characteristic expression, which confirms us in the idea that they are not mere conventional portraits.

They seem to be chiefly tradespeople rather than merchants of the higher class, and of the latter half of the fourteenth century. Here, for example, are William Cheupaign and his wife Johanna, who gave to the Abbey-church two tenements in the Halliwelle Street. One of the tenements is represented in the picture, a single-storied house of timber, thatched, with a carved stag's head as a finial to its gable. This William also gave, for the adornment of the church, several frontals, with gold, roses embroidered on a black ground; also he gave a belt to make a *morse* (fastening or brooch) for the principal copes, with a figure of a swan in the *morse*, beautifully made of goldsmith's work; also he gave to the refectory a wooden drinking-bowl or cup, handsomely ornamented with silver, with a cover of the same wood. He wears a green hood lined with red; his wife is habited in a white hood.

William and Johanna Cheupaign.

The next picture represents Johanna de Warn, who also gave what is described as a well-built house, with a louvre, in St. Alban's town. This house, again, is of timber, with traceried windows, an arched doorway with ornamental hinges to the door, and an unusually large and handsome louvre. This louvre was doubtless in the roof of the hall, and probably over a fire-hearth in the middle of the hall, such as that which still exists in the fourteenth-century

Johanna de Warn.

hall at Pevensey, Kent. The lady's face is strong corroboration of the theory that these are portraits.

Next is the portrait of a man in a robe, fastened in front with great buttons, and a hood drawn round a strongly marked face, reminding us altogether of the portraits of Dante.

A Gentleman in Civilian Dress.

The last which we take from this curious series is the picture of William de Langley, who gave to the monastery a well-built house in Dagnale Street, in the town of St. Alban's, for which the monastery received sixty shillings per annum, which Geoffrey Stukeley held at the time of writing. William de Langley is a man of regular features, partly bald, with pointed beard and moustache, the kind of face that might so easily have been merely conventional, but which has really much individuality of expression. The house—his benefaction—represented beside him, is a two-storied house; three of the square compartments just under the eaves are seen, by the colouring of the illumination, to be windows; it is timber-built and tiled, and the upper story overhangs the lower. The gable is finished with a weather-vane, which, in the original, is carried beyond the limits of the picture. The dots in the empty spaces of all these pictures are the diapering of the coloured background.

William de Langley.

But curious as these early portraits are, and interesting for their character and for their costume, as far as they go, they still fail to give us complete illustrations of the dresses of the people. For these we shall have to resort to a class of illustrations which we have hitherto, for the most part, avoided—that of monumental brasses. Now we recur to them because they give us what we want—the *minutiæ* of costume—in far higher perfection than we can find it elsewhere. Again, instead of selecting one from one part of the country and another from another, we have thought that it would add interest to the series of illustrations to take as many as possible from one church, whose grave-stones happen to furnish us with a continuous series at short intervals of the effigies of the men who once inhabited the old houses of the town of Northleach, in Gloucestershire. This series, however, does not go back so far as the earliest extant monumental brass of a merchant; we therefore take a first example from another source. We have already mentioned the three grand effigies of Robert Braunche and Adam Walsokne of Lynne, and Alan Fleming of Newark; we select from them the effigy of Robert Braunche, merchant of Lynn, of date 1367 A.D. We have taken his single figure out of the grand composition which forms, perhaps, the finest monumental brass in existence. The costume is elegantly simple. A tunic reaches to the ankle, with a narrow line of embroidery at the edges; the sleeves do not reach to the elbow, but fall in two hanging lappets, while the arm is seen to be covered by the tight sleeves of an under garment, ornamented rather than fastened by a close row of buttons from the elbow to the wrist. Over the tunic is a hood, which covers the upper part of the person, while the head part falls behind. The hood in this example fits so tightly to the figure that the reader might, perhaps, think it doubtful whether it is really a second garment over the tunic; but in the contemporary and very similar effigy of Adam de Walsokne, it is quite clear that it is a hood. The plain leather shoes laced across the instep will also be noticed. If the reader should happen to compare this woodcut with the engraving of the same figure in Boutell's "Monumental Brasses," he will, perhaps, be perplexed by finding that the head here given is different from that which he will find there. We beg to assure him that our woodcut is correct. Mr. Boutell's artist, by some curious error, has given to his drawing of Braunche the head of Alan Fleming of Newark; and to Fleming he has given Braunche's head.

We feel quite sure that every one of artistic feeling will be thankful for

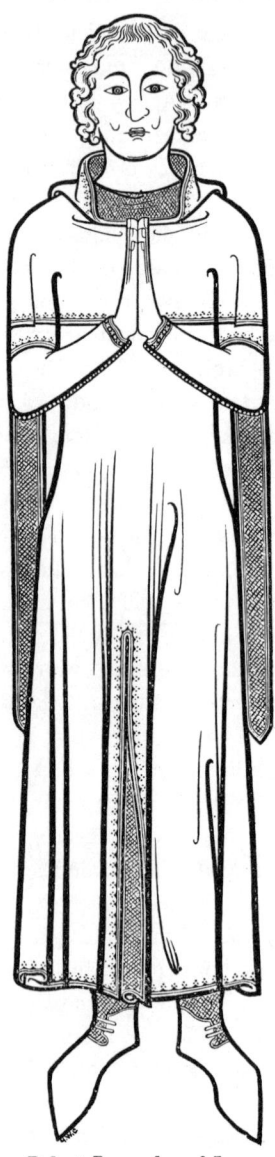

Robert Braunche, of Lynn.   Wool Merchant from Northleach Church.

being made acquainted with the accompanying effigy of a merchant of Northleach, whose inscription is lost, and his name, therefore, unknown. The brass is of the highest merit as a work of art, and has been very carefully and accurately engraved, and is worthy of minute examination. The costume, which is of about the year 1400 A.D., it will be seen, consists of a long robe buttoned down the front, girded with a highly-ornamented belt; the enlarged plate at the end of the strap is ornamented with a T, probably the initial of the wearer's Christian name. By his side hangs the *anlace*, or dagger, which was worn by all men of the middle class who did not wear a sword, even by the secular clergy. Over all is a cloak, which opens at the right side, so as to give as much freedom as possible to the right arm, and to this cloak is attached a hood, which falls over the shoulders. The hands are covered with half gloves. The wool-pack at his feet shows his trade of wool-merchant. Over the effigy is an elegant canopy, which it is not necessary for our purpose to give, but it adds very much to the beauty and sumptuousness of the monument.

Next in the series is John Fortey, A.D. 1458, whose costume is not so elegant as that of the last figure, but it is as distinctly represented. The tunic is essentially the same, but shorter, reaching only to the mid-leg; with sleeves of a peculiar shape which, we know from other contemporary monuments, was fashionable at that date. It is fastened with a girdle, though a less ornamental one than that of the preceding figure, and is lined and trimmed at the wrists with fur. Very similar

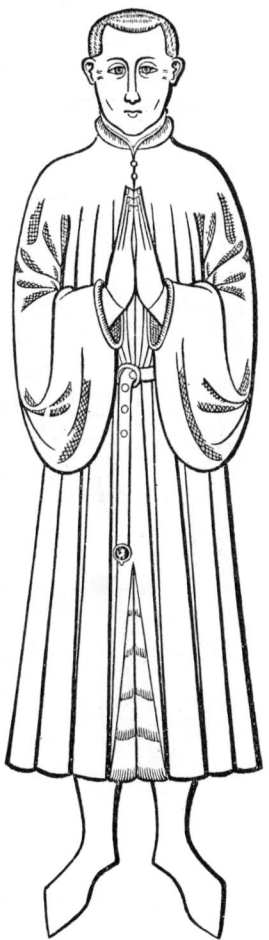

John Fortey, from Northleach Church.

figures of Hugo Bostock and his wife, in Wheathamstead Church, Herts, are of date 1435; these latter effigies are specially interesting as the parents of John de Wheathamstede, the thirty-third abbot of St. Alban's.

The next is an interesting figure, though far inferior in artistic merit and beauty to those which have gone before. The name here again is lost, but a fragment remaining of the inscription gives the date MCCCC.,

Wool Merchants from Northleach Church.

with a blank for the completion of the date; the same is the case with the date of his wife's death, so that both effigies may have been executed in the lifetime of the persons. The date is probably a little later than 1400. The face is so different from the previous ones that it may not be unnecessary to say that great pains have been taken to make it an accurate copy of the original, and it has been drawn and engraved by the same hand as the others. The manifest endeavour to indicate that the deceased was an elderly man, induces us to suspect that some of its peculiarity may arise from its being not a mere conventional brass, such as the monumental brass artists doubtless "kept to order," but one specially executed with a desire to make it more nearly resemble the features of the deceased. If, as we have conjectured, it was executed in his lifetime, this, perhaps, may account for its differing from the conventional type. His dress is the gown worn by civilians at the period, with a *gypcire*, or purse, hung at one side of his girdle, and his rosary at the other.

Lastly, we give the effigy of another nameless wool-merchant of Northleach, who is habited in a gown of rather stiffer material than the robes of his predecessors, trimmed with fur at the neck and feet and wrists. The inscription recording his name and date of death is lost, but a curious epitaph, also engraved on the brass, remains, as follows:—

> "Farewell my frends, the tyde abideth no man,
> I am departed from hence, and so shall ye;
> But in this passage the best songe that I can
> Is requiem eternam. Now then graunte it me,
> When I have ended all myn adversitie,
> Graunte me in Puradise to have a mansion,
> That shed thy blode for my redemption."

The mention of fur in these effigies suggests the restrictions in this matter imposed by the sumptuary laws by which the king and his advisers sought from time to time to restrain the extravagance of the lieges. By the most important of these acts, passed in 1362, the Lord Mayor of London and his wife were respectively allowed to wear the array of knights bachelors and their wives; the aldermen and recorder of London, and the mayors of other cities and towns, that of esquires and gentlemen having property to the yearly value of £40. No man having less than this, or his wife or daughter, shall wear any fur of martrons (martin's?) letuse, pure grey, or pure miniver. Merchants, citizens, and burgesses, artificers and people of handicraft, as well within the City of London as elsewhere, having goods and chattels of the clear value of £500, are allowed to dress like esquires and gentlemen of £100 a year; and those possessing property to the amount of £1,000, like landed proprietors of £200 a year.

There are some further features in these monumental brasses worth notice. Knightly effigies often have represented at their feet lions, the symbols of their martial courage. Some of our wool-merchants have a sheep at their feet, as the symbol of their calling: one is given in the woodcut accompanying. In another, in the same church, the merchant has one foot on a sheep and the other on a wool-pack; here the two significant symbols are combined—the sheep stands on the wool-pack. In both examples the wool-pack has a mark upon it; in the former case it is something like the usual "merchant's mark," in the latter it is two shepherds' crooks, which seem to be his badge, for another crook is laid beside the wool-pack. At the feet of the effigy of John Fortey, p. 523, is also his merchant's mark enclosed in an elegant wreath, here represented.

The initials I and F are the initials of his name; the remainder of the device is his trade-mark. We give two other merchants' marks of the two last of our series of effigies. If the reader cares to see other examples of these marks, and to learn all the little that is known about them, he may refer to a paper by Mr. Ewing, in vol. iii. of "Norfolk Archæology."

We have in a former chapter (p. 498) given from his monumental brass a figure of Alderman Field, of the date 1574, habited in a tunic edged with fur, girded at the waist, with a *gypcire* and rosary at the girdle, and over all an alderman's gown. In St. Paul's Church, Bedford, is another brass of Sir William Harper, Knight, Alderman, and Lord Mayor of London,* who died in A.D. 1573; he wears a suit of armour of that date, with an alderman's robe forming a drapery about the figure, but thrown back so as to conceal as little of the figure as possible. In the Abbey Church at Shrewsbury is an effigy of a mayor of that town in armour, with a mayor's gown of still more modern shape. The brasses of Sir M. Rowe, Lord Mayor of London, 1567, and Sir H. Rowe, Lord Mayor 1607, both kneeling figures, formerly in Hackney Church, are engraved in Robinson's history of that parish. And in many of the churches in and about London, and other of the great commercial towns of the Middle Ages, monumental effigies exist, with which, were it necessary, we might extend these notes of illustrations of civic costume.

In further explanation of civil costume from MSS. illuminations we refer the artist to the Harleian "Romance of the Rose" (Harl. 4,425, f. 47), where he will find a beautiful drawing, in which appears a man in a long blue gown, open a little at the breast and showing a pink under-robe, a black hat, and a liripipe of the kind already given in the citizens of Paris p. 54; he wears his purse by his side, and is presenting money to a beggar. At f. 98 is another in similar costume, with a "penner" at his belt in addition to his purse. There is nothing to prove that these men are merchants, except that they are represented in the streets of a town, and that their costume is such as was worn by merchants of the time.

With these costumes of civilians before our eyes we wish to use them in illustration of a subject which was touched upon in a former section of this work, viz., the Secular Clergy of the Middle Ages. We there devoted some pages to a discussion of the ordinary every-day costume of the clergy, and stated that there was no professional peculiarity

---

* Engraved in Fisher's Bedfordshire Collections, and in the London and Middlesex Archæological Society's Proceedings for 1870, p. 66.

about it, but that it was in shape like that worn by contemporary civilians of the better class, and in colour blue and red and other colours, but seldom black. If the reader will turn back to pp. 244, 245, and 246, he will find some woodcuts of the clergy in ordinary costume; let him compare them now with these costumes of merchants. For example, take the woodcut of Roger the Chaplain, on p. 245, and compare it with the brass from Northleach, p. 522. The style of art is very different, but in spite of this the resemblance in costume will be readily seen; the gown reaching to the ankle, and over it the cloak fastened with three buttons at the right shoulder, with the hood falling back over the shoulders; the half-gloves are the same in both, and the shoes with their latchet over the instep. Then turn to the priest on p. 246, and it will be seen that he wears the gown girded at the waist, with a purse hung at the girdle, and the flat cap with long liripipe, which we have described in the costumes of these merchants. Lastly, let the reader look at these brasses of wool-staplers, and compare the gown they wore with the cassock now adopted by the clergy, and it will be seen that they are identical—*i.e.* the clergy continue to wear the gown which all civilians wore three or four hundred years ago; and in the same manner the academic gown which the clergy wear, in common with all university men, is only the gown which all respectable citizens wore in the time of Henry VIII. and Elizabeth.

CHAPTER VI.

MEDIÆVAL TOWNS.

MEDIÆVAL towns in England had one of four origins; some were those of ancient Roman foundation, which had lived through the Saxon invasion, like Lincoln, Chester, and Colchester. Others again grew up gradually in the neighbourhood of a monastery. The monastery was founded in a wilderness, but it had a number of artisans employed about it; travellers resorted to its *hospitium* as to an inn; it was perhaps a place of pilgrimage; the affairs of the Lord Abbot, and the business of the large estates of the convent, brought people constantly thither; and so gradually a town grew up, as at St. Alban's, St. Edmundsbury, &c. In other cases it was not a religious house, but a castle of some powerful and wealthy lord, which drew a population together under the shelter of its walls—as at Norwich, where the lines of the old streets follow the line of the castle-moat; or Ludlow, on the other side of the kingdom, which gathered round the Norman Castle of Ludlow. But there is a third category of mediæval towns which did not descend from ancient times, or grow by accidental accretion in course of time, but were deliberately founded and built in the mediæval period for specific purposes; and in these we have a special interest from our present point of view.

There was a period, beginning in the latter part of the eleventh and extending to the close of the fourteenth century, when kings and feudal lords, from motives of high policy, fostered trade with anxious care; encouraged traders with countenance, protection, and grants of privileges; and founded commercial towns, and gave them charters which made them little independent, self-governing republics, in the midst of the feudal lords and ecclesiastical communities which surrounded them.

In England we do not find so many of these newly founded towns as on the Continent; here towns were already scattered abundantly over the land, and what was needed was to foster their growth; but our English kings founded such towns in their continental dominions. Edward I. planted numerous free towns, especially in Guienne and Aquitaine, in order to raise up a power in his own interest antagonistic to that of the feudal lords. Other continental sovereigns did the same, *e.g.* Alphonse of Poitiers, the brother of St. Louis, in his dominion of Toulouse. But in England we have a few such cases. The history of the foundation of Hull will afford us an example. When Edward I. was returning from Scotland after the battle of Dunbar, he visited Lord Wakes of Barnard Castle. While hunting one day, he was led by the chase to the hamlet of Wyke-upon-Hull, belonging to the convent of Meaux. The king perceived at once the capabilities of the site for a fortress for the security of the kingdom, and a port for the extension of commerce. He left the hunt to take its course, questioned the shepherds who were on the spot about the depth of the river, the height to which the tides rose, the owner of the place, and the like. He sent for the Abbot of Meaux, and exchanged with him other lands for Wyke. Then he issued a proclamation offering freedom and great commercial privileges to all merchants who would build and inhabit there. He erected there a manor-house for himself; incorporated the town as a free borough in 1299 A.D.; by 1312 the great church was built; by 1322 the town was fortified with a wall and towers; and the king visited it from time to time on his journeys to the north. The family of De la Pole, who settled there from the first, ably seconded the king's intentions. Kingston-upon-Hull became one of the great commercial towns of the kingdom. The De la Poles rose rapidly to wealth and the highest rank. Michael de la Pole "builded a goodly-house of brick, against the west end of St. Mary's Church, like a palace, with a goodly orchard and garden at large, enclosed with brick. He builded also three houses in the town besides, whereof every one hath a tower of brick." Leland the antiquary, of the time of Queen Elizabeth, has left us a description and bird's-eye plan of the town in his day, which is highly interesting. Of our English towns, those which are of Roman origin were laid out at first on a comprehensive plan, and they have the principal streets tolerably straight, and

View of Jerusalem.

crossing at right angles. The great majority of the towns which grew as above described are exceedingly irregular; but this irregularity, so important an element in the picturesqueness of mediæval towns, is quite an accidental one. When the mediæval builders laid out a town *de novo*, they did it in the most methodical manner; laying out the streets wide, straight, at equal distances, and crossing rectangularly; appropriating proper sites for churches, town-halls, and other public purposes, and regulating the size and plan of the houses. It is to the continental towns we must especially look for examples; but we find when Edward I. was building his free towns there, he sent for Englishmen to lay them out for him. A similar opportunity oc-

The Canterbury Pilgrims.

curred at Winchelsea, where the same plan was pursued. The old town of Winchelsea was destroyed by the sea in 1287, and the king determined to rebuild this cinque-port. The chief owners of the new site were a knight, Sir J. Tregoz, one Maurice, and the owners of Battle Abbey. The king compounded with them for their rights over seventy acres of land, and sent down the Bishop of Ely, who was Lord Treasurer, to lay out the new town. The monarch accorded the usual privileges to settlers, and gave help towards the fortifications. The town was laid out in streets which divided the area into rectangular blocks; two blocks were set apart for churches, and there were two colleges of friars within the town. Somehow the place did not flourish; it was harried by incursions of the French before the fortifications were completed, people were not attracted to it, the whole area was never taken up, and it continues to this day shrunk up into one corner of its walled area. Three of the old gates, and part of the walls, and portions of three or four houses, are all that remain of King Edward's town.

The woodcut on the preceding page, from a MS. of Lydgate's "Storie of Thebes" (Royal 18 D. II.), gives a general view of a town, The travellers in the foreground are a group of Canterbury pilgrims.

In these mediæval times the population of these towns was not so diverse as it afterwards became; the houses were of various classes, from that of the wealthy merchant, which was a palace—like that of Michael de la Pole at Hull, or that of Sir John Crosby in London—down to the cottage of the humble craftsman, but the mediæval town possessed no such squalid quarters as are to be found in most of our modern towns. The inhabitants were chiefly merchants, manufacturers, and craftsmen of the various guilds. Just as in the military order, all who were permanently attached to the service of a feudal lord were lodged in his castle or manor and its dependencies; as all who were attached to a religious community were lodged in and about the monastery; as in farm-houses, a century ago, the labouring men lived in the house; so in towns all the clerks, apprentices, and workpeople lodged in the house of their master; the apprentices of every craftsman formed part of his family; there were no lodgings in the usual sense of the word. In the great towns, and especially in the suburbs, were hostelries which received travellers, adventurers, minstrels, and all the people who had no fixed establishment; and often in the outskirts of the town without the walls, houses of inferior kind sprang up like parasites, and harboured the poor and dangerous classes.

The bird's-eye views of the county towns in the corners of Speed's *Maps of the most famous Places of the World*, are well worth study. They give representations of the condition of many of our towns in the time of Elizabeth, while they were still for the most part in their ancient condition, with walls and gates, crosses, pillories, and maypoles still standing, and indicated in the engravings. Perhaps one of the most perfect examples we have left of a small mediæval town is Conway; it is true, no very old houses appear to be left in it, but the streets are probably on their old lines, and the walls and gates are perfect—the latter, especially, giving us some picturesque features which we do not find remaining in the gates of other towns. Taken in combination with the adjoining castle it is architecturally one of the most unchanged corners of England.

We have also a few old houses still left here and there, sufficient to form a series of examples of various dates, from the twelfth century downwards. We must refer the reader to Turner's "Domestic Architecture" for notices of them. A much greater number of examples, and in much more perfect condition, exist in the towns of the Continent, for which reference should be made to Viollet le Duc's " Dictionary of Architecture." All that our plan requires, and our space admits, is to give a general notion of what a citizen's house in a mediæval town was like. The houses of wealthy citizens were no doubt mansions comparable with the unembattled manor-houses of the country gentry. We have already quoted Leland's description of that of Michael de la Pole at Hull, of the fourteenth century, and Crosby Hall in Bishopsgate Street. St. Mary's Hall, at Coventry, is a very perfect example of the middle of the fifteenth century. Norwich also possesses one or more houses of this character. The house of an ordinary citizen had a narrow frontage, and usually presented its gable to the street; it had very frequently a basement story, groined, which formed a cellar, and elevated the first floor of the house three or four feet above the level of the street. At Winchelsea the vaulted basements of three or four of the old houses remain, and show that the entrance to the house was by a short stone stair alongside the wall; under these stairs was the entrance into the cellar, beside the steps a window to the cellar, and over that the window of the first floor. Here, as was usually the case, the upper part of the house was probably of wood, and it was roofed with tiles. On the first floor was the shop, and beside it an alley leading to the back of the house, and to a straight stair which gave access to the building over the shop, which was a hall or common living-room occupying the whole of the first floor. The kitchen was at the back, near the hall, or sometimes the cooking was done in the hall itself. A private stair mounted to the upper floor, which was the sleeping apartment, and probably was often left in one undivided garret; the great roof of the house was a wareroom or storeroom, goods being lifted to it by a crane which projected from a door in the gable. The town of Cluny possesses some examples, very little modernised, of houses of this description of the twelfth century. Others of the thirteenth century are at St. Antonin, and in the Rue St. Martin, Amiens. Others of subsequent date will be found in the Dictionary of Viollet le Duc, vol. vi., pp. 222—271, who gives plans, elevations, and perspective sketches which enable us thoroughly to understand and realise these picturesque old edifices. Our own country will supply us with abundance of examples of houses, both of timber and stone, of the fifteenth century. Nowhere, perhaps, are there better examples than at Shrewsbury, where they are so numerous, in some parts (*e.g.* in the High Street and in Butcher Row), as to give a very good notion of the picturesque effect of a whole street—of a whole town of them. But it must be admitted that the continental towns very far exceed ours in their antiquarian and artistic interest. In the first place, the period of great commercial prosperity occurred in these countries in the Middle Ages, and their mediæval towns were in consequence larger and handsomer than ours. In the second place, there has been no great outburst of prosperity in these countries since to encourage the pulling down the mediæval houses to make way for modern improvements; while in England our commercial growth, which came later, has had the result of clearing away nearly all of our old town-houses, except in a few old-fashioned places which were left outside the tide of commercial innovations. In consequence, a walk through some of the towns of Normandy will enable the student and the artist better to realise the picturesque effect of an old English town, than any amount of diligence in putting together the fragments of old towns which remain to us. In some of the German towns, also, we find the old houses still remaining, apparently untouched, and the ancient walls, mural towers, and gateways still surrounding them. The illu-

A Mediæval Street and Town Hall.

minations in MSS. show that English towns were equally picturesque, and that the mediæval artists appreciated them. The illustrations in our last chapter on pp. 519, 520, give an idea of the houses inhabited by citizens in such a town as St. Alban's. In the "Roman d'Alexandre," in the Bodleian Library, Oxford, a whole street of such houses is rudely represented, some with the gable to the street, some with the side, all with the door approached by an exterior stair, most of them with the windows apparently unglazed, and closed at will by a shutter. We might quote one MS. after another, and page after page. We will content ourselves with noting, for exterior views, the Royal MS. 18 E. V. (dated 1473 A.D.), at 3 E. V., f. 117 v., a town with bridge and barbican, and the same still better represented at f. 179; and we refer also to Hans Burgmaier's "Der Weise Konige," which abounds in picturesque bits of towns in the backgrounds of the pictures. For exteriors the view of Venice in the "Roman d'Alexandre" is full of interest, especially as we recognise that it gives some of the remaining features—the Doge's Palace, the Cathedral, the columns in the Piazzeta—and it is therefore not merely a fancy picture, as many of the town-views in the MS. are, which are supposed to represent Jerusalem,* Constantinople, and other cities mentioned in the text. This Venice view shows us that at that time the city was lighted by lanterns hung at the end of poles extended over the doors of the houses. It gives us a representation of a butcher's shop and other interesting features.

The illustration on the preceding page is also a very interesting street-view of the fifteenth century, from a plate in Le Croix and Seré's "Moyen Age," vol. Corporations et Metiers, Plate 8. Take first the right-hand side of the engraving, remove the forest of picturesque towers and turrets with their spirelets and vanes which appear over the roofs of the houses (in which the artist has probably indulged his imagination as to the effect of the other buildings of the town beyond), and we have left a sober representation of part of a mediæval street—a row of lofty timber houses with their gables turned to the street. We see indications of the usual way of arranging the timber frame-work in patterns; there are also indications of

---

* Take the woodcut on p. 531, from MS. Royal, 15 E. I., f. 436.

pargeting (*e.g.* raised plaster ornamentation) and of painting in some of the panels. On the ground-floor we have a row of shops protected by a projecting pent-house; the shop-fronts are open unglazed arches, with a bench across the lower part of the arch for a counter, while the goods are exposed above. In the first shop the tradesman is seen behind his counter ready to cry "what d'ye lack" to every likely purchaser; at the second shop is a customer in conversation with the shopkeeper; at the third the shopkeeper and his apprentice seem to be busy displaying their goods. Some of the old houses in Shrewsbury, as those in Butcher Row, are not unlike these, and especially their shops are exactly of this character. When we turn to the rest of the engraving we find apparently some fine building in which, perhaps, again the artist has drawn a little upon vague recollections of civic magnificence, and his perspective is not quite satisfactory. Perhaps it is some market-house or guildhall, or some such building, which is represented; with shops on the ground-floor, and halls and chambers above. The entrance-door is ornamented with sculpture, the panels of the building are filled with figures, which are either painted or executed in plaster, in relief. The upper part of the building is still unfinished, and we see the scaffolds, and the cranes conveying mortar and timber, and the masons yet at work. In the shop on the right of the building, we note the usual open shop-front with its counter, and the tradesman with a pair of scales; in the interior of the shop is an assistant who seems to be, with vigorous action, pounding something in a mortar, and so we conjecture the shop to be that of an apothecary. The costume of the man crossing the street, in long gown girded at the waist, may be compared with the merchants given in our last chapter, and with those in an engraving of a market-place at p. 499. The figure at a bench in the left-hand corner of the engraving may perhaps be one of the workmen engaged upon the building; not far off another will be seen hauling up a bucket of mortar, by means of a pulley, to the upper part of the building; the first mason seems to wear trousers, probably overalls to protect his ordinary dress from the dirt of his occupation. Of later date are the pair of views given opposite from the margin of one of the pictures in "The Alchemy Book" (Plut. 3,469) a MS. in the British Museum of early sixteenth-century date. The nearest house in the left-hand picture shows that the shops were still of the mediæval character; several of the houses have signs on projecting poles. There are other examples of shops in the nearest house of the right-

Mediæval Streets.

hand picture, a public fountain opposite, and a town-gate at the end of the street. We see in the two pictures, a waggon, horsemen, and carts, a considerable number of people standing at the shops, at the doors of their houses, and passing along the street, which has no foot pavement.

The accompanying cut from Barclay's "Shippe of Fools," gives a view in the interior of a mediæval town. The lower story of the houses is of stone, the upper stories of timber, projecting. The lower stories have only small, apparently unglazed windows, while the living rooms with their oriels and glazed lattices are in the first floor. The next cut, from a MS. in the

A Town, from Barclay's Shippe of Fools.

French National Library, gives the interior of the courtyard of a great house. We notice the portion of one of the towers on the left, the draw-well, the external stair to the principal rooms on the first floor, the covered unglazed gallery which formed the mode of communication from the different apartments of the first floor, and the dormer windows.

A whole chapter might be written on the inns of mediæval England.

We must content ourselves with giving references to pictures of the exterior of two country ale-houses—one in in the Royal MS. 10 E. IV., at f. 114 v., which has a broom projecting over the door by way of sign; and another in the "Roman d'Alexandre" in the Bodleian—and with repro-

Courtyard of a House. (French National Library.)

ducing here two pictures of the interiors of hostelries from Mr. Wright's "Domestic Manners and Customs of the Middle Ages." They represent the sleeping accommodation of these ancient inns. In the first, from the "Quatre Fils d'Aymon," a MS. romance of the latter part of the fourteenth century, in the French National Library, the beds are arranged at the side of the apartment in separate berths, like those of a ship's cabin, or like the box beds of the Highlands of Scotland. It is necessary, perhaps, to explain that the artist has imagined one side of the room removed, so as to introduce into his illustration both the mounted traveller outside and the interior of the inn.

In the next woodcut, from Royal MS. 18 D. II., the side of the hostelry next to the spectator is supposed to be removed, so as to bring under view both the party of travellers approaching through the corn-fields, and the same travellers tucked into their truckle beds and fast asleep. The sign of

An Inn. (French National Library.)

the inn will be noticed projecting over the door, with a brush hung from it. Many houses displayed signs in the Middle Ages; the brush was the general sign of a house of public entertainment. On the bench in the common dormitory will be seen the staves and scrips of the travellers, who are pilgrims.

A fragment of a romance of "Floyre and Blanchefleur," published by the Early English Text Society, illustrates the mediæval inn. We have a little modernised the very ancient original. Floris is travelling with a retinue of servants, in the hope of finding his Blanchefleur:—

> "To a riche city they bothe ycome,
> Whaire they have their inn ynome *
> At a palais soothe riche ;
> The lord of their inn has non his liche,†
> Him fell gold enough to honde,
> Bothe in water and in lande,
> He hadde yled his life ful wide."

i.e. he had travelled much, had great experience of life, and had gained gold both by sea and land. Besides houses entirely devoted to the entertainment of travellers, it was usual for citizens to take travellers into their houses,

An Inn.

and give them entertainment for profit ; it would seem that Floris and his servants had "taken up their inn" at the house of a burgess; he is called subsequently, "a burgess that was wel kind and curteis :"—

> "This Child he sette next his side,
> Glad and blithe they weren alle
> So many as were in the halle ;
> But Floris not ne drunk naught,
> Of Blanchefleur was all his thought."

---

* Taken. † Like.

The lady of the inn perceiving his melancholy, speaks to her husband about him:—

> "Sire takest thou no care
> How this child mourning sit
> Mete ne drink he nabit,
> He net * mete ne he ne drinketh
> Nis † he no marchaunt as me thinketh."

From which we gather that their usual guests were merchants. The host afterwards tells Floris that Blanchefleur had been at his house a little time before, and that—

> "Thus therein this other day
> Sat Blanchefleur that faire may,
> In halle, ne in bower, ne at board
> Of her ne herde we never a word
> But of Floris was her mone
> He hadde in herte joie none."

Floris was so rejoiced at the news, that he caused to be brought a cup of silver and a robe of minever, which he offered to his host for his news. In the morning—

> "He took his leave and wende his way,
> And for his nighte's gesting
> He gaf his host an hundred schillinge."

One feature of a town which requires special mention is the town-hall. As soon as a town was incorporated, it needed a large hall in which to transact business and hold feasts. The wealth and magnificence of the corporation were shown partly in the size and magnificence of its hall. Trade-guilds similarly had their guildhalls; when there was one great guild in a town, its hall was often the town-hall; when there were several, the guilds vied with one another in the splendour of their halls, feasts, pageants, &c. The town-halls on the Continent exceed ours in size and architectural beauty. That at St. Antoine, in France, is an elegant little structure of the thirteenth century. The Belgian town-halls at Bruges, &c., are well known from engravings. We are not aware of the existence of

---

* N'et, *i.e.* does not eat.   † N'is, *i.e.* is not.

any town-halls in England of a date earlier than the fifteenth century. That at Leicester is of the middle of the fifteenth century. The town-hall at Lincoln, over the south gate, is of the latter half of the century; that at Southampton, over the north gate, about the same date: it was not unusual for the town-hall to be over one of the gates. Of the early part of the sixteenth century we have many examples. They are all of the same type—a large oblong hall, of stone or timber, supported on pillars, the open colonnade beneath being the market-place. That at Salisbury is of stone; at Wenlock (which has been lately restored), of timber. There are others at Hereford, Ross, Leominster, Ashburton, Guildford, &c. The late Gothic Bourse at Antwerp is an early example of the cloistered, or covered courts, which, at the end of the fifteenth century, began to be built for the convenience of the merchants assembling at a certain hour to transact business. The covered bridge of the Rialto was used as the Exchange at Venice.

None of our towns have the same relative importance which belonged to them in the Middle Ages. In the latter part of the period of which we write it was very usual for the county families to have town-houses in the county town, or some other good neighbouring town, and there they came to live in the winter months. When the fashion began we hardly know. Some of the fine old timber houses remaining in Shrewsbury are said to have been built by Shropshire families for their town-houses. The gentry did not in those times go to London for "the season." The great nobility only used to go to court, which was held three times a year; then parliament sat, the king's courts of law were open, and the business of the nation was transacted. They had houses at the capital for their convenience on these occasions, which were called inns, as Lincoln's Inn, &c. But it is only from a very recent period, since increased facilities of locomotion made it practicable, that it has been the fashion for all people in a certain class of society to spend "the season" in London. As a consequence the country gentry no longer have houses in the provincial towns; even the better classes of those whose occupation lies in them live in their suburbs, and the towns are rapidly changing their character, physically, socially, and morally, for the worse. London is becoming rapidly the one great town in England. The great manufacturers have agencies in London; if people are going to furnish a house or to buy a wedding outfit they come up to London; the very artisans and rustics in search of a day's holiday are whirled up to London in an excursion train. While London in consequence is extending so widely as to threaten to convert all England into a mere suburb of the metropolis of the British empire.

THE END.

INDEX.

ABBESSES, costume of, 57
    Abbey, infirmary of, 61
Abbey-church, internal arrangement of, 75
Abbot, duties of, 55; his habit, 57
Abbot-bishop, 5
Abbot's lodgings, 55, 84
Alien Priories, 34
Ampulla, the Canterbury, 171-73
Anchorages, 132
Anchoresses, bequests to, 129; Judith the foundress and patroness of the order of, 120; sketch of, 146
Anchorholds, 130, 134, 138
Anchorites, bequests to, 125-27; rule for, 121; their mode of life, 121
Angel minstrels, 286-88
Anglo-Saxons, St. Augustine the Apostle of the, 6
Arbalesters, the Genoese famous as, 441
Archers, 438; corps of enrolled as body guards by Edward III. and French kings, 412; importance of in battle, 440; mounted corps of, *ib.*; Norman, equipment of at time of Conquest, 438; skill of English, 440
Archery, practice of by commonality of England protected and encouraged by legislation, 445, 446
Armorial bearings, date of invention of, 331
Armour, details of a suit of thirteenth-century, 333; differences in suits of mediæval, 398, 399; little worn in the reigns of Elizabeth and James I., 458; many modifications of in fifteenth century, 452; of King Henry VIII.'s reign, 453; of the fourteenth century, 338 *et seq.*; of the fifteenth century, 394 *et seq.*; various kinds of early, 329, 330, 335, 336
Arquebusier, 458
Artillery, ancient, 446; date of first appearance in field disputed, 447; first evidence as to the existence of, 440, 447
Augustinians, order of the, 18
Austin friars, order of, 44, 94

BANKER, the mediæval, 407
    Bard, anecdotes concerning the, 271-73; the father of the minstrels of mediæval Europe, 270

Basilican Institution, introduction of into Africa by St. Augustine, 4; into France by St. Martin of Tours, *ib.*; into Ireland by St. Patrick, *ib.*; into Syria by Hilarion, *ib.*
Battering-ram, 385, 450, 451
Bede houses, 24
Benedictine monks, habit of, 1-7; orders, 17
Benefices, abuses in connection with, 200
Bonhommes, the, 21
Brigittines (female Order of Our Saviour), 21
Britain, exports of when a Roman province, 463
British Church, early history of the, 4
    coinage, date of first, 463
    commerce, the beginnings of, 461

CAMALDOLI, order of, 17
    Canons, Secular, cathedral establishments of, 196; their costume, 197, 198
Canterbury pilgrimage, chief sign of the, its origin and meaning, 170 *et seq.*
Carmelite friars, order of, 43
Carthusian order, founded by St. Bruno, 15; Charterhouse (Chartreux) principal house of in England, 15
Carthusians, Cistercians, Clugniacs, and the orders of Camaldoli and Vallambrosa and Grandmont, history of the successive rise of the, 10
Castle, mode of assaulting a, 381; various methods of attacking a, 392
Castles, counter-mines used by defenders of mediæval, 387; Greek fire and stinkpots employed in repelling assailants of, 392; mines used for effecting breaches in walls of, 385; places of hospitality as well as of trials of arms, 358
Cells, monastic, 89
Chantry chapels, bequests to, 140
    priests, 136, 204, 206
Chapels, private, curious internal arrangement of, 211; establishments of, 208-10
Chaplains, domestic, 208, 210, 212
Christendom, cœnobitical orders of, 93
Church of England, date of present organization of, 195

Cinque Ports, 480; ships of the, frequently at war with those of other ports of the kingdom, 483
Cistercian order, founded by Robert de Thierry, 16; introduced into England A.D. 1128, *ib.*; St. Bernard of Clairvaux the great saint of the, 17
Clairvaux, external aspect and internal life of, 12; founded by St. Bernard, 11
Clergy, comparison between mediæval seculars and modern, 224, 225; extracts from injunctions of John, Archbishop of Canterbury, on robes of the, 242, 243, 250, 251; form of degradation for heresy, 214, 215; friars a popular order of, 223; parochial, cause of change in condition of the, 193; rivalry between friars and secular, 223; secular, 214; stories illustrating deference of for squire in olden days, 225, 226; wills of the, 248, 249
Clerical costume of archbishop, 234-236; of bishop, 235; of cardinal, 234; of minor orders, 214, 215; of pope, 232, 233
Clericus, meaning of the word, 215
Clugniac, order of, 14
Coffin-stones, mediæval, curious symbols on, 193
Combat, a mediæval, 375, 376
Commerce, checked by the Conquest, 468; discovery of sea-passage to India opens up to a career of adventure, 485; earliest extant document bearing on Saxon, 464; of England greatly increased during reign of Edward the Confessor, 467; receives much attention from Government during fourteenth century, 470; recovers and surpasses its ancient prosperity in reign of Henry II. 469; the pioneers of, 485
Compostella pilgrimage, legend in connection with badge of the, 169; offerings made by pilgrims on return from, 190
Convent, the, officials of: abbot, 55; almoner, 62; artificers and servants, 65; cellarer, 60; chantor, *ib.*; chaplains, 65; cloister monks, 64; hospitaller, 61; infirmarer, 62; kitchener, 63; master of the novices, 62; novices, 65; porter, 62; precentor, 58; prior, 58; Professed Brethren, 65; sacrist, 61; seneschal, 63; subprior, 60; succentor, *ib.*
Council of Hertford, 195; differences affecting parochial clergy reconciled at, *ib.*

Council of Lyons, suppression of minor mendicant orders by, 44; red hat of cardinal first given by Innocent VI. at, 234
Counting-board, the, 501
Cross-bow, not used in war till close of twelfth century, 440; various forms of, *ib.*
Croyland, monastery of, 87
Crusades, objects for which they were organised, 159
Crutched friars, order of, 44

DEACONESSES, order of, 152
De Pœnetentia friars, order of, 44
Dominican friar, Chaucer's, 46
friars, order of, 40
Dunstan, Archbishop, reduces all Saxon monasteries to rule of St. Benedict, 7

EDUCATION, monasteries famous places of, 66
Edwardian period, armour and arms of the, 347
Egyptian Desert, hermits of the, 148
Eremeti Augustini, order of, 94, 96; their habit, 96
Eremetical life, curious illustration of, 2

FAIRS, sole power of granting right to hold exercised by king, 503; great, 506
Feudal system, introduction of into England by William the Conqueror, 326; points of difference between Continental and English, 327
Fontevraud, nuns of, 21
Franciscan friars, order of, 40; the several branches of, 43
nuns, habit of the, 43
Free towns, mediæval, 530; Hull an example of one of the, *ib.*; manner of laying out, 531-38
Friars, orders of: Austin, 44; Carmelites, 43; Crutched, 44; de Pœnetentia, 44; Dominicans, 40; Franciscans, 40
Chaucer's type of a certain class of, 39; convents of, *ib.*; pictures of ancient customs and manners of, 45; the principle which inspired them, 36

GILBERTINES, founded by Gilbert of Sempringham, 21
Godrie of Finchale, 116
Grandmontines, order of, 17

Index.   549

Greek Church, costume of monks and nuns in the, 4; rule of St. Basil followed by all monasteries of, *ib.*
fire, 449; used in the Crusades, *ib.*
Grimlac, rule of, 120, 121
Guesten-halls, 86, 87
Guild priests, 205; bequests to, 206; duties of, *ib.*
Guilds of minstrels, 298; laws regulating them, 299, 300

HAMPTON COURT, shipping of time of Henry VIII. illustrated at, 484
Harper, the mediæval, 271 *et seq.*
Henry VIII.'s army, 455; account of its taking the field, 456; description of the king's camp, 458
Heresy, form of degradation for, 214, 215
Hermit, a modern, 119; form of vow made by mediæval, 98; popular idea of a, 95; service for habiting and blessing a, 99; superstition with regard to a, 100; typical pictures of a, 117-19
Hermitages, localities of, 101; descriptions of, 111-17
Hermit-saints, traditional histories of the early, 95 n.; their costume, 98
Hermits, curious history relating to, 104
Holy Land, early pilgrims to the, 158; pilgrim entitled to wear palm on accomplishment of pilgrimage to, 167; special sign worn by pilgrims to, *ib.*
"Holy Reliques," an account of, 185-87
Horses, equipment of in fifteenth century, 404; trappings of at tournaments, 433
Hospitals of the Middle Ages, 23, 24; foreign examples of, 25
Hospitium, contrast between the Cloister and the, 87; resorted to by travellers, 529
Houses, description of, given by mediæval traders to various churches and monasteries, 519

IMPROPRIATION, evil of, 199
Iona, monastic institution at, 6
Inventories, clerical, 261, 262; of church furniture, 285
"Isles of Tin," 461

JEWELLERY, portable, Saxon goldsmiths famous for, 464
Jousting, 348, 349, 365, 411, 415
Judicial combats, anecdotes illustrative of, 419; various authorities on the subject of, *ib.*

KELVEDON Parsonage, 261, 263, 265
Knight, manner of bringing up a, 406; Chaucer's portrait of a, 409, 410
Knight-errant, armour and costume of a royal, 349, 350; graphic account of incidents in single combat of a, 373-75; squire of a, 352
Knight-errantry, romances of, 354 *et seq.*
Knighthood, won by deeds of arms in the field and in the lists, 409
Knight Hospitaller, a, 31
Knights of Malta, 33
of St. John of Jerusalem, order of, 29-32
of the Temple, order of, 26, 29, 159
Knights, noblemen and eldest sons of landed gentry made, 408; ceremony of making essentially a religious one, 409; equipment of reached its strangest form in reigns of Richard III. and Henry VII. 452
Knights-errant, 369 *et seq.*
Knights of the Middle Ages, armour, arms, and costume of the, 311 *et seq.*; scarcity of authorities for costume and manners of the, 329; quaint and poetic phrases in romances of the, 367, 368

LAURA, the, 3; original arrangement of the hermits in their, 107
Lindisfarne, monastic institution at, 6
Long-bow, the national arm of the English, 441; attains climax of its reputation during fourteenth century, 441
London, burgesses of at battle of Hastings, 467; date of its becoming chief emporium of Britain, 463; importance of its citizens previous to Conquest, 467; interesting account of mediæval, 469; "mysteries," or trades of, 508; regulations as to dress of merchants, citizens, and burgesses of the city of, 525
Lord-monks, 223

MARSEILLES, as a Greek colony, the chief emporium of the world, 462
Mediæval dance, a, 281, 282
England, inns of and their signs, 540-44; picturesque aspect of, 489-92; population of, 503; town-halls of, 545; town houses of county families of, *ib.*
life and characters, sketches of, from an artist's point of view, 1
shops, descriptions of, 509, 510

Mediæval towns, 529; best specimens of to be found in Normandy and Germany, 535; Conway a perfect example of one of the, 534; gradual growth of, 529; houses of, 534, 535; inhabitants of, 533; mode of lodging of population of, *ib.*; numerous on the Continent from eleventh to fourteenth centuries, 530; picturesque views of streets and shops of, 537-40; some built for specific purposes, 529 trade, 503 *et seq.*

Merchant, mediæval, an account of his occupation and way of life, 465, 466; curious epitaph on a brass relating to a, 525; effigy of a at Northleach, 523

Merchant guilds, 489
navy, the, 475
ships, early, 470, 471; king at liberty to impress, 481, 482

Merchants, commerce of England, during thirteenth century, carried on by foreign, 470; details of dresses worn by mediæval, 521; early English, 465; law conferring rank on, 465; munificence of the mediæval, 495; private naval wars carried on between, 482, 483; provision in charter of King John as to, 469; social position of the mediæval, 487, 488; various classes of distinguished by costume, 487

Middle Ages, armour of the, 329-36; archers of England famous during the, 439; combats of the, 411; consecrated widows of the, 152; costume of tradespeople of the, 519; description of the combat between King Arthur and a knight of the, 365, 366; drill and tactics of the soldiers of the, 377-79; engines of war of the, 382, 383; habitations of secular clergy in the, 252-54; harper the most dignified of the minstrel craft throughout the, 271; hermits and recluses of the, 93 *et seq.*; hospitals of the, 23-25; hospitium of a monastery in the, 87; houses of the, 519, 520; itinerant traders of the, 513, 517; manner of bringing up a youth of good family in the, 406; merchant navy of the, 475; merchant princes of the, 493, 494; merchants of the, 461 *et seq.*; minstrels part of regular establishment of nobles and gentry of the, 275; monks of the, 1 *et seq.*; primitive mode of life of rural English population of the, 513;

ships of the, 470-71; sketch of life led by a country parson in the, 262, 263; sumptuary laws regulating dress of merchants of the, 525; system of Pluralities in the, 200

Military engines, 382 *et seq.*
exercises and encounters, 410 *et seq.*
orders: Knights of St. John of Jerusalem, 29; Knights of the Temple, 26; Our Lady of Mercy, 32; Teutonic Knights, *ib.*; Trinitarians, 32-34

Minstrels, mediæval, assist in musical part of divine service, 285; costume of, 304-309; curious anecdotes concerning, 294, 295; duties of, 275 *et seq.*; female, 302, 303; incorporated in a guild, 297; marriage processions attended by, 282, 283; often men of position and worth, 294, 295; part of regular establishment of nobles and gentry, 275-77; patronised by the clergy, 288; singular ordinance relating to, 296; tournaments enlivened by the strains of, 291, 292; welcome guests at the religious houses, 289, 290

"Minstrels unattached," 293, 294

Miracle-plays, parish clerks took an important part in, 220; survival of in Spain, 221

Minstrelsy, in high repute among the Normans, 274; Grostête of Lincoln a great patron of, 288; Israelitish compared with music of mediæval England, 267

Mitre, earliest form of the, 236; transition shape of the from twelfth century, *ib.*

Monachism, origin of, 1-5

Monasteries, Benedictine, 9; British, 5; Saxon, 7; suppression of, 52

Monastery, arrangement of a Carthusian, 71; description of a, 72 *et seq.*; graphic sketch of the arrival of guests at a, 87

Monastic orders, traditional histories of the founders and saints of, 1 *et seq.*; their suppression in England, 52

Monk, cell of a Carthusian, 123; pilgrim, 188

Monks, abodes of, 70; lord, 223

Monumental brasses, 19, 57, 276, 494, 495, 497, 521, 527; *minutiæ* of costume of middle ages supplied from, 521; peculiar features in, 526

Movable tower, a, 387

Music, sketch of the earliest history of, 267-70

Musical instruments, date of invention of, 267; occasions when used, *ib.*; names of, *ib. et seq.*; used in the colleges of the prophets, 269; Saxon, 273; learned essays on mediæval, 274; used in celebration of divine worship, 285; forms of, 309, 310

ORDER for the Redemption of Captives, 33, 34; their habit, 34; their rules, *ib.*
Ostiary, costume of an, 215 n.
Our Lady of Mercy, order of, 32
Our Lady of Walsingham, shrine of, 180, 181; a relic from, *ib.*

PACHOMIUS, written code of laws by, 4
Palmers, 189, 190; graves of three holy, 193
Parish clerk, frequently the recipient of a legacy, 217; his duties, 218, 220; office of an ancient, *ib.*; worth of his office, 220
  priests, early handbooks for, 227; instructions for, 162 n.; points of difference between monks and friars and the, 222
Parochial clergy, 195, 196; domestic economy of the early, 263-65; organization of the established by Archbishop of Canterbury, 195
Parsonage houses, early, 254 *et seq.*; description of, 259; furniture of, 261, 262
Pastoral staff, earliest examples of the, 237
Pedlars, their mode of dealing in mediæval times, 513, 515, 517
Pilgrim, an equestrian, 168; the female, 188; the penitential, 178
Pilgrimage, chief sign of the Canterbury, 170; chief signs of the Roman, 168; Holy Land first object of, 175; mendicant, 176; palmers, on return from, received with ecclesiastical processions, 189; practice to return thanks on returning from, 189; relics of, 191, 192; saying of Jerome as to, 157; special roads to the great shrines of, 178; sign of the Compostella, 169; usual places for, 159
Pilgrimages, a pleasant religious holiday, 176; gathering cry of, 178; popular English, 161, 162
Pilgrims, 159, 160; costume of, 164, 177; description of staff and scrip of, 164-66; graphic sketch of a company of passing through a town, 179; insignia of, 164, 192, 193; office of, 162-64;
special signs of, 167; singers and musicians employed by, 179; vow made by, 164
Pioneers of commerce, the, 485
Piracy, prevalence of in mediæval times, 483, 484
Plate armour, first introduction of, 336
"Pleasure fairs," 507
Priest-hermits, costume of, 97
Priesthood, curious history of way in which many poor men's sons attained to the, 201
Prior, functions of, 59
Prioress, Chaucer's description of a, 58

RECLUSE, service for enclosing a, 148, 150
Recluses, bequests to, 128, 129; canons concerning, 121; cells of female, 142; curious details of the life of, 130; dress of female, 97; giving of alms to, 123; hermitages for female, 130, 131, popular idea as to the life of, 121; sketch of, 146-48
Reclusorium, the, 124, 125, 132
Rectors, Saxon, 198, 199
Reformed Benedictine orders, 17
Regular Canons, Premonstratensian branch of, founded by St. Norbert, 21
Rettenden, reclusorium at, 135, 137
Richard of Hampole, life of, 107-10
Rome, pilgrimage to, 168; number of pilgrims visiting, 168; description of relics at, 182, 183 n.

SACRED music, 284
Salby abbey, staff of servants at, 66
Saxon soldiers, costume of, 312-18, 322-24; ornaments of, 324, 325; romantic fancies in connection with swords of, 320; weapons used by, 316, 318, 319, 321
Saxons, the, a musical people, 272; a pastoral rather than an agricultural race, 466; corn not exported by the, *ib.*; famous throughout Europe for goldsmiths' work and embroidery, *ib.*; rage among the for foreign pilgrimages, 464; traffic in slaves considerable during time of the, 466
Scottish Archers of the Guard, enrolment of the, 442
Secular clergy, comparison between costume of and that of mediæval merchants, 528; costume of the, 232 *et seq.*
Shrines, pictures of, 187

Siege, interesting points in a mediæval, 442
Solitaries, mediæval, 94; curious incident relating to two, 105
Spenser's description of a typical hermit and hermitage, 118, 119
Squires, duties of, 352
St. Anthony, cœnobite system attributed to, 4; monks of, *ib.*
St. Augustine, Canons Secular of, 18; their costume, *ib.*; Canons Regular of, 20; Chaucer's pen-and-ink sketch of one of the order, 19
St. Basil, abuse of great church festivals mentioned by, 513; introduction of Monachism into Asia Minor by, 4; rule of, *ib.*
St. Benedict, his rule, 6, 7; Archbishop Dunstan reduces all Saxon monasteries to rule of, 7
St. Clare, foundress of the female order of Franciscans, 43
St. Edmund's Bury, abbey of, 65
St. Francis, character of, 37
St. Jean-les-Bons-hommes, priory of, 89
St. John the Hermit, 148
St. Mary, Winchester, abbey of, 66
Sumptuary laws, 525; civil costume regulated by, 527, 528

TEUTONIC Knights, order of, 32
Tilting-ground, remains of, to be seen at Carisbrook Castle, 359
Timber fort, 444; used by William the Conqueror, 391
Tournament, 412; a miniature, 415; an historical example of the, 429, 430; description of encounter between French and English knights at a, 432; directions for the, 415-17; form of challenge for a, 431; form of proclamation inviting to a, 412, 413; habiliments required by knights at a, *ib.*; incidents relating to a, 424, 430; manner of arranging a, 423; mode of arming knights for the, 413; pictures illustrating various scenes of the, 432, 433; prizes of the, 427; the *joute à outrance*, 412; the *joute à plaisance*, *ib.*; weapons used at a, 415
Tournaments, feasting and merriment usual at, 424; the mediæval romances safe authorities on all relating to the subject of, 423; unusual deeds performed at, 426, 427
Town-halls, architectural beauty of continental, 544; date of earliest English, 545
Towns, provincial, market-days in mediæval, 511, 572; specimens of various in time of Edward III. 508-10
Traveller, religious houses chiefly the resting-places of the, 103, 490
Trinitarians, order of, 32-34

VALLOMBROSA, order of, 17
Vestments, mediæval official, description of, 237-241; abandoned at time of Reformation, 250

WAGER OF BATTLE, account of a mediæval, 420-22
Walter of Hamuntesham, beating of by rabble, 64
War-ships, cannon of both iron and brass employed on board English, A.D. 1338, 447; costume of sailors and soldiers of mediæval, 477; description of early, 475 *et seq.*; list of English, A.D. 1205, and where stationed, 481
Waverley, Cistercian abbey of, 65
Westminster Abbey, grants made by Henry VIII. to, 79
Whale fishing, early, 474
Widowhood, description of a lady who took the vows of, 155, 156
Widows, order of, 152; dress worn by, 156; profession or vow of, 154; service for consecration of, 152, 153
William of Swynderby, 140
Wills, inventories attached to ancient, 211, 212 n.
Wool merchants, costume of mediæval, 523, 525

THE END.

0652 02 875933 01 4 (IC=2)
CUTTS, EDWARD LEWES 02/25/86
SCENES AND CHARACTE\IDDLE AGES
(S) 1968 901.92 CUT

137340

901. CUTTS
92   SCENES CHARACTERS OF
CUTTS THE MIDDLE AGES 15.50

DATE DUE

137340

901. CUTTS
92   SCENES CHARACTERS OF
CUTTS THE MIDDLE AGES

15.50

To MC due 12-8-83
To MC due 4-9-84
To SCCC-due 5-17-84

83 08x
84
89

APR 13 1972

DISCARD

South Huntington Public Library
Huntington Station, New York

98